PENGUIN BOOKS

BAD MONEY

Kevin Phillips has been a political and economic commentator for more than three decades. A former White House strategist, he has been a regular contributor to the *Los Angeles Times* and National Public Radio and has written for *Harper's* and *Time*. He is the author of fourteen books, including the *New York Times* bestsellers *American Theocracy* and *American Dynasty*. He lives in Litchfield County, Connecticut.

D0366243

Praise for *Bad Money*

"Kevin Phillips' new book, *Bad Money: Reckless Finance, Failed Politics, and the Global Crisis of American Capitalism,* would be sobering enough if it were the first we'd ever heard from him. When you take into account how often he's been right in the past, this fourteenth volume in his continuing commentary on the American condition becomes positively alarming." —Tim Rutten, *Los Angeles Times*

"*Bad Money* is a short book by a practiced artist who specializes in identifying the defining trends of American life. Here Kevin Phillips takes on financial practice in the age of Robert Rubin, Henry Paulson, and the global rule of Goldman Sachs. It's not meant to be pretty and it isn't.... This is an important book. It ranges with stunning clarity over terrain that most political writing, including that of the most prominent voice of the American left, simply ignores." —James K. Galbraith, *The Texas Observer*

"At a time when the Cassandras of finances are looking like realists, there is no gloomier prophet than Kevin Phillips. The author of thirteen previous books, including at least one classic, *The Emerging Republican Majority,* Mr. Phillips sees a perfect economic storm coming.... His warnings have to be taken seriously." —Barry Gewen, *The New York Times*

"A financial policy horror story ... Kevin Phillips, right so often before, castigates both parties for bad times." —*The Philadelphia Inquirer*

"Comes now Kevin Phillips, mighty sage of the political economy, that gray area spanning elections, growth and geography, to condemn the financial services industry. With a recession at the gates, Phillips's previous record as Republican strategist turned skeptic gives *Bad Money* the gravity sure to guide the conversation about what is to be done." —Ross Kerber, *The Boston Globe*

"A pretty grim portrait of the financial services sector and its present role in the American economy." —Tom Acitelli, *The New York Observer*

"His book provides a primer in economics, details but not dull, accessible to the uninitiated and useful to the already well-informed.... His brief against the risky gambits of the venal center in American politics and finance is provocative, and perhaps prescient."
— Glenn Altschuler, *Pittsburgh Post-Gazette*

"This book represents a terrific start on understanding the interplay between past policy, current risk, energy and investments. Without such clear-eyed explanation and thinking, it's hard to see how we're going to move ahead and find solutions in the hard times that seem inevitable."
— Susan Gardner, The Daily Kos

KEVIN PHILLIPS

BAD MONEY

Reckless Finance, Failed Politics, and

the Global Crisis of American Capitalism

PENGUIN BOOKS

PENGUIN BOOKS
Published by the Penguin Group
Penguin Group (USA) Inc., 375 Hudson Street, New York, New York 10014, U.S.A.
Penguin Group (Canada), 90 Eglinton Avenue East, Suite 700, Toronto,
Ontario, Canada M4P 2Y3 (a division of Pearson Penguin Canada Inc.)
Penguin Books Ltd, 80 Strand, London WC2R 0RL, England
Penguin Ireland, 25 St Stephen's Green, Dublin 2, Ireland (a division of Penguin Books Ltd)
Penguin Group (Australia), 250 Camberwell Road, Camberwell,
Victoria 3124, Australia (a division of Pearson Australia Group Pty Ltd)
Penguin Books India Pvt Ltd, 11 Community Centre,
Panchsheel Park, New Delhi – 110 017, India
Penguin Group (NZ), 67 Apollo Drive, Rosedale, North Shore 0632,
New Zealand (a division of Pearson New Zealand Ltd)
Penguin Books (South Africa) (Pty) Ltd, 24 Sturdee Avenue,
Rosebank, Johannesburg 2196, South Africa

Penguin Books Ltd, Registered Offices:
80 Strand, London WC2R 0RL, England

First published in the United States of America by Viking Penguin,
a member of Penguin Group (USA) Inc. 2008
This edition with a new preface and a new afterword published in Penguin Books 2009

·   1   3   5   7   9   10   8   6   4   2

Copyright © Kevin Phillips, 2008, 2009
All rights reserved

THE LIBRARY OF CONGRESS HAS CATALOGED THE HARDCOVER EDITION AS FOLLOWS:
Phillips, Kevin.
Bad money : reckless finance, failed politics, and the global crisis of American capitalism /
Kevin Phillips.
p.   cm.
Includes bibliographical references and index.
ISBN 978-0-670-01907-6 (hc.)
ISBN 978-0-14-311480-2 (pbk.)
1. United States—Economic conditions—20th century.   2. United States—Economic
conditions—2001–   3. United States—Economic policy—20th century.
4. United States—Economic policy—2001–   I. Title.
HC106.7.P52   2008
330.973—dc22   2007045559

Printed in the United States of America

Except in the United States of America, this book is sold subject to the condition
that it shall not, by way of trade or otherwise, be lent, resold, hired out, or otherwise
circulated without the publisher's prior consent in any form of binding or cover other
than that in which it is published and without a similar condition including
this condition being imposed on the subsequent purchaser.

The scanning, uploading and distribution of this book via the Internet or via any other means
without the permission of the publisher is illegal and punishable by law. Please purchase only
authorized electronic editions, and do not participate in or encourage electronic piracy
of copyrighted materials. Your support of the author's rights is appreciated.

To William Russell Phillips,
our new grandson

BAD MONEY

Gresham's Law . . . a general law or principle concerning the circulation of money . . . [named] after Sir Thomas Gresham, who clearly perceived its truth three centuries ago. This law, briefly expressed, is that bad money drives out good money, *but that* good money cannot drive out bad money.

—W. S. Jevons, nineteenth-century economist

In a global free market, there is a variation on Gresham's Law: bad capitalism tends to drive out good.

—Professor John Gray, *False Dawn*, 1998

Preface to the Revised Edition

After the Fall: The Inexcusable Failure of American Finance

Just how well Barack Obama's presidency can address the most severe U.S. financial crisis since the 1930s may not be clear for much of his term. Economic convulsions of a great, once-a-century magnitude do not take hold or let go easily. Nor are they easy to fathom. Disagreement about the causes or avoidability of the 1930s depression still smolders among historians and economists.

The politics of coping also remain uncertain. The election of 2008 was marred by a predictable, yet symptomatic, unwillingness in both major parties to pose troubling overviews or lay out painful economic policy choices for the voting public. Both Republicans and Democrats had contributed to the quarter century onrush of debt and deregulation, albeit the Republicans more so. During the pre-election stock market convulsions that roiled both Washington and Wall Street, panic was more often in evidence than cool analysis of the mega-problems unfolding.

A few pundits even joked that by 2012, the side that had lost the presidency would be grateful for being out of power so that they didn't have to bear responsibility over four difficult years. Reasons for pessimism certainly abound. This edition's new pages—in this front section, a refocus on the financial malpractice and complicitous politics behind the crisis and, at the end, a global look ahead—cannot predict any clear outcome. But some of the autumn 2008 panic seemed unnecessary, tied to Washington's fear-mongering in enacting the early October bailout and mismanaging its implementation.

As 2008 ended, the NBC/*Wall Street Journal* poll found a lopsided 71 percent majority of Americans disapproving the job being done by the federal government in handling the financial crisis. This harsh judgment was upheld by evidence, to which we will return, that the September–

October credit paralysis—the notion of the nation's credit system being at death's door—was exaggerated in order to scare the public and Congress into passing a program that would focus on assisting, even subsidizing, several dozen of the largest U.S. financial institutions.

The hardcover edition of this book was published in mid-April 2008, and though it reached the *New York Times* nonfiction and business bestseller lists, relatively little of its contents have been discussed or publicized by the politicians or by the gatekeepers of the major national media. My analyses and the warnings that accompanied them were, in a word, unwelcome. They were deemed overly pessimistic. For that reason, first-time readers will find information that is still mostly ignored—and is still revelatory. At the same time, more than a quarter of this post-election book is new—a much enlarged and updated preface, plus a twenty-page afterword that sets out the U.S. domestic political and global financial implications for 2009–2012.

Though I stand by my argument, this new edition has a somewhat recast message. Once only a prediction, the grim news is now a reality. I can now update my thesis for recent events, snowballing momentum, trend confirmations, new data, fuddled Washington policy reactions, and surprise reversals during the last four months of 2008. The greatest policy gamble lay in cosseting, intead of severely disciplining, the wayward element among the largest U.S. financial institutions, and abetting an even greater concentration of economic power. To facilitate brevity and avoid repetition, some citations refer the reader to the main 2007 text for relevant explanations, detailed charts, and historical backdrop. The focus is still that summarized in *Bad Money*'s subtitle: "Reckless Finance, Failed Politics, and the Global Crisis of American Capitalism." Once thinking me a catastrophist, few now question the triple premise.

My book locks in on how over the last two decades, speculative finance rose to a counterproductive economic and political dominance in the United States. As we will see, the lesson of modern history—the successive declines of leading world economic powers—suggests that U.S. financialization was dangerous in itself. Then, after riding a long and huge wave of borrowing and liquidity, a grossly overinflated U.S. financial sector—the increasingly commingled excesses of banking, securities, insurance, and real estate—failed the nation's trust through extreme greed, inexcusable speculative leverage, and a streak of sheer incompetence. After first reaching the bestseller charts in spring, *Bad Money* got a second life in September when crashing U.S. and world stock markets prompted more Americans to look for an explanation of how and why the meltdown occurred. I have the opportunity now to flesh out, deepen, and enlarge these explanations. The American people, looking for remedies, first have to understand who did what and why.

The book's thesis had been taking shape over fifteen years. Earlier versions of some arguments and data appeared in three of my previous books: *Arrogant Capital: Washington, Wall Street, and the Frustration of American Politics* (1994); *Wealth and Democracy: A Political History of the American Rich* (2002); and *American Theocracy: The Peril and Politics of Radical Religion, Oil, and Borrowed Money in the 21st Century* (2006). Although the dangers posed by the Religious Right got the spotlight in the 2006 volume, its contents also included sections on debt, finance, and oil. My overriding concern was the extraordinary rise of the U.S. financial sector from 11–12 percent of the gross national product back in the 1980s to a stunning 20–21 percent of the U.S. gross domestic product by 2004–2005. During that same quarter century, manufacturing, for a century the pillar of our economy, slipped from about 25 percent to just 12 percent. This transformation—we could also say *hijacking*—of the U.S. economy has now proven its innate instability as well as its recklessness. Like 1929, the crash of 2008 may become another enduring negative metaphor.

Back in August 2007, when a housing-triggered credit crisis spread from the United States to global markets, I took its tremors to signal that the potential financial mega-crisis I hypothesized in 2006 was beginning to crystallize, and by December *Bad Money* was completed. Obviously, I was hardly the only one to see or write of such dangers; alarm-sounders abounded—which is why the negligence of Washington political leaders and financial regulators, who ignored warning after warning, is as blameworthy as the malpractice of the bankers, brokers, mortgage leaders, and hedge fund buccaneers themselves. The excesses were all too obvious for three to four years *before* the bubbles finally broke. The challenge for Obama and everyone else over the next four years will be to reason from what happened to the imperatives about what must be corrected.

1. FRANKENSTEIN FINANCE:
FIVE MALIGNANT ECONOMIC GROWTHS

The best way to understand what went wrong is to conduct a postmortem on the twenty-five year metastasis by which the financial sector's influence in America grew from a supporting role with 10–12 percent of the U.S. economy circa 1980 to an arguably crippling 20–21 percent predominance. Many of the products, processes, ambitions, and major financial firms conspicuous in this rapid overexpansion fed on one another and figured prominently in the eventual 2007–2009 debacle. This calamitous nexus is worth the closest scrutiny.

Looking back several centuries, little agitates the U.S. economy and its politics—the profound impact is dual—like a new sector grabbing national control. This current upheaval is another such. The last instance, widely remembered for its trauma as well as its modernization, was during the last two decades of the nineteenth century when American railroads and industry shouldered aside a previously supreme farm sector. The dominant survival-of-the-fittest economics so helpful to the emergence of manufacturing simultaneously weakened marginal Southern, Midwestern, and Western agricultural producers. It was this harshness against which Populist politics and the 1896 presidential campaign of William Jennings Bryan mobilized with fervor, yet with no more than partial success.

Meanwhile, in political terms, that subordination of agriculture by industry over three laissez-faire-driven decades stimulated an intense and often poignant debate across much of the United States. Many members of Congress and major newspapers and journals took part. By contrast, the recent displacement of manufacturing and other capital-intensive industry by the paper entrepreneurialism of finance was long neglected, its ramifications barely discussed. From the television networks to the major print media, from the halls of academe to the committee rooms of Congress, mum was long the word. This is a shame. Had there been serious discussion, the abuses now so obvious and the effects now so harsh would almost certainly have been more limited. News executives and journalists have arguably been as negligent as politicians and regulators.

As *Bad Money* details in chapter 2, the rise of a consumer-spending and debt culture in the United States clearly harks back to the nineteen fifties, with acceleration in the sixties and seventies.[1] However, for this postmortem of recent financial recklessness, we dissect only the economic corpus of the last quarter century. Late 1982, indeed, saw the Dow-Jones Industrial Average come off its August bottom (at 780) and begin the spectacular climb that would elevate it to 11,700 by early 2000 and 14,000 by 2007. Several other related indexes rose in tandem: the Jack-in-the-Beanstalk growth of total U.S. credit market debt (see Figure 2.4, p. 43), the ever more disturbing percentage of the gross national or domestic product represented by that debt-surge (see Figure 1.1, p. 7), the expanding share of the economy flying the flag of financial services (see Figure 2.1, p. 31), and the swollen profits of that same financial sector (see also Figure 1.1, p. 7). Hopefully, these pictures are jolting.

For convenience, I call the quarter century ascent the Multi-bubble. The term is doubly descriptive—on one dimension, a simultaneous puffing up of stocks, debt, experimental finance, and the national role of financial services; on the second, a succession of bubbles from the savings-and-loan and junk bond 1980s to the technology-manic nineties and the ultimate great mortgage and debt bubble. The centrality of financial excess, I argue, is not a precursor of postindustrial evolution, but a perilous overconcentration visible in past leading world economic powers as they lost the broad vitality of earlier eras (see pp. 183–85).

It didn't help that, as chastening memory of the Great Depression faded after a half century, Americans were drawn once again to the psychological amusement park of consumption, borrowing, credit, and debt. Even the conservative Reagan administration found it all too convenient—its budget deficits as a share of the U.S. economy reached 6.1 percent in 1983, 4.9 percent in 1984, 5.2 percent in 1985, and 5.1 percent in 1986. Public debt became a tool for simultaneously affording huge tax cuts and a rising defense budget in a period of reduced federal revenues.

The private sector also saw opportunity beckoning. Bankers and savings and loan executives, handed new investment latitude by early 1980s deregulation, got our permissive quarter century off to a raucous start with an orgy of bad real estate loans, scams, financial toga parties, and Texas-sized insolvencies that led, beginning in 1989, to a $200 billion federal bailout. Ambitious financiers, some of whom also wound up in jail, explored grander new frontiers of debt issuance. Michael Milken pioneered high-yield or "junk" bonds for lower-rated corporate borrowers until his firm, Drexel Burnham, failed in 1991. Raiders like Henry Kravis, T. Boone Pickens, and Ivan Boesky made a household expletive out of the term "leveraged buyout"—the lucrative process by which companies were taken over, stripped, loaded up with debt, and sold off. For the first time since the 1920s, both public and private debt had become fashionable again—a social and political convenience, no longer a lingering nightmare (except among aging grandparents).

Liquidity, debt, and leverage provided the essential structure of the Multi-bubble, and its principal architect, from 1987 to 2006, was Federal Reserve Board Chairman Alan Greenspan. He kept the liquidity flowing and declined to regulate the ultimate excesses, be they rogue derivatives, exotic mortgages, mergermania, margin-loan speculation, or a giddy succession of asset bubbles. Over his nearly two decades at the helm of U.S. monetary policy, total credit market debt in the United States quadrupled from under $11 trillion to a mind-numbing $44 trillion. The principal growth, moreover, came not in government debt but in *private* borrowing and credit—the unsung, but indispensable oxygen of grand-scale financial leverage and speculation.

In order to illustrate the essential practices, innovations, and products, all too many unsafe, that enabled the financial sector to engorge from some 12–14 percent of the U.S. economy in the early 1980s to 20–21 percent as Greenspan retired, I employ a quintet of mini-portraits.

Credit Card Nation: The Economics of Manic Consumption

We can begin with national consumption, which ultimately intensified to represent an appalling seven-tenths of the U.S. economy. It drove debt, and vice versa. Between 1960 and 1980, household debt rose from 50 percent of GDP to 60 percent, still below the binge ratios of the 1920s. Then in the 1980s, consumer debt alone more than doubled, and by the early 2000s, the escalation was frightening.

In 2004, economists from Northern Trust and Goldman Sachs began talking about *household* deficits, not just the federal budget variety. For every $1.00 the average American took in as income, he or she spent $1.04. Consumer psychology was the underlying, vital driver. Beginning in 1997, advertisers, retailers, and lenders drummed relentlessly, so that U.S. consumption rose from representing 67 percent of gross domestic product to 69 percent in 2002 and almost 72 percent in 2004.[2] Nowhere else were consumers driven to pull so hard on national economic oars.

The *New York Times* rightly observed that "the machinery of American marketing, media and finance all encourage the consumption habit. Many consumers are unable to resist the overpowering mantra: spend, spend, spend."[3] But because so many households had stagnant or declining incomes, they had simultaneously to borrow, borrow, borrow. And to make that possible, the United States, in the words of sociologist Robert Manning, became a "Credit Card Nation."[4] A vital catalyst had come between 1978 and 1980, when the federal government deregulated credit card and bank interest rates. Ultimately, in 1996, the Supreme Court opened a further Pandora's box of mischief by ruling in *Smiley v. Citibank* that credit card issuers could charge any fees—this included penalties—permitted by the states in which the issuers were based. As author Manning detailed, this deregulation quickly facilitated an "enormously successful mass marketing campaign" that "dramatically altered American attitudes towards consumer credit and debt."[5] Issuers focused on young people—many were teenagers with no job or budgeting experience—and pursued them relentlessly. Consumer historian Peter Stearns noted that for many Americans with decent incomes circa 2001 their lack of savings and paycheck-to-paycheck living flowed from "a sense that so many goods and trips had become absolutely essential."[6]

After the 2001 terrorist attacks, consumption got an additional imprimatur—patriotism. In the words of columnist Daniel Gross, "The message since the September 11 attacks has been . . . a strange and occasionally dissonant message of patriotism and consumption. As New Yorkers flocked to Ground Zero to volunteer Mayor Rudolph Giuliani exhorted Gothamites to patronize TriBeCa restaurants. President Bush appeared in ads urging Americans to fly and stay in hotels. These days, it seems, they also serve those who spend like there's no tomorrow."[7] Astonishingly, the U.S. administration urged a citizenry already over-

FIGURE P.1
The Great American Household Debt Binge, 2008

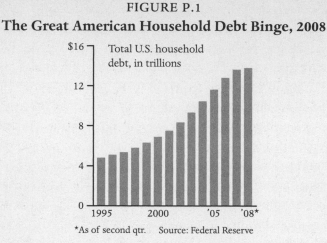

*As of second qtr.   Source: Federal Reserve

burdened by debt that it was their patriotic duty to take on even more of it. Between George W. Bush's first and second inaugurals, household debt increased by 39 percent.

The principal wave of credit card use for debt consolidation and consumption crested in 2005, but industry growth had been enormous. Over the period from 1990 to 2003, the number of card-holding Americans jumped by 75 percent—to 144 million from 82 million. However, the amount that they had charged quadrupled from $338 billion to $1.5 trillion.[8] Issuer profits were further swollen by penalty income. CBS News reported that the portion of credit-card issuer profits that came from fees rose from 28 percent in 2000 to 35 percent in 2003 and hit 39 percent in 2004.

As of that year's end, consumer debt alone had climbed to a record 85.7 percent of GDP. But a glittering opportunity for lenders increasingly became a yoke for borrowers. Between 2000 and 2007, household debt almost doubled, as Figure P.1 shows. By harnessing consumerism, credit card issuers—few major financial firms did not participate—had so enlarged their business that observers talked of a "borrower-credit" industrial complex. By mid-2008, consumer spending finally began to fall like George W. Bush's approval rating, but debt had already become one of America's giant industries.

Paper Entrepreneurialism: Mergers, Acquisitions, and Buyouts

Comparable growth opportunities for the financial sector came from a trio of frenetic, debt-enabled merger and acquisition waves. Until the 1990s, financial services purveyors were constrained by an old New Deal statute—the Glass-Steagall Act of 1933—that kept commercial banks, mortgage finance, insurers, and securities firms apart and unable to collude with each other in the unsafe and speculative practices they had indulged in the 1920s. But cracks were expanding. In 1984, the Bank Holding Company Act was relaxed somewhat, and in 1997, banks were permitted to buy securities firms; in 1998, even before Congress had repealed Glass-Steagall, the Fed had on its own supposed authority approved a merger between Citigroup and Travelers, a leading insurance company. In 1999, Congress passed and President Clinton enthusiastically signed the Financial Services Modernization Act, which reallowed the mergers that had been prohibited six decades earlier and also established a new category of financial holding companies (FHCs).[9]

That Citigroup was the symbol and principal beneficiary of this statute was a travesty itself. During the 1920s, its parent, National City Bank, had been the prime promoter of banks also getting into the securities and speculation business. Discredited by 1933, it became a principal poster child for Glass-Steagall's original enactment. In 2008, the *Wall Street Journal* updated that "while other banks can claim to be the victim of the current panic, Citi is at least a three-time loser. The same directors were at the helm in 2005 when the Fed suspended Citi's ability to make acquisitions because of the bank's failure to adhere to regulatory and ethical standards. Citi also needed resuscitation after the sovereign debt disaster of the 1980s, and it required an orchestrated private rescue in the 1990s."[10] Indeed, the *Journal* omitted two episodes for which Citi had been fined several years years back—pioneering off-the-books gambits for Enron and instituting an "account sweeping program" that automatically removed positive balances (a twice-paid billing, says from credit-card customers' accounts. True connoisseurs can keep up with grassroots opinion by Googling "shittybank"—no further description is necessary.

The 1995–2000 period saw a stunning total of 11,100 bank mergers, and the crescendo peaked during the year following the repeal. Some five hundred new FHCs were also created. The whole process was enormously capital intensive, and the market capitalization of the merged banks and new FHCs was far higher than the sum of the previous individual parts, just what had occurred a century earlier during the consolidation of the U.S. iron and steel industry. For 2000 alone, total merger and acquisitions activity in the United States hit $3 trillion, by far and away a record (see p. 53). By comparison, the total for mergers, acquisitions, and leveraged buyouts for the entire period from 1980 to early 1988 came to only a little over two thirds of a trillion dollars.[11]

Perhaps unsurprisingly, the new mega-firms took advantage of their new size, funding, and deregulation to experiment, like Icarus of Greek mythology, to see how close they could fly to the sun. With regulation all but suspended, competition to innovate, experiment, and return to the collusions of the 1920s became intense. And before the wax attaching their wings melted Icarus–like in 2007–2008, most of the top fifteen to twenty institutions had bet their fortunes on a host of new financial vehicles and instruments—structured investment vehicles (SIVs), special purpose acquisition companies (SPACs), mortgage securitization, collateralized debt obligations (CDOs), credit default swaps (CDSs), and the like.

Although bountiful in their own right, fees for mergers and acquisitions soon paled alongside the larger benefits of bull markets, assets bubbles, and the uber-profitability of exotic financial instruments. Back in the late 1980s, Goldman Sachs estimated that a major portion of that decade's stock market upsurge had come from anticipation of takeover bids or buyouts, and other analysts would make the same point about the later M&A floodtides in 2000 and 2006 (see p. 77). Besides facilitating several bull-market stampedes, this reorganization and rearrangement mania also propelled the financial sector's accelerating GDP share. After 2000, finance replaced the imploding technology sector as the leader in U.S. stock market capitalization. For anybody keeping a mental chart, the M&A game must go down as a second major ingredient, alongside the lucrative inflammation of consumer debt, in the financial services takeover.

I'm sorry if this book doesn't make for pleasant reading. But I can't underscore too strongly how much of the upsurge of financial sector size and clout during its quarter century of self-enlargement came from pretty much the same sort of flawed products, arrogance, and antisocial behavior paraded daily across the headlines. We are not talking about normal, safe growth. We are talking, as more and more commentators intuit, about the economic equivalent of metastasis.

Pigs with Wings: Debt, Credit, and 30:1 Leverage

Facilitator number three involved the financial sector's massive borrowing, which totaled some $15 trillion by 2007. Part of this was necessary to fuel the sector's workaday needs and ambitions—from ensnaring college students through credit-card come-ons or peddling mortgages with initial low payments—but much more of the borrowing funded grand strategies of credit derivatives, leveraged buyouts, or the ability of institutions to take positions with 30:1 leverage. This meant $30 million borrowed dollars in play for every million actually owned. The cheaper the interest rate, the better.

One facet of the quarter century multibubble worth some amplification is how the three U.S. speculative binges born out of booms and financial deregulation—in 1984–1989, 1996–2000, and 2003–2007—each created so much excess, corruption, misjudgment, and threatened (or actual) insolvency that the Federal Reserve had to come to the rescue. Its usual technique was to drop interest rates as low as possible—in 1989–1992, 2001–2005, and 2007–2009. This gave the shaky and hungover financial institutions in particular a chance to get new funds for almost nothing and to loan them out at 8 percent, 12 percent, or even 25 percent (via credit cards). Other less-favored Americans, however, bore the costs—low interest paid on savings accounts or certificates of deposit.

For some reason, government and private economists have almost never paid attention to *private* as opposed to public debt (see pp. 36–41). These gaps of information have inhibited economic historians of the 1920s, and lack of curiosity must cripple any evaluation of credit and liquidity during the 1983–2008 quarter century. These years, bluntly put, were a Mardi Gras, a glittering coming-out party for the many-splendored U.S. debt industry. Debt was becoming to finance what irrigation was to Southern California agriculture.

Figure 2.4 on p. 43, one of the book's key charts, pictures the extent to which private debt in the United States completely dwarfs public debt. Between 1994 and 2004, for example, federal, state, and local debt increased by $1.5 trillion to $6.1 trillion. Private debt, during that same decade, leaped by $21 trillion or some 200 percent to a then record total of over $31 trillion.

The principal pigs at the overflowing trough were, of course, those of private finance. The debt of the domestic financial sector jumped from $3.8 trillion in 1994 to $7.6 trillion in 1999 and $11.9 trillion in 2004. When Treasury Secretary Robert Rubin and others in the Clinton administration boasted of a "virtuous cycle," they meant that several years of balanced federal budgets in late 1990s—principally the result of tax receipts from bull-market-driven capital gains—had helped to keep interest rates low enough to permit a financial and stock market boom. By a deeper interpretation of "virtue," however, the cycle is less benign.

As Figure 2.5 on p. 45 shows, the late 1990s, in particular—but indeed, the entire 1983–2006 quarter century—were a heyday of financial borrowing and a triumph for leverage. True, the late 1990s stock averages initially rode alongside prosperity, but then the broader stock market and tech bubbles popped in 2000—the tech-heavy Nasdaq fell 78 percent from its peak in 2000 to its 2002 nadir and the Dow-Jones Industrial Average slumped by some 40 percent. The incandescence of 1999 was fleeting. Equally unfortunate, as page 47 notes, perhaps half of the $2.5 trillion worth of debt issued by energy and telecommunications firms vanished in the subsequent bankruptcies of politically active firms like Enron, Global Crossing, and WorldCom. Even so, the Multi-bubble soon renewed its expansion as the gauchos of Wall Street found a new thundering herd of bulls to ride in the real estate, mortgage finance, and securitization markets. Expanding leverage enabled new dimensions of miscalculation and instability.

The importance of these borrowed trillions also changed and enlarged the financial sector's institutional profile. For starters, banks and insurance companies in general lost relative ground and prominence. Whereas the two groups had enjoyed 71 percent of financial sector assets back in 1966 and 52 percent in 1986, their share as of 2006 had shriveled to 30 percent. Figure 4.3 on page 108 details the rest of the participants.

Mutual funds and federally related mortgage pools rose from 6 percent in 1966 to 31 percent forty years later.

The most revealing surge, however, took place in the fast-money, highly leveraged, or regulation-evading categories—securities brokers and dealers, hedge funds, private equity firms, issuers of asset-backed securities, funding corporations, structured investment vehicles (SIVs), and the like. Although some categorizations muddle as much as they clarify, these groups soared from 1 percent of the assets in 1966 and then 4 percent in 1986 to about 18 percent in 2006. Nearly one fifth of the financial sector's ships flew pirate or privateer flags.

Hedge funds, still virtually unregulated, mushroomed from a couple of hundred in the early 1990s to roughly ten thousand in 2007, boasting assets of close to $2 trillion. Some funds were stereotypical gunslingers in derivatives or commodities. However, many operated in the credit markets or became major lenders, shading into our hypothesized U.S. debt industry. Some, playing in what insiders labeled the shadow banking system, were also nicknamed as liquidity factories—enterprises able to manufacture the near equivalent of something formerly reserved to banks: money.

This interpretation was not fanciful. Mohamed El-Erian, president of the Harvard Management Company, observed in 2007 that "Over the past two years, markets have developed powerful liquidity factories . . . as more investors have embraced debt in an attempt to increase the impact of their investments." He cited hedge funds and private equity firms. Bond manager Bill Gross reminded clients that much as circa 1950 economics texts had described how money deposited at a local bank could be multiplied five- or sixfold by the operations of the banking system, latter-day financial innovators had done an "end run" around the banks: "Derivatives and structures with three- and four-letter abbreviations— CDOs, CLOs, ABCP, CPDOs, SIVs (the world awaits investment banking's next creation: IOU?)—can now take a 'depositor's' dollar and multiply it ten or twenty times" (see pages 108–111).

It makes sense, although none of the materials I have read precisely explain the new mechanics. The upshot seems twofold. First, that the nearly $15 trillion the financial sector borrowed during the last quarter century had a steroidslike effect. And second, that some of the

new and unregulated designer debt shops established—the so-called
liquidity factories—were busy creating moneylike debt instruments
that usurped the banks' fomerly exclusive role in increasing the U.S.
money supply. Small wonder the financial sector grew like Topsy.

The Ascent of Exotic Finance: Derivatives and Securitization

The fourth major expansion platform of our twenty-five year chronicle relied on the huge profits and ever expanding zoo of exotic financial
flora and fauna—derivatives, securitization, and the like. This animal
watch was more lighthearted back in the late 1980s and early 1990s
when derivatives in circulation included the acronyms CATs (Certificates of Accrual on Treasury Certificates), LYNX (Liquid Yield Note
Exchanges), OPPOSSMS (Options to Purchase or Sell Specific Mortgage-
backed Securities), and LIONs (Lehman Investment Opportunity Notes),
and in a different vein when wisecrackers had fun with SURFs (Step-Up
Recovery Floaters) and SLOBs (Sale-Leaseback Obligation Bonds). Figure 2.3 on page 35 sets out the chronology of derivatives and securitization. Alas, the money and stability at stake is too great for humor.

Let me preview some basic definitions. *Derivatives* are contracts
whose value is derived from assets including stocks, bonds, commodities, and currencies or from events like changes in interest rates. The
process of *securitization,* in turn, involves the bundling of consumer
loans and home mortgages into packages of securities that are then resold. Alas, Warren Buffett was talking sense back in 2003 when he
warned that "the range of derivatives contracts is limited only by the
imagination of man or, sometimes so it seems, madmen."[12] But madmen or not, most Wall Street leaders, in the mounting stages of avarice
and glee, embraced the whole seeming opportunity. Not only would
these products sell like hotcakes in the United States, but their believers
predicted they would carve out a huge international market. Merrill
Lynch, Lehman, and the others could almost smell the money.

By 2008, as the financial pages trembled with the global downgrades
and default problems undercutting American-made and American-
exported CDOs, CDSs, CMOs, ABSs, MBSs, and ABCP, the numbers
began to look a good deal more cautioning. Yes, the profits had indeed
been huge. JPMorgan Chase estimated that in 2006, banks globally

brought in $30 billion from their asset-backed securities business, and
Bloomberg News later surmised that securitized products produced
one-fifth of bank revenues during the preceding decade. In 2008, the
fixed-income research firm CreditSights Inc. estimated that over-the-
counter sales of derivatives accounted for as much as 40 percent of the
profits of firms like Goldman Sachs and Morgan Stanley.[13]

However, the potential vulnerabilities were mind boggling. Back in
1993, the notional or nominal value of U.S. derivative instruments had
been some $14 trillion. By 2001, it was approaching $100 trillion. Then
over seven years, one of the most extraordinary and perilous transformations in world financial history would lift the 2008 total to $600 tril-
lion. Figure P.2, below, illustrates the rocketing derivatives volume,
along with the naive reassurances (and consequent failure to regulate)
from Federal Reserve Chairmen Alan Greenspan and Ben Bernanke.

FIGURE P.2
Wild About Derivatives

Global Derivatives Market
$ trillions (Nominal Value)

$615 Trillion ▶

■ Over-the-counter instruments
□ Exchange-traded instruments

2005
2003
1999
1987 Crash

88 90 92 94 96 98 00 02 04 06 08*
*First-half 2008

Data: Intl Swaps & Derrivatives Assoc; Bank of Intl Settlements
Source: InvesTech Research, Oct. 17, 2008

"I think, generally speaking, they
[derivatives] are very valuable. They
provide methods by which risks can be
shared, sliced and diced and given to those
most willing to bear it."

Ben Bernanke, *Chairman, President's Council of
Economic Advisors—11/15/05
(Current Federal Reserve Chaiman)*

"The use of a growing array of derivatives
and the related application of more
sophisticated methods for measuring and
managing risk are key factors underpinning
the enhanced resilience of our largest
financial intermediaries . . . the benefits
of derivatives, in my judgment, have far
exceeded their costs."

Alan Greenspan, *Federal Reserve
Chairman—5/3/03*

"By far the most significant event in
finance during the past decade has been the
extraordinary development and expansion
of financial derivatives."

Alan Greenspan, *Federal Reserve
Chairman—3/19/99*

Because the practices and predicaments of securitization are described in chapter 4 of the main text, these pages will focus on derivatives and securitization—both "exotic finance"—as the fourth great nurturer of the financial sector. To be sure, the notional value shown in Figure P.2 gives a much overstated picture of the real sums at risk in any plausible default scenario. Several attempts have been made in the latter direction. Using 2007 data, the Bank for International Settlements first broke out the notional values: a total of $596 trillion split between interest rate derivatives ($393 trillion), credit default swaps ($58 trillion), and currency derivatives ($56 trillion) with the remainder put into an unallocated category. Then, to assess real-world vulnerability, the BIS set what they called *net risk* at $14.5 trillion, and put a plausible *gross credit exposure* at $3.256 trillion.[14]

Abstract as these trillion-dollar references may seem to laypeople, global fears of a second wave of exotic financial implosions took shape during 2008. In 2007, mortgage-backed securities and mortgage-linked packages of collateralized debt obligations (CDOs), contaminated by subprime mortgage ingredients, had been the top sources of heartburn. By autumn 2008, financial institutions had already written off some $700 billion of these products. In the meantime, credit default swaps (CDSs), as well as the so-called Synthetic CDOS in which credit swaps also figured, had become the new front burner of crisis management. Commentators were identifying them as the next set of financial dominoes positioned for a costly tumble.

Credit swaps, in a nutshell, allow an investor—or a gambler—to take out a contract for an agreed upon period on the credit worthiness of a borrower or lender, whether bank, brokerage firm, insurance company, or even sovereign government. Because these swaps represented insurance of a sort, the American International Group (AIG), the giant U.S. insurance company, emerged as the leading issuer or writer. Other firms were also drawn into what was an unregulated, but initially lucrative field. The issuer—AIG or some other enterprise—didn't have to put up any collateral on its swaps so long as it could maintain its triple-A credit rating. On top of which, the writer could book a profit, based on a benign expected default rate, as soon as the contract was sold. Taking out credit swap "insurance" appealed to institutions anxious to hold a lower-rated but high-yielding asset.

Several of these innovations notably facilitated financial sector expansion. Credit default swaps were insurance contracts, but unregulated because they fell into a jurisdictional crack. Banks, in particular, could use these initially cheap pseudo-insurance policies as wraparounds to upgrade their speculative investments to triple-A, respecting which the bank in question would not have to hold collateral. This allowed banks to leverage themselves to the hilt and shrug off low assets quality—"we're insured, aren't we?"

High returns drove the marketing. "It was a quest for yield," said Don Kowalchik, fixed-income strategist at St. Louis–based A.G. Edwards. "As soon as you get all of these synthetic products based on other products, it's a cancer that refuses to stop spreading."[15]

Nonspecialist readers who have gotten this far may be starting to chuckle. Between 2001 and 2008, according to Bloomberg News, credit default swaps surged from a notional value of $681 billion to a notional value of $62 trillion. Intensifying the jeopardy, added Bloomberg, "ninety percent of the trades were concentrated in the hands of seventeen banks, according to the Federal Reserve Bank of New York."[16] Should one of those institutions fail, and AIG was an even bigger bomb, the falling dominoes could become the financial equivalent of the Black Death. In the fearful global credit conditions after August 2007, skittishness sent the cost of these swaps climbing. That strain intensified in the weeks leading up to September 2008, the month when four major institutions—Merrill Lynch, Wachovia, AIG, and Lehman Brothers—lost triple-A ratings, faced insolvency, or were obliged to let themselves be acquired. Panic was not only in the air; it was in the elevators, toilet stalls, and executive suites.

We will come back to these private interrelationships and to Washington mismanagement—sometimes collusive—in a later part of this preface. Suffice it to say for now that as 2007 drew to a close, elements of the financial press speculated that financial institutions might have to take write-downs with respect to credit default swaps (and related synthetic CDOs) comparable to the $700 billion they were taking for instruments connected to the subprime mortgage crisis. While that future amount was conjectural, insiders knew that amid autumn's maelstrom, the credit swap counter-party nexus surrounding AIG was a driving force behind the enactment of mammoth federal bailout legislation.

We cannot turn away from this fourth engine of financial sector expansion—the embrace and promotion of exotic products—without noting that in 2006 and 2007, confident Wall Streeters predicted that derivatives, securitization, and structured finance were becoming this country's biggest and most profitable export, replacing yesteryear's manufactures. For several years, the market seemed promising, but foreign sales tanked in late 2007 and 2008. "Securitization was based on the premise that a fool was born every minute," Columbia University economics professor Joseph Stiglitz told a congressional committee in October 2008. "Globalization meant there was a global landscape on which they could search for these fools—and they found them everywhere."[17] Not exactly, though. The other fools—or worse—were some Americans sitting in large corner offices.

Foreclosing on the American Dream: Mortgage Finance and Housing

The fifth vehicle of the financial sector's mega-expansion, hardly a great disclosure, can be treated quickly, in light of the great 2000–2006 media focus on housing, mortgage finance, and related securitization. The buildup was huge, just like the eventual 2007–2008 implosion.

As Figure 2.6 on page 51 shows, between the first quarter of 2001 and the first quarter of 2007, total mortgage debt in the United States doubled from $4.92 trillion to $9.96 trillion. As for mortgage origination, that had tripled from 1997 levels to reach a total of $2.5 trillion in the year 2006 alone (see pp. 112–119). United States banks, in the meantime, were moving into mortgage finance in a big way. Figure 2.2 on page 32 shows the mushrooming of the percentage of total bank earning assets that fell into the mortgage-related category. From some 28 percent in 1985, the ratio jumped to 40 percent in 1989, about 50 percent in 1998, and some 60 percent in 2006. Banks, and brokerage firms with them, were placing a whopping bet.

Now "mortgage-related" went well beyond plain vanilla mortgage loans to individual homebuyers. These were only the beginning of the profit chain. As the mortgage-related ratio of bank assets made its big leap between 2001 and early 2007, exotic financial products were also coming to the fore, as we have just seen. Of the $2.5 trillion in mortgages originated in 2006, three-quarters went on to a pseudo-sophisticated reincarnation in mortgage-backed securities (see p. 116 for more detail). At this point, though, even the mortgages themselves had often taken on unprecedented variations. In 2005, the *Washington Post* reported that about two hundred different mortgage products were available, and David Duncan, chief economist of the Mortgage Bankers Association, opined that a recent reference to "exotic" loans by Fed Chairman Alan Greenspan probably meant the "option adjustable rate mortgage." This contract extraordinaire permitted borrowers to themselves decide how much to pay, the length of the loan, and when they chose to convert from a fixed rate to a variable rate or back again.[18] Who, you might wonder, could offer such a mortgage?

In fact, there was a powerful new reason why banks and other lenders were offering such wide-ranging come-ons to get people to sign up for loans they probably couldn't afford. That was the heavy demand from securitization shops and bank departments for new carloads of mortgage loans to repackage into mortgage-backed securities or collateralized debt obligations. With the help of misleading or even rigged ratings, these would then be sold for a fat fee to a pension fund in Baton Rouge or a savings bank in Bavaria. The fees were paid up front. It didn't matter too much what quality of meat was being stuffed into the securitized sausages. In fact, it was often subprime. Financial writer Michael Lewis noted that "In 2000, there had been $130 billion in subprime mortgage lending, with $55 billion being repackaged as mortgage bonds. But in 2005, there was $625 billion in subprime mortgage loans, $507 billion of which found its way into mortgage bonds."[19] Many of these bonds received absurdly high ratings.

Besides banks, many brokerage firms and investment houses were also heavying up in the business of mortgage finance. The *New York Times*'s Gretchen Morgenson, in a far-ranging analysis, described how the giant Merrill Lynch brokerage firm, "went on a buying spree. From January 2005 to January 2007, it made twelve major purchases of residential or commercial mortgage-related companies or assets. It bought commercial properties in South Korea, Germany and Britain, a loan-servicing operation in Italy and a mortgage lender in Britain. The biggest acquisition was First Franklin, a domestic subprime lender. The firm's goal, according to people who met with Merrill about possible deals, was to generate in-house mortgages that it could package into CDOs."[20] Regulators, said Morgenson, "are finding that exotic products known as derivatives . . . transformed a financial brush-fire into a conflagration."

In the halls of the Federal Reserve, meanwhile, a vital accomplice, chairman Greenspan, had a long-standing interest in how amid periods of rising home prices, Americans would refinance their existing homes or buy new ones, using their gains to support other outlays. He had seen them do exactly that in the 1970s and 1980s (see pp. 11–12, 33–34, and 104). In 2001–2002, he probably considered how they might do so again, especially if the Fed pushed its key interest rate down to 1½ percent or even 1 percent. The Fed did just that, the home-owning (and would be home-owning) public took advantage, and pumped some of their proceeds into the rest of the embattled U.S. economy. As described in the main text on pp. 10–12, not a few economists have underscored the importance of this stimulative increment, especially between 2003 and 2006. Harvard economist Martin Feldstein noted that in 2004 alone, net mortgage borrowing not used for new home purchases, about $600 billion, represented nearly 7 percent of disposable personal income. In a related vein, over five years the housing sector was calculated to have provided nearly 40 percent of the increase in U.S. GDP and employment.

The further benefit was that rising home prices offset much of the nationwide loss of wealth—some $7 trillion—occasioned by the 2000–2002 collapse of the stock market bubble, most notably the implosion of the tech-laden Nasdaq Index (see pp. 11–13, 62). In California, for example, the price of homes essentially tripled between 1995 and 2006, as you can see in Figure 4.4 on p. 114. Wealth-wise, this increase was gangbusters.

It was also a powerful tool of financial expansion, mortgage finance being one of the sector's weightiest pillars. Virtually all the mega-firms were enthusiastic participants. I don't think it is any coincidence that the peak of financial services' share of GDP came in 2004, amid the hey-day of low-interest rate refinancings and before California real estate, in particular, started showing early hints of a downturn in 2006. In the end, of course, housing and mortgage finance also led the contraction.

It would be convenient to be able to say that these five circum-stances accounted for three-quarters or four-fifths of the financial sec-tor's takeover, so that the chickens coming home to roost in 2007 and afterward were related hatchlings of that same arrogant and miscon-ceived expansion. Obviously, though, no such precision is possible. It's my surmise, but guesswork is not proof. In societal terms, though, the balance must tip toward condemnation. Hyping Americans into some-thing like card-carrying indentured servants obliged to support 70 per-cent of the U.S. economy was unforgivable. Letting the merger and acquisitions process run wild and create mega-firms beyond effective national regulation but disposed to experiment and speculate hither and yon was disastrous. Allowing the financial sector to metastasize us-ing $15 trillion of borrowed money over a quarter of a century was calamitous. So was permitting the derivatives and securitization busi-ness to create its $11 trillion of this and $53 trillion of that with the most incestuous and uncontrolled webs of distribution and counter-party re-lationships. And turning the core of the American dream, home owner-ship, into a trap for the rest of that dream staggers belief. For these transgressions, combined with a malfeasance that has jeopardized tens of millions of jobs, turned some suburbs into incipient ghost towns, and bushwhacked retirement plans, university endowments, and pension funds, the principal blame can fairly be placed on big finance and on largely ineffective federal regulators and political overseers.

Readers will have noted that I place the financial mega-firms, formed after the 1999 repeal of prior constraints, at the center of all five of the opportunities, mentalities, exotic innovations, and circumstances just described. My discussion of the flawed 2008 bailouts will focus on how these relief measures were preoccupied with rescuing or subsidizing the five biggest commercial banks, the five biggest investment banks, four top players in the mortgage sector, and the insurance industry gi-ant AIG. I call them the Frankenstein Fifteen because of their size, reck-lessness, and in some cases, very prominent culpability—JPMorgan, before its merger, had been a principal nursery of credit derivatives, Merrill Lynch was the principal underwiter of CDOs, Countrywide and Washington Mutual were the sultanates of subprime, and Citigroup led the field with a 25 percent national share of off-the-books structured investment vehicles. Breaking them up and letting them fail might have been the better course. But first, a quick look at that ineffective regulation.

2. 1929 REDUX: FEDERAL PERMISSIVENESS AS CONTRIBUTORY NEGLIGENCE

When we look back to the Great Depression for precedents, comparisons between the minimal regulation of the Roaring Twenties and the permissiveness of the years from 1996 to 2008 have some validity. However, there is also a pivotal difference. During the 1920s, there was very little prior U.S. financial regulation to repeal or ignore, and the fault lay in governmental failure to come to political and legal grips with new economic relationships and financial practices. That could be—and generally was—corrected by the New Deal reforms of the 1930s, even if some enactments were worthier than others.

By comparison, the financial sector's malpractice from the mid-1980s through 2008 was more corrosive than the earlier negligence. This is because in many ways the politics, permissive ideology, and interest-group lobbying during the Multi-bubble years was obliged to be deliberate and uprooting. This involved the capture and disarming of existing agencies and boards, as well as the gutting or repeal of existing statutory protections. Besides Congress and the White House, the centers of this "disregulation" usually included the Federal Reserve Board and often the Treasury department.

By the end of 2008, however, the American people clearly grasped what had taken place. As the data later in this preface will show, large majorities believed it was critical or very important for President Obama to impose stricter regulations on financial institutions.

The deregulation of the savings and loan industry set in motion by the Reagan administration in 1981 is a jumping-off point. Edwin Gray, a California Republican who headed the Federal Home Loan Bank Board, agreed that philosophy encouraged the scandals and bad loans because oversight was generally neglected: "The White House was full of ideologues, particularly free-market types. They'd say 'The way to solve the problems is more deregulation,' and by the way, deregulation means fewer examiners" (see p. 41).

Even one bank lawyer looked back with dismay on the 1996 Supreme Court ruling deregulating credit-card fees. Duncan MacDonald, a lawyer for Citibank, commented that "I didn't imagine that some day we might have ended up creating a Frankenstein."[21]

The 1999 repeal of the Glass-Steagall act and its restraints on financial mergers, pushed by Democratic President Clinton and his treasury secretary, Robert Rubin, as well as by Congressional Republicans, wound up creating the regulatory equivalent of the Cumberland Gap. Nomi Prins, a former managing director at Goldman Sachs, described the crippling result this way: "Another festering problem created by the Financial Services Modernization Act was so-called functional regulation. The act claimed that each component of these new conglomerate institutions would be regulated by a different governmental regulatory body. This meant that different federal and state entities had oversight for different components of the same business, yet nobody had full oversight for the entire institution's activities as a whole. . . . So, functional regulation could more appropriately be called 'disfunctional regulation.'"[22]

A second consequence of the repeal of Glass-Steagall's bar on banks participating in the securities underwriting business was to legitimize a late 1920s reenactment. Repeal was a major enabler of the 2002–2007 collusion between mortgage lending and booming mortgage-backed security and collateralized debt obligation issuance.

The tale of how Fed Chairman Greenspan and Treasury Secretary Rubin had blocked regulators anxious to take a close look at derivatives has been well reported. In 1998, when Brooksley Born, chairwoman of the Commodity Futures Trading Commission, urged that a study be made of regulating over-the-counter derivatives, Greenspan and Rubin led the counterattack. In 1999, Greenspan and Rubin recommended that Congress permanently strip the CFTC of regulatory authority over derivatives, and in 2000, Congress passed a law keeping them unregulated.[23]

The resulting multitrillion-dollar boom and bubble has already been described.

As for the administration of George W. Bush, its eight years of pro-permissiveness attitudes and refusals to regulate or inhibit were predictable. One pattern deserving of particular notice lay in how the Federal Reserve Board and the Bush era Securities & Exchange Commission supported bank lobbyists in keeping the Financial Accounting Standards Board from cracking down on banks' remunerative use of off-the-books entities (SIVs, QSPEs, and the like) to hold and distribute high-profit securitized products. The dangerous nexus was summarized by one Bloomberg News analysis: "Securitization's biggest innovation was off-balance-sheet accounting. If a bank couldn't sell a bond or didn't want to, the asset could be sold to a trust within a so-called special purpose entity, incorporated in a place such as the Cayman Islands or Dublin, and shifted off the books. Lending expanded, and banks still booked profits."[24] The sums involved were vast. Citigroup, which had earlier developed such entities for Enron, had $1.18 trillion in off-balance-sheet holdings as of June 2008.

Another Bush regulatory culpability involved predatory lending practices—hidden fees, deceptive "teaser rates," and the like. In 2004, after a barrage of state laws and lawsuits, the Treasury Department's office of the comptroller of the currency used an obscure federal statute to nullify state laws against predatory lending with respect to national banks. This crimped state-level action against the abuses of subprime lending.

Over the last twenty-five years, few financial regulatory objectives have been less seriously pursued in the United States than the bridling of speculation in its more destabilizing forms—first, the activities of hedge funds; second, Federal Reserve refusal to control speculative or assets bubbles; and third, the practices and big-firm domination of commodities trading. Because that speculative tendencies are central in defining the differences between Anglo American capitalism and the state capitalisms of Asia or parts of Continental Europe, this is a debate certain to grow—and possibly even to produce some new regulation in Washington. Hedge funds have stumbled and been weakened financially, but their close ties to many leading Democrats may keep them essentially unregulated (see pp. 169–74). As for the refusal of Fed chairmen like Alan Greenspan and Ben Bernanke to try to stop speculative bubbles, Bernanke has indicated some willingness to reconsider and foreign central banker opinion has also moved in that direction. In 2008, at least, Congressional Democrats seemed most interested in trying to block or constrain the effects of commodity speculators. Exhibit A was the role speculators appeared to play in pushing up oil prices as high as $147 a barrel by July 2008, then pushing them down sharply again in the second half of the year. Michael Masters, a hedge fund operator who studied energy trading because of his own investments in airlines, gained considerable attention on Capitol Hill. He argued that one of the reasons oil prices came down after June is that traders worried about potential Washington regulation reversed their bets. Masters singled out three of New York's "large financial players" as the "primary source of the recent dramatic and damaging price volatility." The extent to which many OPEC officials and oil ministers bitterly blamed speculators for excessive price increases and decreases also adds to the prospect for some regulation.

Regulatory and malpractice with respect to the 2008 federal bank bailouts also became a heated ethical and legal issue. A number of Washington tax lawyers and former tax officials charged that a Treasury notice issued in September giving a potential $140 billion tax break to bank mergers was illegal and amounted to "a backdoor way of providing aid to banks."[25] House Financial Services Committee Chairman Barney Frank likewise opined that giving the portions of the $700 billion bailout money to banks as investments without strings, as the Treasury did, was improper: "Any use of these funds for any purpose other than lending—for bonuses, for severance pay, for dividends, for acquisitions of other institutions, etc.—is a violation of the act."[26] The Government Accountability Office, for its part, complained in December that Treasury officials lacked internal controls and ways of monitoring what the banks did with the funds provided under the Troubled Assets Relief Program (TARP). That same month, the Federal Reserve Board rejected a lawsuit under the Freedom of Information Act to disclose the (financial sector) recipients of over $2 trillion in loans from eleven different FRB lending programs, as well as the collateral those recipients had left with the Fed. Secrecy would continue. Clearly, neither the Treasury Department nor the Fed had any interest in disclosure or transparency, despite earlier broad assurances by both Secretary Paulson and Chairman Bernanke. One is hard-pressed to disagree with skeptics convinced the whole thing was planned this way.

In politics, what looks like malevolence is often mostly incompetence, but the cynical explanation of the Bush administration approach to financial regulation in general and the Troubled Assets Relief Program in particular does have another building block—the October 2008 article in the Minneapolis Federal Reserve Bank's monthly Working Papers. Authored by three economists affiliated with the Minneapolis Fed—Patrick Kehoe, V. V. Chari, and Lawrence Christiano—the paper contends that actual data on bank lending, interbank lending, and commercial paper issuance do not support the case for the federal bailout legislation set forth by Treasury Secretary Paulson and Fed Chairman Bernanke. Indeed, a separate version of the analysis published by Boston-based Celent Communications, a financial consultancy, under the title "Facts and Myths About the Financial Crisis 2008," contended that "It is striking that many of Chairman Bernanke and Secretary Paulson's data are not supported or are flatly contradicted by the data provided the very organizations they lead." Octavio Marenzi, the head of Celent, said that the Bernanke-Paulson view wrongly generalizes from the situation of a few big institutions.[27]

What the data may ultimately prove is that yes, there was a credit crisis, but that a disproportion of it was concentrated in fifteen or so large U.S. financial institutions, many of which were flirting with insolvency because of their recklessness as just described. This would also help to explain the unusual and much exaggerated panic that was sown by Bernanke, Paulson, and their allies supporting the bailout legislation (see pp. xxxviii–xl). Telling the truth about the apparent preoccupation was not an option. Certainly much of the money Paulson quickly passed out went to these big firms, and the institution-by-institution data on which megafirm had to take what amount of write-downs makes the same point. By December 2008, North American financial institutions had taken some $700 billion worth of writedowns, and the "Frankenstein Fifteen" seem to have accounted for 60–70 percent of them.

The Minneapolis Fed was not the only one of the regional reserve banks to make a stab at truth in labeling. Kansas City Fed President Thomas Hoenig, in an October 13 speech to the Institute of International Bankers in Washington, said this: that regulators, while weighing changes to oversight, should consider "the degree to which we should be concerned and address the rising levels of concentration of financial resources among, if you will, a financial oligarchy that will wield vast powers in the future."[28]

Economist Henry Kaufman, one of Wall Street's few remaining grand old men, proposed in mid-2008 that some sort of federal regulatory authority be set up to deal specifically with the megafirms, and as October and November proved the depth of his fears, he listed them to another international audience. Recent events, he said, have increased the domination of the top fifteen institutions, which now hold over half of the nation's non-financial debt. "These were the very firms," he said, "that played a central role in creating debt on an unprecedented scale through a process of massive securitization via complex new credit instruments" and who "pushed for legal structures that made many aspects of the financial market opaque." In years ahead, he warned, these giants "will limit any chance for the U.S. to move toward greater ecomonic democracy," riddled as they are with conflicts of interest from multiple roles "in securities underwriting, in lending and investing, in the making of secondary markets and in the management of other people's money."[29] True, all of it, and you have to wonder: if all this can happen, does the financial regulatory system the United States operates under today even merit the pretense of that description?

Over the years since 1987, however, no single person's responsibility in these matters can match that of Greenspan, the libertarian and erstwhile follower of Ayn Rand. In testimony to a newly hostile Congressional committee in 2008, he allowed to being shocked, just shocked, at the failures of his beloved free market and self-regulation on the part of the financial sector. In a sense this was perjury, albeit of a philosophic and non-indictable nature. The Fed chairman well knew, from decades of personal experience, that Washington had long since ceased to leave the fortunes of banking and financial services to free-market vicissitudes. Part of federal regulators' reluctance to interfere with asset bubbles or questionable financial sector practices lay in undoubted awareness that high Washington officialdom had, for decades, implicitly signed off on a bias toward assets bubbles and bailouts. Overall, banking and finance constituted the sector of the economy that the Federal Reserve Board and the Treasury not only strongly favored, but had bailed out time after time, pumping money in where necessary to overcome bad managerial judgment or to stave off unwelcome free marketplace judgments.

For a decade and a half now, I have described this flagrant practice as "financial mercantilism" and discussed it at some length (see pp. 54–58). Twelve of the major Washington bailouts and rescues since the policy's de facto launch in 1982 are capsuled on page 57 in Figure 2.7. This is necessary background before our next topic: the implications of multi-trillion dollar federal bailouts of Wall Street put in motion in 2008 by Treasury Secretary Henry Paulson and Federal Reserve Chairman Ben Bernanke.

3. THE GREAT 2008 BAILOUT: SHREWDNESS OR NEO-HOOVERISM?

The gray autumn of 2008 brought Herbert Clark Hoover back into the news pages. The crumbling U.S. economy, some thought, faced another Great Depression, turning George W. Bush into the Republican Party's second Hoover. But a handful of historians argued that the Bush-Hoover analogy did not ring true.

Hoover, they pointed out, was an activist, a man famous for his humanitarian food relief leadership during the World War era. As president in 1929, he criticized his party's laissez-faire wing, later prodding the Federal Reserve Board to expand credit and businessmen to maintain wage levels. By 1931, he was proposing a global moratorium on First World War debt payments and gaining Congressional approval for an unprecedented federal-level Reconstruction Finance Corporation. In the words of historian William Leuchtenburg, "He advocated legislation to undergird mortgages and to liberalize requirements for the issue of Federal Reserve notes. Today, these measures seem modest, but, at the time, *BusinessWeek* called the law to ease credit 'perhaps the most powerful dose of monetary medicine that has ever been applied to the strengthening of the banking system'" in a similar period.[30]

Hoover boasted, in his 1932 Republican national convention speech accepting renomination, that, "We might have done nothing. That would have been utter ruin. Instead, we met the situation with proposals . . . of the most gigantic program of economic defense and counterattack ever evolved in the history of the Republic. Some of the reactionary economists urged that we should allow the liquidation to take its course until we found bottom. We determined that we would not follow the advice of the bitter-end liquidationists."

The point, though, is that Hoover's activism didn't succeed. Cross-pressured Republican presidents do these things poorly. Between 1929 and 1932, Congress had worsened matters with new tariffs and tax increases. The Federal Reserve Board, after taking interest rates down to 1½ percent, put them up to 3½ percent again in 1931. The several branches of the U.S. government coordinated poorly, and stepped-up White House activism failed to keep a recession from morphing into something worse. And this is why we can talk legitimately about a second round of confused interventionism in 2008 as the "neo-Hooverism" in which the Bush regime embroiled itself.

Not a few old-line Republican stalwarts grumbled, after Hoover left office, about how he had paved the way for Democratic "socialism" under Franklin D. Roosevelt. Similar complaints were predictable in 2009–2010. Presidentially weak as Bush was, he chose as his top economic managers an activist treasury secretary and a willing Federal Reserve Board chairman, who orchestrated unprecedented and massive intervention in the private sectors. In September and October, editorialists and pundits boggled about Republican socialism, bank "nationalization," and weeks in which "capitalism changed forever." This was exaggeration, given the number of times since the early 1980s that the financial sector had been bailed out under both Republican and Democratic regimes. Nevertheless, the Bush administration, by its last months in office, had reiterated Hoover's essential failing: insufficient skill to keep a major speculative debt buildup from imploding, followed by an activist brand of crisis management that was flawed, and in some ways made matters worse.

These unfolding policies, between August 2007 and December 2008, represented a slow, reactive response to the implosion of a quarter-century bubble that the White House hadn't understood and which, to shift metaphors, took the form of a huge slow-motion train wreck around grand-scale vulnerabilities. Two of the president's choices for top economic posts played leading roles.

One of them, a top Wall Street financier, ensured that Washington's eventual rescue policies would concentrate on trying to bail out the leading financial sector firms while ignoring the spreading cancer of their innovations and malpractices. The second, by career a university professor, overemphasized academic research about how to guard against severe downturns by attempting to refight the onset of the 1930s depression—his doctoral specialty.

Henry Paulson, Bush's pick as treasury secretary, was not your ordinary gray-flannel investment bank CEO. One 2006 *BusinessWeek* article spotlighted the new secretary as a high-roller: "Think of Paulson as Mr. Risk. He's one of the key architects of a more daring Wall Street where securities firms are taking greater and greater chances in their pursuit of profits." That, the magazine added, "means taking on more debt . . . it means placing big bets on all sorts of exotic derivatives and other securities."[31] Those were items like collateralized debt obligations (CDOs) and credit default swaps (CDSs), arcane U.S. innovations we now know to have spread toxicity, opacity, and paralysis.

Economics professor Ben Bernanke, before he replaced Alan Greenspan as Federal Reserve Board chairman in early 2006, had served almost three years as the Chairman of George W. Bush's Council of Economic Advisers. There he had been an enthusiast of Bush economic policies, including upper-bracket tax cuts, Social Security privatization, "securitization" of assets, and "safe" financial derivatives. No expert on exotic finance, he was an academic specialist in monetary policy—a man held out to Congress and the public as understanding how to prevent or ameliorate a great depression. The Fed, in Bernanke's view, would have to expand the money supply or extend liquidity enough to overcome any credit crunch. As a card-carrying monetarist, he also insisted that no meaningful inflation was building in 2007 and early 2008 even though global commodity price indexes had begun to soar.

Thus, and without foresight, did a hapless George W. Bush assemble his last economic team. They would pick up where the original bubble-blower, Alan Greenspan, Fed Chairman between 1987 and early 2006, had left off. Together, the two would steer U.S. policy toward a blend of experimentation and panic—an outcome not unlike Hoover's, albeit reached through new biases and myopia.

Wall Street's "Mr. Risk," calling the shots at Treasury, would focus the Bush administration's 2008 economic "rescue" policies not on the broad national interest but on bailing out the "Frankenstein Fifteen" top U.S. financial institutions—the big five investment firms (Morgan Stanley, Goldman Sachs, Merrill Lynch, Lehman Brothers, and Bear Stearns), the five largest commercial banks (Citigroup, JPMorgan Chase, Bank of America, Wells Fargo, and Wachovia), the four mortgage gamesters (FNMA, FRMC, Washington Mutual, and Countrywide), and American International Group, the high-rolling insurance giant. Along with the barely regulated hedge funds, these were the big firms that borrowed huge sums, overleveraged, merged grandiosely, experimented with all "the exotic derivatives and other securities," and led the multitrillion-dollar metastasis through which finance ballooned to take over domination of the U.S. economy. They had a lot of vocational turf and a big political and gross domestic product beachhead to protect. They also had a huge lead in write-downs and institutional vulnerability. Although in mid-2007, Paulson initially contended that the emerging crisis involved no more than bad real estate lending practices, the cynical observer can reasonably assume that "Mr. Risk," the archinsider, knew much of what he was ignoring—how deeply the malpractice and deception ran—and on whose behalf.

If Paulson wanted to keep the spotlight off the real culprits—the financial and mortgage giants with their leverage laboratories, multiple trillions worth of exotic mortgages, toxic CDOs, and Las Vegas–like credit swaps—then academician Bernanke at the Fed was a good partner. The narrow-gauge theory in which the economics Ph.D. had immersed himself basically ignored twenty-first-century mega-innovations and looked back seven decades to the crash of the 1930s and how that long-ago, pre-computer-age debacle might have been prevented. Too little of that outdated context applied more than seven decades later.

Foremost among Bernanke's economist heroes were the late Milton Friedman and the latter's wife, Anna Schwartz. Some four decades earlier, they had coauthored a landmark volume entitled *A Monetary History of the United States,* which made them the preeminent theorists of how the Federal Reserve deserved principal blame for letting the circumstances of 1929–1933 deepen into depression—and also of how the Fed might have prevented that deflationary descent. It was noteworthy, then, that on October 18, in an interview published by the *Wall Street Journal,* Anna Schwartz opined that Bernanke, their acolyte, was simply getting Fed policy wrong. The problem, she said, did not lie with the money supply or liquidity as it had in the 1930s. There was a sufficient amount. The problem lay in all these toxic securities the Wall Street geniuses had dreamed up, gorged on, and sold around the globe in huge quantities between 2003 and 2007. "They're toxic," said Ms. Schwartz, "because you cannot sell them, you don't know what they're worth, your balance sheet is not credible, and the whole market seizes up." And by giving transfusions to otherwise insolvent banks, she said, Paulson and Bernanke had prolonged the crisis. "They should not be recapitalizing firms that should be shut down. . . . Firms that made wrong decisions should fail."[32]

Letting bad decision makers fail was how things worked in the old days when "creative destruction" kept capitalism on its toes. Now, of course, too many institutions in the United States were perceived as too big to fail, which made creative destruction unacceptable. And that inacceptability, in turn, denied U.S. capitalism some of its capacity for renewal.

Had Paulson and Bernanke been willing to take a blowtorch to the Frankenstein firms and their practices and products back in late 2007 or early 2008, some six or eight might well have had to be broken up, taken over, or forced into bankruptcy or receivership—indeed nine more or less were anyway. However, the stock market and credit crisis of autumn 2008 might have been avoided or greatly mitigated. Instead, up to that point, Paulson publicly pretended that nothing serious was wrong, perhaps because he was out to save Ober-Kommand Wall Street—the pivotal leaders and institutions who were at the heart of the underlying negligence. Bernanke, in turn, could not sufficiently transcend his student-of-the-1930s academic focus. "This was [his] claim to be worthy of running the Fed," said Anna Schwartz.[33] However, Bernanke miscued because he was fighting the last war, not the present one—much like the French generals of the 1930s who constructed the Maginot Line superfortifications along the German frontier to keep Berlin from mounting another 1914-type attack.

The eighteen months between the credit crisis of August 2007 and the ignominious departure of the George W. Bush administration in January 2009 will probably seed hundreds of chronicles over the next decade, and to attempt one before the economic dust has settled would be senseless. Besides which, after October 2008, the two major paths diverged somewhat—that of Treasury's Paulson, who planned to leave with the other Republicans, and that of Bernanke, who planned to stay at the Fed and hope for reappointment from the Democratic president in 2010.

Paulson's role, a far cry from the further deregulation of Wall Street he had at first hoped to orchestrate, stumbled over a mounting succession of ad hoc financial bailouts that segued into stock market panic in September and October 2008. Then embarrassment widened in November and December as contradictions and miscalculations piled up and fault-finding mounted among Democrats empowered by the national elections.

Complaints that the treasury secretary had seemed more reactive than proactive dated back to August 2007 when he downplayed the initial credit crisis as mostly a matter of bad mortgage lending decisions that shouldn't hurt the "real economy." Then in the early autumn he proposed his first Wall Street bailout—a Treasury-backed plan for a "super-SIV" fund to buy $80 billion worth of assets from structured investment vehicles set up by major banks to house off-the-books activities. However, the Dow-Jones Industrial Average set a new record in October, and the big banks dealt with their SIVs in various ways, so the Paulson proposal was shelved. Soon thereafter, the secretary and his aides turned back to the question of a new Washington regulatory approach. Calling for a federal regulatory rollback was no longer politic, but in late March the former Goldman Sachs chairman discussed some of his "blueprint" for centralizing broader monitoring of systemic risk to financial markets together with related new regulation in the Federal Reserve. If any federal regulator was seen as generally benign by the financial sector, it was the Fed, for reasons one European scholar, Professor Willem Buiter of the London School of Economics, would distill a few months later: "The Fed listens to Wall Street. Throughout the twelve months of the crisis, it is difficult to avoid the impression that the Fed is too close to the financial markets and leading financial institutions, and too responsive to their special pleadings, to make the right decisions for the economy as a whole."[34]

Nor was there any coincidence about Paulson's March timing with respect to proposing expanded Fed authority. That month, Paulson and Bernanke had to put aside other concerns, particularly the troubles of the two mortgage giants, Fannie Mae and Freddie Mac, to deal with an immediate crisis—a liquidity squeeze and mounting desperation at Bear Stearns, the fifth largest New York investment bank. Over the weekend of March 17–18, the two officials, through the good offices of the New York Federal Reserve Bank and a $29 billion Fed loan, arranged a bailout in the form of a shotgun marriage between JPMorgan Chase and the hapless Bear. The latter was not too big in size to fail. However, it was too *interconnected* to fail because of its super-leveraged involvement in the trillion-dollar webs of mega-firm counterparty exposure, principally with respect to credit derivatives. Meanwhile, the Fed jumped with both feet into a new role of lending to previously ineligible investment banks and setting up three new financial lending mechanisms at the New York Fed—most notably the Term Securities Lending Facility (to which the fearful could turn in weak securities for treasuries, as long as the second-rate paper had the pretense of a triple-A rating). On March 27, the *Wall Street Journal* ponderously described the period since March 18 as "Ten Days That Changed Capitalism"—or at least its American variety.

Alas, many more such days would follow as the deleveraging of America continued to outpace the belated comprehension of plutocrats, professors, and pundits alike. Among the handful of journalistic exceptions, the most conspicuous was columnist Gretchen Morgenson of the *New York Times,* herself at one time a stockbroker, who mocked the Fed's "trash for cash" program by noting that "in early April, for instance, the Fed had to turn away many of the nation's largest broker-age firms when they showed up, trash bags a-bulging. These firms hoped to unload securities valued at almost twice what the Fed was willing to lend." She concluded by urging the Fed to tighten its lending entities' collateral requirements and stop being "a monetary bordello."[35] Paul-son, however, said in May that the credit crisis was abating, and then in late July, the Associated Press quoted the treasury secretary as saying that "It's a safe banking system, a sound banking system. Our regulators are on top of it. This is a very manageable situation."[36]

Obviously not. Six weeks later, fear and incompetence began giving way to panic. September 7–14 saw the first of several weeks of financial hell, this one centered on problems and/or bailouts relating to Fannie Mae, Freddie Mac, Washington Mutual, and Lehman Brothers, as well as the Bank of America's sudden acquisition of Merrill Lynch. In the background, AIG, the giant insurer at the epicenter of the $60 trillion global web of credit default swaps, began talking to the Fed about pos-sible assistance in asset sales.[37] By September 16 or so, global investors were trying to figure out why Paulson and Bernanke had decided to let Lehman Brothers go bankrupt while rescuing AIG. Lehman was also a major player in the global derivatives tangle. Apparently Washington had not as yet worked out a clear and intelligible bailout yardstick.

Shortly thereafter, Paulson, enlisting Bernanke, decided to swing for the fences. On September 18 the stock market surged after hearing of his reported plan to set up a new mega-entity to buy up bad debt, thereby taking it off the books of the major banks. Even hedge funds might be able to participate. But when the treasury secretary, still un-wise in the ways of Congress, submitted his proposal on September 19, it was a short and haughty two-and-one-half page emergency docu-ment. Approved by President Bush, it proposed that Paulson be made America's financial czar and empowered to use $700 billion of taxpayer funds to bail out wall Street by buying up the half-worthless financial products that other Wall Street geniuses—all too many working in the same major firms—had pioneered.

Congress quickly produced a larger and somewhat different bill, but in the same vein. The public, however, rightly perceiving a staggering ego trip and shameless bailout, inundated Congress with a wave of letters, telephone calls, and e-mails, and on September 22, the House of Representatives voted to reject the Treasury-Fed power grab. This stunned the financial community, and global markets shuddered. Within ten days, the Senate had acted on a new rescue package—further loaded with $100 billion worth of baubles, tax breaks, and fresh pork to sway public and congressional opinion. It passed, and on October 3, the House accepted this version. Even so, global stock markets scoffed and sank for several days. The legislation enacted was never sufficiently credible.

Especially in the week before October 3, Bush administration and Congressional supporters of the bailout, and others in Wall Street, left no available panic-button unpushed. A talking head on CNBC said that if the package didn't go through, people might not be able to get cash out of ATMs. Ben Bernanke had actually told a Congressional committee in September that "if we don't do this, we may not have an economy on Monday."[38] Washington economist Kevin Hassett, an adviser to John McCain, whose presidential hopes came unglued amid this late September and October disillusionment, said it certainly "looks like a panic. Markets are pricing in catastrophes beyond modern experience."[39] Anti-bailout conservatives complained that backers kept visiting the rhetorical cemetery with this or that death prediction. At the Kansas City Fed's big end-of-August conference at Jackson Hole, Wyoming, C. Fred Bergsten, director of the Peterson Institute for International Economics, had regretted that "the alarms of the financial sector have been overstated. The real economy has slowed down but is not yet in severe difficulty."[40] The momentum was that the *real* real economy, finance, *was* in severe difficulty.

In Greek mythology, panic came when Pan frightened the Titans in their great battle with the gods, so that terror displaced rationality. Autumn generated a similar mood. By mid-November, even the *Wall Street Journal* referred to the Street's "race . . . for the title of uber-bear." Whereas Merrill Lynch chief John Thain said the slump would resemble 1929 rather than lesser contractions, former Goldman Sachs chairman John Whitehead told Reuters that this economic crisis "could be worse than the Depression."[41] No major financial elite in an embattled leading world economic power had ever talked this way before. Normally, authority prefers happy talk.

So why were the panic buttons pushed so relentlessly and at so many intervals? Because, if I may venture a hypothesis, Frankenstein finance needed a speedy rescue from its trillion or so of toxic products (or a massive infusion of de facto subsidies) before it faced multiple indictments—in political assemblies, judicial halls, and courts of both domestic and international public opinion. Furthermore, benefits were to be had from widespread popular belief that the world, and not just the United States, was in a severe economic crisis, a point to which we will shortly return. But for ordinary Americans, the damage from this special-interest manipulation and panic was disastrous. Bloomberg News calculated that as of mid-October, "the crisis of confidence has destroyed about $27 trillion of value in the global stock market. That isn't a typographical error. The combined market capitalization of the world's publicly traded companies is down to about $36 trillion, from a high of $63 trillion reached a year ago."[42] The additional fallout ranged from devastated private retirement accounts and corporate pension funds to beaten-down university endowments and anticipated state and municipal insolvencies and cutbacks in services.

For the treasury's Paulson, though, his high profile began to turn into personal and political embarrassment as contentions grew that in early autumn he had stumbled from one short-lived government bailout yardstick to another. September's major misstep had been the seeming inconsistency of treatment between an unrescued Lehman Brothers and an extravagantly Band-Aided American International Group. To add insult to inadequacy, Paulson admitted that in late September, he had changed his mind about the central proposal before Congress to bail out the big financial institutions through a government entity to buy up their toxic paper. This while it was still being considered! Paulson's explanation? The number of conditions being tacked on to the toxic paper sales and the investor wariness signaled by the plummeting stock market. These had made him shift, he acknowledged, to a second objective: taking the $700 billion in the new federal Troubled Asset Relief Program

(TARP) set up by early October's legislation and using it instead to buy equity stakes in financial institutions, thereby giving key banks substantial funding. However, Paulson didn't tell anyone, and for several weeks Treasury staff continued to say that the distressed assets plan was being implemented even though focus had been shifting to the plan to use TARP to directly subsidize banks.[43] Congress was more than annoyed.

In the meantime, skepticism had also accumulated around Paulson's loose manner of investing federal dollars from TARP in selected banks and other financial firms. Complaints included concern that much of the first $250 billion was going to healthy mega-banks that didn't really need it like JPMorgan Chase, Bank of America, Goldman Sachs, Wells Fargo, et al. Getting these powerhouses to expand lending seemed to be more Washington lip service than true priority. In some quarters, Treasury selections were interpreted as something of a seal of approval intended to bless selectees' stock prices and merger capacities. Moreover, Treasury favoritism—its apparent vocation in picking winners and losers among the top fifty or top one hundred banks—put weaker rivals at risk of being taken over or shut down.[44] Worse, said critics, instead of being required to make loans, banks were allowed to apply the federal investment dollars to pay high salaries and bonuses, as well as to take over other banks. Washington even went so far as to provide new federal tax-break support for the would-be mergers. A related ruling by the Internal Revenue Service and the Treasury Department on September 30 gave banks a special merger-related provision that would facilitate such acquisitions but potentially cost taxpayers $100 billion.[45] This made potential acquisitors receiving a Treasury imprimatur even bigger winners.

As for the separate lending mechanisms set up by the Federal Reserve in the wake of the Bear Stearns bailout, these—unlike the $700 billion to be spent under TARP—were not obliged by actual disclosure requirements. So although heavy Fed lending topped $2 trillion by early November, an increase of $1.172 trillion just in the seven weeks since the Fed's September 14 relaxation of its collateral standards, details were withheld. Media and investors alike fumed at not being able to find out who borrowed how much and with what quality of collateral. Information on how the Fed valued collateral could unclog the markets, some

said, and the unwillingness of the Fed and Treasury to provide that detail sparked a lawsuit under the Freedom of Information Act, which
was unsuccessful.[46]

Demands by critics to force informed valuations on Frankenstein
financial products went to the heart of both government misbehavior
and the troubled assets enigma. In their eyes, the government should
have been much tougher and less concerned with financial sector profits and negative publicity in breaking the "trash" logjam. One strong
voice, Janet Tavakoli, the president of a structured finance consultancy,
blamed the inadequacy of federal officials, suggesting to the *New York
Times* that regulators ought to impose a form of martial law allowing
them to rewrite derivatives contracts: "Just start straightening out these
books. Start stripping them down and simplifying contracts so people
can start to understand what they own. It would be unprecedented, but
so is everything else that we are doing."[47] Many other proposed solutions pointed in the same general direction, albeit without the extreme
measure of martial law.

In any event, as late 2008 slipped into the slowed-down turkey-dinner-
and-eggnog holiday season, Paulson's TARP, in particular, had become
a Treasury embarrassment and a tempting Congressional piñata. Invec-
tive ballooned after his mid-November volte-face that had ruled out
distressed asset purchases and announced that the program would now
be used only for capital injections into financial firms and to increase
the availability of auto loans, credit cards, and student loans. Demands
grew on Capitol Hill that TARP dollars be made available to the near-
death automobile industry and to hard-up cities like Phoenix, Philadelphia, and Boston. Elements of the investment community complained
about changing rules in the middle of the game. "It's really thrown the
markets into a tizzy," said one brokerage firm strategist. Former House
Republican majority leader Dick Armey, himself an economist, minced
no words: "Paulson's very public and frantic panic of a few weeks ago,
along with his current state of bewilderment and indecisiveness, is most
likely the single greatest explanation for the persistent doldrums in the
market." Indeed, on November 13, the Dow-Jones Industrial Average
closed 27 percent below where it had been when Paulson first announced his plan.[48] The future of TARP, pundits said, would have to

await the arrival of the new Democratic president and the new and more Democratic Congress in January 2009.

By this point, Bernanke, whose Fed term ran until early 2010, was increasingly colluding with Democrats like House Financial Services Committee Chairman Barney Frank. The Fed chairman's fortunes were diverging from those of Paulson, whose time in office was nearly over. Bernanke, to be sure, shared some of Paulson's embarrassment over TARP. However, since September, much of his own effort had concentrated on Federal Reserve projects like the $100 billion bailout of the American International Group, tailored to favor banks, as well as his multitrillion dollar outreach to make the U.S. central bank the domestic and international lender of last resort. This mission took a prominent page from the post–World War II internationalist playbook of how authorities should have defused the 1929–1933 disaster. Of course, the Fed Chairman was also taking a prominent page from his own well-advertised doctoral thesis. On top of the huge loans given to domestic financial institutions, massive dollar credits were extended to foreign central banks—not just to the traditionally collaborative ones in Western Europe, Canada, and Australia, but to central banks in upper-tier emerging-market nations like Mexico, Brazil, Singapore, and Korea.

On the surface, these actions were shrewd. In September and October, panicked global investors fled to security in U.S. treasury debt, which simultaneously buoyed the dollar and put downward pressure on oil prices. Moreover, Bernanke's largesse slowly displaced the initial perception of a bumbling United States spreading toxic financial products around the world with the affirmative image of a deep-pocketed Uncle Sam generously extending giant loans and credits to other countries which, it now seemed, might be even worse off. Besides the $1 trillion steered into the U.S. financial system, the Fed provided another $450 billion of dollar liquidity to European central banks to spread around, and then a further dollop to central banks in Canada and Australia and to the four in Latin America and Asia. There were even predictions that Fed distributions might hit the $3 trillion mark by New Year's.

These huge undertakings, on the heels of Washington's scare rhetoric about the U.S. and world economy seizing up unless Congress passed the Paulson-Bernanke bailout, worked to internationalize what had appeared to be a U.S.-centered crisis. It also anointed the U.S. dollar as the apparent currency of the *rescue* instead of the vulnerable and blameworthy currency of the underlying *implosion*. Something similar had happened back in August 2007, when for four to five weeks a flight to "safety" and U.S. treasury debt buoyed the U.S. dollar, after which foreigners resumed their dimmer view. A year later, the flight to safety and related gain by the hitherto embattled dollar was even larger, but the bills coming due would be mind-boggling.

Skeptics warned that no lender of last resort had emerged after 1929 for a good and practical reason. The United States, although it had become the world's principal creditor nation after World War I, had yet to establish the dollar as the world's reserve currency. Britain, meanwhile, was clearly a faded global military and political hegemon, but through 1931 sterling remained the leading and most trusted currency. Neither nation fit the role of lender of last resort—the United States didn't want to be, and Britain didn't have the wherewithal.

As 2008 ended, kindred warning flags flew. China was the leading creditor nation, with huge currency reserves. The United States was the weakening principal power that still printed the accepted reserve currency.

The crux was whether the United States, having become the world's principal debtor nation, could afford to provoke its global creditors with its biggest ever round of massive budget deficits and monetary expansion. By the year's end, autumnal prediction that the Paulson-Bernanke financial rescue programs might cost $3 trillion had doubled and trebled, although the numbers were vague. In mid-December, the *Wall Street Journal* noted that "by the most expansive counting possible, the U.S. has pledged to spend, invest or loan as much as $10 trillion," yet "the final tab is likely to be much, much smaller."[49]

Through the early summer of 2008, informed opinion had come to see the world facing its biggest inflation wave since the fifteen-year commodity cycle between 1966 and 1981. The international monetary fund said just this in July. The world is "in the midst of the broadest and most buoyant commodity price boom since the early 1970s." Then the panic came in September and October. As a result, and with financial institutions in the lead, opinion—certainly among elites in the United States, Britain, and Europe—enthusiastically shifted to the view that deflationary forces had replaced inflationary pressures. By these assumptions, Bernanke's behemoth reflationary outlays would succeed yet also be neutralized. Few questions would be more pivotal for the next decade, but before we turn to the potential for an inflation trap, it is necessary to review the underlying inadequacy of U.S. inflation and economic growth statistics and their potential to become an American Achilles' heel.

4. LIES, DAMN LIES, AND ECONOMIC AND FINANCIAL STATISTICS

Amid everything else, the Obama administration has to wrangle with the decades of bad statistics, both private financial and official, that previous Washington regimes tolerated, smiled on, or even colluded with. In a period of great stress, weak and untrustworthy U.S. government economic data could be as dangerous as the phony triple-A bond ratings of American mortgage-backed securities and collateralized debt obligations peddled around the world through 2007. The inaccuracy of government statistics is real, as several top Obama economic advisers had recognized in earlier comments.

University of Chicago professor Austen Goolsbee, appointed to Obama's Council of Economic Advisers, described in a 2002 *New York Times* op-ed column how the federal government had "cooked the books" with regard to unemployment data.[50] Clearly, he suffered few illusions.

In May 2008, former Federal Reserve Board Chairman Paul Volcker, already a prominent Obama counselor, allowed to the Joint Economic Committee of Congress that he thought the Consumer Price Index understated inflation. He told members a tale of "an old lady, who used to, when I was in the Federal Reserve, (say) there's a lot more inflation in the economy than in those figures." Now Volcker saw the same thing. He added that CPI data hadn't reflected the sharp run-up in the housing market before the 2007 credit crisis, that food and energy prices shouldn't be excluded when judging inflation's long-run trend, and that "we're much more inclined to say there are improvements in quality" rather than rising inflation.[51] This was a concern for global investors, because GDP growth data, as well as the CPI, pivots on inflation or its lack.

If such complaints rarely stirred partisan divisions, that was because of a forty-year record of both Republican and Democratic presidents abetting what outsider critic John Williams called "polyanna creep"— making federal economic data more friendly to incumbents and cheerleaders (see pp. 80–89). Besides, human nature includes a chiseling component, and during the centuries of gold and silver coinage, precious-metal debasement was common. The twentieth century transition to paper money obliged a shift into debasement through both printing presses and statistics.

Politically, regimes can find weak or nonexistent statistics convenient. For roughly a century, government and private economic data in the United States and Britain has usually been behind the times rather than ahead of them in spotlighting the major changes overtaking the two nations. A venturesome scholar might argue that "establishments" have little reason to introduce measurements. Take the late nineteenth century United States, where the displacement of farming wracked the Midwestern and Western political economy. Data was sparse. According to agricultural historian Fred Shannon, with respect to costs of production, prices, interest rates, and farm credits, "no collected data exist for most of these." Furthermore, "no attempt was made by the census takers of the nineteenth century to enumerate farm population . . . and the basic data for farm income are probably even less dependable than those for farm population."[52]

Or consider Britain at the beginning of the twentieth century where another debate over economic decline involved the strength of that nation's manufacturing and wealth relative to the rest of the world. Aaron Friedberg, author of *The Weary Titan: Britain and the Experience of Relative Decline, 1895–1905*, noted that "there were at the turn of the century no good measures of national income or total production. When the question of Britain's economic performance was raised, those who favored a continuation of present policies used raw output figures to make crude demonstrations of absolute progress, but they could not show at what rate overall growth was occurring."[53] Data would have aided critics to make their case.

Nor had U.S. statistics been informative as the Great Depression unfolded from 1929 to 1933. Because the federal government did not know how many people were out of work, the American Statistical Association in 1928 urged Washington authorities to put such a question in the 1930 census. That was done, and by one account Washington "enumerated the unemployment and soon afterward reported that 2,429,069 were out of work and 758,885 were on lay-off, a total of 3,187,947. Even this relatively modest figure was not low enough for [President] Hoover. He asserted that between 500,000 and 1,000,000 of those persons were not 'unemployed' because they had no intention of seeking work, mainly in the seasonal trades. Hence the President 'corrected' the Census figure to 1,900,000, which he declared was not out of line with unemployment in the twenties."[54] Later reconstructions put a correct figure for April 1930 in the neighborhood of 4.4 million.

In 2008, U.S. economist N. Gregory Mankiw, suggesting that even today's data may not facilitate effective prediction, also harked back to the Depression as an example. He cited a 1988 paper by three reputable economists entitled "Forecasting the Depression: Harvard versus Yale," which showed "that the leading economists at the time, at competing forecasting services run by Harvard and Yale, were caught completely by surprise by the severity and length of the Great Depression. What's worse, despite many advances in the tools of economic analysis, modern economists armed with the data from the time would not have forecast much better."[55] The related issue for the next decade is what *foreign* investors may be able to rely on for accuracy with respect to U.S. debt, inflation, and growth.

The politicization of government data, although not much acknowledged by U.S. opinion molders, helps to explain its weakness. In the May 2008 *Harper's,* I wrote an article entitled "Numbers Racket," which focused principally on political considerations and how most presidents from John Kennedy on made cumulating efforts to have government economic statistics say what presidents, treasury secretaries, and Federal Reserve Board chairmen (and for that matter, the emerging debt industry and financial sector) would be more comfortable with. In a nutshell, John Kennedy wanted to minimize unemployment in Camelot, Lyndon Johnson was rumored to tinker with gross national product data, and Richard Nixon ordered up what became the distinction between headline and core rates to de-emphasize inflation. Jimmy Carter fell victim to soaring inflation, and the Reagan regime defanged part of the Consumer Price Index by substituting a mild so-called owner's equivalent rent computation for the prior home-ownership cost estimates. The George H. W. Bush administration pushed revamping the CPI Index to reduce the inflation computation, curb Social Security and pension increases, trim runaway federal deficits, and bring down interest rates, and Bill Clinton presided over the implementation of this controversial agenda.

The upshot, under Bush the Younger, was a CPI that no longer measured the cost of a constant basket of goods. Thanks to product substitution and so-called hedonic pricing, the new math came in at a much lower and government-friendly rate as shown in Figure 3.3 on p. 83. The hedonic adjustment—reducing prices to make up for supposed quality increases—was the one criticized by Paul Volcker a few pages back. One wonders what he has said to Obama.

Unemployment numbers, for their part, are in the process of soaring as the economy confronts its possible Hoover era analogy. Here it is vital to remember that U-3, the semi-official government figure—at least the one always cited in the media—is not the one that best reflects the inclusive measurements used in many European nations. True, U-3 is the one that Hoover's ghost would presumably recommend. However, U-6, the broader count, describes what is the harsher reality. From 8.3 percent in mid-2007, it jumped to 9.1 percent in March 2008, 10.3 percent in July, and 12.5 percent in October.

Other pivotal government statistics, like the gross domestic product calculation, also have *Fantasy Island* characteristics. We should begin by noting a switch in definitions. Washington used gross *national* product data until the early 1990s, but because that portrait encompassed imports and other embarrassing international trends, decision-makers switched to the gross *domestic* product, which tends to be a half point more positive. The current GDP calculation, however, is also more a matter of imagination than precision because it relies on manipulable ingredients like imputed income, a life-and-death-of-businesses adjust-ment, and a GDP price deflator component that some experts feel might as well be made up.

In September, *Barron's* columnist Alan Abelson commented that "these days, alas, those initials [GDP] more typically signify 'Gross Distorted Pap.'" He singled out the GDP deflator, which alleged that inflation grew at a rate of 1.33 percent during the April–June quarter, which would be the lowest in five years—this while even CPI reports showed a much higher rate.[56] A year earlier, Peter Schiff of EuroPacific Capital had wryly noted that Washington orchestrated its latest growth rate only by declaring a mere 8/10 of 1 percent inflation level, the lowest deflator claim since the Eisenhower era.[57] The reader must keep in mind the importance of an honest inflation deflator. For example, as-suming nominal GDP growth of 3 percent, a 1 percent deflator would mean 2 percent real growth, whereas a 5 percent deflator would turn real growth negative by 2 percent. Iconoclast John Williams, who watches the federal data for ShadowStats, calculated in late 2008 that real GDP growth had been negative since 2006.[58]

Critical characterizations could fill a book. Bloomberg columnist Caroline Baum noted that the two economic performance reports pub-lished more or less simultaneously by the federal Bureau of Economic Analysis—the GDP and gross domestic income (GDI)—should resem-ble each other but recently have displayed a conspicuous overperfor-mance by GDP. Robert Barbera, chief economist at brokerage firm ITG, called the $300 billion shift over eighteen months "breathtaking. We have no employment, no income, and a jump in output. It's like the virgin birth."[59] Merrill Lynch economist David Rosenberg took the same second quarter 2008 GDP report with a "very large grain of salt" for another reason. The profits figure in the GDP was helped by a non-sensical claim that profits in the crumbling financial sector ballooned at a 27 percent annual rate. Rosenberg's succinct comment: "Are you kid-ding me?"[60]

It's hard to see who could believe that government statistics bureaus successfully defy political pressure. However, I do think that most of the professional staffers support their data out of some conviction. They are caught up in their own guidelines, methodologies, and information, just like the U.S. intelligence specialists who were certain that Saddam Hussein had weapons of mass destruction and the financial ratings people at Standard & Poor's, Moody's, and Fitch, who confidently relied on computer programs that assigned triple-A ratings to assets-backed securities now eight levels lower and all but worthless. Bureaucrats tend to go with the conceptual flow.

Finally, it's important to underscore that a lack of statistical, informational, and accounting integrity was at the heart of the financial sector's recent crisis and panic. An extensive list of lies and damn lies came to light in 2007–2008. Mark-to-market accounting had frequently turned into mark to make-believe. With respect to Fannie Mae and Freddie Mac, Senator Richard Shelby, the ranking Republican on the Senate Banking Committee, accused the two mortgage giants of keeping books that were "a house of cards." Several analysts have published evaluations showing banks' gross abuses of so-called goodwill accounting. One bank claimed $11.5 billion worth of goodwill to pump up its assets even though its market capitalization was only $7.4 billion. The ratings given to structured securities by companies like Standard & Poor's and Moody's were so shoddy and opportunistic that the *Wall Street Journal* headlined one early 2008 analysis "Moody's Weighs Warnings Labels for Its Ratings."[61] In this milieu, why should CPI or GDP data be presumed pristine?

Although these shortcomings and deceptions have gotten some attention amid the crisis, they are likely to get more in the near term as political leaders and prosecutors contemplate financial reforms, remedies, and punishments. The flaws and misrepresentations of U.S. government economic statistics, in particular, may be an unexploded bomb waiting to go off. During much of 2007 and 2008, candid foreign investors made occasional reference to hard-to-believe U.S. inflation and growth statistics as one reason for the American dollar's decline in value and support. The greenback's upsurge in the summer and autumn of 2008 temporarily curbed that discussion. However, the Federal Reserve's massive reflation campaign, in embracing a role as domestic and international lender of last resort, was thought by some to pose the threat anew. Were inflation to remain or return as a powerful global force, bolstered by Washington's expected record budget deficits and the Fed's profligate balance sheet, then the believability of politicized U.S. inflation and GDP data—flawed well beyond opacity—could again pose major difficulties.

5. THE 2010S: A GLOBAL INFLATION TRAP?

Nothing, of course, matches inflation and high interest rates for potential menace to the orderly winding down of a massive twenty-five-year bubble of debt and credit instruments blown up around low interest rates. Figure 1.1, on page 7, shows that as of 2007, the present-day U.S. debt bubble on the right side of the page had swollen to a record 340 percent of GDP. This was up from 159 percent in 1975 and 200 percent in the early 1980s at the launching of the Multi-bubble. Amid such levels, prime-rate interest levels in the 8–9 percent range could be devastating, and 5–6 percent inflation figures combined with large-scale borrowing needs could bring such constrictions in their wake.

FIGURE P.3
Commodity Plateaus and Rises

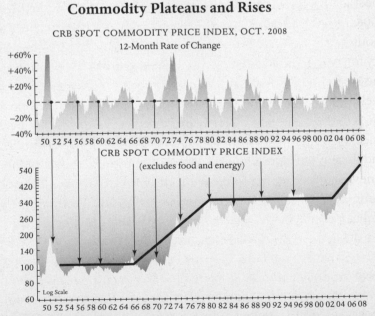

CRB SPOT COMMODITY PRICE INDEX, OCT. 2008
12-Month Rate of Change

CRB SPOT COMMODITY PRICE INDEX
(excludes food and energy)

Source: Commodity Research Bureau

Back in late spring and summer of 2008, as consumer and commodity prices in the United States appeared to peak, investors like Jim Rogers, the motorcycle-riding commodities guru, had a ready counterclaim: commodity prices will dip for a while because of recession, but they'll be back on the rise soon enough, borne aloft by the winds of a ten-to-twenty-year cycle. Had one of those began in 2002 or 2003, as Commodity Research Bureau charts and precedents hint, then energy, metals, and grains could start climbing again in 2010 or earlier. Economic historians generally agree on three such commodity up-cycles in the twentieth century—first, between 1897 and 1920; second, between 1933 and 1950; and third, between 1965 and 1981. Figure P.3, above, shows the ups and downs between 1950 and 2008, and it's easy to see the distinctive 1965–1981 upthrust surrounded by the relative price plateaus on either side.

An Ongoing Commodity Cycle?

The current eruption seems to have started in 2002, accelerating in 2006, and dedicated traders in the commodity pits believe it's another long-term phenomenon. Federal Reserve Chairman Bernanke and most of his fellow economists, however, dismissed the idea in 2005 and 2006, sweated in 2008, and then contended as 2009 began that any previous inflation gathering had been stopped in its tracks by the deflationary forces of the credit implosion and slumping stock market. However, the 1965–1981 behavior patterns suggest that a full-fledged commodity cycle doesn't get extinguished that easily. Figure P.4, with fuller detail for 1965–1981, reveals a sequence of three relatively short commodity price dips—in the growth recession of 1966, in the recession of 1970, and then in the deep recession of 1974—that were quickly followed by renewed upward spikes. Only in the double recession of 1980–1982 did commodity prices dip and then remain on a lower plateau, and the second half of that double downturn included Fed Chairman Paul Volcker's once-in-a-century decision to crush inflation with a federal funds rate that peaked at 19–20 percent in early 1981. In particular 1974's sharp but brief commodity price nosedive was quickly followed by a 1975–1976 rebound, which occurred notwithstanding the brief deflationary impact of a severe 48 percent bear market in 1973–1974.

FIGURE P.4
Commodity Prices and Recessions

CRB SPOT COMMODITY PRICE INDEX, NOV. 2008
(12-Month Rate of Change)

The point to underscore with respect to the 1970s commodity boom is that it was interrupted in 1969–70 and again in 1973–74 by two wicked bear markets notable for assets deflation. Besides the well remembered 1973–74 dive, the 1969–70 bear market savaged hedge funds, and between November 1969 and November 1970 roughly one hundred brokerage firms disappeared or were acquired (see p. 33). Commodity prices slumped both times, and presumably both bear clawings raised (false) specters of inflation turning into deflation. Overall, the assets deflation was misleading because economic histories summarize the 1970s as inflationary.

Not that this 1970s portrait represents firm proof of a renewed commodity cycle. No precedent says that a deeper stock market and bond market debacle in 2009–2010 couldn't stop it. However, the Fed does appear determined on reflation. Whereas Paul Volcker "took the punchbowl away" in 1980, Bernanke in 2008 was filling it up with steroids and amphetamines never before distributed in the hallowed halls of the Federal Reserve Board. One longtime credit watcher (and Fed critic), publisher James Grant, described late 2008's liquidity excitement this way: "Over the past year, the Central Bank's balance sheet has grown by 133 percent. It was only yesterday when annual growth of 13 percent seemed aggressive. Ten times that aggressive-if-not-reckless-and-certainly-inflationary rate of expansion is a fact that takes some getting used to."[62] Although Bernanke and his colleagues initially argued that their bailout would not produce inflation, that pretense weakened in December after the National Bureau of Economic Research pronounced that the United States had already been in a recession for a year despite inconclusive GDP data. That increased the likelihood that the sharp commodity declines in 2008 were recession-linked and that the end of the downturn would see a price rebound.

It is also relevant, however, that at the end of 2008, most of the world's population were experiencing steep levels of inflation that stood in sharp contrast to their circumstances in the deflation-colored yesteryear of 1925–1933. Also, the 2002–2009 period differed from the 1925–1933 example in half a dozen additional ways—mostly debt, currency, and trade circumstances—that further undercut the case for parallel remedial measures. The several contexts posed different challenges. But the yes-or-no of global inflation is a good starting point.

Studying American political history over fifty years has taught me a lot about when the farm states hurt and when they prospered, and from 1925–1933, the U.S. commodity states suffered, along with kindred areas in Asia, Latin America, Canada, and Australia. One economic history summed up the severity: "Between 1925 and 1929, the combined average price of the leading agricultural commodities fell about 30 percent. . . . Then came the Depression. Between 1929 and 1933, the price of coffee and most other agricultural commodities hit rock bottom."[63] In the United States, the wholesale price index dropped from 93 in 1925 to 78 in 1930 and 59 in 1933. I doubt that any government bureau measured the price levels of that era in Brazil, Mexico, China, India, Korea, Indonesia, the Philippines, Pakistan, Russia, Nigeria, Egypt, Turkey, or Saudi Arabia because some were colonies and most had no budgets for such things. This was an eight-year global deflation that deserved the name.

Today, these nations' central banks muster some of the world's largest foreign currency reserves, and together these countries count ten times the population of the United States. Most of their governments issue inflation statistics monthly. The data was easy to find, and here are the published annual inflation rates as of October 2008: Brazil, 6.4 percent; Mexico, 5.78 percent; China, 6.5 percent; India, 11.8 percent; Pakistan, 25 percent; Korea, 4.8 percent; Indonesia, 11.8 percent; Philippines, 11.2 percent; Russia, 11.5 percent; Turkey, 12.0 percent; Egypt, 20.2 percent; Saudi Arabia, 10.9 percent; and Nigeria, 14.7 percent.[64, 65, 66, 67, 68, 69, 70, 71, 72, 73, 74, 75, 76, 77] In several cases, autumn saw a small decrease;

in just as many, the trend was still up. Culprits cited ran the gamut from housing, education, clothing, and footwear to food, fresh fish, utilities, kerosene, and transportation. But currency relations were also at work.

Parenthetically, in a third of these nations, inflation intensified during late 2008 because of the depreciation of their local currencies, some of which reflected global panic and some effects of Westerners bailing out of emerging markets' securities. This depreciation, in turn, intensified local inflation by raising the cost of imported goods and foreign loans. Chaotic currency relationships create their own Pandora's box of inflationary and disinflationary side effects.

The Federal Reserve and Inflation

As figure P.3 shows, the CRB Commodity Price Index had been rising since 2002. For the next five years, however, Federal Reserve Board members professed to be unworried. Inflation was not a problem; the CPI was tame; American popular expectations of inflation were "anchored." Skeptics scoffed. Bill Gross of PIMCO, the well-known U.S. bond manager, cited global inflation in 2008 to explain why he disbelieved Washington's CPI numbers. Over the past decade, he said, worldwide inflation has averaged nearly 7 percent while the U.S. official inflation rate has averaged 2.6 percent. "Does it make any sense that we have a 3 percent to 4 percent lower rate of inflation than the rest of the world?"[78]

By that spring, even Bernanke was nervous. If inflation was really gathering force on a scale to match the 1970s, his basic model of where the early twenty-first century U.S. economy was vulnerable would be drawn into question. The decline of the dollar and the rise in oil prices made the threat worse. But then the autumn panic brought an ironic rescue. Frightened investors sold emerging market assets and moved to U.S. treasuries, and this bolstered the dollar. So did the collaboration of the Federal Reserve Board with foreign central banks. A stronger dollar, in turn, put downward pressure on commodity prices, which eased inflation and further bolstered the dollar. By reversing the 2002–2008 trend of the dollar going down and oil prices going up, U.S. policymakers put foes like Iran, Venezuela, and Russia on the defensive. These countries' previous strategic edge—see pp. 148–150—had turned into an Achilles' heel. Niccolò Machiavelli couldn't have taken better advantage of a previously weak economic hand.

What remained unclear was for how long it would work. Oil prices, driven too low by depression-and-deflation panic, were close to a rebound. The United States—the Fed, in particular—was making huge outlays and taking huge obligations onto its books. One compilation put the mid-November total at $4.284 trillion—$2.910 trillion belonging to the Fed, $1.375 trillion to the Treasury and other governmental institutions.[79] December estimates climbed higher. At some point, holding the paper money and debt of a great power whose financial system might come unglued would not be smart.

Anna Schwartz, Milton Friedman's widow, told *Barron's* she was sorry that her husband was no longer alive to lecture the Fed, but she would try: "The problem comes from a lack of ability to price the [arcane] instruments, not a lack of liquidity. Evidence of the banks' unwillingness to lend can be seen in the most basic Federal Reserve statistics, which show that in the week ended Oct. 1, the banks had $167 billion of balances with the Federal Reserve, whereas on July 2 there was only $14 billion. Clearly the banks are holding the money and failing to pass it on in new consumer loans and business, preferring instead the safety of the vault."[80]

And, she added, the result of the Fed's approach would be inflation. "Up until the middle of 2008 the Federal Reserve balance sheet had not experienced an annual growth rate well above the traditional 5 percent. Since midsummer, Fed credit appears to have ballooned greatly, and that's behind the upward pressure in the consumer price index. The Fed pooh-poohs inflation because of a perceived slowdown in oil and gas prices. But theoretically, any increase in the monetary base must be met with tightening if inflation is to be avoided. Right now the Fed is pursuing a pro-inflation strategy by lowering interest rates and showering the banking system with liquidity. They're not even considering inflation. Paul Volcker learned that success in fighting inflation comes from tightening monetary policy, even if the public holds you responsible for disinflation."[81] As 2009 began, this debate hung over the currency and credit markets.

A Second Price Revolution in the Works?

Early twentieth century historians came up with the term "price revolution" to describe the great surge of inflation visible across Europe from the mid-1500s to the early 1600s. The New Cambridge Modern History even split the sixteenth-century volume's title: *The Counter-Reformation and the Price Revolution, 1559–1610*.

I'm not pedantically fishing for precedents. If we are indeed caught up in a second of these sweeping price redefinitions, it would be front-page stuff. Based on some twenty-five years of intermittently reviewing Spanish and Dutch economic history from that distant era, I think the analogy has considerable plausibility. The half-century that began in the late 1960s may represent a comparable upheaval in prices, wealth, and geopolitical realignment, and one that is hardly finished.

The first price revolution is generally said to have been propelled by the arrival in Spain and subsequent dispersal across Europe of the gold and silver brought by treasure fleets from the new world. But as the editor of the New Cambridge Modern History volume explained:

> We no longer regard the "price revolution" as solely the product of the sudden influx of silver from America after the opening of the Potosi mine in 1543 any more than we think of the Renaissance as caused by the sudden influx of Greek scholars after the fall of Constantinople in 1453. Nevertheless, the flood tide of American silver, pouring in on top of other deeper and longer-term movements of population, of trade and of finance, did quicken and steepen the price rise and make this a more difficult time for governments and for all whose incomes were comparatively inflexible.[82]

Geopolitically, the original price revolution encompassed a period in which European ships armed with cannon, a breakthrough, combined the gold and silver of the Americas and control over African and Asian sea routes to establish Europe's primacy in global wealth and power. In military and economic terms, Asia, while still much more populous, slowly fell behind. The possibility of a second grand upheaval starting in the late 1960s begins with two Asian successes—in Vietnam and in OPEC's oil price achievements in 1973 and 1979—and extends through the early twenty-first century commodity and wealth realignments tied to the rise of Asia and the chastisement of U.S. finance in the 2008 Crash. As power began to realign in the early 2000s, prices rose even more rapidly than they had four hundred years earlier—except, in the ultimate crush, the prices of battered U.S. financial assets.

The complexity of this half-century transition will be amplified in the new afterword, but for the moment the critical significance lies in price upheaval—the possibility of Asia-linked inflation.

6. THE NEW POLITICS OF (DISGRACED) FINANCE

A weird parlance of depression chic edged into American conversation in late 2008. The unnerving financial analogy between 2008–2009 and 1932–1933 kept cropping up. The mood indigo of the post-election stock market—darker than that of 1932—was deemed to fulfill the inky gloom registered in pre-election charts. Standard & Poor's noted that its S&P 500 Index rose or fell at least 1 percent in 86 percent of October's trading days, making it the second most volatile month—only November 1929 was worse.[83] The next day the S&P 500 was identified as heading for the worst annual decline since 1931, and Goldman Sachs predicted that the magnitude of stock market swings—the recognized volatility index—was on track to top 1929.[84, 85] This dark chronicling was a boon for those Democrats hopeful that Inauguration Day would have the aura of a Rooseveltian rescue.

But if the 1932 analogy had some validity regarding the market for stocks, it had less regarding the 2008 national elections. Republican nominee John McCain had even led in some Labor Day period polls, losing any chance for the White House only when September's financial fear syndrome set in. Seventy-six years earlier, Franklin D. Roosevelt had defeated Herbert Hoover by a whopping 57 percent to 40 percent majority. In 2008, Obama led McCain by 52.7 percent to 46 percent.

This was not a mandate-filled margin. Aside from stimulus, popular demand for a second New Deal did not leap out. Nor was it important to add that Roosevelt hadn't been very specific about his own plans during the 1932 election campaign.

Besides FDR's own margin, the 1932 Congressional elections had also been a blowout. The Democrats won a 59 to 36 margin in the Senate and a gaping 313 to 117 seat edge in the House. Taken together, the 1930 and 1932 elections had tidal wave characteristics—in the Senate Democrats gained eight seats in 1930 and twelve in 1932; their pick-up in the House was fifty-three seats in 1930 and ninety-seven in 1932.[86] By contrast, the Democrats' gains in 2006 and 2008 were impressive but less than overwhelming. Their twenty-seat House gain of 2008, disappointing to earlier hopes, in part reflected the reduced vulnerability of House Republicans who opposed the Bush White House on the unpopular Wall Street bailout proposal.

The 1932 election stands in rare company as a full-fledged realignment. It produced the strongest presidential margin for the Democrats since Martin Van Buren overwhelmed William Henry Harrison in 1836. The Democratic performance in 2008, however, most resembled the outcome in 1976—Obama exceeded Jimmy Carter's 50 percent to 48 percent presidential victory, but the Democrats of 2008 fell well short of their 1976 Congressional ratios. Distilling the several elections into relative mandates, the Democrats of 1932 got more or less carte blanche. For 2008, *carte gris* might be more accurate—a slightly ambivalent gray. The incoming party, though, did get some more help in November and December when George W. Bush again disappointed on a world economic stage and Treasury Secretary Paulson's bailout missteps and retractions worsened the departing Republicans' image.

But victory also had a further caveat. Considerable post-election mention was made in the press of how the Democratic and Republican presidential contenders never referred to the troubled U.S. economy's below-the-surface obstacles—massive debt, the ascendancy of finance, its hold on both parties, the conflicts of interest in the regulatory role of the bank-linked Federal Reserve System, the ballooning federal budget deficit, and the rapidly closing window of opportunity for Washington to deal with the ever nearer Social Security and Medicare crisis.

Both parties were complicit, and no clear partisan advantage was obvious. The unmentionables loomed large.

Hardly anyone moved to the next interpretive level. What kind of responsiveness could be expected from the two major party coalitions, their constituencies, and financial backers? Why would a 2009–2012 Democratic administration be unusually bold? What would be politic for the new president to attempt and at what stage of his administration?

Finance and the New Democratic Coalition

Since the New Deal years of the 1930s, the two major parties have, to a revealing degree, shifted bases. Obama got most of his white votes in the Northeast, Great Lakes, and Pacific Coast, where he carried unusually high percentages of better-educated and wealthier voters. He swept black voters everywhere. Ironically, this was much closer to the social geography of Herbert Hoover's support in 1932 than to the regionalism and race of those backing FDR. Of Roosevelt's top nine states in 1932, only one—Florida—went for Obama. Of McCain's top nine states in 2008, all had gone for FDR seventy-six years earlier. By and large, FDR's best regions in 1932—the South, Rocky Mountains, Border, and Great Plains—backed McCain in 2008. For Democrats, the Obama coalition represented a considerable post–New Deal metamorphosis.

Which brings us to how that changing Democratic presidential coalition may or may not be able to deal with critical economic issues in a time of deep popular economic frustration. Besides FDR, there are no previous examples of success. The 1960s regimes of presidents Kennedy and Johnson governed during a period of relative prosperity and uptrending stock markets, as did Bill Clinton over his two terms. The animosities the three produced were related to war, social issues, and scandals. No real economic-tension precedents there.

Jimmy Carter did face four years of troubled economics, and the Democratic coalition splintered in 1980 after liberal Edward Kennedy attacked Carter's relative economic conservatism in the Democratic primaries. Harry Truman and Woodrow Wilson both held office during reasonably prosperous times, and negative judgments on them were largely noneconomic and partially war-related. However, if we jump back from Wilson to the previous Democratic president, Grover Cleveland (1893–1897), we find another prime occasion of economic policy and tension splitting the Democratic coalition like a ripe melon. Cleveland, a Wall Street–friendly conservative Democrat from New York, did little to combat the hard times that started in 1893. So radical Western forces wound up seizing the 1896 nomination for William Jennings Bryan, "the boy orator of the Platte," who led the Democrats into a coalition with the Populist Party. They lost, but not by much. The post–Civil War Democratic coalition came unglued.

Normally, devoting attention to a nineteenth century presidency would be pointless. However, the Democratic party over the last decade and a half has been "Clevelandizing"—giving a growing amount of attention and weight to a well-heeled financial-sector faction based in the New York–New Jersey–Connecticut region. These ties, accelerated by Bill and Hillary Clinton—and therefore also describable as "Clintonizing"—are dealt with at length in the main text (see pp. 172–74). In these pages, I will simply update them for the Obama ascension, which added Chicago.

Support for Democratic candidates, including Obama, increased substantially in Northeastern, Great Lakes, and Pacific upper-income areas in 2008. Moreover, financial-sector political contributions also realigned in favor of the Democrats. Public Citizen, the consumer advocacy group, charged that by giving Obama a record $11.7 million to McCain's $8 million, Wall Street had gained a disproportionate influence over the new administration's regulatory agenda.[87] Indeed, absent Obama taking provocative positions on issues he generally sidestepped during the campaign, this embrace is not likely to reverse. Most financial-sector donors to the Democrats assumed by election day the inevitability of significant re-regulation between 2009 and 2012. What they did expect was that the change would be reasonably collaborative, implemented by Democrats acceptable to Wall Street. That expectation proved out with Obama's November 18 comment that "The answer is not heavy handed regulations that crush the entrepreneurial spirit and risk-taking of American capitalism," along with his subsequent naming of New York Federal Reserve Bank President Timothy Geithner as Treasury secretary and former secretary Lawrence Summers to head the National Economic Council (and perhaps replace Chairman Bernanke at the Federal Reserve in 2010).

On the other hand, dissatisfaction could easily grow among nonaffluent white Democrats anxious for a powerful response to their needs from the erstwhile party of labor, working-class, and middle-class Americans. As we will see in more detail, the financial panic of September and October radicalized much of the U.S. electorate—traditional low- and middle-income Democrats were in the vanguard—against the financial sector, its bonuses, and demand for bailouts at taxpayer expense. The range of 2009–2012 issues able to crystallize intraparty tensions would include: 1) expansive funding of Social Security and Medicare versus budget deficit priorities; 2) consideration of finger-pointing investigations like those of the 1933 Pecora Committee; 3) ongoing Wall Street bailouts, especially those raising collateral bonus and pay issues; 4) any de facto "industrial policy" in which Washington picks economic winners and losers; and 5) any White House plan to centralize additional regulation of finance in the hands of the unpopular Federal Reserve Board, with its intimate ties to banking and Wall Street.

Potential fault lines took early shape in attacks by leaders of the AFL-CIO on the influence within the Obama camp of former Clinton Treasury Secretary Robert Rubin, for almost a decade chairman of the executive committee of Citigroup, the controversial bank which itself obtained a federal bailout in late November 2008.[88] Liberal economist Joseph Stiglitz, for his part, warned Obama against appointing Democratic deregulationists from the Clinton years: "Many of the people whose names have been floated around have actually been implicated in some of the deregulation initiatives that got us into this mess."[89] The Consumer Federation of America, joining the battle, described consolidating regulatory power in the Fed, which isn't responsible to Congress, as a recipe for lax oversight. The federation's head of investor protection emphasized pressuring the new administration to reject the Paulson plan to emphasize the Fed: "You can't just assume that because Barack Obama is a Democrat that he's going to come in and fundamentally change that [Paulson] approach."[90]

Publications from the *Wall Street Journal* to *The Nation* commented on the number of actual and rumored Obama appointees to top jobs who had strong ties to the financial sector. It was a powerful list. Chicago Congressman Rahm Emanuel, quickly named White House chief of staff, had been a managing director of the investment firm of Wasserstein Perella and a director of both Freddie Mac and the Chicago Mercantile Exchange. The *Journal* noted that in 2008, he "collected more money than any other House member from hedge funds, private equity firms, and the broader securities and investment industry, even though he faced no serious opposition." Geithner, picked for Treasury, came from the presidency of the New York Federal Reserve Bank, where he had been the Fed's chief liaison with securities firms and bond dealers and a key figure in all the major bailouts. Summers, named to head the National Economic Council, was managing partner at D. E. Shaw, a $39 billion Boston-based hedge fund and private equity firm with a specialty in esoteric math-based investing strategies.[91, 92] Press reports also noted that during the Wall Street panic, Obama himself regularly traded text messages with Robert Wolf, CEO of UBS Americas, Timothy Collins, head of the buyout firm Ripplewood Holdings, and Mark Gallogly, managing partner of the private equity firm Centerbridge Holdings.[93]

In allocating political responsibility for the quarter-century Multibubble, I would give the Republicans, in office for sixteen of the twenty-four years, about 70 percent of the blame and the Democrats some 30 percent. The tricky aspect for the incoming Obama administration is that most of this three-tenths portion of Democratic fault and complicity rests on the people and policies of the two Clinton terms. Failures include the deregulatory embrace of exotic finance and the 1999 repeal of Glass-Steagall in part to legitimize the unfortunate creation and unbridled ambition of Citigroup. Several ex-Clintonians named to major jobs by Obama were involved in these or in the bailouts of the mid- and late nineties.

Most pundits expected the new Democrats to prove more competent than the Bush crew. But many have some belief in a managed economy, and may enjoy a few years of trying to pick winners and losers in finance, transportation, and other sectors. The Japanese, however, have been trying to do this for almost two decades without any lasting success. As for breaking up some of the new financial mega-firms or rolling back the financial sector's excessive size and influence, I doubt that Obama will try. But never say never. The minority view in January 2009 had Obama surrounding himself with so many Wall Street and party establishment figures as initial cover that would enable him to undertake bolder moves in later years.

Senior managers of the Democratic coalition may also expect some serious opposition from the Republicans. John McCain sometimes sounded like a populist in his denunciations of Wall Street, and Repub-lican members of the House of Representatives, in particular, profited from their September decisions to oppose the Bush White House and to attack the $700 billion financial sector rescue package. Soon after the November results were tabulated, two of the three top House Republi-can leaders, Roy Blunt and Adam Putnam, both federal-rescue advocates, decided to step down. They were replaced by bailout opponents.

A related context, often ignored, is that without a Republican presi-dent and a White House apparatus sensitive to the financial sector and the party's web of large donors, the GOP members of the Senate and House—the latter, in particular—are far more likely to respond to the economic viewpoints and discontents of their Western, Southern, and Middle American constituents. That was certainly true in 1994, when House Republicans opposed the Clinton administration's bailout of the Mexican peso on behalf of U.S. bond holders. Meanwhile, moderate Northern Republicans from districts with large numbers of financial-sector executives were almost an endangered species. Although the GOP coalition is sure to remain schizophrenic regarding finance, the balance of power within the Congressional party has shifted.

In a lingering slow-growth economy—a parallel to Japan's stagna-tion in the 1990s was one of many such scenarios—politics suggests a Republican temptation to seize upon economic and financial issues that will sharpen divisions within the Democratic coalition.

Growing Public Anger at the Financial Sector

Critics may not have to look far. October and November opinion polling charted a watershed movement as voters were inflamed by the bailouts and the huge pay packages and bonuses paid on Wall Street despite most firms' ongoing mismanagement. In late July, journalist James Grant, a longtime Wall Street critic, wrote an article complaining that "Through history, outrageous financial behavior has been met with outrage. But today, Wall Street's damaging recklessness has been met with near-silence, from a too-tolerant populace."[94]

Three months later, though, Grant's doubts were as dated as a black and white television. Week after week, the airwaves had hummed with stories about Wall Street's exotic products, outrageous pay, dishonest accounting, and crumbling brokerage firms, as well as the government's demand for $700 billion and later much more to bail them out. As the stock market indexes plummeted, public anger intensified.

From the start, most surveys had shown opposition to the bailout idea. But the ratios were not lopsided. By late September, that had changed.

The *Washington Post* described how Republican and Democratic challengers alike sought to use the issue against vulnerable incumbents.[95] Congressional offices reported that phone calls and e-mails were running ten, twenty, or thirty to one against the administration's proposal. On October 10, the Reuters/University of Michigan Consumer survey, having sampled amid that mood shift, reported that "The credit crisis has shattered U.S. consumers' faith in financial institutions, including a stunning loss of confidence in the Federal Reserve." Some 57 percent of those sampled reported having lower confidence in the Fed than they had five years ago, including 29 percent who admitted to having a "lot less" confidence.[96] Belief in banks, thrifts, brokers, and mutual fund companies also soured, only sparing credit unions. The next month's numbers were similar.

By November, the *USA Today*/Gallup Poll found just 21 percent of Americans favoring aid to financial companies, with 51 percent dismissing it as not important. This was "not important" as in not needed or worthwhile. By contrast, 60 percent of Americans strongly favored "stricter regulations on financial institutions," and only a mere 10 percent thought that unimportant.[97] Autumn's Bloomberg/*Los Angeles Times* polling also turned up public indignation. In late September, Americans by 55 percent to 31 percent said "it's not government's responsibility to bail out private companies with taxpayers' dollars even if their collapse could jeopardize the economy." A month later, only 38 percent approved of how Fed Chairman Bernanke was handling his job, down from 50 percent in March.[98, 99]

In December, that month's *Wall Street Journal* poll found 71 percent of Americans critical of the government's handling of the financial crisis. This mostly meant the Republican excutive branch, but some jeopardy for the incoming Obama regime lurked in those same numbers. The new treasury secretary, as president of the New York Federal Reserve Bank, had been part of the troika running the rescue programs. The incoming Roosevelt administration of 1933 had no similar link.

Gallup's November poll had found 60 percent of those sampled calling it critical or very important for Obama to impose stricter regulation on financial institutions. Then December's revelation of the $50 billion Ponzi scheme run by financier Bernard Madoff further soured the public. In December's CNN/opinion research poll, 74 percent of those sampled said they believed Madoff's behavior was common among financial advisers and institutions, and 59 percent said that government regulated the stock market and financial institutions too loosely, up from 50 percent in September.

Surveytakers may continue to record such answers. The financial crisis became an intense national experience, imprinting psychologies that voters will not easily forget. Even so, it is unclear whether Congress and the executive branch can enact the sort of tough-minded regulation achieved by the New Deal back in the 1930s. In those days, the Democratic Congress and president did not represent the party favored by financial executives and contributors, and they were free to represent public indignation. Now, though, finance has shifted the bulk of its chips to Democratic federal officeholders. How much serious reform this relationship can yield will not be answered for several years, but the history of other leading world economic powers does not reassure. Either they have not tried very hard to roll back financialization or they have failed to overcome the interest group obstacles and inertia involved. These several precedents are discussed on pp. 162–68 in the main text. The odds probably favor a similar incapacity in the United States. It is not a happy thought.

As a personal aside, my first book, *The Emerging Republican Majority*, published in 1969, made me one of the theorists of the GOP presidential cycle that dominated the White House for twenty of the next twenty-four years, and by the 1990s, I was especially sensitive to what I thought was the general incapacity of the Bush dynasty. When George W. Bush became the second Bush president, I began what became a series of books appearing each election year—2002, 2004, 2006, and 2008—that framed what I thought were critical problems facing the United States. All four became bestsellers, but *Bad Money* will be the last. The White House having changed hands, the Bush family's failings spur me no longer. I voted for Barack Obama, although I do not have much confidence that the problems coming down the road can be managed. So I have no desire to monitor his success or failure for election-year readers and will leave any near-term attention to younger observers and to close students of the new Democratic coalition.

Finally, the new structure of this paperback edition deserves a bit more explanation. Back in 1929, economist Stuart Chase had written the book *Prosperity: Fact or Myth* about the 1922–1929 period which was at the printer's when the Crash came that autumn. It was a good explanation of why the bubble was about to break, and Chase published it in December 1929 with a new introduction and a few changes of tense or detail. Otherwise, he let it stand as a historical document. After I appeared on a national broadcast in April 2008, one of Chase's descendants got in contact to point out the similarities between our books, which I appreciated, having read his several times. In my case, however, while I have added a large amount of new analysis at the beginning and in an afterword at the end, I have not changed anything in the first material written in late 2007, not even dates or tenses. Most of it still stands, and now we can look further ahead. Doing so is just as important in 2009 as it was in 1933.

Contents

BAD MONEY

ONE

Introduction

The Panic of August

We are living through the first crisis of our brave new world of securitised financial markets. It is too early to tell how economically important this upheaval will prove. But nobody can doubt its significance for the financial system. Its origins lie with credit expansion and financial innovation in the U.S. itself. It cannot be blamed on "crony capitalism" in peripheral economies, but rather on irresponsibility in the core of the world economy.

—Martin Wolf, *Financial Times*, September 2007

The "crack cocaine" of our generation appears to be debt. We just can't seem to get enough of it. And, every time it looks like the U.S. consumer may be approaching his maximum tolerance level, somebody figures out how to lever on even more debt using some new and more complex financing. For years, I have watched this levering up process, often noting that it was taking an ever increasing amount of debt to produce a dollar's worth of GDP growth.

—Jeff Saut, chief investment strategist, Raymond
James & Associates, September 2007

Virtually nobody foresaw the Great Depression of the 1930s, or the crises which affected Japan and southeast Asia in the early and late 1990s. In fact, each downturn was preceded by a period of non-inflationary growth exuberant enough to lead many commentators to suggest that a "new era" had arrived.

—Bank for International Settlements, June 2007

For centuries, the importance of harvesttime in the affairs of men made August and September months notorious for declarations of war, crop failures, and, eventually, bank crises. The last connection was simple enough. Under the tight U.S. monetary reins of the nineteenth-century gold standard, late-summer demands for cash by rural banks usually skirted financial panic but sometimes brought it. In the United States, observed one master chronicler, crises came in August and September, most notably in 1837, 1857, and 1873, when western banks required large inflows from the East to finance shipments of cereals.[1]

If shortages of credit reflected the seasonality of farming, so periodically did a dearth of soldiers and military reserves. Armies have always had to watch the agricultural calendar. George Washington and other patriot commanders in the American Revolution knew that militia, in particular, would stay home for the harvest. Even in July 1914, Austria-Hungary could not mobilize its armies for a quick invasion of Serbia to avenge the assassination of the Hapsburg heir, Archduke Franz Ferdinand. Too many troops had been given farm furloughs through July 25.[2] In consequence, what might have been a short, localized suppression of Serbia dragged out into fatal weeks of great-power ultimatums, mobilization, and countermobilization—the Guns of August, which initiated the forty million casualties of World War I.

By the twenty-first century, of course, farm calendars no longer guided major events in North America or Europe, save for well-attended fairs and festivals or the pleasure of buying raspberries, peaches, sweet corn, and cider at roadside stands. However, in the United States, a new economic seasonality—the high point in late spring and summer of new and existing home sales—helped set the time frame for the financial markets' 2007 mortgage and credit spasms. Falling prices fanned concern that housing's giddy five-year buoyancy had created a bubble, indeed one already starting to pop; concern crystallized into panic, at least in the mass media and the financial markets, when June and July data dashed any lingering hopes for a sales and price rebound.

Nearly a year earlier, very different public concerns—a quagmire in Iraq, and Republican sexual scandals and attendant moral hypocrisies—had taken over the 2006 midterm elections, returning control of Congress to the Democrats after twelve Republican years. Worry about soon-to-be-inadequate world oil supplies and the mountainous U.S.

buildup of public and private debt, particularly home mortgages, were merely clouds on the horizon—perils, but not ones determining how people voted . . . yet.

That changed in mid-2007. Surging gasoline demand as springtime put motorists back on the road had focused May attentions on oil prices. Now roiling financial markets took global center stage, spooked by home foreclosure data, several hedge fund problems, and ominous projections of further foreclosures and price declines to come. As the days passed, fear spread—from subprime mortgages to the collateralized debt obligations (CDOs) into which asset loans had been opaquely repackaged. In August, apprehensions also stalled leveraged buyouts for want of funds, made banks unwilling to loan to one another, and froze the normal activity in commercial paper and other suddenly hard-to-value situations and product innovations. The impact was worldwide. From London to Tokyo, credit market after credit market froze toward illiquidity. Buyers sat on their hands, kept inactive by too little information about the new products' enigmatic content and wary of undisclosed risk. The once-sought-after CDOs could no longer be valued or "marked to market," or even marked to model, the next resort, but only, as skeptics remarked, marked to make-believe, a poisonous perception. Investors heard talk of the possible deleveraging of the global credit bubble—the privately feared "great unwind." Recession and deflation might be just over the hill. Other financial shivers—trembling municipal bonds, money market funds, and plain vanilla stocks—added to the worst August market chills since the mobilizations of 1914 had shut down bourses on both sides of the Atlantic. (The New York Stock Exchange, closed on July 31, 1914, did not resume full trading for four months.)

The 2007 crisis quickly revealed watershed characteristics. The great credit bubble, over two decades in its shaping, had since the 1980s been kept aloft and generally expanding by uplifts of monetary expansion from the U.S. Federal Reserve and other central banks. Having taken so long to form, cycle watchers thought, it would take years, not months, to unwind and deleverage. Proximate and wobbly currency and petroleum situations might add their own domino effects. Nor was the process assured of a happy ending through the wave of a central bank magic wand. Not unless, as the old adage says, God once again took particular care of fools, drunks, and the United States of America.

It is the thesis of this book that far-reaching economic and political events and consequences began to unfold in midsummer's melee— developments that at least in part followed the direction that many specialists had foreseen—regarding U.S. housing prices, credit-bubble risk, the instability of so many financial innovations never crisis-tested, the ever-more-apparent inadequacy of global oil production, the re- lated vulnerability of the dollar, and, behind it all, the false assurance of American "imperial" hubris. The administration of George W. Bush, rarely known for strategic grasp, miscued again in the early days of the crisis. Statements by the president, the secretary of the treasury, and the chairman of the Federal Reserve Board that the low-quality-mortgage meltdown would be short-lived and safely contained were disproved almost overnight. The principal catalysts of marketplace panic were some $500 billion of collateralized debt obligations seen to be tainted by subprime mortgages: "Ninja" loans, so called because unqualified borrowers had "no income, no job or assets." The CDOs quickly spread wider destruction than had been rumored for the vaunted weapons never found in Iraq (investor Warren Buffett, in 2003, had prophetically nominated derivatives as the "weapons of mass destruction" especially to be feared).

History does seem to repeat itself, if only in outline or rhyme. Un- fortunately, vague memories of past financial bubbles almost never suf- fice to inoculate a people or nation against repeating an earlier generation's mistakes. Despite highly cautioning precedents, the U.S. financial services circa 2007, swollen to an unprecedented and unstable 21 percent of gross domestic product, had laid down a national and in- ternational playing field no more controllable than the earlier venues of the Gilded Age and the Roaring Twenties. Technology, quantitative mathematics, and leverage allowed more to go wrong more quickly, and with much greater global reach. Twenty-first-century risk turned out to be spread and distributed in a negative rather than positive way.

Aggravating matters, America's sprawling financial debtscape of 2007—some $11 trillion in federal, state, and local obligations, plus a towering private issuance of $37 trillion (mostly financial, corporate, and mortgage)—had attained most of that size and clutter over the two previous frenetic decades. When Alan Greenspan had taken up the eagle feathers of Federal Reserve Board chieftainship in 1987, public and private debt in the United States had totaled $10.5 trillion. By 2006, following his departure, total credit market debt had quadrupled to $43 trillion. The best-publicized part of the surge, in various forms of mortgage borrowing, came when the Fed, anxious to stimulate the weakened post-9/11 economy, dropped the key overnight interest rate, already low, several times more to an ultrastimulative 1 percent in July 2003. In the abstract, this mortgage bet was plausible; in its multiyear government and private implementation, though, the mistakes and abuses are still surfacing.

Huge sums were involved. Debt in record quantities had been piled on top of the trillions still extant from the binges of the eighties and nineties, so that by 2007 the nation's overseers watched a U.S. economy in which public and private indebtedness was three times bigger than that year's gross domestic product. This ratio topped the prior record, set during the years after the stock market crash of 1929. However, in contrast to the 1920s and 1930s, when manufacturing retained its overwhelming primacy despite the economy's temporary froth of stock-market and financial ballyhoo, the eighties and nineties brought a much deeper transformation. Goods production lost the two-to-one edge in GDP it had enjoyed in the seventies. In 2005, on the cusp of Greenspan's retirement, financial services—the new übercategory spanning finance, insurance, and real estate—far exceeded other sectors, totaling over one-fifth of GDP against manufacturing's gaunt, shrunken 12 percent. During the two previous decades (and only marginally stalled by the early 1990s debt bailouts), the baton of economic leadership had been passed.

In the new century, a burgeoning debt and credit complex—vendors of credit cards, issuers of mortgages and bonds, architects of asset-backed securities and structured investment vehicles—occupied the leading edge. The behemoth financial conglomerates, Citigroup, JPMorgan Chase, et al., were liberated in 1999 for the first time since the 1930s to marshal banking, insurance, securities, and real estate un-

der a single, vaulting institutional roof. Hedge funds, the bold bou-
tiques, had multiplied from just a couple of hundred in the early 1990s
to roughly ten thousand in mid-2007, deploying over $1.8 trillion in
assets. Like digital buccaneers, and hardly more restrained than their
seventeenth-century predecessors, they arbitraged the nooks and cran-
nies of global finance, capturing even more return on capital than casino operators made from one-armed bandits and favorable
gaming-table odds.

As the mortgage markets seized up in mid-2007, shrewd players understood the virginity of the terrain. Jack Malvey, the chief global fixed-
income strategist for Lehman Brothers, explained: "This is what we
would characterize as the first correction of the neo-credit market.
We've never had a correction with these types of institutions and these
types of instruments."[3] Others distilled the doubts about hedge funds
themselves—the exotic quantitative mathematics, the obscure language of fixed-leg features and two-step binomial trees, and the humon-
gous bank loans needed for the fifteen- or twenty-to-one leverage that
alchemized mere decimal points into financial Olympic gold medals.

New products often turned out to have Achilles' heels, like the mis-
behaving index arbitrage of so-called program insurance, the derivative
innovation widely blamed for the 1987 crash, and the junk bonds dero-
gated after their inventor went to jail. In 2007, the failures were multiple: besides the CDO and exotic mortgage embarrassments, hedge funds'
mathematical vulnerabilities included too many copycats doing the
same thing, as well as an inability to deal with anarchic, almost random,
volatility. . . . Some future congressional investigating committee
would have a field day. Mathematically, what was theoretically impossible often manages to occur anyway. But the hedgies were big players,
first-tier customers of first-tier lenders, and their bets sometimes accounted for as much as half the daily trading volume on the New York
exchanges.

The average American, with other things to worry about, had little
inkling of the financial sector's gargantuan size and clout or its resemblance to a laboratory of digital wagering. Straightforward, candid discussion was about as easy to find in popular publications as a five-leaf
clover in a vacant lot full of weeds. In 1987, and again in the late nine-

ties, financial journals had occasionally featured sobering barbell-shaped charts in which a Roaring Twenties debt mountain on the left was connected by mild undulation (the forty years from 1935 to 1975) to the current-day Mount Everest rising on the right. During August's subprime panic, however, few similar charts appeared. Analogies to the late 1920s would have been too disconcerting. But figure 1.1 updates the portrait through 2006.

Two-step binomial trees might baffle most non–Wall Streeters, but home prices and mortgages were something the average American thought he or she understood. Or had thought so until 2003, when mortgage firms and bank mortgage departments started offering new and exotic variations—"interest-only" mortgages, payment-option adjustable-rate agreements, "piggyback" loans, negative amortization mortgages, and suchlike. The trickiest, as we will see, generally earned salesmen the biggest fees, so that was where buyers were steered. By

FIGURE 1.1
The Great American Debt Bubble

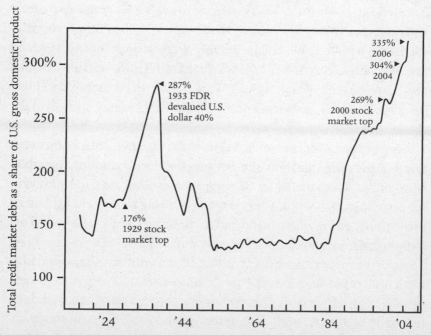

Source: *Barron's*, February 21, 2005, updated for 2006.

2005 and 2006, half of the new borrowers, usually less affluent, were signing up for one of the delayed-fuse versions. Besides the Ninja wise-crack, some brokers aptly called subprime applications "liar loans" or, quasi-scientifically, "neutron" loans (kill the people but leave the houses standing, borrowed from the Pentagon's neutron bombs). Many buy-ers, for their part, were quite ready to be misled or to fib themselves. "Housing inflation," pundits pointed out, was also "the American na-tional religion."

Investment strategists at Charles Schwab, a brokerage firm with no mortgage involvement, pointed a finger at 2003–6 lending practices: "The excesses in this housing cycle went beyond what was reasonable. Sub-prime originations totaled 20% of all originations in 2006, at an estimated value of over $600 billion. Alt-A loans (to borrowers with weak credit but decent incomes) were another nearly 20% of 2006's originations. Many are performing as badly as sub-prime loans, accord-ing to Moody's."[4] *Fortune* magazine hinted that the drawn-out pattern of nonchalance verged on negligence: "For the past five years, risk has been the invisible man of Wall Street. Banks, hedge funds, and lenders behaved as if home prices always rise, borrowers never miss a payment, and companies never blunder into bankruptcy."[5] The FBI, vocationally excited by actual crime, cited a fivefold increase in its mortgage fraud caseload between 2002 and 2007, further highlighting a strong correla-tion between borrower default and foreclosure and prior borrower vic-timization.[6] It was, as they say on the multiple-choice tests, (d) all of the above.

Many insiders, of course, had sensed for months, even years, what was coming. The valuation of U.S. homebuilders' stocks hit a zenith in 2005, pulled down thereafter by sagging new-home demand and slow-ing price appreciation. New mortgage borrowing by households peaked in the third quarter of 2005, and had declined by 45 percent a year later. Building permit applications topped out in late 2005. The index of real estate investment trusts crested in 2006. California was already a patch-work quilt of cut-rate sales and unraveling prices. Housing foreclosures were setting national records during the last quarter of 2006 and the first quarter of 2007, even though the April–May–June peak-season di-saster got the page 1 headlines.

By September 2007, the Mortgage Lender Implode-O-Meter—real enough, and easily found on the Internet—listed 150 U.S. mortgage lenders as having gone out of business or stopped making certain loans since December 2006, including American Home Mortgage and Ameriquest, once the nation's largest subprime lender.[7] Even in late winter and spring, several dozen had already closed their doors. In May and June, endangered hedge funds also came to light. By late July and August, the bond and credit markets should not have been surprised. On the other hand, neither should markets have been surprised nine decades earlier when war came in August 1914. But they were. British bonds (consols) did not plunge until July 27, 1914, just days before.[8] If markets are not always rational, the same is true of their willingness to anticipate bad news.

August 2007 was when the bad numbers became market movers, and charts of the slumping stock market averages, after a July August 10 percent decline, showed an intraday bottom on August 16. On the next day, fulfilling the previous afternoon's rumors, the Federal Reserve rode to the rescue with a surprise half-percent cut in the discount rate that its decision makers had all but ruled out a week earlier. Overall, global markets were sinking, central banks were injecting liquidity, and negative housing- and mortgage-related data kept pouring in. Twice as many houses were foreclosed in July as had been a year earlier. Moody's Economy.com estimated that the total for 2007 would reach 1.7 million, up from 1.26 million in 2006, through a "self-reinforcing downward cycle" of falling home prices, loan defaults, and credit tightenings.[9] The public-relations-minded National Association of Realtors was slow to accept the inevitability of an outright decline—it finally did so in late summer—because year-over-year slippage would mark the NAR index's first anual downturn of home prices since its launch in 1950. But outside measurement-takers had less compunction. The relatively new S&P/Case-Shiller Home Price Index, monitoring home prices in twenty major metropolitan areas, reported a 3.4 percent decline between June 2006 and June 2007.[10] More scarily, Robert Shiller, the Yale economist who made his name predicting the fate of the technology stock bubble, pictured housing's downfall in comparable terms. He told a late-August conference that home prices in some cities might fall by as much as half if the gathering bust could not be contained.[11] If so, losses by U.S. homeowners could reach $10 trillion, more than the $7 trillion lost in the 2000–2002 stock market bust led by the decline of the technology-heavy NASDAQ index.

August saw predictions of a downward spiral begin to dwell on "resets"—the upward revisions of monthly payments after two years, specified in many subprime mortgages, that were to replace low initial teaser rates. The post-reset amounts, often 50 to 100 percent higher, were already persuading some borrowers to fold their residential tents even before the date arrived. Within the larger and somewhat more prosperous universe of *all* adjustable-rate mortgages (ARMs), over a half trillion dollars' worth signed for in early 2006 carried reset dates during the first half of 2008. Figure 1.2 shows the highest-volume reset months and their overlap with the peak delegate selection periods of the 2008 Democratic and Republican presidential nomination processes. Fulsome Washington sympathy and attempted rescue, then, was all but baked in the election-year cake. Where analysts disagreed was over whether federal relief would notably ease things or merely drag out the predicted spiral of resets, abandonments, and foreclosures, and a material decline in home prices.

Huge stakes also drove the intense politics. In the United States, the UK, Canada, and Australia, your-home-is-your-castle nations where ownership reaches the 70 percent level, housing-centered crises are usually the ones that cut deepest into middle-class well-being. The explanation is simple. By some hypotheses, an informal, broadly defined "housing sector" of the U.S. economy—mortgage finance, construction, furnishings, lumber, and related industries—might represent a 25 percent share of the notional gross domestic product, enough to include several million vulnerable jobs on top of the frightening blow to the national psyche's sense of well-being and stability.

And on top of that, between 2001 and 2006, an unprecedented number of Americans used their homes as ATMs, turning huge chunks of residential equity into borrowed, but spendable, cash. Harvard economist Martin Feldstein, a former Republican chairman of the White House Council of Economic Advisers, calculated in 2007 that over "the past five years, the value of U.S. home mortgage debt has increased

FIGURE 1.2

**Monthly Amount of Adjustable-Rate Mortgage Resets,
January 2007–December 2008**

2007		2008	
January	$22 bil.	January	$80 bil.
February	25	February	88
March	35	March	110
April	37	April	92
May	36	May	76
June	42	June	75
July	43	July	50
August	52	August	35
September	58	September	26
October	55	October	20
November	52	November	15
December	58	December	17

Source: Millennium Wave Advisors.

by nearly $3 trillion. In 2004 alone, it increased by almost $1 trillion."
He went on: "Net mortgage borrowing that year *not* used [my italics]
for the purchase of new homes amounted to nearly $600 billion, or al-
most 7 percent of disposable personal income."[12] In short, borrowing
against homes enabled stressed consumers to keep consuming.

Indeed, over five years, the housing sector seems to have provided
some 40 percent of the growth in U.S. GDP and employment, representing stimulus on a grand, almost 1930s scale. Kevin Feltes, associate
director of New York's Jerome Levy Forecasting Center, was categori-
cal: "The wealth effect [from rising home prices], equity extraction and
excessive homebuilding were absolutely necessary for this expansion to
continue as long as it has or even continue at all."[13] Based on Greenspan's own earlier discussions of how turning home ownership equity
into cash had pumped needed spending into the 1975–78 economy, the
Fed chairman probably hoped for a threefold or fourfold replay during
the 2001–3 period as he dropped the Federal Reserve's main interest
rate to just 1 percent, the lowest level in four decades.[14] It would remain

below 2 percent, continuing to support feverish mortgage activity, until the end of 2004.

Whatever the Fed's strategy, official data later released showed that between 2001 and 2005, net household wealth in the United States actually increased. Despite the steep decline in *financial* assets between 2000 and 2002, new *housing*-based wealth, bolstered by a stock market rebound starting in 2003, more than made up the difference, as set out in figure 1.3. The *Economist* saluted the assets renewal with an article titled "The Houses That Saved the World."[15] Or so it appeared at the time. Housing's own weakness in 2006–7, however, raised a question that added steam to the pressure cooker of the August debate: Could housing's eight years or so (1998–2006) of price gains be lost in a return to the mid-1990s base level?

Some thought so, and they had a historical case. Real estate slumps, particularly in the English-speaking world, had unleashed greater economic dislocation (and across a much broader swath of society) than comparable stock market downturns. Home prices mattered more than stocks, a point dwelled upon by economist Shiller and supported in a lengthy study by the International Monetary Fund published in 2003. Thomas Heibling, the IMF study's principal author, explained that "the output loss associated with the typical housing price bust of about 8 percent of GDP was twice as large as that associated with a typical equity price bust."[16] Kurt Richebächer, a noted German economist, added that "housing bubbles . . . entangle banks and the whole financial system as lenders. For this reason, as a matter of fact, property bubbles have historically been the regular main causes of major financial crises."[17]

In short, a major mortgage debacle and housing-price decline might be enough to catalyze a painful deleveraging of the overall 1987–2007 debt bubble. Collapsed real estate had also stood out in the deleveraging effect of the Depression, 10 percent of U.S. housing having gone into foreclosure by 1933. But not all the conditions in historical precedents reliably apply in later years. Major oil price increases, for example—unknown in the thirties—abetted or caused major inflationary dislocations and recessions in the United States in 1973–75 and again in 1979–82. The latter period was when the black stuff reached a price

FIGURE 1.3
Stocks, Homes, and the Wealth Roller Coaster, 1998–2004

Wealth Rises Again in 2003–4
After the 2000–2002 Stock Collapse

Year-over-year percentage change in household net worth

Source: Federal Reserve, Global Insight Inc.

The Replacement of Stocks by Housing
as the Pillar of U.S. Wealth Creation

Value of U.S. stocks and homes, as a percentage of GDP

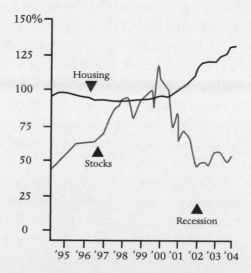

Source: Federal Reserve, Commerce Department via Economy.

equivalent to roughly $80 in today's dollars. However, when prices in 2007 notoriously hit the $75–$85 per barrel range, the effect was much less. The changed U.S. economy was less petroleum-intensive, and to match the absolute peak price of a quarter century earlier, not just a monthly average, a barrel would have to reach $100 or so in current dollars.

Nevertheless, if housing, mortgage, and credit problems grabbed the main spotlight in August's financial angst, oil was close behind. That month's UBS/Gallup Index of Investor Optimism fell, with energy costs ranked first and housing and real estate problems ranked second in "fueling investor skepticism about the U.S. economy." A midsummer sampling of members of the National Association for Business Economics, though, found them agreeing that bad credit, the immediate hobgoblin, had supplanted terrorism as the top immediate economic risk. The credit panic was their priority.[18] Still, oil prices prompted several August White House meetings and anxious telephone calls to the Middle East by the energy secretary, Samuel Bodman. As we will see, these brought a brief respite.

Some further amplification is useful. The energy insecurity infusing the U.S. economy in 2007 lay at least as much in the changing supply consciousness of the Organization of the Petroleum Exporting Countries (OPEC) and in Machiavellian foreign oil and dollar politicking as in straightforward per barrel cost. Relative stagnation in global output—Energy Information Administration data for 2005–7 showed it plateauing at 84 million to 86 million barrels per day—seemed to partially validate the so-called peak-oil theory. This is the contention by many geologists that oil is finite, that existing resources are overstated (even in pivotal Saudi Arabia), and that sparse new discoveries are falling behind fast-accelerating global demand.

Taken together with international currency realpolitik, foreigners' oil-related strategies pose mischief on a level with the overreach and instability of the nation's financial sector. Historically, it is vital to remember the United States as the nation that, beginning 150 years ago, linked its fate to its vast oil reserves and its commercial and military ability to maximize them. In 1919, 1946, or even 1973, oil was a proud U.S. flag, not just a fungible energy commodity. The twentieth century became America's golden era partly because it was also petroleum's. Under Washington's military and geopolitical aegis, oil remained a pillar of U.S. economic and great-power dominance even after OPEC orchestrated the steep price increases of 1973–74 and 1979–80. But by 2005–6, the success of the Nixon-Kissinger era's critical bargain—unofficially, Washington would arm and protect the Persian Gulf, in return for which the Saudis and the Gulf sheikhdoms would require that their oil be paid for with dollars, thereby keeping the greenback on a de facto oil standard—was coming undone. Reasons abounded.

The figurative soup into which the United States had fallen during the early 2000s was a broth of bile. For now, it suffices to list outlooks and complaints—some fair, others exaggerated—that we will revisit in chapter 5. First place went to deepening international loss of respect for the United States after the miscalculated invasion and bloody occupation of Iraq. This ebb was global. Other elements in the hostile atmosphere involved the clash of religions: (1) secular Europeans and international elites in general believed that the American religious Right and its biblical interpretations had too much power over the Bush administration and domestic and foreign policymaking; (2) many Muslims angrily conceived that the United States was fighting an anti-Muslim religious war in the Middle East (witness the references to Crusaders); and (3) many Muslims had been aroused by a conviction that the post-1991 presence of U.S. troops sullied holy places in Saudi Arabia. It goes almost without saying that resentment of the U.S. alliance with Israel also throbbed across much of the Middle East.

Some opinion leaders in oil-producing nations believed that the invasion of Iraq mirrored a U.S. blueprint to pump and market large quantities of Iraqi oil in order to break OPEC and drive down petroleum prices. But by 2006 and 2007, oil- and dollar-related psychologies were getting more complex and economically justifiable. Four stand out: (1) worry among producer nations that their own oil output had peaked or soon might make even erstwhile U.S. allies in the Persian Gulf reluctant to pump oil at anything less than near-record prices; (2) obligation to accept payment for oil in dollars, a declining currency, cheapened the prices received by exporting nations that depended on petroleum for much of their government revenue; (3) pegs that tied local currencies to a fading dollar made, for example, Saudi or United Arab Emirates imported goods more expensive and drove up local inflation rates; and (4) how much people in Dubai, Doha, and other Persian Gulf boom cities, to which even U.S. corporations (Halliburton in 2007) and a few business groups were relocating, already believed that the future lay in Asia, not North America.

For the more sophisticated in Washington, the $60- to $95-a-barrel cost prevalent in 2006 and 2007 was only the most obvious of the energy-related problems. Dismissing memories of $12 oil in 1998 and $25 oil in 2003, the expert consensus was that the era of low-cost petroleum was done and gone. With the United States of 2007 producing only 35 percent of the crude it consumed—by 2010, possibly as little as 30 percent—the cost of buying the remainder elsewhere had become inescapable. Annual outlays for imported petroleum, $50 billion to $75 billion during most of the late eighties and nineties, had swollen to $100 billion in 2002, $130 billion in 2003, $180 billion in 2004, $232 billion in 2005, and $302 billion in 2006.[19] The ever-larger checks written for black gold also weighed heavily in the broadest annual measurement of the U.S. trade gap: the current account deficit ($857 billion in 2006). Overall, oil-related optimism and promises by the U.S. government had not worked out since peace in occupied Iraq deteriorated into insurgency and regional separatism.

The world also had to begin to face up to the real crisis: a global oil supply on the verge of reaching a plateau or peak and unable to support demand. Absent a global recession, world demand was predicted by the International Energy Agency (IEA) to increase by 1.5 percent in 2007 and 2.4 percent in 2008, largely because of rising consumption in China, India, and Latin America, and even within the diversification-driven OPEC nations themselves. In 2006, Charles Maxwell of Weeden & Company, a top U.S. oil analyst, dramatized the simultaneous shortfall in new discoveries: "In 1930, we found 10 billion new barrels of oil in the world and we used 1.5 billion. We reached a [new discovery] peak in 1964 when we found 48 billion barrels and used approximately 12 billion barrels. In 1988, we found 23 billion barrels and used 23 billion.

That was the crossover when we started finding less than we were using. In 2005, we found about 5 billion to 6 billion and we used 30 billion. These numbers are just overwhelming."[20] Many well-informed geologists and industry consultants considered top producers like Russia, Saudi Arabia, and Mexico to have reserves well below what their governments publicly claimed. Each year, when members of the Association for the Study of Peak Oil convened in congenial cities like Uppsala, Sweden; Pisa, Italy; or Cork, Ireland, new evidence seemed to support their pessimistic calculations, while new speakers added luster to the cause. The sixth annual meeting in autumn 2007 saw Lord Oxburgh, a former chairman of Shell UK, predict $150-per-barrel petroleum, while James Schlesinger, the former U.S. CIA director and energy secretary, told the attendees that "the battle is over and the partisans of peak oil have won."[21]

No one doubted that more fuel could be had from ultradeep drilling in the Gulf of Mexico and the South Atlantic; from submerged Arctic mountain ranges claimed by nearby Russia; from the western Canadian oil sands; from the heavy and superheavy oil deposits in the Orinoco Belt of eastern Venezuela; from shale oil in the U.S. Rocky Mountains; and from hard-to-reach, expensive portions of already-tapped fields the world over. The catch was twofold: deepwater drilling aside, new production was unlikely to be great, and these prospects assumed costly technology and prices remaining at or above $50–$60 per barrel. Furthermore, the up and down "market" forces generally prevalent during the twentieth-century heyday of the privately owned American and European oil giants, the famed Seven Sisters, were giving ground to the realities of lopsided control (three-quarters of world reserves) and overtly nationalist agendas of the leading state-owned oil companies. In 2007, the *Financial Times* described Saudi Aramco, Gazprom, Petro-China, National Iranian Oil Company, Petrobras (Brazil), Petronas (Malaysia), and Petróleos de Venezuela as the "New Seven Sisters."[22] Christophe de Margerie, the chief executive of Total, the top French firm, described the supramarket calculus of these state companies, now that global capacity no longer sufficed to meet global demand, as marking "a revolution" in the industry.[23]

Seventy-dollar oil hardly doomed the U.S. car-and-driver culture, which stands next to homeownership in the American pantheon of privileges. Still, the global scramble for increasingly strategic oil did have rippling consequences for financial markets. For years, CNBC, the market-watching U.S. cable network, prominently displayed on-screen "bugs" that carried current oil and gold prices and interest-rate data, along with the latest readings of the Dow Jones Industrial Average, the S&P 500, and NASDAQ. As August began, oil had reached $78, and Washington proposed a $20 billion arms package tailored for the Persian Gulf oil producers. Energy Secretary Bodman, saying prices were in the "danger zone," called on OPEC to step up production. A favorable response came from Mohammed al-Hamli, the oil minister of the United Arab Emirates, and the Saudis reduced the per-barrel price of extra light crude to U.S. customers by $4. Powerful Dow Jones rallies on August 1 and August 6 were attributed to oil's downward price movement, which bought some time.

Provocative foreign economic tactics generated too little attention from the U.S. mainstream media. In 2005 and thereafter, there was more open scheming against U.S. energy interests by actual or incipient energy blocs: by OPEC; by the fast-emerging Shanghai Cooperation Organization (begun in 2001 and including Russia, China, and the central Asian republics of Uzbekistan, Kyrgyzstan, Kazakhstan, and Tajikistan); by left-leaning nations in Latin America; and by an Iran ambitious to restore the ancient Persian glories of Darius and Xerxes through an inner Asian alliance with China and Russia. Venezuelan strongman Hugo Chavez's strident efforts to shape a new South American energy grouping around his own country, Argentina, Uruguay, Bolivia, and Ecuador could not be dismissed, given Venezuela's oil and gas resources. Russia, for its part, worked off and on to bring Iran into the Shanghai Conference Organization, which in mid-2007 held joint military maneuvers—observed by Russian president Vladimir Putin and Chinese president Hu Jintao—in the Chelyabinsk region of Russia's southern Urals and then in northwestern China's Xinjiang Province.[24] China, petro-hopping with investments in Africa from Somalia and the Sudan to Angola and Nigeria's offshore Akpo deepwater oil and gas field, was even proselytizing in Canada, where the out-of-office Liberal Party, if returned to power in Ottawa, might cut new oil sands deals with Beijing at Washington's expense. All of this took place as the United States floundered in Iraq, inviting old and new rivalries and prompting global disrespect.

A second ambuscade, less direct, involved hopes and actions by a number of nations, many of them oil producers, to (1) diversify their central banks' reserves by cutting back U.S. dollar holdings; (2) eliminate pegs that tied their local currency to the dollar; or (3) require that foreign purchasers of oil from their (Iranian and Venezuelan) fields pay only with euros or Japanese yen. Both these foes were particularly angry with how the greenback could retain world primacy and reserve-currency status because years earlier it had been designated the currency through which oil had to be bought and sold internationally. Unsurprisingly, the first nations to openly move against the dollar—Saddam Hussein's Iraq, Iran, North Korea, and Venezuela—all had political motivations. By 2007, however, other complaining nations could give good reasons to be leery of a dollar steadily losing its international purchasing power—against the euro, for example, the loss over five years was some 40 percent.

The drumbeats for competing, even hostile, currencies gained volume in 2007. Foreign rivals knew that if they could manage to end the dollar's semiofficial role in oil transactions, a further decline might trigger a major economic downturn (and full-scale financial crisis) that would further weaken Washington. China, although cautious, held a particularly strong gold and currency hand. A mixture of naïveté and patriotism made it hard for many Americans to believe that so many foreigners would work against the United States. Aren't we the good guys? people asked at Rotary lunches in Indianapolis and church picnics in Nashville. However, international polling by the U.S.-based Pew Research Center, the Program on International Policy Attitudes, the BBC World Service/Globescan, and various consortia of foreign newspapers, as well as overseas tabulations by WorldPublicOpinion.org, documented the hostility. Respondents around the world distrusted U.S. world leadership and called the actions of the Bush administration a threat to world peace (see appendix). Such global disdain affected both oil and the greenback.

But we are getting ahead of ourselves. The convergence of a bursting debt and credit bubble, an increasingly reckless financial sector, a decreasingly friendly global oil chessboard, and the dollar's reenactment of the old-time Perils of Pauline requires an extended explanation. I've given this book the title *Bad Money,* and part of the explanation is caught up in what I think of as the malfeasance of "money," including lax oversight of the financial sector by Washington past and present. These failures laid the foundation for both of this volume's main concerns: first, the deadly interplay of financial sector growth and debt hubris with a hot-wired American housing crash; and second, the intertwined vulnerability of U.S. oil supremacy and the embattled, targeted dollar. Should both perils impact the U.S. financial markets simultaneously, as August 2007 hinted, the word "crisis" might prove to be an inadequate description.

In recent decades, many book titles and names for television programs have placed hot, flavorful adjectives—"old," "new," "easy," "dirty," "mad," "smart," and "dumb"—in front of greed's best-loved noun, "money." The pairing for this volume, *Bad Money,* is not intended to evoke nineteenth-century robber barons, twentieth-century salad oil swindlers, or twenty-first-century Enron architects. For now, that is too parochial. The reason for applying a negative characterization is historical and institutional, with a deep bow to the inherent vulnerability of human nature exposed to pecuniary temptation, witnessed today on an unprecedented scale. Money is "bad," in the historical sense, when a leading world economic power passing its zenith—before the United States, think Hapsburg Spain, the maritime Dutch Republic (when New York was New Amsterdam), and imperial Britain just before World War I—lets itself luxuriate in finance at the expense of harvesting, manufacturing, or transporting things. Doing so has marked each nation's global decline. *To institutionalize the dominance of minimally regulated finance at this stage of U.S. history is a bad idea.*

"Bad" in the systemic sense further applies to letting a financial elite elevate, expand, and entrench itself as a country's GNP- and profits-dominating sector, as has been done in the United States over the last quarter century. Doing this so hurriedly has wound up institutionalizing runaway public and private debt, gross speculative biases, tenfold and twentyfold leveraged gambling, unchecked and barely regulated "product" innovation, and a tendency toward periodic panics and insta-bility. In such a short time frame, though, finance could probably not have consolidated and entrenched in a meeker or more civic-minded fashion. Former Federal Reserve chairman Alan Greenspan has openly stipulated, now that he is again a private citizen free to speak, what most people know well: that manic boom and bubble periods bring the weakness of human nature to the fore. As for the financial sector's be-havior in such circumstances, surely there must be some applicable variation of Lord Acton's famous thesis about the greater the power, the greater the abuse and corruption.

It's also "bad" to promote an overbearing financialization of Amer-ica's economy and culture, lesser versions of which in both U.S. and world history have led to extremes of income and wealth polarization, a culture of money worship, and overt philosophic embrace of specula-tion and wide-open markets. Minimally bridled finance, extraordinarily rewarding to the top 1 or 2 percent of the population possessing capital, skills, and education, indulges all of these tendencies. Bridling that sec-tor was possible in 1933, when Franklin D. Roosevelt orated about throwing the money changers out of the temple. To a degree, at least, he did. Tossing political and governmental nets around the giant, cy-berspatial King Kong who prowls early-twenty-first-century Manhattan (or, for that matter, the City of London financial district) represents an entirely different magnitude of challenge.

Economists, political scientists, and energy experts, usually eager to make forecasts, have arguably predicted nine of the last five recessions—a joke about economists seen occasionally in the media—or made comparable miscalculations in the other disciplines. Neverthe-less, many have hoisted accurate warning flags about exactly the trends now visible, not least the dangers of financial and real estate bubbles. A view of finance as debt-driven and panic-prone goes way back. Some twentieth-century scholars, especially before World War II, explained economic or business cycles as an unfolding progression: First came normal expansion; next, some catalyst, an unusual event or a fear able to trigger a crisis (or panic). This flash point then led to economic reces-sion or contraction, after which came revival of economic activity. Prosperity, by nurturing excess, led to crises, although economists usually disagreed on what and how. Europeans, in particular, embraced this weighty theory—*la crise* in French, *die Krise* in German. A crisis, wrote French business-cycle theorist Jean Lescure for the *International Encyclopedia of the Social Sciences,* "may be defined as a grave and sudden disturbance of economic equilibrium."[25]

Economic historian Charles Kindleberger, in his classic work *Manias, Panics, and Crashes,* took a related view, often discounted during three decades of free-market orthodoxy, fatuous insistence on efficient and rational stock behavior, and homage to the ups and downs of the nation's all-explaining money supply. Kindleberger's concern was with "speculative booms in the cycle and in the crises at the peak, and especially with their financial aspects. By no means is every upswing in business excessive, leading to mania and panic. But the pattern occurs sufficiently frequently and with sufficient uniformity to merit renewed study."[26]

The Austrian School of economics, for its part, taught that booms brought about by credit expansion must ultimately collapse. Basically, these economists concentrate on economic booms and what distorts them. Every boom, they say, comes from extraordinary credit expansion out of proportion to real economic growth. One Austrian School acolyte, Kurt Richebächer, had predicted just that unhappy fate for the U.S. housing bubble several years before his death during the summer of 2007. Hyman Minsky (1919–96), part Keynesian, part disciple of Joseph Schumpeter, became so well known for preaching the financial system's vulnerability to speculation and risk that admirers labeled the August panic a "Minsky Moment." Certainly the Austrian-Minsky fusion, so specific in its finger pointing, will rise or fall on the economic outcome of the next several years.

Parallel inflections have been suggested for energy: the insistence that fossil-fuel history has also had dramatic break points that prompted government, commerce, and society to redirect how energy was used and to recast the global structure of its production and consumption. For proponents, the last break point and rebalancing came in the 1970s, when prices surged enough that conservation and attention to new energy sources mobilized to cut oil demand, if only for a while.[27] The hints of another watershed snowballed between 2005 and 2007—inadequate world oil and gas reserves; clearly insufficient new discoveries; stepped-up belief in peak oil; the unprecedented new demand from Asia, the Middle East, and Latin America; and the increasing salience of energy-security issues and even resource wars.

The tumultuous 1970s were the last decade to experience an economic crisis alongside an energy break point, a precedent few populations would want to repeat. The politics of our current double dislocation is treated in chapter 6, albeit without much conviction that it can still be fixed. The U.S. political system is not broken—weak presidents can plummet in the polls, voters can still mobilize, Congress can change hands—but both political parties have calcified in terms of interest-group domination and limited strategic capacity. The problem of dynasty, which I analyzed in detail with respect to the Bush family and the Republicans in 2004, has since confirmed its power in the Democratic Party as well, through the Clinton family.[28] The drawbacks include a particular legacy of family biases, funding, precedents, and immobility operating within the related entrenchments and limitations of the 150- to 200-year-old political parties. Parenthetically, the inheritability of civic office in the later years of Rome, Spain, and the Dutch Republic was an earlier symptom of calcification.

Neither of the major parties will find it easy to discuss long-evolving U.S. predicaments, including energy and financial excesses, which reflect on both, if not necessarily equally. This should not be surprising, because the existing parties, factions, and movements weren't able to achieve much in late-stage Rome, seventeenth-century Spain, the eighteenth-century Dutch Republic, or Britain in the first half of the twentieth century, either. The dynamics of this failure will be reviewed in chapters 6 and 7.

My sense of what constitutes a U.S. watershed and what does not obviously owes much to three decades of research, most intense during the last ten years, into the common attributes and eventually debilitative weaknesses of the earlier leading world economic powers: Spain when the Hapsburgs ruled much of Europe, maritime Holland, and imperial Britain. The backdrops to U.S. energy, debt, and financialization trends mentioned in this book have been developed at considerably more length in *American Theocracy,* with its subtitle-cum-précis,

The Perils and Politics of Radical Religion, Oil, and Borrowed Money in the 21st Century. Because the comparison between the United States and these past hegemons (Rome, too) has only grown over the last two years, it seems useful to include here a short capsule of the contexts and circumstances they shared in their years of slippage and decline. The reader can make his or her own judgments.

To begin with, there was a popular sense of national decay, with economic, moral, and patriotic components. Rome and the later three all had that discomfort, although the lower orders and their sympathizers worried more about the decline of economic livelihood, treatment, and opportunity, while conservatives deplored national erosion more in terms of patriotism, family, virtue, and morality.

Religion tended to intensify in unfortunate ways. Common forms included a pride of global mission and conquest (Spain) or a smug evangelical drive (Britain); intolerance, torture, or persecution by a powerful state church (Christian Rome, Spain); or a quest to somehow recapture an earlier, more vital patriotic religion and era (the Dutch).

Resurgent or intensifying faith typically came into conflict with science. Examples included the later days of Rome (libraries and astronomical observatories were shuttered) or Spain (superstition and theology suppressed science). Nineteenth-century Britain provided the first arena for conflict between scientific Darwinism and biblical Christianity.

Imperialism and military overreach brought a damaging mutual stimulus. Rome extended its boundaries too far and later couldn't defend them against "barbarian" auxiliaries the Romans had trained. Spain overreached in Europe as well as the rest of the world, and spent itself fighting for the Catholic Counter-Reformation in the Thirty Years' War. Maritime Holland overstretched in both commercial globalization and the draining cost of international wars fought between 1688 and 1713. Britain, in turn, could not manage the size of the empire it had to defend and the crushing expense of two world wars (1914–18 and 1939–45).

Excessive debt usually became crippling. Spendthrift and fiscally inept Spain had a series of royal bankruptcies but muddled through until the fiscal coup de grâce of the Thirty Years' War. The Dutch of the eighteenth century polarized into a nation of rentiers in which the wealthy lived off interest while industry, fishing, and shipping declined. The world's largest creditor in 1914, Britain was broken over roughly three decades by the economic transformation and debt of two world wars.

Each time, finance rose at the expense of industry, agriculture, and other earlier forms of economic activity. This alone could fill an entire book. The provincial parliaments of Spain complained about how wealth was being taken away by foreign bankers, lenders, and merchants. Holland's example worried Britons who were all too well aware of it, but the United Kingdom ultimately followed a similar path.

The seventh precedent, applicable only to the more modern Dutch and British economies, involves the idiosyncratic nature of fuel and energy achievements and hegemony. For the Dutch, that regime was wind and water—sails, windmills, navigation, pumps, drainage, and land reclamation. They lost headway when coal took over, which was the idiosyncratic resource and talent of Britain. Coal, in turn, prevailed until the rise of oil-powered industry and oil-fueled military success played to the unique skills and resources of the United States. While I believe that this overall pattern has validity, few of its details will be repeated in these pages. However, the immediate topicality of precedents relating to debt, financialization, and a vulnerable U.S. energy regime takes on greater credibility and urgency from America's own late-stage-of-empire setting. One vital distinction, which chapter 2 will develop, is that in the United States during the Bill Clinton and George W. Bush years, the excesses of *private* credit and debt—mortgage, consumer, corporate, and financial—have developed into a more immediate contemporary danger than the relatively tame dimensions of *public* (federal, state, and local) debt. To be sure, future Social Security and Medicare costs promise to balloon to oversized public sector burdens five, ten, or twenty years hence, but the immediate predicament lies with an explosion of private debt and credit.

Few senators, congressmen, and treasury officials, however happy to bluster on the fiscal ramparts attacking federal deficits, showed any parallel disturbance over private sector debt and fiscal legerdemain—at least not before August opened the private debt sector equivalent of

Pandora's box. Before long, scrutiny had exposed the largest array of financial abuses since congressional hearings on 1920s practices amplified the basis for an eventual barrage of New Deal statutes. Some of these had involved *regulating* securities markets, undocumented securities issuance, short selling, margin trading, and housing loans; others called for *requiring* federal deposit insurance and the divorce of commercial banking from the securities business; and still others specified *prohibiting* open-market operations by individual Federal Reserve banks, the operation of "pools" within exchanges, so-called bucket shops, the private ownership of gold, and more. The seventy-year-old list itself is less important than its strong hint of yet another regulatory wave. In 2006, the average member of Congress didn't know a swap contract from an option contract, or a "conduit" (a vehicle for off-the-books financing) from a clogged suburban drainpipe. By 2008, they knew a lot more.

Some pundits simply referred to August 2007 or the "August panic." The Dow Jones Industrial Average had peaked on July 16, and on July 27 President George W. Bush convened leaders of the Working Group on Financial Markets, headed by Treasury Secretary Henry Paulson, a former Wall Streeter. Their immediate concern was the 311–point loss the Dow had suffered the day before, largely because of jolting housing news. But the underlying problem was in how the major market indexes, the Dow and the S&P 500, were being cut down by a psychological crossfire—on one side, credit-bubble fears sharpened by housing tremors, and on the other, oil prices climbing as U.S. foes like Venezuela's Chavez gleefully predicted $100 a barrel. The second two weeks of August were the nadir, culminating in frozen commercial paper markets, stricken interbank lending, and a week of intense stock market gyrations and volatility between August 13 and 17. Finally, the thirty-first day of a painful month concluded with a much-publicized conference in Jackson Hole, Wyoming, the majestic onetime fur trappers' rendezvous, the twenty-ninth in an annual series underwritten by the Federal Reserve Bank of Kansas City. This assemblage neatly bookended the month's surprises as participants came away from speeches— by Harvard's Martin Feldstein, Robert Shiller the home-price Cassandra, German central bank chief Axel Weber, and others—convinced that a rougher endgame than they had hoped for was likely. "I came to Jackson Hole thinking there would be no recession," said Susan Wachter, a professor of real estate at Pennsylvania's Wharton School, "but I'm leaving thinking we could well have one."[29]

When those events pass into the history books, the more detailed accounts will surely confect some of those unexpected German state bank casualties, fearful New York Stock Exchange openings, extraordinary final-hour Dow surges (possibly Washington-orchestrated), mortgage-lender death spirals, $700 billion of central bank liquidity injections, Venezuelan and Iranian rants, eerie "Hindenburg Omen" fulfillments,* hedge fund disgraces, and trillion-dollar meltdowns into the sort of breathless *You Are There* chronicles that have offered insider-type postmortems on previous notable financial crises. There is rich material aplenty.

Looking ahead, many informed observers of the 2007 gyrations were quick to raise analogies to one or more of the prior eruptions going back a century (the panic of 1907, the summer market closings of 1914, the August–October breakdown of 1929, and the OPEC revolutions and the stagflation of the seventies) and to more recent market blowups (the short-lived crash of 1987, the Asian currency crisis of 1997, the Russian debt default of August 1998, and the NASDAQ-led stock market swan dive of 2000–2001). The analogies between 2007 and 1929, although common enough and backed by surprising resemblances, were mostly made in private. Not only was this understandable, but a disguised stock market decline like 1973–82 (or 1967–82), its ultimate severity veiled to the populace by substantial inflation, struck most as the better bet. Few financial pundits doubted the willingness of Fed chairman Ben Bernanke and his monetarist colleagues on the Federal Reserve Board to print money or monetize debt.

Alan Greenspan himself had invoked nearly "identical" resemblances to the crises of 1987 and 1998, and the centennial of the brief financial panic in 1907, ironically another August-launched event, had elicited a new book, *The Panic of 1907*, which further invited comparison.[30] Experts analogizing 2007 events to those of 1987, 1997, or 1998

---

* The Hindenburg Omen involves a little-known stock market measurement that attempts to predict a forthcoming crash. It is named after the 1937 crash of the German zeppelin of the same name.

generally did so in a reassuring way, suggesting that just as those upheavals had surprisingly little long-term effect despite their initial severity, so might the latest August eruption, which was indeed followed by
a quieter, if still taut, September. Several market watchers, however,
took a deeper breath and reminded their audiences that 1987 had led
into the 1990–91 downturns, and that interest-rate cuts hastily provided
in 1998 had wound up feeding the speculative bubble and eventual market debacle of 2000–2002. Treasury Secretary Paulson told a financial
audience that he thought the 2007 crisis would last longer than individual shocks like those of 1987 and the 1990s. And some representatives of the most pessimistic school—Robert Shiller and other
housing-crash worriers—outlined the case for a much more powerful
downturn.

    This book does not predict, or select among, any of these outcomes.
This is too early a stage. It does, however, take note of the variety of
scenarios laid out, most relevant to the circumstances and problems
described in these pages. Time will tell, but 2008 being an election year,
politicians will also have a voice, and chapter 6 looks at how changes in
the dynasties, party alignments, and interest-group access to U.S. politics have already laid new foundations.

TWO

Finance

The New Real Economy?

The money that's made from manufacturing stuff is a pittance in comparison to the amount of money made from shuffling money around. Forty-four percent of all corporate profits in the U.S. come from the financial sector compared with only 10% from the manufacturing sector.

—Raymond Dalio, Bridgewater Associates, 2004

Corporate profits, household incomes, asset prices and economic performance have all evolved to the point of acute dependency on ongoing leveraged specula-tion and rampant credit inflation. . . . Aggressive profit-seekers today pursue their outsized share of wildly inflated financial fortunes with confidence that policymakers have no alternative than to sustain the boom.

—David Tice, Prudent Bear Fund, 2007

The one-two punch of income vulnerability and rising costs has weakened the middle class at the same time that the revision of the rules of financing deliv-ers a death blow to millions of families each year. Since the early 1980s, the credit industry has rewritten the rules of lending to families. Congress has turned the industry loose to charge whatever it can get and to bury tricks and traps throughout credit agreements. Credit-card contracts that were less than a page long in the early 1980s now number thirty or more pages of small-print legalese.

—Professor Elizabeth Warren, Harvard Law School, 2006

Some in Henry Paulson's attentive Washington audience of mort-gage and banking executives took the September 12, 2007, com-ments of the U.S. treasury secretary slightly amiss. Paulson had opined on the August subprime crisis by saying that "unlike periods of financial turbulence I've witnessed over many years, this turbulence wasn't precipitated by problems in the real economy. This came about as a result of some bad lending practices."[1]

Most of the attendees, who were from the mortgage units or subsidiaries of big banks like Wells Fargo, Citigroup, JPMorgan Chase, and HSBC, doubtless wondered exactly what the secretary meant: which lending practices? Certainly not just those of local mortgage brokers. And weren't they all part of the financial services sector, no remote vocational periphery but the biggest and richest chunk of American private enterprise? Financial services now represented a fifth of the gross domestic product, thank you. And it wasn't local mortgage lenders who had divided the loans into tranches, packaged them into collateralized debt obligations, and handed the CDO papers to salesmen (few of whom fully understood them) to offload, especially to foreigners—to banks like BNP Paribas in France, Landesbank Sachsen in Germany, and the Industrial and Commercial Bank of China. Many customers also lacked understanding, but eagerly sought the high interest carried by these products, most reassuringly rated AAA or AA. Half of the financial services sector food chain had been in on the act—local lenders, banks, rating agencies like Standard & Poor's and Moody's, securitization counsel, hedge funds, special purpose vehicles, overseas sales offices.

Politically, though, Paulson's message had the effect he sought. The television news programs carried his sentences about no problems in the real economy, just some collateral mishap. That was the message to Main Street: arcane finance wouldn't hemorrhage into the real economy at the grass roots. However, this did leave a related issue to be finessed: the unappreciated hugeness of a U.S. financial sector that in many ways dictated the circumstances of the erstwhile real economy rather than vice versa.

The average voter wouldn't have guessed the numbers involved; the average investor might not have done much better. But the U.S. Commerce Department has set them out clearly enough, as shown in figure 2.1. As of 2004–5, the financial services sector of the United

FIGURE 2.1

The Rise of Financial Services and the Decline of Manufacturing

Manufacturing and Financial Services:
Changes in Share of U.S. Gross Domestic Product, 1950–2005

	1950	1960	1970	1980	1990	2000	2003	2004	2005
Manufacturing	29.3%	26.9%	23.8%	20.8%	16.3%	14.5%	12.7%	12.1%	12.0%
Financial services	10.9	13.6	14.0	15.0	18.0	19.7	20.5	20.6	20.4

Source: "Gross Domestic Product by Industry," Bureau of Economic Analysis, November 11, 2004. For historical data, see table B-12, Gross Domestic Product by Industry, 1987–2003, *Economic Report of the President, 2005*; and table B-38, Manufacturing Output, 1943–1971, *Economic Report of the President, 1972*.

The Reversing Origins of U.S. Corporate Profits, 1950–2004

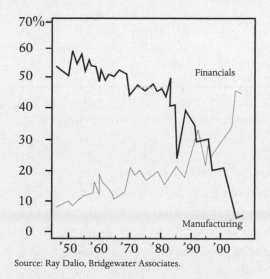

Source: Ray Dalio, Bridgewater Associates.

States represented between 20 and 21 percent of the nation's GDP—essentially the same share, for comparative purposes, as the seven-state Farm Belt combined with the eight Rocky Mountain states.

Shrewd cabinet members and elected officials also preferred a less revealing GDP figure. New York City mayor Michael Bloomberg and Senator Charles Schumer, in releasing an in-depth portrait of New York

FIGURE 2.2

Banks and the Mortgage Business, 1952–2004

U.S. Banks: Mortgage-Related Assets/Total Earning Assets (in Percent)

Source: Northern Trust Company, Paul L. Kasriel, director of economic research.

finance in 2007, described the national financial services sector as just 8 percent of GDP by using an outdated definition that excluded mortgage lending and real estate operations.[2] But it's silly to cavil. Since the Financial Services Modernization Act of 1999 dissolved old legal separations and constraints, commercial banking, insurance, securities, and mortgage lending have intertwined like tossed four-colored linguine in a bowl. They are, for all purposes, indivisible. As figure 2.2 shows, over the last two decades, mortgages have soared to represent over 60 percent of bank loans, and the financial services sector is now bigger than any other, including manufacturing, health, and wholesale/retail. This interaction, mass, and momentum, alas, have become critical elements of the problem. Driven by a metastasizing debt and credit industry, the financial sector got too big too carelessly, and in way too much of a hurry.

DEBT AND THE EMERGENCE OF THE
U.S. FINANCIAL SECTOR

When John Kennedy, Lyndon Johnson, and Richard Nixon were in the White House, the manufacturing share of U.S. GDP was almost twice that of financial services. The Depression of the 1930s had made debt a four-letter word—debt service hit a painful 20 percent of national income in 1932—and it remained one until the fifties and sixties opened up new vistas of consumerism and consumer borrowing. Then, memories of the dust bowl, WPA projects, and grown men selling apples were put aside.

The sixties, while remembered more for the war in Vietnam and protest demonstrations than for speculative capitalism, did have its go-go side—a wave of merger-mania and the modern era's first spate of corporate "conglomerates," the first wild ride of hedge funds, the Dow Jones Industrial Average hitting 1,000, and the ballooning of credit cards and installment debt. Mortgage debt doubled from $162 billion in 1960 to $338 billion in 1970. But much of the speculative element washed out of stocks in the Dow Jones's 36 percent minicrash of 1969–70. Between January 1969 and October 1970, the twenty-eight largest hedge funds saw 70 percent of their assets disappear; and between November 1969 and November 1970, roughly a hundred brokerage and financial firms were acquired or disappeared. Indexes cobbled together by *Dun's Review* around the ten leading conglomerates and parallel tensomes for technology and computers tumbled between 77 percent and 86 percent.[3] Those excesses, by and large, were purged.

The seventies were a confused era, marked by two major oil-price shocks (1973–74 and 1979–80) that bred a pair of serious stagflationary recessions in more or less the oil-shock time frames. However, mortgage debt expanded like gangbusters as housing prices soared between 1976 and 1979, letting owners refinance and tap spendable funds. Alan Greenspan, who was chairman of President Gerald Ford's Council of Economic Advisers, would keep those supportive precedents in mind almost thirty years later as Fed chairman. And 1979 also brought the first leveraged buyout of a public company, Houdaille Industries, by a private equity firm, Kohlberg Kravis Roberts & Company, although the real LBO tide would await the more exuberant eighties.

In 1977, *Time* saluted another symptom, credit card growth, with a lengthy analysis of how "the Affluent Society has become the Credit Society, and an insistence on buying only what can be paid for in cash seems as outmoded as a crew cut."[4] Since 1950, the U.S. consumer installment debt outstanding had soared twelvefold to roughly $179 billion, omitting mortgage debt, which had risen comparably. Lacy Hunt, an economist at Philadelphia's Fidelity Bank, enthused that "the ability of the consumer to take on more debt will be the underpinning of the economy in 1977. This year is the year of consumer credit."[5]

The mortgage debt that so impressed Greenspan, along with the credit card volume saluted by Hunt, slowed down as interest rates soared from 1979 to 1981, and it's probably fair to say that the deep 1980–82 recession squeezed the debt hangover out of the U.S. economy while it hammered down the inflation rate. With the slate of past excesses at least partly wiped clean by a federal funds (overnight) rate briefly taken up to 18 percent, the eighties emerged as the decade in which debt and financial debtsmanship really came into their own. And here, I think, is where the financial sector's rise to power truly began.

The prerequisites for this takeoff included a series of innovations and circumstances dating back to the 1970s. When Richard Nixon "closed the gold window" in 1971, ending Federal Reserve authority to let foreign central banks buy gold with dollars, he "floated" the currency on restless global seas. Currency trading and foreign exchange markets boomed, with currency futures launching in 1972, and foreign exchange in one form or another growing into the world's largest financial market. The extent to which financial firms and markets were rapidly computerizing was likewise essential to this kind of trading, and together with the pioneering work of Fischer Black and Myron Scholes in options theory in 1973, the elements of primordial soup were set for a new hedging and speculative universe, one that supported so-called derivative instruments. The first two introduced were foreign currency futures in 1972 and equity futures in 1973; T-bill futures and futures on mortgage-backed bonds followed in 1975. Figure 2.3 shows the early emergence of derivatives in the seventies, together with their much

FIGURE 2.3
The Evolution of Critical Derivatives, 1972–2005
A Chronology of Risk Management Techniques

So-called risk management techniques proliferated in the 1990s and thereafter, but the products that became famous in 2007–8 (mortgage-backed securities, collateralized debt obligations, collateralized mortgage obligations, credit default swaps) had varied origins, catching hold in the 1990s but ballooning in the 2000s. Mortgage-backed securities (MBSs) arose from the secondary market in 1970, and in 1983, FNMA introduced the first collateralized mortgage obligation (CMO). Sperry Leasing Finance Company developed the first asset-backed security (ABS) in 1985. The collateralized debt obligation (CDO) was invented in 1987 by Drexel Burnham but developed during the 1990s. Credit default swaps (CDSs) came into use during the early 1990s, but their volume metastasized only during the 2000s.

	1992 ——	Differential swaps
Portfolio swaps ——	**'91**	
Equity index swaps ——	**'90**	
Three-month euro-DM futures ⌐	**'89** ⌐	ECU interest-rate futures
Captions ⌐	**'88**	Futures on interest-rate swaps
Average options ⌐	**'87** ⌐	Bond futures and options
Commodity swaps ⌐	**'86**	Compound options
Eurodollar options ⌐	**'85** ——	Futures on U.S. dollar and
Swaptions ⌐	**'84**	municipal-bond indices
Interest-rate caps and floors ——	**'83** ⌐	Options on T-note futures
	'82	Options on currency futures
		Options on equity-index futures
Equity-index futures ⌐	**'81**	T-note futures
Options on T-bond futures ⌐	**'80**	Eurodollar futures
Options on bank CD futures ⌐		Interest-rate swaps
Currency swaps ⌐	**'79**	
	'78	Over-the-counter currency options
T-bond futures ——	**'77**	
	'76	
T-bill futures ——	**'75** ——	Futures on mortgage-backed bonds
	'74	
	'73 ——	Equity futures
Foreign currency futures ——	**'72**	

Source: Chase Manhattan; 1993–2005 discussions from various sources.

grander and sophisticated permutation in the upward-bound eighties
and nineties. With booming currency markets, soaring derivative volume, and the enabling effects of large-scale computerization, the basic
backdrop for the sectoral triumph of finance was in place.

Back in 1977, *Time* had titled a lengthy essay on credit card issuers "Merchants of Debt" but had examined none of the bolder new financial
products. Perhaps unknowingly, the magazine had adopted a phrase
used in the 1930s by Joseph Schumpeter, an economist of the Austrian
School, and then in the 1970s by Hyman Minsky. Both men argued that
downturns evolved from financial and credit excesses. "Merchants of
debt" was their epithet for banks and other financial entities that strove
to market debt in as many (innovative) forms and to as many buyers as
possible. The longer good times persisted—a description most of the
last quarter century would fit—the more likely the financial sector was
to be marketing unwise or risky products.[6]

   The omissions and fallibilities of U.S. census and economic data are
not a principal concern of this book. However, a brief comment is necessary. For anyone trying to track great upheavals, such as manufacturing displacing agriculture as America's top economic sector in the late
nineteenth century, or financial services recently performing the same
requiem for manufacturing, the available data leaves much to be de-
sired. Either officialdom didn't really understand what was happening
or there wasn't much interest in measuring it. Economic historian Fred
Shannon, a chronicler of U.S. agriculture, elaborated on how
nineteenth-century census takers failed to count farmers and shuffled
the definitions of agricultural workers. Farm income data, Shannon
thought, was essentially unreliable.[7] Some years back, I had the same
difficulty in tracking the manufacturing sector's climb to preeminence,
and finally settled for official value-added figures that showed goods
production pulling ahead in the 1880s. The rise of financial services at
the expense of manufacturing is clear enough as of 2007, but that was
not true in the 1970s or during most of the 1980s.

   A second information gap also deserves note. The ups and downs of private as opposed to public debt have rarely been a focus for U.S. economists or historians. Canadian economist John Hotson, after likewise faulting Canadian statistics, commented that "one can read through almost every principles of economics text, or even money and banking texts, without learning that private debts are several times larger than public debts and growing in a wholly unsustainable fashion." Several economic portraitists of the 1920s have complained about the thin data and insufficient discussion of that decade's high private debt levels, especially installment credit. Even now, critics point out, the National Income and Product Accounts (NIPAs) published by the U.S. Department of Commerce's Bureau of Economic Analysis contain no statistics on entrepreneur debt or private debt. In consequence, "Persons referring to the NIPAs are left with the impression that private debts or deficits are of little or no significance insofar as the process of growth in national income or national product is concerned."[8] Even in 1996, *The Indebted Society,* in which liberal-leaning economists James Medoff and Andrew Harless criticize several negative effects of corporate debt, omitted surging financial sector debt and made no reference to the new sector's debt-powered emergence.

Turgid as this may sound, a lot of people are missing something awfully big. These pages will not revisit the academic wars of the mid- and late twentieth century, which rival Keynesians on one side and monetarists on the other effectively controlled, partly smothering alternative interpretations of panics, crashes, and business cycles, including those that tied financial crises to innovative, excessive, and unstable private debt. Small matter now who prevailed back in 1937 or 1979. What matters nearly a decade into the new century is that recent circumstances—the 2007 global freeze-up of speculative and overextended credit markets—provide considerable affirmation of the maverick viewpoints centered on financial crises, private debt, and credit excesses.

Figure 1.1, back on page 7, is a double presentation. On its left side, it illustrates the extraordinary public and private debt surge associated with the 1929 crash and aftermath, while the summit on the right, higher still, marks the peak of indebtedness achieved as the U.S. housing and debt bubble quivered and sagged in the summer of 2007. To explain what had built up, we must now turn back the clock to a critical threshold: the embrace of securities-market capitalism and financial sector renewal that took form in the United States and Britain some three decades ago.

PRIVATE DEBT, FINANCIAL INNOVATION, AND ECONOMIC INSTABILITY

The British acted first, electing in 1979 a Conservative Party government that chose free-market lioness Margaret Thatcher as prime minister. She immediately embraced a program of minimally fettered capitalism, and over more than a decade in office largely implemented it. The Republicans under Ronald Reagan, in turn, won the U.S. presidency in November 1980. They soon supported, albeit with some reservation, a harsh crackdown on double-digit inflation by the chairman of the Federal Reserve Board, Paul Volcker. More enthusiastically, they embraced a policy of returning to the old-time economic religion. Secretary of the Treasury Donald Regan, formerly the chairman of the Wall Street securities giant Merrill Lynch, announced, "We're not going back to high-button shoes and celluloid collars. But the President does want to go back to many of the financial methods and economic incentives that brought about the prosperity of the Coolidge period."[9] As a further pledge of allegiance to the eighteenth-century British free-market apostle, many Reaganites took to wearing Adam Smith ties. On both sides of the Atlantic, and after a considerable hiatus, finance and its allies were back in power.

The economic tale of the eight Reagan years has been told often enough to necessitate only a short condensation. Harking back far beyond the presidency of "Silent Cal" Coolidge, Washington free marketeers anxious to overcome demand-side Keynesian economics took up nineteenth-century economist Jean-Baptiste Say's half-forgotten thesis that supply (i.e., production or commerce) created its own demand. In the nation's capital, this was political shorthand for "Unleash capital through tax cuts." Washington did so in 1981, but so extravagantly that, in tandem with the 1981–82 recession, too much revenue was lost and some of the reductions had to be rescinded in 1982. Still, the economy did start to rebound, and late that summer there began an eighteen-year bull market in stocks that would carry the Dow Jones Industrial Average from 775 to 11,700 in early 2000.

Republicans and Democrats predictably disagreed about the breadth and quality of the 1980s recovery and early bull market. Despite a near recession in 1986, the official growth cycle was a long one, lasting until mid-1990. Republican architects crowed over reduced regulation of business and the climbing stock market, and although the tax cuts helped to bring about a quartet of serious federal budget deficits, most Reaganites believed that tax reduction counted more. For their supporters and swing voters, Republicans had a bevy of talking points. As the economy grew, so did spending on defense to rebuild U.S. military strength. The tax cuts and stock market gains revived venture capital, entrepreneurship, and technological development. New business formation jumped. Capitalism and its leaders had regained stature.

Many Democrats wouldn't have minded increasing federal indebtedness to pay for broader stimulus, health care, and education, or benefits programs for farmers, blue-collar workers, or the poor. In many states, the pain of manufacturing decline was all too apparent. However, leading Democrats complained, as did many economists, that the benefit of the GOP tax reductions went disproportionately to corporations, commercial real estate, stock owners, and so-called paper entrepreneurs—the designers and promoters of mergers, assets shuffling, corporate takeovers, or debt-fueled corporate leveraged buyouts. The rich, critics argued, were the principal beneficiaries. In general, this was true. Even LBOs and debt speeded manufacturing's ebb, inasmuch as goods producers constituted a disproportion of companies affected, and when they were stripped of some assets and loaded up with debt, blue-collar jobs and futures were usually at risk.[10]

These chapters will note only in passing the questions of fairness or polarization of income and wealth within the United States, albeit the polarization is sharper than ever. This book's premise, now that a quarter century's results are in hand, is that the eighties can be identified as the launching pad of a decisive financial sector takeover of the U.S. economy, consummated by turbocharged, relentless expansion of financial debt and eventual extension of mortgage credit to subprime and other unqualified buyers. The two converging pumps helped to swell the housing, mortgage, and credit bubble that began imploding in the summer of 2007.

Not that leaders in the early eighties sat down and planned it. Aside from Marxists mostly given to repeating ideological doctrine, there was relatively little perception of spreading financialization and a burgeoning debt mentality until the second half of the decade. In 1982, business magazines were still running cover stories on the death of equities. What first helped to establish a new reliance on debt finance was the provocative string of major-league federal budget deficits resulting in part from the loss of tax revenues: $208 billion (6.1 percent of GDP) in 1983, $184 billion (4.9 percent) in 1984, $212 billion (5.2 percent) in 1985, and $221 billion (5.1 percent) in 1986. In 1989, Harvard economist Benjamin Friedman published *Day of Reckoning* (New York: Random House), a well-received indictment of the deficits. But he also made a relevant critique of private debt:

> The 1980s has been by far the worst period for business investment in physical assets like plant and equipment since World War II. Instead of borrowing to build new facilities or even to build liquidity, the corporate business sector as a whole has mostly used the proceeds of its extraordinary volume of borrowing since 1980 to pay down equity through mergers and acquisitions, leveraged buy-outs and stock re-purchases. . . . This massive substitution of debt for equity, in conjunction with the onset of record high real interest rates, has sharply raised the debt service burden that the average American business faces.[11]

In retrospect, we can now see another transformation. From the end of World War II until the beginning of the eighties, the share of the U.S. gross domestic product represented by the totality of outstanding debt remained roughly stable. However, this was because the share represented by government debt was going down while economic growth rode the rapid expansion of private sector debt—household, corporate, and financial. Overall, the eighties began a quarter century in which the totality of debt as a share of GDP would balloon, but with a heavy bias toward private debt, which would figuratively rocket.

Thomas Synnott, an economist at U.S. Trust, in 1991 published "The Debt Explosion of the 1980s," an article that ventured far beyond budget deficits. He detailed how much larger dollar amounts propelled a wave of private debt, both household and corporate, that financed overinvestment in residential and commercial real estate. Another large slug of corporate debt, in the form of high-yielding "junk bonds," was issued to finance leveraged buyouts and recapitalizations.[12] These are not dry numbers of distant commerce accumulating well-deserved cobwebs. On the contrary. They are milestones, and they even furnish an essential backdrop to a time most of us better remember for dubious and corrupt finance, culpable politics, and a sequence of Washington bailouts.

Bluntly put, some of the private debt expansion of the eighties helped to bring about three reckless or scandalous episodes. First was the S&L mess—the mid- to late-1980s collapse and post-1988 federal bailout, at a cost over $200 billion, of much of the nation's network of failing and discredited savings and loan institutions. These once solid institutions had been deregulated at the urging of the Reagan administration in 1981 and given effective carte blanche to borrow and invest (read: wheel and deal) in commercial real estate, junk bonds, and other temptations. Edwin Gray, the California Republican who headed the Federal Home Loan Bank Board under Reagan, agreed that deregulation was culpable because oversight was so badly neglected: "The White House was full of ideologues, particularly free-market types. They'd say 'the way to solve the problems is more deregulation'—and by the way, deregulation means fewer examiners."[13]

The second example involved the Federal Reserve–orchestrated rescue of New York's Citibank and others. These, too, had fed at the trough of initially profitable but ultimately unsound loans made for unnecessary real estate projects advantaged by 1981 tax provisions. At first, this stimulus produced an assets boom, but overbuilding soon became clear, and then after 1989 a sharp price decline took place in both residential and commercial real estate. Citi's stock market quotation had collapsed into single digits, and the bank could have failed if examiners had strictly interpreted the definition of a bad loan. They did not. New York Federal Reserve Bank president Gerald Corrigan used his good offices to arrange a billion-dollar investment-cum-bailout by Saudi prince Alwaleed bin Tawal.

Episode number three involved the Federal Reserve Board's early-1990s bailout of junk (high-yielding) bonds through sharp interest-rate reductions that took the federal funds rate down to twenty-year lows. Some of these bonds were issued to raise money for weaker corporate borrowers, but others funded the leveraged buyouts that became so notorious. Such bonds also lost cachet as Michael Milken of Drexel Burnham, the architect and promoter of the junk bond concept and distribution system, was indicted on ninety-eight counts in 1989, eventually plea-bargained, went to jail, and paid a fine of $600 million. Drexel itself filed for bankruptcy in 1990.

Let me hypothesize: If these innovations and misadventures—prototypical "bad money"—hadn't been bailed out, the recession of 1990–91 would probably have deepened into the multiyear crisis of 1990–93 or some such. Cleansing, perhaps, but also horrible publicity for the "merchants of debt." So discredited, the financial sector might never have been able to manage its 1990s ascent. However, because these several collusions between political permissiveness and financial recklessness *were,* in fact, absolved by alternating currents of government rescue and monetary ease, sector momentum survived. The prevailing wisdom, well reassured, still recalls the era's officially measured recession as a short and mild one.

More accurately, it was also a close-run thing. During those years, the *Wall Street Journal* ran an early example of a chart genre comparing the decade's escalation of debt (or of the stock market indexes) to the surge in the pre-1929 decade. In a related vein, Bert Ely, a northern Virginia–based banking expert, calculated that the percentage of total U.S. deposits held in financial institutions ultimately forced into FDIC and FSLIC rescues in the late 1980s and early 1990s wound up *surpassing* the portion of national deposits lost in the failing institutions that had *actually shut down* in the years surrounding the 1929 crash.[14]

How textbook authors and others can consider private debt unimportant and how Washington bean counters can omit it from the National Income and Product Accounts I can't imagine. If more attention had been paid to private debt back during the S&L playpen years and in the early 1990s, the critical mass reached in 2007 might have been kept smaller and possibly manageable. But as things worked out, of course, the 1990s got to extend the trends and mind-sets of the 1980s, and to further expand private indebtedness to new heights. Figure 2.4 sets out the striking growth of public and private debt—federal, state and local, household, domestic and foreign financial, and corporate nonfinancial—across three profligate decades.

The table is actually easy reading, although depressing. Public debt—federal, state, and local (nearly $11 trillion all told)—was neither the immediate danger point nor the fastest-growing category. What went ballistic over the last quarter century is exactly what dissidents hold up for more attention: private debt (household, financial, and nonfinancial corporate) that wound up totaling some $36 trillion. Under Democratic president Bill Clinton, inaugurated in January 1993, the influence of the financial sector continued. Indeed, almost from the start, his principal economic adviser, former Goldman Sachs chairman

FIGURE 2.4
Debt Outstanding by Sector ($ billions)

	1974	1984	1994	2004	2006
Domestic financial	$258	$1,052	$3,791	$11,868	$14,184
Foreign financial	81	233	443	1,431	1,764
Total nonfinancial business	821	2,315	3,830	7,650	9,031
Total household	680	1,943	4,541	10,593	12,873
Federal government	358	1,364	3,492	4,395	4,885
State and local government	208	514	1,107	1,683	2,007
Total U.S. financial and nonfinancial debt	2,407	7,422	17,205	37,620	44,744

Source: *Flow of Funds*, D.3: "Debt Outstanding by Sector," September 17, 2007.

Note: Columns may not add up to the stated totals because of rounding.

Robert Rubin, persuaded the new president to defer to the debt markets, prompting the new chief executive's famous reply: "You mean to tell me that the success of my [economic] program hinges on the Federal Reserve and a bunch of f——ing bond traders?" James Carville, a Democratic strategist of populist bent, was moved to comment, "I used to think if there was reincarnation, I wanted to come back as the president or the pope or a .400 baseball hitter; but now I want to come back as the bond market. You can intimidate everybody."[15]

Clinton, somewhat like conservative Democratic president Grover Cleveland at the height of the late-nineteenth-century Gilded Age, slowly drifted into the orbit of New York finance. He got along well with the Republican chairman of the Federal Reserve Board; promoted Rubin to treasury secretary; raised a lot of reelection money on Wall Street (which, as we will see, was also becoming more Democratic); joined with Citigroup chairman Sanford Weill, an active Democrat, to promote the sweeping federal financial deregulation act of 1999; exulted over the rocketing stock market averages; gravitated to resorts like the Hamptons and Martha's Vineyard; and on the occasion of one visit found himself hailed by a Hamptons chronicler who called the ebullient president "the spirit of the bull market." Before leaving the White House in 2001, Bill and Hillary Clinton moved their residence to New York, where Mrs. Clinton had won a U.S. Senate seat in 2000.

Principally because of the large sums the U.S. Treasury collected from capital gains taxes on bull market stock profits between 1998 and 2000, the federal budget deficit itself reversed into a temporary surplus. With respect to private debt, however, Clinton voiced no criticism of what had become frenetic issuance. Between 1993 and Clinton's retirement early in 2001, total U.S. credit market debt rose from $16.1 trillion to $27.7 trillion, a 72 percent increase. More than $10 trillion of that growth involved private debt, of which the financial category alone represented about half.[16] In light of this excess, continued federal budget deficits in the $100 billion to $200 billion range would have been less pernicious.

Obviously, this flood of private credit provided high-octane fuel for the expansion, leverage, and ambition of the financial sector, which seems to have passed manufacturing in the GDP data during the mid-nineties. Figure 2.5 measures the trot, canter, and gallop of the 1969–2006 advance of financial debt, which left all other private debt expansion in the dust. *The Flow of Funds Review & Analysis,* published by the Virginia-based Financial Markets Center, offered one of the few explanatory backdrops as financial debt hit a crescendo in the year before the stock market bubble popped in 2000:

> These figures are the latest manifestation of a remarkable rise in financial sector indebtedness that dates to the late 1960s, when U.S. banks began borrowing Eurodollars in huge volumes from their offshore branches. . . . In each decade since 1969, the ratio of financial sector debt to GDP has nearly doubled. During this 30-year period, the financial sector's share of total U.S. credit has quadrupled (from 7.5 percent in 1969 to 29.7 percent in 1999) and its share of annual flows has grown precipitously. In 1999, financial firms absorbed 49 percent of the total increase in credit (in the second quarter, their share topped 55 percent). With financial institutions channeling half of new lending to other financial

FIGURE 2.5

The Triumph of Leverage

Growth of Debt of the U.S. Financial Sector, 1969–2006

	1969	1979	1989	1999	2004	2006
Total outstanding ($ billions)	100 (est.)	505	2,399	7,607	11,868	14,184
Financial sector's share of outstanding debt of all sectors	7.5%	11.8%	18.7%	29.7%	31.5%	31.7%
Domestic financial debt as a percentage of U.S. GDP	12%	21%	44%	82%	104%	107%

Source: Federal Reserve System, *Flow of Funds Accounts of the United States.*

firms, credit markets increasingly are being used less to facilitate economic activity and more to leverage bets on
changes in asset prices.[17]

Exactly. But if the financial sector couldn't power its own economic
and political winning sprint with steroids, who could? Besides which,
federal bailouts continued apace, and bolder structured products and
derivatives were invented and marketed every year. Collateralized mortgage obligations (CMOs) had begun in the late 1980s, and CDOs had first
appeared in 1995. Because this financial pseudoscience elevated the gross
domestic product a lot less than it did hedge fund assets and Manhattan
penthouse prices, the national ratio of outstanding debt to (less outstanding) GDP kept growing. In 1997, debt hit 250 percent of national GDP;
ten years later, it peaked, precariously, just short of 340 percent. Debt
and finance, we can now see, pretty much grew together—the profits of
the former helped to fuel the triumph of the latter.

One can hardly blame the Democrats for what was a private sector
frenzy. However, the Clinton administration was relatively collusive
with an increasingly Democratic set of elites. To borrow the phrase
of another era, men like Robert Rubin, Jon Corzine, Sandy Weill,
Roger Altman, and Richard Grasso were "present at the creation."
A shrewd young Democratic writer, Daniel Gross, argued in a 2000
book, *Bull Run,* that northeastern finance was realigning toward
the Democrats, but in contrast to the "Arrogant Capital" dominat-
ing the Republican Party, the Democratic financial element represented "Humble Capital."[18] Eight years later, Wall Street showed signs
of tipping Democratic, as chapter 6 will pursue. However, the behavior of hedge funds, private equity houses, derivatives packagers,
the compensation committee of the board of the New York Stock
Exchange, and überbanks like Citigroup showed a striking continuity
with the heyday practices of previous elites. Humble proved to be
humbug.

Indeed, the great waterfall of private lending, liquidity, and leverage that spilled over the financial sector during the 1997–2000 stock mania, at its brashest in the energy and telecommunications sectors, produced a lot of the same recklessness and grand jury attention so visible in the late eighties. More than one analyst has linked this second peak flow of lending and debt—$2.5 trillion of issuance by energy and telecommunications firms, both opened wide by recent deregulation—to the temptations epitomized by Enron (energy) and WorldCom and Global Crossing (telecommunications). All three were politically active, and when money sloshed around Washington, corner cutting and legal violations followed. Perhaps half of the money pumped into energy and communications debt vanished through bankruptcies and bear market clawings. The partially burst debt and credit bubbles of 2000–2002 had more than a little in common with the burst bubbles of 1969–70 and 1989–92. The floodtides of financial and nonfinancial corporate debt always leave a mess when the waters recede. Indeed, the high-tech and stock market bubble had popped while the Clinton administration was still in office.

In its initial months, with a recession already at hand, the administration of George W. Bush was dogged by his family's and political associates' closeness to Enron. Thereafter it was plagued well into 2002 by the Texas firm's failure and apparent criminal culpability. Even so, the attack on Manhattan's World Trade Center and the Pentagon on September 11 had pushed economic issues into a new, subordinated position. In a caricature of the U.S. government's World War II advice to the public to save and buy war bonds, after 9/11 Americans were told to spend, charge away on their credit cards, or travel to help keep the private economy in a growth mode. George W. Bush himself had urged as much. He even appeared in a travel industry television commercial. For several years, the United States would be at war, giving debt a slight tint of red, white, and blue.

AFTER 9/11: THE DEBT CULTURE TRANSFORMED

Economic favoritism in Washington is also as American as apple pie. In the decades after the Civil War, federal policy had certainly favored manufacturers and railroads over the restive millions of U.S. farmers. Tariffs, railroad land grants, and tight money (tied to gold) all subsidized capital, not agriculture. Farm families, especially on the grain-dependent Great Plains, came to understand that they were fighting for their livelihoods. The leading histories of agrarian populism describe giant meetings, sometimes literally thousands of wagons gathered on the prairies, to discuss railroads, banks, unbearably low grain prices, free coinage of silver, and the need, in the famous words of Kansan Mary Elizabeth Lease, "to raise less corn and more hell." Economic pamphlets were passed from farm to farm, periodicals like the *National Economist* had a hundred thousand subscribers, and William H. "Coin" Harvey enjoyed the fruits of bestsellerdom with his book *Coin's Financial School*. Compared to early-twenty-first-century torpor and lack of serious financial debate, the nineteenth-century agrarian civic engagement had an almost Fourth of July quality.

Over the last three decades, finance cannily sidestepped the spotlight, like mushroom cultivation doing best in rich soil and darkness. Far from flagging its ascendancy with every new track or belching smokestack in the nineteenth-century manner, the financial sector—not that the singular noun implies any single voice—practiced a form of false modesty. References to the "real economy" in 2007 continued to suggest that U.S. finance occupied some small periphery where a hundred thousand Masters and Mistresses of the Universe collected rare wines and endlessly bought and sold structural products and derivatives with a notional value of $500 trillion, all the while never—or hardly ever—disturbing the safety and serenity of West Virginia, Wisconsin, and Wyoming. Even as the August 2007 panic subsided into autumn jitters, no serious debate about the transformation of the U.S. economy had been sparked.

In January 2001, when George W. Bush was inaugurated for the first of his two terms in the White House, he may or may not have known that financial services—the niche in which most of his own family had greatly prospered over four generations—had become the nation's top economic sector. If he had heard, it is hard to imagine he had any qualms. His father, ex-president George H. W. Bush, had been spoofed, during a 1988 Gridiron Club dinner, with these words:

If your daughter's in cotillion
And your son's enrolled at Choate
And your wife is worth a million
I'm sure to get your vote.

During his first years in office, the son's tax proposals, in particular upper-bracket rate cuts, more capital gains advantage, and a farewell to the estate tax, proved to be a chip off the old block—the solid mahogany conservatism of Bush family economics. But the September 2001 attack by al Qaeda that brought down the World Trade Center's twin towers, in addition to targeting America's symbolic preeminence in global finance, shut down the New York Stock Exchange for several days, promised to strip additional trillions of dollars from the U.S. stock indexes, and threw into great uncertainty a national economy already in recession in the aftermath of the 2000 stock market crash. What would happen next no one knew, although Greenspan in his memoirs recalled that "for a full year and a half after September 11, 2001, we were in limbo. The economy managed to expand, but its growth was uncertain and weak. Business and investors felt besieged. . . . Behind everything loomed the expectation of continued terrorist attacks on U.S. soil."[19]

This terror-framed milieu was what the Bush administration also propounded and upheld. Nobody guessed that no major attempt would be made to strike North America again. Meanwhile, given the financial symbol destroyed in the principal September 11 attack, it would have been negligent for Washington not to devise a financial counterplan to support U.S. markets by backstopping financial institutions and exchanges and related communications systems. If the U.S. government had been unwilling to pick "winners and losers" back in the early 1980s when some advocates had promoted a strategic commitment to high-tech or high-value-added manufacturing, by late 2001 the choice had been made. In the late 1980s, as we will see, without making any official or public decision, the United States had effectively opted to put its economic chips on a finance-dominated national future. A "financial strategy" existed in practice, if not in name. Thus, when al Qaeda struck a nerve center of the U.S. financial economy, all but throwing down a gauntlet, finance became a battlefield.

Private credit and debt quickly became a priority of post-9/11 U.S. economic management. Greenspan knew that economic activity had to be maintained or spurred, and although $40 billion to $50 billion a year was spent for homeland security, serious stimulus had to involve harnessing those sturdy global workhorses, U.S. consumers. Bush had similar ideas, but expressed himself ineptly. When he urged people to participate in the economy—to shop, go to the malls, and travel—many pundits assailed him for urging consumption, not the shared sacrifice usually propounded in wartime. In one sense, this critique was mistaken. Consumption and commercial activity served a real public economic purpose amid national disarray and despondency. However, the charge was correct in terms of Bush's civic misjudgment. He was all but barred from talking about shared sacrifice because of his insistence on increasing tax favoritism to upper-income Americans, so contrary to the usual wartime ethic.

George Bush Sr. had shown a similar weakness. In 1992, two *Time* correspondents, Michael Duffy and Dan Goodgame, in a book titled *Marching in Place,* had described the elder Bush's economic philosophy as favoring breaks for the rich, who were capitalism's creative force. In the meantime, burdens could be put on "ordinary Americans, who are not a creative force in the economy and who anyway have no choice but to work and scrimp."[20] However, Bush senior was unable to keep economic discontents from regaining the whip hand over Iraq and national security in 1991–92. Perhaps similar favoritisms guided the younger Bush during the economic aftermath of 9/11. In any event, many consumers, having no great choice in 2001, did indeed take up Washington's hints to borrow and spend.

Financing a new house, or borrowing against the value of one already owned, became the decision into which Washington policymakers aimed to tempt John and Jane Doe, especially as the Federal Reserve dropped interest rates to 1 percent, a low unseen since the early sixties. It was a strategy that, superficially at least, succeeded beyond all expectation. When the debt and deficit hallmarks of the George W. Bush years are carefully examined, the three fastest-growing forms of indebtedness—mortgage debt, financial debt, and the current account deficit

FIGURE 2.6
Leading Components of the 2001–7 Debt Explosion

Category	Amount in 1Q 2001 ($ billions)	Amount in 1Q 2007 ($ billions)	Percentage increase
Outstanding foreign debt	872	1,783	104%
Outstanding home mortgage debt	4,923	9,961	102%
Outstanding domestic financial debt	8,482	14,529	71%
Annual U.S. current account deficit*	420 (for year 2000)	857 (for year 2006)	104%

Source: Federal Reserve, "Debt Outstanding by Sector," September 17, 2007.

*Broadest measure of U.S. international trade in goods and services.

(U.S. net foreign borrowing)—paint an extraordinary picture. Figure 2.6 lays out the numbers.

Pouring $11 trillion into housing and the financial sector obviously stimulated the value of financial assets and homeowner real estate. And Bill Gross, the nation's largest bond fund manager, explained the similar assets-boosting effect of the U.S. trade deficit or the broader current account deficit. "There is likely near unanimity," he says, "that it is now responsible for pumping nearly $800 billion of cash flow into our bond and equity markets annually. Without it, both bond and stock prices would be much lower, the $800 billion for instance representing 3–4x our current federal budget deficit. Almost perversely, then, an increasing current account deficit supports and elevates U.S. asset prices as the liquidity from it is used to buy stocks and bonds."[21]

By comparison, the other categories—public (federal, state, and local), consumer, and business debt—all showed smaller increases. The figure shows where the action was. The doubling of mortgage debt during these years was the $5 trillion contribution assumed by American households. Through 2006, as we have seen, mortgage money did provide massive, vital stimulus. By 2007, though, the collateral abuses of mortgage finance were returning, like any boomerang. As for the even greater $6 trillion of new debt taken on by the financial sector, much of it went to expand the sector's moneymaking capacity and leverage its speculative profits ten-, twenty-, or thirtyfold. How much of a monkey wrench that recklessness had thrown into the economic future remained to be seen.

Debt to foreigners expanded, as the enlargement of the annual U.S. current account deficit, in turn, required more and more foreign loans and investments to finance the things the United States needed to import—oil and manufactures—because our factories and oil fields no longer made or produced enough. The current account deficit had been $79 billion in 1990, then $420 billion in 2000, before mounting to $857 billion in 2006. Some economists thought that, too, constituted a potential menace. International economists Kenneth Rogoff and Maurice Obstfeld argued that "any sober policymaker or financial analyst ought to regard the United States' current account deficit as a potential sword of Damocles hanging over the global economy."[22]

Let me stipulate: there is a banal side to throwing around figures like $5 trillion or $6 trillion or even $857 billion. They lose their bite and capacity to scare, even when put into a comparative or real-world context. The $5 trillion increase in outstanding mortgage debt, a sum equivalent to roughly 40 percent of the U.S. gross domestic product, can best be thought of as the soap and air for one hell of a bubble. And "bubble" is a term that conveys its own danger.

Many people today think that today's finance is too complicated for ordinary citizens to fathom or handle. Bubbles aside, other financial terms used by the media—credit derivatives, securitization, and even current account deficit—do not lend themselves to conversations in neighborhood bars or beauty parlors. Americans are excusing themselves accordingly. Still, if the farmers of more than a century ago could study and understand Sherman Silver Purchase Act provisions and details of the nationwide currency shrinkage—and many studied and somehow managed—can't we expect as much today? Alas, probably not.

The limited, parochial benefit of swollen corporate and financial debt, meanwhile, is all too clear. The debt the United States has been piling on in the last few years has provided only 30–40 percent as much stimulus per dollar to the national economy as did the debt added twenty-five or forty years ago. Why? Because money borrowed in 1970 or 1984 to be spent on factories, new jet fighter aircraft, teachers, or interstate highways had a lot more grassroots impact than money borrowed by ten thousand hedge funds to double the leverage of their various self-serving speculations.

Futures trading, for example, has grown to a huge volume, but 92 percent of it involves bets placed in the financial sector—even trickle-down has lost much of its old juice. The report in the *New York Times* that "during the first half of 2006 the global market in credit derivatives grew 52% to $26 trillion" did little or nothing for people who rode the subway more than four stops or lived in Yonkers.[23] Likewise for the *Wall Street Journal*'s revelation that 2006 merger and acquisition activity would exceed the $3 trillion total reached at the height of the last frenzy in 2000.[24] Any impact on the "real economy"—say in job-losing manufacturing towns—was at least as likely to be negative.

Disinterested experts, of course, could pull back the curtain. The prestigious Bank for International Settlements, headquartered in Basel, Switzerland, pointed in June 2007 to a quartet of troubling indicators: issuance on a huge scale of complicated new credit instruments, reckless tolerance for risk, unprecedented household debt levels, and major imbalances in the world currency system. The bank dismissed financial cheerleaders, recalling that "virtually nobody foresaw the Great Depression of the 1930s, or the crises which affected Japan and southeast Asia in the early and late 1990s. In fact, each downturn was preceded by a period of non-inflationary growth exuberant enough to lead many commentators to suggest that a 'new era' had arrived."[25]

Economists tied to the Austrian School or admirers of the iconoclastic Hyman Minsky were almost beside themselves. In January 2007, Kurt Richebächer wrote that "measured by its level of indebtedness, today's U.S. economy is the worst bubble economy in history."[26] Speaking to his shareholders in May, money manager David Tice, a Minskyite, deplored "the massive expansion of credit instruments—large swathes of which have little or no transparency but have nonetheless evolved into the speculative instruments of choice for a monstrous global leveraged speculator community. Today, previously unimaginable 'credit arbitrage' financial profits are doled out to the holders of myriad securitizations, CDOs, derivatives and other structured instruments and products. It is within this peculiar mania in highly leveraged risk intermediation where we discern the type of acute fragility associated with Minsky's 'Ponzi finance.'"[27] Five or ten times as many investors, being hopeful in outlook, would have endorsed the prevailing expectation of Wall Street muddling through. However, Richebächer, Tice, and others represented the essence of a critique that dwelled on the particular fallibility of the financial sector. No other economic school had been so bold.

More U.S. mortgage lenders were shutting their doors. In-house hedge funds were in trouble at Bear Stearns and Goldman Sachs. By this point, the August turbulence was only weeks away.

FINANCIAL, MONETARY, AND ASSETS-PRESERVATION MERCANTILISM

One intriguing sidebar to the intensifying August debate over the debt and housing bubble was a slowly spreading perception by the financial media of trends toward protectionism, mercantilism, and economic nationalism. Semantic disagreements vied with the political variety, but one could identify a number of strands. Summer's seeming defeat of the Doha Round of world trade negotiations bespoke a resurgence of trade-related protectionism. The rise of sovereign wealth funds (huge government-run investment agencies) in China, Russia, Qatar, Abu Dhabi, and elsewhere grabbed attention as new vehicles of economic nationalism, simultaneously producing countermovements as France, Germany, the United States, and other nations expressed skepticism about letting state-owned foreign companies buy up important or strategic firms. The ballooning accumulation of large currency reserves by

Russia and China, but also by Japan, Taiwan, and Korea, gave them the wherewithal to defend their own currency (or attack some other). This quickly drew a pejorative label—"monetary mercantilism." In addition, the practice of some nations—China, Russia, India, Angola, Sudan, and others—of bypassing the global marketplace and cutting oil and gas deals directly with other nations was called "energy mercantilism."[28]

Finally, as U.S. finance received something of a black eye from its CDOs and other tainted products, a further behavior became evident. Other regions of the world, besides stepping up their interest in buying or opening new financial or mercantile exchanges, began to insist on mandating more transparency for asset-backed securities and structured investment vehicles. Perhaps more debt could be issued or packaged locally rather than imported from the United States. Indeed, foreigners sold U.S. securities heavily in August.

Clearly, elements of marketplace globalization are in some retreat, not least in the United States. Over the last fifteen years, I have used the term "financial mercantilism" to describe a collaboration in which Washington and the U.S. financial sector seek to minimize certain unwanted marketplace forces. The purpose is to suppress what economist Joseph Schumpeter called "creative destruction"—for the United States, circa 2008, that would include the failure of a major financial institution or the deflation-cum-downward-revaluation of financial assets. My book *Arrogant Capital* (1994), following several notable bailouts, used this phraseology: "Financial mercantilism—government-business collaboration calculated to suspend or stymie market forces—has at least partly replaced yesteryear's vibrant capitalism." *Wealth and Democracy* (2002) expanded the concept, detailing the two-decade U.S. history of financial bailouts beginning in the early 1980s.[29]

Others have principally used the term "financial mercantilism" to describe a nation's favoritism to its own exports through subsidies or easy financing. When I Googled the term for this chapter, several of the first ten citations related to my prior usage, so let me reopen the question here. If we are headed into an era of rekindling government economic activism sufficient to resurrect an old term like "mercantilism" and embellish it with four, five, or six subcategories, then some greater precision may be in order.

Take the three-decade pattern of bailouts extended by Federal Reserve chairman Ben Bernanke in his August–September minuet of full-fledged rate cuts, discount window enlargements, and emergency liquidity injections. The old pomposity "moral hazard" has lost relevance as "assets hazard" has become the feared bogeyman. Sometime back in the naive eighties, Milton Friedman rightly called banking "a major sector of the economy in which no enterprise ever fails, no one ever goes broke. . . . The banking industry has been a highly protected, sheltered industry. That's because the banks have been the constituency of the Federal Reserve."[30] Political foes have called the bailout procession "Wall Street socialism," and financial markets watcher James Grant, seeking cooler precision, has coined the term "socialization of credit risk." Figure 2.7, a chronology of federal bailouts and rescues I first published in 2002, has been updated for the Bernanke Fed. No further commentary is necessary, but read it and weep—for the integrity of markets, if nothing else.

A further dimension of financial mercantilism, much in the news since the stock market crash of 2000–2001, is the question of how the Federal Reserve should deal with asset bubbles—financial, real estate, or otherwise. Should policy be to pop them at an early stage, or should they be allowed to attain full spherical shimmer and then eventually deflate messily, as was the case at the turn of this century? Former chairman Greenspan chose shimmer and pop. Board members of the Federal Reserve get the question after speeches; prominent economists pen articles; and foreign central bankers, so the news stories say, favor the "let the air out early if you can" viewpoint.[31] Some of these foreign bankers feared the global consequences of a largely American-made bubble, a valid worry that will be revisited in chapter 7.

Depending on the popping, reinflation, or slow subsidence of the Great Bubble on so many minds in the heat of August 2007, history may dictate a clear verdict. Possibly, however, observers may come to understand a second reality: that Federal Reserve Board chairmen and top-level federal officials did not enjoy a full range of options after late 1987. The stakes of institutional protection, failure prevention, and assets maintenance have been too high.

FIGURE 2.7

U.S. Financial Mercantilism: Bailouts, Debt, and the Socialization of Credit Risk, 1982–2007

Year	Rescue	Government methodology
1982–92	Mexico, Argentina, Brazil debt crisis	Federal Reserve and treasury relief package to avoid domino effect on U.S. banks.
1984	Continental Illinois Bank aid	$4 billion Fed, treasury, and FDIC rescue package.
Late 1980s	Discount window bailouts	Fed provides loans to 350 weak banks that that would later fail, giving big depositors time to exit.
1987	Post–stock market dive rescue	Massive liquidity provided by Fed, and rumors of Fed clandestine involvement in futures market.
1989–92	S&L bailout	U.S. spends $250 billion to bail out hundreds of S&Ls mismanaged into insolvency.
1990–92	Citibank and Bank of New England bailouts	$4 billion to help BEN, then government assistance in arranging a Saudi infusion for Citibank.
1994–95	Mexican peso rescue	Treasury helps support the peso to backstop U.S. investors in high-yield Mexican debt.
1997	Asian currency bailout	U.S. government pushes IMF for rescue of embattled East Asian currencies to save American and other foreign lenders.
1998	Long-Term Capital Management bailout	Fed chairman Greenspan helps arrange bailout for shaky hedge fund with high-powered domestic and international connections.
1999	Y2K fears	Liquidity pumped out by Fed to ease Y2K concern helps fuel final NASDAQ bubbling.
2001–5	Post–stock market crash rate cuts	Fed cuts U.S. interest rates to 46-year lows to reflect U.S. financial and real estate assets and protect the U.S. economy's newly dominant FIRE sector.
2007	Structured investment vehicle and subprime mortgage bailouts	Treasury Secretary Paulson proposes super-SIV fund to rescue top banks and negotiates subprime mortgage relief mechanism.

I wrote back in 1994 that "the investment community also buzzed with another rumor that the Federal Reserve, sheltered in the secrecy of its unsupervised, free-from-audit status, had gone even further by quietly buying S&P futures to prop up the stock market on critical days."[32] Actually, what would later be nicknamed the Plunge Protection Team may have been sheltering such activity behind something far more reassuring: stated but imprecise presidential authority, contained in a proclamation establishing the President's Working Group on Financial Markets issued by Ronald Reagan on March 18, 1988, four months after the October 1987 crash. The secretary of the treasury and the chairman of the Federal Reserve Board were the designated big hitters, but others—the several stock market chief executives, for example, and the president of the New York Federal Reserve Board—could be added to the attendees as needed. The Working Group's purposes, as elaborated in a 1997 *Washington Post* article, were to enhance "the integrity, efficiency, orderliness and competitiveness of financial markets and [maintain] investor confidence." It set up something of a war room, maintained a global as well as a national list of key contacts, and carried out simulated emergency drills.[33]

There is even a suspicion, discussed in Edward Chancellor's history of financial speculation and several other publications, that the Fed first practiced its rescue techniques during the 1987 crash itself, helping to stabilize stocks by manipulating the futures markets.[34] By this reading, the 1988 presidential proclamation was issued to provide a loose legal basis should a repetition be necessary.

Just how much power the Working Group was allowed to exercise was never publicly made clear. A year after its launch, Robert Heller, a retiring member of the Fed's Board, wrote in a widely discussed op-ed for the *Wall Street Journal* that there was a better alternative in emergencies than rate reduction: "Instead of flooding the entire economy with liquidity, and thereby increasing the danger of inflation, the Fed could support the stock market directly by buying market averages in the futures market, thus stabilizing the market as a whole."[35] Besides being relatively inexpensive, the focus on futures market activity made sense. No conclusions were ever reached in writing, but Heller's recommendations may have been accepted backstairs. Over the next two decades, that was certainly the gist of the rumors as to what the Working Group was actually doing. In a January 1997 speech in Leuven, Belgium, Greenspan—just one month ahead of the eye-opening *Post* article—defined the Fed's authority more broadly than usual. Beyond cutting rates and bailing out banks, the Fed could pursue "direct intervention in market events."[36] Central banks in other countries sometimes did, most notably the Bank of Japan.

Apart from the one groundbreaking article in the *Washington Post,* the opinion-molding journals in the United States generally let the group's operations go without serious investigation or comment. The overseas English-speaking press, however, was more intrigued. The *Telegraph* in London ran several articles, in 1998 and 2006, eventually describing the Plunge Protection Team as a "shadowy body with powers to support stock index, currency and credit futures in a crash." The newspaper also quoted George Stephanopoulos, the former top aide to Bill Clinton, as saying that the PPT—the preferred handle in the press—had "an informal agreement among the major banks to come in and start to buy stock if there appears to be a problem."[37] In September 2001, the *London Observer* reported that the PPT was "ready to coordinate intervention by the Federal Reserve on an unprecedented scale. The Fed, supported by the banks, will buy equities from mutual funds and other institutional sellers if there is evidence of panic selling in the wake of last week's carnage."[38]

The financial press also was intrigued. In March 2002, the *Financial Times* quoted a Fed official anxious not to be named as saying that Fed policymakers had considered "buying U.S. equities" and not just futures. The official told the *FT* that the Fed could "theoretically buy anything to pump money into the system." That included "state and local debt, real estate and gold mines, any asset."[39] Two months later, the *Australian Financial Review* weighed whether a 234-point intraday New York Stock Exchange surge could be attributed to the PPT: "There is a belief that this team represents a powerful and secretive hand that is ready to act any time the Dow looks ready to tank big-time."[40]

American financial journalists, more cautious, qualified their stories. One began with a paragraph of insistence that he didn't believe in conspiracies but did know about the buy orders from friends in the S&P

futures pit. Another, the assistant managing editor (money and business) of *U.S. News & World Report*, James Pethokoukis, described how, in the last two hours of August 16, 2007, the Plunge Protection Team might have put the word out to a major institution or two to buy stock index futures: a 300-point Dow decline was relentlessly wiped away. He closed with the caveat that "there's never been any official confirmation" of this, and that people in Washington and on Wall Street "totally dismiss" these reports, albeit confirming that back in late 2006 Treasury Secretary Paulson began to reinvigorate the Working Group.[41]

Revealingly, press coverage of the Working Group turning into the PPT—like Clark Kent turning into Superman—has concentrated during three periods: the Asian and Russian crises of 1997 and 1998, the aftermath of 9/11 and its continuation well into 2002, and the 2006–7 period of preparation for the housing and credit panic and its hurricane-like arrival in August. Frequent intervention in nonemergency situations would only prompt unwelcome investigative reportage. Drawn-out credit-market problems could also increase that likelihood.

I have no personal firsthand knowledge and am not interested in becoming a conspiracy investigator. Proof of federal orchestration, could it be established, might lead to some very messy lawsuits. But I do have a deep strategic interest. After the financial markets' narrow escape in the stock market crash of 1987, some kind of high-level decision seems to have been reached in Washington to loosely institutionalize a rescue mechanism for the stock market akin to that pursued on an ad hoc basis (by the Fed and the U.S. Treasury) to safeguard major U.S. banks from exposure to domestic and foreign loan and currency crises. Thus the coinage of the phrase "financial mercantilism." For Washington to have made such a tentative choice in 1988 was momentous. Finance became the chosen sector of the U.S. economy—the one that would be protected and promoted because it was too important to fail. Manufacturing would receive no such help, however excited members of Congress might get from time to time.

Smiled upon and protected in this backstairs fashion, the financial sector was free to take on greater risk—indeed, greater and greater— and to maximize its growth and profitability through product innovation, massive borrowing, and expanded leverage. Its movement ahead of manufacturing in the GDP numbers came in the midnineties, and by 2007, the results in terms of wealth and profits were staggering, as the next several pages will show.

Yet the same could also be said about the nation's rising vulnerability in terms of debt, volatility-cum-instability, and hubris. Was all or most of this contemplated back in 1988? Almost certainly not. But the steady flow of innovative risk taking and national and international debt and monetary crises served as grist for the mill of incremental government bailouts and supportive intervention. After September 11, 2001, the Washington dialogue also hinted at a growing federal role in national assets management—perhaps better described as national wealth and assets *maintenance,* to which we now turn.

FINANCE: THE WEALTH-MAXIMIZING SECTOR

Adam Smith would have been amazed at the new financial services sector and its close interconnection with government, politics, and power; Jean-Baptiste Colbert, the French architect of seventeenth-century mercantilism, would simply have smiled.

Treatises on the origin of scientific economics leave out mercantilism, and its preoccupation with gold, silver, and national aggrandizement of precious metals, as unscientific. But economics can be emotional as well as scientific—the psychologies of human nature, panic, and bubbling, for example. Indeed, this emotional explanation is becoming chic—witness the recent spate of books and articles on emotions trumping rationalism, the case for "black swan" (supposedly impossible) events, and the unlikely specialty of neuroeconomics.[42]

The early mercantilists propounded an economics based on the accumulation of precious-metal assets. These were the measure of a monarch's or nation's wealth. One got them from mines, from conquest, from captured ships, from colonies, and from exporting manufactures or commodities. What counted was amassing them. Now there are signs in the early-twenty-first-century United States that assets, both financial and real estate, are taking on a growing importance in economic thinking and policy calculations.

The Federal Reserve Board pays close attention to asset prices and what should be done about them. As of August 2007, the policy seemed to be: Let them build or bubble, and don't interfere. During his years as Fed chairman, Alan Greenspan kept a close eye on the nation's net worth numbers: Are assets rising faster than liabilities? If so, good. Back in 2002 the Fed needed housing values to climb so that net worth gains in that category would compensate for the $7 trillion lost between the stock market top in 2000 and its nadir in 2002. Then in 2006, as housing weakened, Treasury Secretary Paulson reinvigorated the Plunge Protection Team—even the nickname smacked of assets worship—to keep a close watch. Achieving and consolidating a 2,000-point climb in the Dow Jones Industrial Average could restore wealth in those financial ledger accounts even as home values dipped. Through mid-2007, that seemed to be on track. Financial journalists, in turn, noted how the Dow, since Paulson had taken over, had broken records for the amount of time passing without a 10 percent correction. And revealingly, on August 15 and 16, at the peak of financial market nervousness, wave after wave of stock index buys kept the correction from reaching 10 percent at any market close and thereby establishing bear market or correction status.

Product innovation in the financial sector was also focused on asset values because of their burgeoning role in securitization, Wall Street's new profits machine. The dollar value of asset-backed securities issuance had jumped from $108 billion in 1995 to $1.07 trillion in 2000, then $1.1 trillion in 2005 and $1.23 trillion in 2006. In 1996, a much discussed article in *Foreign Policy* titled "Securities: The New World Wealth Machine" had set out the ultimate paper entrepreneurial opportunity: high-quality stocks and bonds could be issued against clusters and pools of existing loans and assets, an innovation that "requires that a state find ways to increase the market value of its stock of productive assets." By such a strategy, "an economic policy that aims to achieve growth by wealth creation therefore does not attempt to increase the production of goods and services, except as a secondary objective."[43] Alan Greenspan, too, had wondered whether wealth still required any kind of manufacturing.

Ten years later, most of the other major wealth strategies pursued in the financial sector also involved asset values and rearrangements: private equity and leveraged buyouts, corporate stock buybacks, and mergers and acquisitions. In contrast to the old corporate outlays that used to bestow major benefits on communities and workers, the new ones favored few but investors and shareholders. In addition to being major profit centers, these transactions also fed the upward momentum of the various national stock indexes, derivatives of which were another big business. As assets became the raison d'être of economics, the barons, princes, and monarchs of finance turned to alchemists, this time advanced mathematicians and options theorists, just as the fifteenth- and sixteenth-century princes and monarchs seeking gold and silver had turned to metallurgical alchemists, who boasted of what they could make out of mercury, lead, arsenic, or antimony.

Old-fashioned bankers, Austrian School economists, and Minsky disciples found little to cheer. Back in 1986, Minsky had written in *Stabilizing an Unstable Economy* that whereas a banker's orientation to cash flows was sober, "an emphasis by bankers on the collateral value and expected value of assets is conducive to the emergence of a fragile financial structure."[44] Twenty years later, in a report entitled "Monetary and Prudential Policies at a Crossroad?" the Bank for International Settlements delivered its own verdict: "We have shifted from a cash-flow constrained to an asset-backed economy."[45] It was not a good augury.

But we are getting ahead of ourselves. The flight of the economy from tangibles to money manipulation is enriching a broad cross section of the upper-echelon institutions and practitioners of U.S. finance, and the potentially dangerous transformation represented by the ascendancy of securitization will be dealt with in chapter 4. However, as befits the cavalcade of great wealth in the United States, hedge fund and private equity money was creating enough individual billionaires in 2005, 2006, and 2007 to dominate discussions of the changes in the Forbes 400 Richest Americans list published in the summer of 2007. The changing importance of financial leaders in the various lists of the richest Americans since the early 1980s is, all by itself, a vivid representation of the sector's growing importance and shifting currents.

Figure 2.8 (page 65), comprising data from the 1980s and 1990s, illustrates the rising annual take of Wall Street's biggest individual earners as calculated by *Financial World*. Between 1986 and 1996, the average compensation jumped three- to fivefold. Even so, the increase was greater among two other classes of Americans whose income and wealth were tied to the stock market: the nation's thirty top individual and family fortunes, up roughly tenfold between 1982 and 1999 (see figure 2.9, page 66), and top executives, whose compensation gains between 1981 and 2000 are shown in figure 2.10 (page 67). These were up an average of fortyfold, a measure of that decade's profound and parallel financialization of corporate America.

This was an important reflection. Top executive compensation soared largely because of stock options tying pay to the markets, if not to actual performance of that firm's stock. Companies with names famous in manufacturing—Ford, General Motors, General Electric—became substantially dependent on financial divisions and profits.

During the bull market run-up of 1999–2000, of course, the big gains came among technology entrepreneurs whose companies had soared, but that flow ebbed in 2002 and 2003. By 2007, as shown in that year's Forbes 400 listings, much of the star power and wealth breakthrough capacity had moved to financial entrepreneurs—23 private equity and leveraged-buyout operators (9 of them new in 2007) and the 22 hedge fund stalwarts (13 of them new). A second survey found that the twenty highest-paid hedge fund managers made an average of $657.5 million in 2006. In the meantime, of course, heads of the giant New York banks enjoyed growing wealth, although of their number only Citigroup's Sandford Weill appeared on the Forbes 400 list.[46] Financiers were now making much the same breakthrough in the wealth sheets that finance had made in the sector comparisons a decade earlier.

Part of the reason for sketching some of the realignment of wealth that has flowed from the rise of the financial sector is simply to underscore how yesteryear's support for the creative destruction of a free and fast-flowing marketplace would logically have evolved into support for an assets "Plunge Protection Team" or a federal assets-maintenance strategy instead. Keep the markets up. Please, gentlemen, especially with all of those crazy people in the Middle East and the dollar coming unglued. Meanwhile, the new economy is breeding more stratification and inheritance than mobility. Money makes money. When *Barron's* published its 2007 survey of the top forty wealth-management firms in the United States—most part of banks or other large financial institutions—

FIGURE 2.8
The Great Bull Market and Soaring Wall Street Earnings, 1986–96

The Top Ten from Financial World's *Annual Surveys of Wall Street's Top One Hundred Earners ($ millions)*

CALENDAR YEAR 1986	
Michel David-Weill, Lazard Frères	125
George Soros, Soros Funds	90–100
Richard Dennis, C&D Commodities	80
Michael Milken, Drexel Burnham	up to 80
J. M. Davis, D. H. Blair	60–65
Jerome Kohlberg, KKR	50
George Roberts, KKR	50
Henry Kravis, KKR	50
Ray Chambers, Wesray	45–50
William Simon, Wesray	45–50

CALENDAR YEAR 1991	
George Soros, Soros Funds	117
Julian Robertson, Tiger Mgt.	65
Paul Tudor Jones, Tudor Group	60
Bruce Kovner, Caxton Corp.	60
Michael Steinhardt, Steinhardt Partners	55
John Henry, J. W. Henry & Co.	50
Henry Kravis, KKR	45
Michael Ovitz, Creative Artists Agency	40
Robert MacDonnell, KKR	35

CALENDAR YEAR 1996	
George Soros, Soros Funds	800
Julian Robertson, Tiger Mgt.	300
Henry Kravis, KKR	265
George Roberts, KKR	265
Stanley Druckenmiller, Soros Funds	200
Robert MacDonnell, KKR	200
Sam Fox, Harbour Group	190
Thomas Lee, Thomas H. Lee Co.	130
Nick Roditi, Soros Funds	125
Jerome Kohlberg, KKR	112

Source: *Financial World.* Adapted from chart 3.17 in Kevin Phillips, *Wealth and Democracy: A Political History of the American Rich* (New York: Broadway Books, 2002), p. 145.

FIGURE 2.9

Ten Times Richer: Comparing the Top Thirty Family and Individual Fortunes, 1982 and 1999

The thirty richest families and individuals of 1982 (amounts only)	The thirty richest families and individuals of 1999	
$8.6 bil.	Bill Gates (Microsoft)	$85 bil.
6.6 bil.	Walton family (Wal-Mart)	80 bil.
3.3 bil.	Paul Allen (Microsoft)	40 bil.
2.0 bil.	Warren Buffett (investor)	31 bil.
2.0 bil.	Steven Ballmer (Microsoft)	23 bil.
2.0 bil.	Fisher family (The Gap)	20 bil.
1.6 bil.	Michael Dell (computers)	20 bil.
1.4 bil.	Cox family (media)	19 bil.
1.2 bil.	Mars family (candy)	16 bil.
1.0 bil.	Gordon Moore (Intel)	15 bil.
1.0 bil.	McCaw family (cell phones)	13 bil.
1.0 bil.	du Pont family (inheritance)	13 bil.
1.0 bil.	Bass family (oil)	13 bil.
1.0 bil.	Dorrance family (food)	11 bil.
1.0 bil.	Johnson family (Fidelity Inv.)	11 bil.
1.0 bil.	Philip Anschutz (fiber optics)	11 bil.
1.0 bil.	John Kluge (media)	11 bil.
1.0 bil.	Pritzker family (real estate)	10 bil.
950 mil.	Mellon family (inheritance)	10 bil.
800 mil.	Sumner Redstone (media)	9 bil.
750 mil.	Newhouse family (media)	9 bil.
700 mil.	Koch family (oil)	8 bil.
650 mil.	Rockefeller family (inheritance)	8 bil.
650 mil.	Jeff Bezos (Internet)	8 bil.
600 mil.	Kirk Kerkorian (enterntainment)	7 bil.
600 mil.	Ted Turner (media)	7 bil.
550 mil.	Rupert Murdoch (media)	7 bil.
550 mil.	Charles Schwab (finance)	7 bil.
525 mil.	Phipps family (inheritance)	7 bil.
500 mil.	Hearst family (media)	7 bil.

Source: Forbes 400 for 1982 and 1999. Adapted from chart 3.1 in Kevin Phillips, *Wealth and Democracy: A Political History of the American Rich* (New York, Broadway Books, 2002), p. 145.

FIGURE 2.10
Financialization in the Executive Suite: The Rise of Top Corporate Executive Compensation, 1981–2000

The Top Ten from Each Year's BusinessWeek *Survey of the Highest-Paid U.S. Executives*

Name/Firm and Compensation ($ millions)

1981

R. Genin/Schlumberger	5.7
F. Hickey/General Instrument	5.3
J. Kluge/Metromedia	4.2
J. Riboud/Schlumberger	3.0
H. Gray/United Tech	3.0
R. Adam/NL Industries	2.9
R. Cizik/Cooper Industries	2.8
D. Tendler/Philbro	2.7
A. Busch/Anheuser-Busch	2.6
F. Hartley/Union Oil	2.3

1988

M. Eisner/Disney	40.1
F. Wells/Disney	32.1
E. Horrigan/RJR Nabisco	21.7
F. Johnson/RJR Nabisco	21.1
M. Davis/Gulf & Western	16.3
R. Gelb/Bristol-Myers	14.1
W. Stiritz/Ralston-Purina	12.9
B. Kerr/Pennzoil	11.5
J. Liedtke/Pennzoil	11.5
P. Fireman/Reebok	11.4

2000

John Reed/Citigroup	290
S. Weill/Citigroup	225
G. Levin/AOL Time-Warner	164
J. Chambers/Cisco	157
H. Silverman/Cendant	137
L. Koslowski/Tyco	125
J. Welch/GE	123
D. Peterschmidt/Inktomi	108
K. Kalkhoven/JDSU	107
D. Wetherell/CMGI	104

Source: *BusinessWeek*, May 10, 1982; May 1, 1989; and April 16, 2001. Adapted from chart 3.23 in Kevin Phillips, *Wealth and Democracy: A Political History of the American Rich* (New York: Broadway Books, 2002), p. 154.

among them they appeared to have some seventy thousand private client managers.[47] Wealth management has become a large and growing business in the United States, and wealthy Americans are no more likely to submit their swollen and cherished assets to the unfettered whims of the free market than Japanese asset owners were when Japan's real estate and stock bubble began to deflate in 1989.

THREE

Bullnomics

Its Favoritism and Fictions

The U.S. consumer price index continues to be a testament to the art of economic spin. Since wages, Social Security cost-of-living increases and some agency budgets are tied to it, the government has a vested interest in keeping it as low as possible. Yet your real cost of living— what you keep after taxes, medical bills, college expenses, and other household costs—is probably much higher than the 2 percent annual rate the government reported in July.

—Columnist John Wasik, Bloomberg News, 2007

Anyone who ever claimed that the modern global capital markets were rational or efficient, in other words, clearly never anticipated the pernicious impact of geopolitics—or the financial innovation that has turned so fiendishly extreme.

—Gillian Tett, capital markets editor, *Financial Times*, November 2007

A spin cycle is a lot more than an option on the dial of a washing machine. Politicians and pundits take up where Whirlpool, General Electric, and Maytag have left off, spinning an event or circumstance into something new and often unexpected. And it's not just events—entire national moods and belief structures have been recast or spun anew. The catch is that these can't be managed overnight or even in a few years. The most successful spin cycles, like the economic one that peaked in and around the millennium, take a generation or more to reach fruition.

American finance has been both a shaper—a grand shaper—and a beneficiary of finespun upheaval. Without the powerful new mythology woven since the 1960s, recent economic superlatives—the Great

Bull Market, the Great Housing and Credit Bubble, take your choice—
could not have been achieved. The United States would have had less
bull, less bubble, and certainly a less complete breakthrough of the U.S.
financial sector into its twenty-first-century digitalized nirvana. But so
promoted, and in less than half a century, finance has ascended from its
image as a mistrusted casino (a memory from 1929) to secular altar,
from emotional cockpit to Efficient Market, from a battlefield of scamps
to a playing field of such Efficient Market exemplars as speculators, arbitrageurs, credit-derivative designers, and corporate raiders. Hedge
funds were useful participants, erudite citadels of Ph.D.'s and professors. Derivatives, even though mere fifteen- to twenty-year-old conceptual adolescents, were, well . . . as safe as houses. "Democratization of
capital" had allowed "We the People" to end-run around yesteryear's
elite market riggers. Bubbles did not really exist, being merely ex-
tensions of rational enthusiasm, and business cycles no longer had
primitive time limitations.

This gradual investiture of U.S. financial markets as centers of integrity and rational behavior, however vital to their success and popular
appeal, should not be confused with the larger transformation of American politics, economics, and culture that has suffused each of the nation's three capitalist-conservative heydays—the late-nineteenth-century
Gilded Age, the Roaring Twenties, and the crisis-spangled boom that
began in 1982 (and that, depending on one's calculus, either ended in
the 2000 crash or double-bubbled into 2007–8). I have described these
eras in other books, and figure 3.1 capsules ten important characteristics shared by all three. Self-interest, mass emotion, and even capitalist
utopianism appear to proceed hand in hand.

My task here is somewhat narrower: to set out several securities-
market-related dimensions unique to the last three decades, clearly the
deepest of the three transformations. The financial sector cut its teeth
in the Gilded Age, in the years of J. P. Morgan and the initial emergence
of the great corporations and trusts. In the Roaring Twenties came the
first broad American stock mania, replete with Ponzi schemes and
bucket shops. But amid the blood, sweat, and jeers of the Depression,
tickertape ballyhoo collapsed into caution. Contemporary finance was

FIGURE 3.1

Ten Recurring Characteristics of U.S. Capitalist Heyday Booms

*The Late-Nineteenth-Century Gilded Age, the Roaring Twenties, and
the Post-1982 Second Gilded Age*

Conservative politics: Mostly Republican presidents but several conservative
Democrats.

Normative support for reduced government: Laissez-faire, reduced regulation,
deregulation, privatization.

Poor climate for labor: Hostility to unions, declining labor union membership,
loss of influence.

Large-scale corporate restructuring: Rise of trusts, consolidation and merger
waves, holding companies, leveraged buyouts.

Tax reduction: Reduction or elimination of wartime taxes, reduction of top
personal income tax rates.

Disinflation or deflation: Return to hard currency, productivity gains, tight
monetary policy.

Two-tier economy: Difficult times in agricultural and mining regions and old
industrial areas; booms in emerging industrial, service, and financial
centers.

Concentration of wealth: Huge gains in the top 1 percent of wealth and
income relative to the rest of the population.

Increased debt and speculation: Major increases in individual and corporate
debt, innovation in types of credit and debt instruments, heavy
speculation.

Speculative implosions and stock market crashes: 1873, 1893, 1929, 1987,
2000, and 2007.

---

able to seize and hold the nation's reins, in part by selling markets as a
participatory experience and democratic empowerment only when the
1980s and 1990s brought support from pension funds, Internet trading,
and 401(k)s.

It makes sense to dub the first of this era's new dimensions "Bullnomics": the exaltation of financial markets as a rational and safe underpinning for public well-being and the stewardship of a leading world
economic power, and then as a millennial rainbow's end. The role and
sweep of finance in Edwardian Britain pales by comparison with its

reach and pervasiveness in the United States a century later. And the achievement of that success over three decades is a historical phenomenon in its own right.

The second dimension examined in this chapter is what a growing group of dissidents labels a grand statistical misrepresentation—a con—by the U.S. government. This involves the debasement, amid inflationary trends Washington cannot acknowledge, of official statistics, the consumer price index, rather than of the official coinage, the principal plaything in earlier times. Lehman Brothers, in a 2007 report, described the notorious Hapsburg coinage debasement of 1621–22, during the sixteenth- to seventeenth-century price revolution, as the first modern financial panic. The debasement of the CPI, by contrast, won little attention, having been quietly orchestrated amid the political excitement and the bull market hubbub of the late nineties.

The third dimension—a different breed of suasion—is the importance of Christian fundamentalism, of evangelical preoccupation with personal salvation, and of widespread "God wants you to be rich" prosperity gospeling, in making the 2000–2008 Republican national electorate a coalition uniquely willing to accept a period of speculative indulgence and conspicuous favoritism to the upper income brackets. Something like 40 percent of the national GOP electorate—those who voted for Bush in 2000 and 2004—put aside the sort of populist economics that once described and roused their grandparents and great-grandparents in Georgia, Oklahoma, the Dakotas, and Nevada. Their new preoccupation, in many cases, was to concentrate on Jesus their redeemer, to imbibe fear of Islam, and to watch a crescendo of seeming biblical prophecy unfold with a roar in the Middle East. Nothing so large and excitable marked the Republican Party's northern-based capitalist heyday coalitions of the 1880s or the 1920s. The latter-day religious hotbed and hitherto most populist section of the United States, the South, was not in either of those national coalitions. In George W. Bush's, it led the parade.

The place to start, though, is with Bullnomics, the pied-piping of America toward a misleading financial ideology (the efficiency and reliability of markets), buttressed by a spectrum of dubious thinkers, doctrines, and enablers: monetarist economists with their dismissal of government; economic-deregulation enthusiasts; and gurus of the Efficient Market Hypothesis, with its validation of speculators, corporate raiders, assets shuffling, debt, and derivative instruments. That is not the entire tool kit, but it is a fair summary.

MARKET WORSHIP:
ITS DEITIES, DISCIPLES, AND DOCTRINES

Many Americans of the late 1940s, the 1950s, and the early 1960s still adhered to the nation's powerful Depression-era disillusionment with speculation, finance, and big business. Feisty Democratic president Harry S. Truman flogged speculators and war profiteers, and even called Republicans "bloodsuckers with offices in Wall Street" during the 1948 presidential campaign. But Republican chief executives shared some of the sentiments. Dwight Eisenhower maintained a skepticism of munitions makers left over from the investigations of the thirties, and he declined, during his 1950s presidency, to publicly support repeal of a widely accepted 91 percent top income tax rate. Richard Nixon, in turn, signed legislation capping tax rates for earned (wage and salary) income at a lower level than unearned (interest and dividend) income, and condemned speculators: "Because they thrive on crises, they help to create them."[1]

Nevertheless, by the late 1960s Keynesian and progressive economics were losing credibility in the United States because of soaring government spending, inflation, and deceitful fiscal management of the war in Vietnam. Milton Friedman, a conservative economist whose work combined emphasis on the nation's money supply as the key to inflation with a staunch belief in the market as a self-correcting mechanism, began to sell these positions within the Republican Party. So did other colleagues from the academic seat of American free-market economics, the University of Chicago.

From Barry Goldwater and Ronald Reagan in the United States to Margaret Thatcher in Britain, conservatives harked to Friedman's and the Chicago School's essential message: that government interference with the operation of the market was ill-advised and doomed to failure. They also took quiet and secondary comfort from his defense of speculators and greed, a tolerance welcomed by party contributors. By the end of the 1970s, Friedman was probably the world's most famous economist, and two of his admirers, Thatcher and Reagan, were on the cusp of power.

Even as political leaders and university economics departments were heeding Friedman's doctrine, business schools, banks, and investment firms were embracing its workaday cousin—the Efficient Market Hypothesis. Abstract theorizing about finance did not have a long history in the practical and commercial United States, but it was about to gain an audience. The essence of the EMH was that at every moment, shares priced themselves in the market through attracting the input of all information relevant to their value. Further price changes depended on further information. Over the long haul, the Efficient Market Hypothesis maintained, no one could outstrategize the market. Modern Portfolio Theory, in turn, emphasized that it was less risky to shape individual portfolios around the full universe of stocks rather than pick them one by one. Investors, for their part, were motivated seekers of wealth. Mr. Market was a friend, not a Charles Ponzi.

It was economics, but with strong political implications. Markets were held to be inherently rational and efficient, thus rebutting the Keynesian assumption that they were unstable, and by the 1960s beginning to submerge the old New Deal insistence that they were little more than rigged casinos. Moreover, the notable advances during the late 1960s and 1970s in information technology, automated trading, and the computerization of financial markets were assumed to make already "efficient" markets all the more so. One could almost imagine the seething, converging informational flow. The Model Ts carrying Okies west to *Grapes of Wrath* country were from another era.

By the end of the 1970s, according to Edward Chancellor in *Devil Take the Hindmost,* a learned history of speculation, the Efficient Market Hypothesis had become "the working ideology of financial capitalism."[2] It also framed a reinterpretation of the markets that helped to renew their credibility. Still, it had flaws. The obvious loose thread was that if markets were often efficient and rational, from time to time they were neither, indulging both moodiness and irrationality. Critics of the EMH made especially telling points with respect to the crash of 1987, when the Dow Jones Industrial Average lost 23 percent of its value—508 points—on one shocking, stunning day in late October. Few could find much rationality there. But the EMH was too important as a theoretical foundation to be pushed aside or abandoned. The financial sector had too much at stake to risk losing popular acceptance of markets and their relentless innovations.

Looking back on three decades of financial sector growth culminating in domination of the GDP, that success couldn't have occurred without politicians and opinion molders alike believing that the various U.S. stock and mercantile exchanges, fixed-income markets, and over-the-counter markets were rational and efficient, well able to function on their own and self-regulate without the heavy hand of government. They also had to look like safe places for ordinary folk to put their money. Following several government-facilitated bailouts in the early nineties after the looting and raiding of the eighties, markets were about to be exalted and embraced by Republicans *and* Democrats, populists *and* bankers, in the bull run-up to the great millennial stock market peak and crash of 2000–2002.

Thomas Frank described the reinvention, sometimes hinting at idolatry, in his 2000 book, *One Market Under God: Extreme Capitalism, Market Populism, and the End of Economic Democracy.*[3] "Today," he lamented, "American opinion leaders seem generally convinced that democracy and the free market are simply identical." Also, he mocked the pretensions of "market populists" that "since markets express the will of the people, virtually any criticism of business could be described as an act of despicable contempt for the common man." Once, the arrogance of the elite had involved an attempt to impose their values and sociology; now their arrogance was economic, "revealed by their passion to raise the minimum wage, to regulate, oversee, redistribute and tax."[4] The viewpoints Frank comprehensively cataloged—support for a market democracy of "one dollar, one vote," insistence that workers had all become "businesspeople," and belief that the late-nineties "market consensus" represented the high point of Western civilization—seem ludicrous a decade later. But at the time, he captured the excesses of the "extreme capitalism" and "market populism" posited in his book's subtitle.

Looking back to its introduction in the late 1960s, the Efficient Market Hypothesis provided a vital framework for eventually justifying hitherto controversial practices. By way of example, we can note the origins of four such practices that proved vital to the ascent and high profitability of finance: (1) persistent economic deregulation; (2) debt-dependent mergers, takeovers, and leveraged buyouts; (3) the economic utility of speculation; and (4) the usefulness and facilitation of markets provided by derivatives. All four found support in definitions by friendly academicians of what justified abandoning old suspicions in the name of promoting marketplace stability, efficiency, or liquidity.[5] Just as earlier capitalism turned the vice of greed into the virtue of self-interest, market efficiency became a new pavilion for another, similar change of clothing.

Deregulation of industry, popular during the 1920s, was for decades after World War II unacceptable. Regulation itself had brought reform during the 1930s. Suspicion of what business would do if it got another chance lingered on. When it finally took hold during the 1980s, deregulation did make obvious sense in specific situations. When inflation hit double digits, for example, it was logical to abandon the old single-digit federal ceiling on the interest rates that banks could pay on deposits. However, the larger phenomenon of economic deregulation likewise reflected the spreading conservative viewpoint that markets delivered better results than government-controlled economies.

The 1980s, 1990s, and 2000s were also decades in which the stock market averages were propelled by high levels of mergers, reorganizations, and leveraged buyouts. Under the new Internal Revenue provisions of the 1980s, debt seemed rational from a tax standpoint, rather than immoral or indulgent. That same decade saw corporate raiders posture as outsiders tackling a bloated "corpocracy," as promoters of the ability of the small to challenge the big, and as standard-bearers of "a democratization of capital" that unlocked "shareholder value." Business school realpolitik was more appealing to the public when rephrased to emphasize commitment to shareholders.

That being said, in each of the three decades, the most important effect of mergers, acquisitions, and reorganizations was to goose the stock indexes and increase fees and profits. During the mid-1980s, Goldman Sachs estimated that a major portion of the stock market's rise came from anticipation of takeover bids, and others specifically credited the boom in leveraged buyouts.[6] Similar claims would be made for the late 1990s and the 2005–7 period. All the while, arbitrageurs, raiders, and private equity operators thrived under the aegis of the Efficient Market as its supposed agents and as disciplinarians of inefficient managements. But none of this resolved the underlying conundrum: Is the "efficiency" served by these various doctrines and enablers that of the broad economy of three hundred million Americans, or that of a much narrower financial sector and the richest 1 to 2 percent of Americans?

Speculators enjoyed a new respectability—academics lavished them with encomiums for how they made markets efficient and helped markets assimilate new information. And, claimed defenders, they provided needed liquidity, assumed the risks inevitable to the processes of capitalism, and contributed to the effective distribution of scarce resources. At the Federal Reserve Board, Alan Greenspan essentially agreed. Hedge funds, the quintessential speculators, thrived and multiplied in this friendly milieu, ballooning their assets under management from several hundred billion dollars in 1997 to $1.81 trillion in late 2007, but this underestimated their true importance because leverage further increased it by some disconcerting multiplier.

As for derivative instruments, many had been conceptually pioneered by mathematicians and other academicians, who routinely invoked efficiency theory to proclaim them reliable and essential risk-management tools. One pioneer, Professor Merton Miller, for years a board member of the Chicago Mercantile Exchange, enthused over derivatives as "essentially industrial raw materials" created to deal with uncertainty and volatility. He argued that "contrary to the widely held perceptions, derivatives have made the world a safer place, not a more dangerous one."[7] But professors frequently go overboard. In 1990, when U.S. economist William Sharpe, in accepting his Nobel Prize, insisted that unrestricted short selling was necessary for efficient markets, wags pointed out that it was restricted even in the United States.[8]

Over the years, a handful of critical academicians and several billionaire investors—Warren Buffett, George Soros, and William H. (Bill) Gross—would emerge as relentless critics of derivatives, bubbles, and alleged market efficiency. Yale's Robert Shiller scoffed at the Efficient Market Hypothesis, commenting after the 1987 crash that the "efficient market hypothesis is the most remarkable error in the history of market theory. This is just another nail in its coffin." Harvard professor Lawrence Summers, who later became the treasury secretary, likewise opined that "if anyone did seriously believe that price movements are determined by changes in information about economic fundamentals, they got to be disabused of that notion by Monday's 500 point movement."[9] Two decades after 1987, the coffin remained unbuilt, partly because EMH supporters had developed watered-down versions tolerant of exceptions, but also because critics were so disparate. Nevertheless, as market crises, quantitative failures, and bubbles recurred in the 2000s, it became harder for professors with financial interests to repeat the tired mantra of these events being mathematical flukes, mere one-in-ten-thousand possibilities.

In September 2005, one columnist for the *Financial Times* reported that "most fund managers think that efficient market theory is nonsense. They believe it is possible to find stocks that are wrongly priced by the market."[10] Warren Buffett, given to jokes about business school professors, had once said, "I'd be a bum on the street with a tin cup if markets were always efficient."[11] And in the wake of the mid-2007 financial panic, the *Wall Street Journal* updated the embarrassing state of market informational efficiency:

> Since the invention of the ticker tape 140 years ago, America has been able to boast of having the world's most transparent financial markets. The tape and its electronic descendants ensured that crystal-clear prices for stocks and many other securities were readily available to everyone, encouraging millions to entrust their money to the markets. These days, after a decade of frantic growth in mortgage-

backed securities and other complex instruments traded off
exchanges, that clarity is gone. Large parts of American financial markets have become a hall of mirrors.[12]

Ordinary investors are starting to pay a price for what is fast becoming a tattered pretense. Information is deficient, not efficient; the theory
behind the EMH has spurred a dubious shift toward passive index funds
and the "buy and hold" approach and away from market timing and
active management. The EMH assumption that the stock market provides the best guide to the value of corporate assets is undercut by the
lack of attention to private debt in U.S. and British data collection. In
addition, the investment theory taught in U.S. business schools may be
useless with respect to East Asia, where complex social networks differ
from those of the West. Sooner or later—sooner would be preferable—
these critiques (many others have been omitted for brevity) must start
converging into a revisionist framework and into a new "spin."

More disconcertingly, the fallibility of derivatives and their underlying mathematical calculations and assumptions now spans *two* decades—so-called program insurance in 1987, the flawed convergence
plays and risk arbitrage of Long-Term Capital Management in 1998,
and the multiple miscalculations of 2007 (flawed quantitative analysis,
risk myopia, and the crippling opacity and toxic "contagion" of collateralized debt obligations). The risk of risk is no longer just a bad pun.
Members of the Austrian School, bubble blamers, and Minsky acolytes
indicting Ponzi finance have made some valid criticisms. So, too, have
those identifying "black swans"—supposedly impossible occurrences—
as a valid field of study. Emotion theorists, for their part, were beginning to hit Efficient Marketeering with countertheses that had manic
mood swings cavorting with financial utopianism. Between the 1930s
and the 1960s, none of these varied viewpoints managed to seed a rival
economic school to match the Keynesians and Friedmanite monetarists, who went on to dominate the late-twentieth-century debate.
Whether a new Western fusion can emerge in this new century—or
whether Asian state capitalism will establish a new paradigm to replace
the Anglo-Saxon one—remains to be seen.

However, it is now necessary to turn to a second element of

Bullnomics: the warping since the 1990s, by some arguments inten-
tional, of the collection and presentation of U.S. economic data to make
it more market-supportive.

THE CONSUMER PRICE INDEX AND STATISTICAL DEBASEMENT

To deal with inflation, an old and recurring problem, the governments
of yesteryear often debased the coinage. They clipped silver coins or re-
minted them with a lower fineness—less silver, more of something else.
Because the United States had taken the silver out of its coinage in the
1960s, that option no longer existed. The alternative pursued in the late
1990s, which may yet boomerang, was to debase the consumer price index statistics maintained by the federal Bureau of Labor Statistics (BLS).

This tinkering did not go unanswered. By 2007, most top officials of
the central banks or new sovereign wealth funds of China, Japan, Russia, Saudi Arabia, Qatar, Kuwait, and the United Arab Emirates, nations
with major U.S. dollar holdings or local currencies pegged to the dollar,
would have heard of California-based Bill Gross, managing director of
the Pacific Investment Management Company (PIMCO). Sometimes
called the world's leading bond investor, billionaire Gross was colloquially known as "the bond king." Were he to send these bureaucrats notes
saying, "My sense is that the [U.S.] CPI is really 1% higher than official
figures and that real GDP is 1% less," they would quickly infer his advice: Rethink your treasury bonds and notes before people get wise and
their values tumble.

Not that Gross would send any foreign official that kind of commu-
nication. However, the quote above is taken from one of his monthly
Investment Outlook letters posted on the PIMCO Web site.[13] Gross
included his terse estimate within a broader complaint about "the con
job perpetually foisted on the American public about the low level of
inflation. 'Inflation under control'—(ex food and energy, of course)
shout the carnival barkers." From there he delivered a double machete
swipe at (1) "substitution bias" and (2) "hedonic" adjustments for product quality, two of the CPI's most controversial post-1995 revisions
(more on both these topics shortly).

Gross noted that he had been joined in his dismissal of the CPI by Stephen Roach, James Grant, Peter Bernstein, and "a host of other voices in the inflationary wilderness." Ah, but much like California in the first decade of the twentieth century, today it's a wilderness no longer. Dissenters have been stirred not just by the emerging scarcity of oil, with its finite supply, but by a new fear—agflation, or soaring food costs. Wheat, grains in general, and other produce are all climbing in price. Besides droughts that may be linked to climate change, experts cite new demand for foodstuffs from India, China, and the rest of Asia, as well as from the biofuels industry's pursuit of corn for ethanol. One senior government minister in Australia raised the possibility of a global "food shock" to match the already obvious "oil shock."[14] The Russian government imposed retail price controls on some basic foodstuffs, Germany buzzed with newspaper headlines about milk and vegetable prices, and the director-general of the United Nations Food and Agricultural Organization noted in late 2007 that food prices in developing countries were up about 11 percent in the past year, spurring concern about food riots.[15] In the United States, food represents 14 percent of the consumer price index, but the ratio is much higher in China (33 percent) and India (46 percent).

Two economists at Merrill Lynch coined the term "agflation" in spring 2007, referring not just to short-term price increases for grain, soybean, corn, and corn product but to "a secular price rise we have seen in the global agricultural business that may be more long-lived."[16] The contention of PIMCO's Gross, well displayed in figure 3.2 (page 82), is that the food and energy element in the CPI is likely to be the best 2005–8 predictor of overall inflation, just as it was back in the 1970s. This, he said, "may bias more central banks to begin considering headline numbers in their policy decisions like Japan and the ECB do already."[17] Washington's insistence on using a "core" measurement that excludes food and energy because of "volatility" may not be able to stand much more evidence on peak oil and agflation.

The larger problem is that the federal government just isn't measuring inflation the way it used to. Until the 1990s, the CPI quite straightforwardly measured the cost of a fixed basket of goods using prevailing market prices. No statistical opportunity for clipped coinage or reminting to a lower standard existed in that constant. The current interlacing of gimmicks, by contrast, far from representing the costs of a *constant* standard of living, has been described by critics as measuring downward mobility—an index that, in the words of one, "more closely represents the costs of holding to an ever declining standard of living," such as a family shifting between hamburger, pork, and chicken depending on the price.[18]

The push to abandon the longtime fixed-basket-of-goods yardstick began in the early 1990s with Federal Reserve chairman Alan Greenspan and Michael Boskin, chairman of the Council of Economic Advisers under President George H. W. Bush. During the 1980s, Greenspan had chaired a presidential commission on Social Security that achieved no great long-term benefits changes, and by the mid-1990s he wanted to

FIGURE 3.2

Headline Inflation Numbers Predict Inflationary Surges Better Than "Core" Inflation

Sources: Bureau of Labor Statistics, Pacific Investment Management Company.

reduce Social Security outlays in the worst way, arguably just what the Boskin Commission, appointed by the new GOP Congress, recommended in its 1995 report. Social Security payments were not vulnerable to frontal political and legislative attack, so attention shifted to the CPI determination of how much retiree payments would rise each year. Greenspan and Boskin charged that the CPI overstated inflation by as much as 1.5 percent, and the Boskin Commission recommended a set of revisions to the Bureau of Labor Statistics, which generally concurred. These changes were implemented between 1997 and 1999, while the public and the politicians were preoccupied by bull market euphoria and the actions in Congress to impeach Bill Clinton.

Unfortunately for the government, a former journalist in Oakland, California, named John Williams took it upon himself and his small firm, ShadowStats.com, to calculate the CPI using the old criteria and to publish those figures alongside the new numbers. The results are disconcerting. As figure 3.3 shows, if the methodology used in 1990 still held sway, the government would have been reporting 5 to 7 percent

FIGURE 3.3

Inflation Calculated Under the Old CPI Compared with Inflation Calculated Under the New CPI, 2001–7

*Alternate CPI Measures Year-to-Year Change,
Not Seasonally Adjusted, to August 2007*

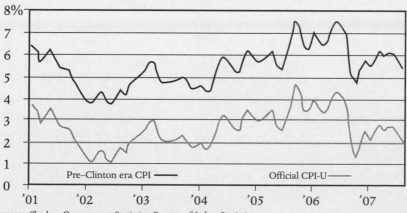

Sources: Shadow Government Statistics, Bureau of Labor Statistics.

inflation between 2005 and 2007 instead of essentially 2 to 4 percent. Statistically, that's a huge difference. For example, if 2 to 3 additional percentage points had been subtracted from the official GDP numbers in order to give inflation its due, that would have dropped the U.S. economy into recession or to its borderline.

Critics of the new methodology usually emphasized three or four deceptions. The best place to start is with the emphasis on consumer substitution that so inspired Greenspan and Boskin. The 1990–92 downturn was deep enough that suburbanites from Denver to Washington to Boston were turning to food stamps and charitable pantries; there is little reason to doubt that many were also price-shopping between hamburger, chicken, and canned stew.[19] But we can assume others had also done so in the deep recession troughs of 1958 and 1974 without prompting the government to institutionalize such defensive approaches as a normal feature of the American dream.

Yet just this occurred in 1999, when the Bureau of Labor Statistics adopted so-called geometric weighting for its now-flexible basket of goods. Items going up received less weight, thereby easing inflation, while items becoming less expensive received more weight, likewise easing inflation. As critic Joseph Stroupe explained, "Since, in the absence of significant price inflation, consumers would be unlikely to engage in substitution on a meaningful scale, then it is also an indirect but powerful admission that significant price inflation does exist, for why else would consumers switch from more expensive items to less expensive ones?"[20]

Which brings us to the born-again CPI's principal controversy—the use of "hedonics" (a government attempt to measure increased pleasure) in order to moderate prices by reducing them for the increased satisfaction a consumer derives from some improvement. Caught out on a shaky limb, the government dropped its large-scale hedonic reduction of computer prices in 2003 after a critical letter from the National Science Foundation's Committee on National Statistics.[21] Moreover, according to the BLS, the consumer electronics category, heavy with declining prices (usually exaggerated by hedonics), accounted for only 1 percent of the CPI, minimizing its practical importance.

What remained, however, was powerful data on how hedonic calculations had falsely ballooned computer sales and thereby artificially enlarged GDP growth. Steve Milunovich, a well-regarded computer analyst at Merrill Lynch, explained in a 2004 report that the federal Bureau of Economic Analysis, responsible for ascertaining the gross domestic product each quarter, had stopped reporting the real computer hardware shipment figure that was used to calculate GDP growth. The government, it seemed, decided that between the second quarter of 2000 and the fourth quarter of 2003, real tech spending had risen by $111 billion, from $446 billion to $557 billion. However, in nominal (price-tag) terms, it had climbed only from $42 billion to $88 billion. The BEA hypothesized the rest to represent the added value it perceived in computer quality![22] In 2007, economic historian Peter Bernstein wrote in the *New York Times* that because of the distortions of hedonic pricing, it might be more realistic to have a new auxiliary CPI measure that included food and energy but *excluded* consumer durables.[23] Other nations have declined to use the hedonic approach. The Japanese earlier took the matter under study, and Germany's Bundesbank noted that hedonics would have increased that nation's GDP by 0.5 percent.[24]

Even critics acknowledge that the great majority of U.S. economists favor some sort of hedonic adjustment in the CPI. One wonders if economic historians would share that view. Why now? Why not earlier? I was a teenager in the 1950s, and after spending a year in Europe, I came home in 1960 well reminded that the United States was paradise for the middle-class consumer. If hedonics properly apply to watching a current-day fifty-inch high-definition television by upgrading from a forty-two-inch version, why not back in 1952, when TV screens got big enough to watch from more than five feet away? A short list for legitimate fifties hedonics could include air conditioners, air travel (jet), automatic transmissions, barbecues, color photography, dishwashers, drugs (over-the-counter and prescription), electric shavers, Frigidaires, frozen foods—and that's just to the letter F. To answer the question "Why now?" we must look at the historical trajectory—and the answer is essentially inglorious.

The third fiddle in the ever-changing CPI involves how the 70 percent of Americans who own homes fail to see anything resembling their actual expenses included in the official measurement. Housing represents 40 percent of the CPI, but what the BLS computes is quite misleading. The bureau's yardstick is called "owners' equivalent rent"—the amount that homeowners could get were they to rent out their homes. To illustrate how unresponsive this figure has been to recent homeowning realities, consider three situations. First, let us suppose the Smiths just bought a house that they had previously rented for $2,000 a month, and that their new monthly total of mortgage, insurance, and property taxes is $3,000. The effect on the CPI: zero, no increase. Now suppose they had always owned and their property tax bill just went up 40 percent. Effect on the CPI? Nil. Now suppose they bought in 2005 under an "exotic" mortgage, and the monthly payment has just reset from 4.5 percent to 7.5 percent. What would be the effect of those circumstances on CPI? Again nil. None of these would affect owners'

FIGURE 3.4

**Changes in the Case-Shiller Home Price Index vs. Inflation
Under the "Owners' Equivalent Rent" Calculation
Used in the CPI**

Year-over-year percent change

Source: www.seekingalpha.com.

Note: Instead of being based on homeowners' actual expenses, such as mortgage payments, insurance, property taxes, and the like, the CPI includes an estimate called owners' equivalent rent.

equivalent rent, even though in the real world, they were out of pocket mightily.[25]

Here, just as with food and energy, the measurement shunned because of "volatility"—yes, housing costs are volatile—is the one that meaningfully reflects trends. Consider, for example, the 2003–6 difference between the 5 percent yearly increase in owners' equivalent rent and the 10 to 20 percent annual increase in the S&P/Case-Shiller Home Price Index. Obviously, the OER and the home price index are not parallel. An index of mortgage payments, insurance costs, and property taxes would serve better. Still, the comparison shown in figure 3.4 is worth noting. Using the housing price data yields a CPI increase 2.5 to 4 percentage points above the official one released by the Bureau of Labor Statistics.

An indictment of the CPI penned in 2007 by Bloomberg News columnist John Wasik, besides charging that "the government casts a blind eye to total homeownership expenses," made the same case regarding inadequate treatment of medical expenses: "It wasn't that long ago when employers could cover almost all of an employee's health-care bills. Now workers are shelling out an average of $3,281 from their paychecks for family coverage, according to the Kaiser Family Foundation, a nonprofit organization based in Menlo Park, California. The average premium for a family policy is more than $12,000 annually. Since 2001, health premiums have risen 78 percent while wages have only gained 19 percent. The government's inflation measure during that stretch was 17 percent."[26]

The United States is hardly the only major Western nation where the public disbelieves the low-inflation assertions of the official bean counters. Wolfgang Munchau, an associate editor of the *Financial Times,* reported a similar experience in Germany:

> The first time I ever began to doubt my country's cost-of-living index was in 2002 when euro banknotes and coins were introduced. In Germany, where I was living at the time, the prices charged by many hotels, restaurants and dry cleaners effectively doubled. If you spent a lot of time travelling, as I did at the time, the personal inflation shock was

severe. . . . The central bankers were in denial because the
official inflation index did not register any significant movements. It must have been in people's heads. But this was
nonsense. The problem was that the official inflation index
no longer reflected many people's personal shopping basket.
The index basket is full of manufactured goods largely produced in Asia, while we spend most of our money on services, such as childcare, education, heathcare, transportation,
travel and gastronomy.[27]

If German central bankers are in denial, perhaps the position of U.S.
central bankers could be called deceitful denial. Foreign bond buyers
are being gulled. Nor is gamesmanship confined to the CPI (or to the
GDP calculation). Beginning in March 2006, the new Fed chairman,
Ben Bernanke, ordered that the government cease publishing data on
changes in the broadest measurement of the U.S. money supply, the
so-called M3. It was expanding at a 10–12 percent annual rate in 2006;
outsiders calculated that as of August 2007, that growth had accelerated
to a high-powered 14 percent. This category, pulling away from the
narrower measurements, M1 and M2, was arguably the one that picked
up the explosion of money and credit taking place in financial sector
debt. Continued publication of M3 reports would have undercut the
assertion of Bernanke and Federal Reserve Board colleague Frederic
Mishkin that the inflationary expectations of the public had been safely
"anchored" at a low level by the tame core CPI.[28] This suppresion of
data, alas, went a long way to prove Sir Walter Scott's adage about
what a tangled web people weave when first they practice to deceive.

Occasionally a commentator interjected some welcome humor. Michael Shedlock, a U.S.-based global economic analyst, penned an analysis that turned to mockery in suggesting that U.S. personal income
included an imputation of $335.2 billion because of free checking ac-
counts banks should have charged for. At this point, he wondered about
the TOAD—Total of All Distortions—in the U.S. GDP (Gross Distorted
Procedures), and surmised that "the real TOAD is far uglier" than what
the government admits.[29]

Ugliness abounds. The most obvious unfairness is to U.S. retirees whose Social Security payments have been clipped, and to workers whose cost-of-living wage increases have been minimized. Gross of PIMCO and others found this especially shabby. However, a different danger for the United States has arisen in perhaps a score of dollar-watching nations—countries with dollar-pegged currencies, oil revenues paid in dollars, central banks with dollar-stuffed vaults, or huge sovereign wealth funds boasting war chests worth $100 billion or more. In many of these nations, rising prices have bred worries about inflation rates—their own, the world's, and even those in the United States being so clumsily minimized. For Persian Gulf oil exporters like Saudi Arabia and the United Arab Emirates, the stakes keep enlarging. To continue to require oil revenues to be paid in U.S. dollars and to tie their currencies to the weak dollar serves to (a) reduce what these producers actually clear from their overseas oil sales, and (b) increase the cost of other goods they import from Asia and Europe. Pegging to the dollar raised their own domestic inflation levels. During the months after the August 2007 crisis, the English-language press in the Gulf region was full of such cost-of-using-the-dollar discussions. But close Middle Eastern attention to the fallibilities of U.S. economic data might be even more troublesome.

RELIGION AND THE ANESTHESIA OF AMERICAN POPULISM

Beyond homage to financial assets and market efficiency, along with reliance on misleading government statistics, Bullnomics as a discernible political and economic force had a third, little appreciated, dimension. This was the de facto anesthetizing, over the last twenty years, of onetime populist southern and western constituencies prominent in the George W. Bush–era conservative coalition. The principal ethers at work were evangelical, fundamentalist, and Pentecostal Christianity, infused with a millennial preoccupation with terrorism, evil, and Islam that greatly strengthened after September 11.

Let me frame the numbers: at least 30 percent of those who supported Bush in 2000 and 2004 (and by some polls, perhaps even a small majority) were end-time believers. The highest ratios of Bush supporters came from the southern, border, Farm Belt, and Rocky Mountain areas of peak support for William Jennings Bryan in 1896, and for Franklin D. Roosevelt in 1936. These were the sections that had rallied to Bryan's attacks on Wall Street, banks, the great trusts, and the gold standard, and forty years later to FDR and his New Deal support for farmers, miners, and industrial workers against big business, Wall Street, and archetypal Rotary Clubs. If white economic populism has a historical geography in U.S. elections, that is it.

On the surface, then, it is ironic that this same geography underpinned Bush's two narrow presidential election victories. But although Bush appealed to these regions as a cultural outsider, he evoked neither economic populism nor its memories. What counted much more was culture and religion—not just his own born-again beliefs but his frequent faith-based rhetoric and his links to well-known conservative preachers, religious Right groups, and large denominations like the Southern Baptist Convention and the Pentecostal Assemblies of God. Those ties, in turn, had been reinforced by late-1990s domestic politics—the dislike for Bill Clinton and his moral values by some 70 to 80 percent of southern white churchgoers—and even more by global events. These trends accelerated with the evangelical and fundamentalist focus on the Middle East spurred by the collapse of the Soviet Union, the Gulf War of 1991, the demonization of Iraq's Saddam Hussein, the late-decade launch of the Left Behind book series about the imminent end-time, the sense of the great biblical battleground taking center stage again with the approach of the millennium, and then the good-versus-evil confrontation framed by the events of 9/11.

These transformations are described at length in my *American Theocracy*. As explained by Richard Cizik, vice president of the National Association of Evangelicals, "Evangelicals have substituted Islam for the Soviet Union. The Muslims have become the modern-day equivalent of the Evil Empire." In a poll of evangelical leaders, two-thirds of them called Islam "dedicated to world domination" and a "religion of violence." Three-quarters of U.S. evangelicals believed that the world would end in Armageddon and that the Antichrist was already on earth, and 55 percent of white evangelical Protestants considered "following religious principles" a top priority for U.S. foreign policy.[30] Not surprisingly, support among these voters for George W. Bush and his engagement in the Middle East was huge, at least through 2004. Their separate criticism of conservative economics was rare. In short, a very large electorate, the historical constituency of U.S. economic populism, was essentially taken out of the domestic policymaking equation. For all practical purposes, Bush and congressional Republican leaders had their full political proxy.

The preoccupation of Americans awaiting the Rapture or the tremors of Armageddon, or pursuing the alternative theology that true believers must first build a godly kingdom on earth before Jesus will return, kept another band of voters essentially unconcerned about budget deficits, peak oil, or the perils of the U.S. dollar. No one can calculate these numbers. However, Tim Weber, professor of church history at Northern Baptist Theological Seminary, caught the practical implication: "If Jesus may come at any minute, then long-term social reform or renewal are beside the point. It has a bad effect there."[31]

What merits "Bullnomic" attention in this arena, though, is the further evidence in 2006 and 2007 of Americans turning to success-ethic belief systems—to the "prosperity gospel" and to "name it and claim it" and "God wants you to be rich" theology. Economic hopes were imitating religious conviction. To many mainstream Christian theologians, this trend pulled Christianity further toward an unacceptable materialism. Some even found hints of blasphemy. Rick Warren, author of *The Purpose-Driven Life,* dismissed the prosperity gospel as "baloney: It's creating a false idol. You don't measure your self-worth by your net worth."[32]

Arguably, though, such religion was a logical outgrowth of an angst-threaded economic consumerism, powered by incessant "be all you want to be" advertising and funded by home equity withdrawals and credit card debt, in which a relatively small population at the top reveled in a large and rising percentage of the nation's income and wealth. While this took place, average household incomes stagnated, personal debt soared, and hints of a credit and housing crash added new worries. For some among America's less successful, the prosperity preachers and churches were probably the last resort between lost jobs or ambitions and the deeper embarrassments of home foreclosures, divorces, or bankruptcy courts.

Indeed, history offered an unfortunate precedent. Similar politicians, preachers, and places of worship had gained attention in the 1920s. New York Republican congressman Bruce Barton described Jesus as the world's greatest marketer, and author Sinclair Lewis's fictional Elmer Gantry brought a similar spirit to huckstering religion. Real-life gospeler Aimee Semple McPherson packed them in on Sunday. Guru Émile Coué—"Every day, in every way, I am getting better and better"—was the decade's top spielmeister of self-help. Many of these delusions crashed with the 1929 stock market.

Pentecostalism, ten million to fifteen million strong and home to several of America's fastest-growing denominations, was—as it had been in the twenties—the fertile seedbed of the new twenty-first-century "prosperity gospel." If the rest of Protestantism found money a theological taboo, prosperity doctrine rose to the opportunity. It blended Pentecostal emotion over God's gifts with the power of positive thinking and the thesis of a spiritual contract: plant a seed, make a donation, and God will repay you many times over.

But in 2006 and 2007, as Americans declared less respect for U.S. institutions and high ratios identified the United States as being on the wrong track, the prosperity gospel metastasized beyond the usual Pentecostal setting. According to a fall 2006 *Time* cover story ("Does God Want You to Be Rich?"), of the four biggest megachurches in the United States, three emphasized prosperity or "prosperity lite": Joel Osteen's Lakewood Church in Houston; T. D. Jakes's Potter's House in Dallas; and Creflo Dollar's World Changers near Atlanta. Equally to the point, a poll taken for *Time* showed the prosperity theme commanding support far beyond self-identified Pentecostals. Some 17 percent of Christians told the survey takers that they considered themselves part of such a movement, and a surprising 61 percent believed that God wanted individuals to be prosperous. And fully 31 percent—that would project to 90 million Americans—agreed that if you give money to God, he will bless you with more money.[33]

We cannot know how closely such views overlapped support for George W. Bush in 2000 and 2004. But despite the substantial black and Hispanic membership in the megachurches, logic supports a strong correlation. By the 1990s, white Pentecostal voting was often over 90 percent Republican, and whereas Hispanic Catholics were lopsidedly Democratic, Hispanic Pentecostals leaned Republican.[34] In addition, some of the black prosperity gospel churches in metropolitan Atlanta were Republican strongholds, based on a unique fusion of rap music with a doctrine of money, power, and respect.[35] Houston's Methodist megachurch pastor Kirbyjon Caldwell, who gave the benediction at George W. Bush's 2001 and 2005 inaugurals, was a prosperity lite preacher.[36] Should prosperity gospel adherents opt to group together in a newly formed denomination, its membership would be among the nation's largest.

Bestselling books in vivid forms of the prosperity genre also confirmed just how far these outlooks had spread beyond Pentecostal churches. The "name it and claim it" movement, sprung from Oral Roberts's Oklahoma ministry, broke the barrier at the end of the nineties with preacher Bruce Wilkinson's five-million-volume bestseller *The Prayer of Jabez*. Jabez, the hero, prayed that God would "enlarge my territory," and author Wilkinson claimed that "if Jabez had worked on Wall Street, he might have prayed, 'Lord, increase the value of my investment portfolios.' "[37] In 2007, Rhonda Byrne's runaway bestseller *The Secret* rose several notches higher on the chutzpah ladder. Those who are well off, she wrote, deserve their success because they attracted it. One weekly paraphrased the technique this way: "Mired in debt? No problem, just start visualizing checks and paste a phony $1 million bill on the ceiling above your bed (so you'll see it in the morning). . . . The universe, *The Secret* asserts, is akin to a mail-order business, and 'your job is to declare what you would like to have from the catalog.' "[38]

Even New York City boasted new prosperity gospel churches, notably the northern branch of Creflo Dollar's Atlanta temple to Mammon. In lower Manhattan, former commodities trader Dan Stratton, author of *Divine ProVision: Positioning God's Kings for Financial Conquest,* served as founder and pastor of the professionals-oriented Faith Exchange Fellowship.[39]

Alabama is not known as a prosperity gospel stronghold, but in 2003 the state held a very relevant referendum on a tax reform program put forward by Republican governor Bob Riley, who favored easing the burden on the poor by shifting it to the rich in the name of Jesus. "What would Jesus tax?" he asked. But although the unfairness of the Alabama tax code was beyond debate, Riley's proposal was defeated by 68 percent to 32 percent. Just months after the invasion of Iraq, the martial Jesus of "Onward Christian Soldiers" handily defeated the Jesus of the book of Matthew.

Revealingly, beyond the Pentecostal orbit, the only major U.S. denomination that has something akin to its own prosperity gospel—the five-million-member Church of Jesus Christ of Latter-day Saints, or Mormons—is also the most overwhelmingly Republican in politics and ideology. Utah, the historic Mormon stronghold, was George W. Bush's top state in both 2000 and 2004. Mormonism is often caricatured, but it has a long, open history of emphasizing financial success, and fraud has been epidemic in the state. Salt Lake City, for example, is the nation's smallest city to have its own local branch of the federal Securities and Exchange Commission. In 1989, the *Ogden Standard-Examiner* reported that "the cultural emphasis in the Mormon Church that equates financial success with spiritual success, and an unquestioning allegiance to authority figures, may partly explain why 10,000 Utah investors have been swindled out of more than $200 million during the last decade."[40] A topical compendium of press stories over the years turns up the following descriptions: the nation's "stock fraud capital," "a leading center of financial shenanigans," and "the sewer of the securities industry."[41] Clearly, the local emphasis on finance is not altogether wholesome.

It would be unfair to broadly tie Mormonism and the prosperity gospel to the gestation of Bullnomics, but it is not unfair to suggest an unfortunate cousinship between prosperity theology and the Bush administration's unsuccessful promotion of the conservative "Ownership Society" or "Opportunity Society," which insisted on individuals naming and claiming economic fulfillment through self-help, individual accounts, and the all-rewarding marketplace. In August 2007, as the partly delusional aspects of subprime homeownership cast larger doubts on what was true opportunity and what wasn't, commentator James Pinkerton, a longtime GOP political and policy activist, offered his own wry three-decade retrospective. He noted that Karl Rove, the Utah-educated chief political adviser in the Bush White House, was deeply influenced by the "libertarian-universalist" school of Republican thinking, which blended awareness of the religious element in the Republican base with an economic theology that emphasized a bigger piece of the prosperity pie for everyone. One ardent libertarian-universalist was former New York congressman Jack Kemp, a leading tax-cut evangelist and political pie man. And Rove, according to Pinkerton, embraced Kemp's vision: "What really matters is the miracle of the market. . . . More immigrants equals more economic growth and a higher stock market, which means we can privatize Social Security and make everyone a rich investor, whether he or she speaks English. That was the domestic policy vision of the White House and, seemingly, the foreign policy vision, too."[42]

Pinkerton may exaggerate a bit, but New York congressman Bruce Barton, the fictional Elmer Gantry, Charles Ponzi, Aimee Semple McPherson, and Émile Coué would presumably have understood. Unfortunately.

FOUR

Securitization

The Insecurity of It All

A rising tide of defaults among borrowers with shaky credit histories has, thanks to the way that their debts have been securitised and sold globally, triggered chaos in the world's credit markets as asset-holders struggle to re-evaluate their risk.

—*Economist*, August 31, 2007

Collateralized debt obligations . . . have gotten much too sophisticated, are priced by extraordinary mathematical models, and are very difficult to value. I think people are going to be frightened to deal with those things for a long time. A lot of them are just going to disappear, because they've been tried; they don't work.

—Former Federal Reserve chairman Alan Greenspan, September 2007

Wall Street has produced a credit crisis for banks by securitizing more than $900bn of subprime mortgage loans. The ultimate default rate on these loans could rise as high as 20–25 per cent, so there is $200bn–$250bn of bad paper now circulating in the financial system. As the credit rating agencies have issued widespread downgrades of securities that previously had scores of triple or double As, investors have taken fright and been fleeing all asset-backed securities.

—Economist David Hale, November 2007

In 1996, as that decade's bull market began to paw and snort, a Latin American specialist, Professor John C. Edmunds, published an article that built a brassy trumpet into its very title: "Securities: The New World Wealth Machine."[1] Widely discussed, the article's underlying theme was that wealth could be increased without creating or manufacturing anything, save for paper that rearranged and added value and marketability to new and existing loan agreements. There was a deeper social and legal logic in Peru or Bangladesh, but in the English-speaking nations, "securitization" tapped an established penchant for paper entrepreneurialism. Edmunds never made another such splash, but the securitization of assets, just getting started, spread like wildfire, especially in the United States.

Securitization, as a business, includes two principal product categories: mortgage-backed securities (MBSs), followed by asset-backed securities (ABSs). The latter includes within its half dozen subcategories two products frequently or always tied to housing—collateralized debt obligations (CDOs) and home-equity loan (HELs). The reader must note that HELs are *not* the same thing as mortgage-backed securities. Like a second mortgage, they borrow against the homeowner's equity, not the amount covered by the mortgage. From some $400 billion a year back in 1995, by 2003 the annual volume of securitization issuance had jumped to $4 trillion. Excitement ran high. Lenders applauded the opportunity to sell loans quickly and get them off their books, to spread the institutional risk of the weaker loans, and to collect most of their payment up front, obtaining the wherewithal to make even more loans. Wall Street, in turn, exulted in an enormous opportunity for profits, globally as well as domestically. As late as 2005, 80 percent of global securitization issuance was in U.S. hands.[2]

The perversity was that outside the high towers of finance, the risks facing ordinary American households were growing. Securities were a financial business, but financial insecurity was a bona fide public apprehension. The average citizen could sense what was happening, but not fully explain it. Corporations, financial institutions, and the federal government were all shifting risks and expenses they had once routinely borne onto the figurative balance sheets of ordinary families. Some pundits thought that one short word—"risk"—was about to become a major force in U.S. politics. By the end of 2007, however, government officials, mortgage lenders, packagers of asset-backed securities, and top financial executives faced an unexpected risk of their own: potential blame for what was starting to be imagined as the biggest U.S. housing crash since the Great Depression.

ORDINARY AMERICANS:
A NEW AND GROWING RISK BURDEN

The economic uncertainty and disillusionment of Middle America has become a commonplace. The five-year stagnation of median family incomes, the additional millions lacking health insurance coverage, and the increasing share of personal income required for debt service have taken the wind out of the sails of even new-economy soothsayers. If household-sector risk consciousness had a quantifier, it would be at or near a record.

If risk—more specifically, its minimalization or its widest feasible dispersal—has been a major preoccupation of the financial sector, corporate America and the federal government have been moving in comparable directions, dumping this or that onetime responsibility. Corporations facing Darwinian markets and globalization pressures have spared few efforts to curb defined-benefit pension obligations, minimize wages, and reduce employee and retiree health costs. Conservative White House regimes and Congresses, in turn, especially between 2003 and 2006, proposed variations on what they called the Opportunity or Ownership Society—through it, Social Security would be partly privatized, Medicaid would be cut back to encourage personal responsibility, and a variety of "personal accounts" would drive a stake into the heart of the federal insurance state. But voters withheld support, and most of these ideas had already failed by 2006, when the Democrats recaptured Congress.

Two important books helped to explain the new angst. Yale professor Jacob Hacker, in *The Great Risk Shift*, identified two vital pillars of economic security—the family and the workplace—that had been weakened as political leaders and corporations cut back protection of income security, health care, and retirement pensions. Income *instability*, said Hacker, had grown even faster than income *inequality*. He emphasized data showing that family income had become increasingly volatile from year to year—for example, the chance that a household would at some point experience a 50 percent drop in income rose from minimal in 1970 to almost 1 in 5 in 2002.[3] From the workplace to health-care centers and retirement communities, insecurity was spreading.

Elizabeth Warren, a professor at the Harvard Law School, put more emphasis on harmful financial practices and changes. In a 2007 article following up her 2003 book, *The Two-Income Trap,* she set out a fiercely argued thesis: "Middle-class families have been threatened on every front. . . . Even with two paychecks, family finances are stretched so thin that a very small misstep can leave them in crisis. As tough as life has become for married couples, single-parent families face even more financial obstacles in trying to carve out middle-class lives on a single paycheck. And at the same time that families are facing higher costs and increased risks, the old financial rules of credit have been rewritten by powerful corporate interests that see middle-class families as the spoils of political influence."[4] Here she is talking about the deregulation of finance, and in particular the facilitation of the sky-high interest rates and penalties credit card issuers found so profitable.

Figure 4.1 (page 100) displays Warren's assessment of how rising basic costs—mortgage, child care, health insurance, car, and taxes—have been consuming more and more of the "discretionary" remainder of family income. By a different but overlapping calculus, the percentage of household disposable income spent on debt service—principally mortgage, auto loan, and credit card debt—had risen from just over 10 percent in 1983 to 14.5 percent in 2006.[5] The sort of households that preoccupied Hacker and Warren simply did not enjoy flush times in the early years of the new century. Presumably, their ire will grow if future CPI clarifications retrospectively show that inflation was considerably worse than the government acknowledged, confirming that many Americans were shortchanged for many years in their cost-of-living adjustments to wages and Social Security payments.

But that same grassroots America will be even more aroused should the values of their homes drop by 8–10 percent or even 15–20 percent over a year or two. This could occur if Alan Greenspan's prophecy about malfunctioning CDOs quoted at the beginning of this chapter proves correct, and the connections to unworkable securitization deepen and prolong the mortgage and housing crisis. Then the Wall

Street financial architects who packaged mortgage-backed securities or
structured CDOs to include subprime exposure might come to realize
that they should have thought more broadly: not just about the difficulty of tracing where the original mortgage made in Cleveland or San
Diego eventually wound up, or anticipating blowback over the subprime content of the CDOs sold to dummkopf provincial bankers in
Germany, but also about domestic political backlash—the prospect that
aroused homeowners in Hackerville or Warrentown might begin to
take their first serious look at the new U.S. financial sector and what it
has become.

FIGURE 4.1

The Shrinkage of Family Discretionary Income

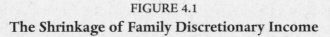
Fixed Costs as a Share of Family Income

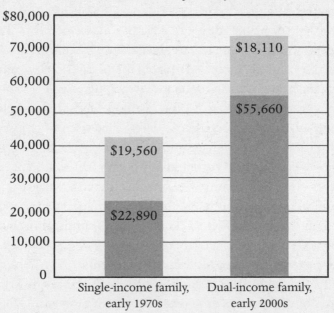

■ Discretionary income
■ Fixed costs (mortgage, child care, health insurance, car, taxes)

Source: Elizabeth Warren, "The Middle Class on the Precipice," *Harvard Magazine*, January–February 2006,
p. 30. Inflation-adjusted. Updated from sources cited in Warren and Tyagi, *The Two-Income Trap*.

PROFIT APPETITES AND RISK REFLUX

For an interested layman, one of the first things to ponder about mortgage- and asset-backed securities and credit-related derivatives, two huge product categories, is that despite their importance, even the inventors, architects, and marketers of these products didn't (or couldn't) entirely understand how the new creations would fare in a major liquidity crisis. Asset-backed securities, for example, had been weak in the 1998 Russian debt imbroglio, when credit markets seized up. However, proponents insisted, that was a decade earlier, when such products were new and their volume was small. By year's end, the more critical 2007–8 test was going even less well, as witness the angry description of *Financial Times* associate editor Wolfgang Munchau:

> The reason why this crisis is so nasty has to do with the deep inter-linkages within the credit market, and between the credit market and the real economy. Take, for example, a synthetic collateralised debt obligation, one of the most complicated financial instruments ever invented. It consists of a couple of credit default swaps, credit linked notes, total return swaps, all jointly connected in a wiring diagram that looks as though the structure was about to explode.[6]

The amounts involved were mind-boggling. Besides CDOs, explosive or otherwise, the great bulk of credit derivatives are credit swaps, a category at first incidental to this housing- and mortgage-focused chapter. However, their large-scale emergence after 1998 was what "turned credit from a dull backwater into a financial market blockbuster. . . . The outstanding notional value of credit derivatives contracts has doubled every year since the start of this decade to reach $26 [trillion] in the middle of last year [2006]."[7] By October 2007, the newly merged Chicago Mercantile Exchange reported that the notional value of credit derivatives had climbed to $45.5 trillion. By year's end, as bank and investment bank losses began to pile up, some exporters began to fear that problems might spread into the corporate credit markets, principally through credit default swaps with their purpose of allowing risk managers and speculators to bet on a company's ability to repay debt. The *New York Times* half-joked that if 2007 was the year readers and reporters learned about CDOs and SIVs, 2008 might be the year of credit default swaps.

Unfortunately, it is entirely relevant to note the greed factor: the amount of money the financial sector was making out of these hot new products and huge volumes, at least until mid-2007. Between 2002 and 2006, volume in these financial sector bestsellers swelled enormously, creating a cumulative total of roughly $2.3 trillion in residential mortgage-backed securities and $1.7 trillion in CDOs. Here we are talking more or less real valuation, as opposed to the gauzy notional value used to measure credit default swaps. With profits and fees probably running to $100 billion or more, inexcusable excesses were to be expected. Figure 4.2, with its components, displays the rise—and then the near implosion in August—of CDOs and asset-backed commercial paper.

Relatively little information is available on the category-by-category profits of the big investment banks—Citigroup, JPMorgan Chase, Bank of America, Goldman Sachs, Morgan Stanley, Merrill Lynch, et al. Nevertheless, it is clear that they had placed huge bets on these new derivative track stars. Analysts at JPMorgan Chase estimated that just in 2006, banks globally took in profits of about $30 billion from their asset-backed securities business.[8] That made it as least as big a moneymaker as equity derivatives or cash equities trading—and it was faster growing. Parenthetically, JPMorgan, before its merger, had been the principal nursery of credit derivatives; Merrill Lynch was the largest underwriter of CDOs; and Citigroup led the field with a 25 percent share ($100 billion) of so-called—and helpfully off-the-books—structured investment vehicles (SIVs) or conduits.

As figure 4.2 shows, the credibility and issuance of CDOs and asset-backed commercial paper was chilled by late summer's credit implosion. Subprime had become a dirty word. For comparison, during the 1995–2001 period, speculative euphoria, scandal news, and ultimately embarrassing business failures had all pointed to the same chic sectors:

FIGURE 4.2

Waterloo: The Rise and Fall of Collateralized Debt Obligations and Asset-Backed Commercial Paper, 2005–7

Global Issuance of Collateralized Debt Obligations ($ billions)

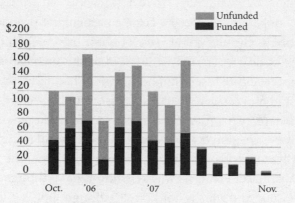

Source: "Out of the Shadows: How Banking's Secret System Broke Down," *Financial Times*, December 16, 2007.

Asset-Backed Commercial Paper Outstanding ($ billions)

Source: Agora Financial, "5 Minute Forecast," January 4, 2008.

technology, telecommunications, and Enron-type energy merchants. When history applies that same retrospective yardstick to the failures of these several years, its conclusions should echo the frustrations of August: an unprecedented housing bubble, reckless mortgage lending and securitization, extreme debt and credit excesses, and gross insensitivity to risk.

Indeed, looking back at 2000–2002, a particularly provocative contention is that as the technology stock bubble burst and dragged other stock markets down, shrewd eminences of the financial sector concluded that real estate assets and home prices had to be the follow-up strategy—and if necessary, even a successor bubble. As we have seen, back in the late 1970s Alan Greenspan had been fascinated by data showing that extraction of homeowners' equity amid rising residential prices had been a prop of the larger economy. Whether the President's Working Group on Financial Markets might have thought that same way in late 2001 and 2002 is not known, though, nor is it likely to be. John Crudele of the New York Post, for example, achieved little from a later demand for different information under the Freedom of Information Act.[9]

Certainly no one doubts that important parts of the financial sector were excited over asset- and mortgage-backed securities. These were sectoral growth hormones as well as profit makers. Instead of being kept on firm ledgers, mortgage loans could be stripped of risk by a derivative contract, or in most circumstances sold off in a mortgage-backed security or structured CDO. The money received could be used for another loan or mortgage, then again—and again. Lending limitations became nonlimitations. However, as volume swelled, loan- and mortgage-making standards dropped. Enticements to sign up marginal borrowers—through the "exotic" forms of mortgages little used before—took on an ever-larger role.

All of which laid vital groundwork for the eventual problems. Just as expansion-crazed U.S. and British railroads in the nineteenth century laid pointless track to unwise destinations or overcompeted for markets already well served, in 2004 and 2005 U.S. loan-making standards fell as demand grew. Securitization and mortgage resale through mortgage-backed securities appeared to push risk far enough out the distribution chain to make it somebody else's problem. The ratings agencies—Standard & Poor's, Moody's, and Fitch—were collaborative (some said complicit) in bestowing high-safety classifications that are in hindsight almost mind-boggling. Drexel University finance professor Joseph Mason told the Associated Press of bonds backed by delinquent credit card accounts in which up to 40 percent of the accounts in the security were rated AAA.[10] However, institutional customers at home and abroad were clamoring for the high yields attached, and perceptions of "moral hazard" were minimal, especially in New York. The nation's seventeenth-biggest bank based somewhere out in the hinterland might not rate a bailout, but Manhattan megabankers were confident of their own place on Helicopter Ben's chopper route.* Indeed, New York's Citigroup had already benefited from a bailout arranged by the Federal Reserve back in 1991.

Another attraction that asset-backed securities and structured CDOs held for the financial community was turnover—no waiting around for payment over the life of an individual loan. With respect to CDOs, the bulk of the receipts came up front, in fees and net proceeds from the sale.[11] In terms of safety and rigorous standards, however, laxity became an obvious downside of high-volume securitization and its mortgage-demanding momentum.

Indeed, most of the shortcomings that became routine complaints by August and September were understood in important quarters earlier. Hedge fund crises in New York drew negative attention to CDOs in May. Opacity, which means lack of transparency, or impossibility to figure out, brought a particular drawback in practical terms of identifying market value. Often, value had to be assigned because CDOs weren't listed and sold on open exchanges; they were drawn up as contracts between the packager-cum-seller and the buyer. Frequently, there were no clear prices or sources for hard offers, although dubious techniques were sometimes used to create the illusion of offers. The upshot, when prices came under stress, was what we might call the

---

* Federal Reserve chairman Ben Bernanke, then a Federal Reserve Board member, had joked back in 2002 that if needed in a crisis, money could even be dropped from helicopters.

Three-M Conundrum. Because CDO values couldn't be marked to market—usually none existed—they would be marked to model, and if demand was weak, they would be marked to myth or to make-believe, depending on whose sarcastic description was being quoted. Warren Buffett was associated with the "mark to myth" put-down.

The minority of experts initially worried by opacity and potential pricing difficulties often shared a related insight: that CDOs, far from distributing risk broadly enough to reduce it to inconsequence, would in especially nervous markets sometimes wind up in weak hands where uncertainty itself would be psychological dynamite. Michael Panzner, author of *The New Laws of the Stock Market Jungle*, prophesied as much months earlier:

> Few would argue with the notion that sharing risk helps to cushion the blow from small "shocks." Unfortunately, shoveling layers and layers of myriad risks into every nook and cranny of the global financial system also boosts the odds that a "black swan event"—an unexpected economic or financial rupture—could also bring down the entire house of cards. Some policymakers argue, in fact, that securitization ensures that large-scale upheavals will be anything but contained.[12]

Probably so. Tracking down a mortgage situation easy to fix in one or two individual loans became difficult to impossible when a structured megaconcoction was involved. "For the last couple of years," noted Michael Gordon, global head of fixed income at Fidelity International, "everyone seemed so comforted that debt and risk were spread so widely. . . . Now everyone is panicking because they don't know where it is."[13]

That same uncertainty about what had been dispersed to where also fed "contagion." If CDOs and mortgage-backed securities were radioactive, and some had turned up to great dismay in money market funds run by BNP Paribas in France, then money market funds in general became suspect. By mid-August, the most severe of the contagion problems all but froze the commercial paper market.

The Swiss-based and tradition-conscious Bank for International Settlements had issued its cautions in June, and Austrian School economist
Kurt Richebächer had been even more damning in earlier warnings.
Some of the August crisis gestated in banks within the Federal Reserve
Board's regulatory and rate-reduction orbit, but at least as much of the
reckless behavior originated in the burgeoning financial sector's less-
regulated "Wild West"—the phalanx of mutual funds, hedge funds, private equity firms, mortgage entities, conduits, and "liquidity factories"
sometimes called the "shadow banking system." By year's end, the
shadow system rivaled experimental securitization as a whipping
post.

THE FINANCIAL WILD WEST—HEDGE FUNDS, PRIVATE EQUITY, LEVERAGE FACTORIES, MORTGAGE POOLS, AND THE WEALTH MANAGEMENT INDUSTRY

The suitability of the term "Wild West" lies in the relative lack of regulation and enforcement in these newly important financial precincts.
Some of the new enterprises, particularly hedge funds, fit the gunslinger
image. Hedge funds live on the barely regulated edge, and many take
advantage. Not that this should be surprising. No sectoral breakthrough
of the magnitude that U.S. finance achieved in the 1990s and 2000s occurs without creating a new economic infrastructure. Parts of it verged
on swagger—for example, the off-the-books SIVs that Citigroup set up
to do what it could not do as a bank. Although hedge funds and private
equity operators stand out in the public perception, especially in terms
of bravado and wealth, they have plenty of company.

As profiled in figure 4.3 (page 108), a key development within the
financial sector over the last several decades has been the decline in
relative importance of depository institutions. Banks and savings and
loan associations had been the big guns through the 1970s, along with
insurance companies. Then they lost their old sway before the advance
of the new or expanding forces—mutual funds, nonbank lenders, hedge
funds, federally related mortgage entities, issuers of asset-backed securities, security brokers and dealers, and others. In 1976, the depository
institutions and insurance companies accounted for a ponderous 67.6

percent of the sector, and the new crowd just 13.1 percent. Three decades later, the old crowd had dropped to 30.1 percent while the new-
bies had ballooned to 50.1 percent.

Portions of the transformation are well understood. Mutual funds
now hold more assets than banks do, while money market funds outweigh checking and savings accounts. Economists like to talk about
how markets have been replacing banks as "the engine room of the financial system."[14] But the change has left gaping regulatory holes.
Hedge funds, for example, have come to dominate trading in the equity
markets, likewise becoming major lenders, all the while enjoying a
Wild West minimum of supervision.

History helps to explain how hedge funds, private equity firms, and

FIGURE 4.3

The Makeup of the Financial Sector, 1956–2006

By share of financial sector assets

	1956	1966	1976	1986	1996	2006
Depository institutions	57.2%	54.6%	55.9%	42.6%	27.2%	23.8%
Insurance companies	21.1	16.4	11.7	9.3	8.7	6.3
Pension funds*	12.2	16.5	19.3	23.1	25.6	19.3
Mutual funds	2.7	4.0	2.2	7.5	15.1	18.3
Nonbank lenders†	4.3	4.9	4.3	4.3	3.4	3.6
GSEs and federally related mortgage pools	1.4	2.4	5.1	9.0	12.1	12.8
Issuers of asset-backed securities	–	–	–	0.8	3.5	6.8
Securities brokers and dealers	1.1	1.1	1.3	1.9	2.8	5.2
Others‡	–	0.1	0.2	1.6	1.7	4.6

Source: Federal Reserve, *Flow of Funds Accounts;* updated March 2007, Insurance Information Institute.

Note: Percentages may not add up to 100 because of rounding.

*Includes insured pension assets.
†Includes finance companies and mortgage companies.
‡Includes real estate investment trusts and funding corporations.

some of the liquidity factories should be so well-heeled and effectively positioned yet so little constrained. Politics and regulation tend to lag behind great sectoral upheavals. If you go back to the 1880s, when manufacturing was pulling ahead of agriculture in the national statistics, federal regulation of railroads and heavy industry was de minimus. The fight to bring them under public control wasn't won until a quarter of a century later, when World War I was at hand.

In cultural geography, to be sure, there's nothing wild or western about the shadow sector. It's chic, and favors places with high ratios of Michelin- and Zagat-saluted restaurants. As summarized by the *Financial Times*, "Wall Street has been usurped by Greenwich, Connecticut, and the City of London by Mayfair. A rising proportion of hedge funds, most often in the limelight with gambits in equities or commodities, are now dealing in corporate credit. The players who used to dominate credit investing, such as traditional pension funds and insurers, are jostling for space with a spectrum of new layers, including specialist credit funds and new lending businesses such as managers of collateralised debt obligations, the vehicle of choice for today's credit investors."[15]

Since the U.S. deregulation of financial services in 1999, which broke down many old barriers, neat lines and subject-matter distinctions have faded. Effective regulation has itself suffered from the scrambling effect. For this book's purposes, trying to catalog the new contours is hardly essential. Still, one new überdimension taking shape commands political as well as financial inquiry: how the expansion of credit and money within the United States, once tied to banks and bank lending, has been partly assumed by the firms, funds, and paper vendors of the new secondary system, or shadow banking sector.

It seems extraordinary that such an influential new complex was allowed to emerge largely outside of the existing U.S. financial regulatory structure. Small wonder that respected investment strategists could talk of debt and credit being abused like cocaine. Small wonder that legal issues raised by locally originated mortgages being absorbed into CDOs meant that a Bermuda Triangle of uncertainty now hovered over the interaction of state and federal regulation and contract law. Small wonder that no Environmental Protection Agency existed to deal with the financial equivalent of toxic waste (CDOs nicknamed "Chernobyl

Death Obligations"). Small wonder that, with no equivalent of the Consumer Product Safety Commission, buyers worldwide found themselves with structured products that lacked (1) opacity and responsible description, (2) disinterested and careful credit ratings, (3) reliable markets to which they could be marked, and (4) practical testing under major credit-crisis conditions. Manufacturers negligent in these ways would be facing large fines or even jail terms.

A further problem is that U.S. regulators caught up in market efficiency or deregulation theory either didn't understand what was happening or philosophically rejected interference with the magic of the marketplace. Unfortunately, this included Federal Reserve chairman Alan Greenspan, who smiled permissively at hedge funds, asset bubbles, and the new mortgage gambits, while shunning closer attention to the abuses of mortgage lenders.[16] This may be why it took a European, Axel Weber, president of the German Bundesbank, to become the first central banker to explain that the August crisis was just like a classic banking crisis or run, save that it was taking place in the nonbank financial system.[17] Washington seems to have ignored a profound and trouble-making transformation.

In the meantime, the new nonbank financial sector, or shadow banking system, had also taken over some of the prerogatives formerly reserved to banks of creating money. This explained why some market watchers were giving the various leveraged debt and credit merchants catchy new monetary descriptions. Mohamed El-Erian, president of the Harvard Management Company, wrote in early 2007, "Over the past two years, markets have developed powerful liquidity factories," in forms ranging from private equity to hedge funds, "as more investors have embraced debt in an attempt to increase the impact of their investments." These "market drivers of liquidity," he argued, "currently exceed influences coming from traditional monetary policy instruments."[18] To David Tice at the Prudent Bear Fund, credit derivatives had enabled "a credit apparatus unlike any in history with endless capacity to create 'money'-like debt instruments."[19] Derivatives expert Satyajit Das called the new quasi currency "candyfloss money," explaining that "by the early 2000s, the new liquidity factory had created a money pyramid that had no parallel in history."[20] Bill Gross, from the bond-market viewpoint, made a pointed analogy in his October 2007 Investment Outlook:

> Remember those old economics textbooks that told you how a $1 deposit at your neighborhood bank could be multiplied by five or six times in a magical act of reserve banking? It still can, but financial innovation has done an end run around the banks. Derivatives and structures with three- and four-letter abbreviations—CDOs, CLOs, ABCP, CPDOs, SIVs (the world awaits investment banking's next creation; perhaps IOU?)—can now take a "depositor's" dollar and multiply it ten or 20 times. Reserve banking, and the Federal Reserve that regulates the system, appear anemic in comparison.[21]

These pseudomonetary products fit neither of the two current definitions of money employed by Washington—the narrow M1 (essentially cash, traveler's checks, and checking accounts) and the slightly broader M2 (M1 plus most savings accounts, retail money market fund balances, and time deposits under $100,000). However, some think that the new moneylike debt instruments overlap with the definition of M3, the broader money supply that formerly reached measurement into the innards of the financial sector. By definition, M3 includes all of M2 plus large time deposits, institutional money market funds, bank repo agreements, and some overseas Eurodollars. This is the money-supply data that the Federal Reserve decided to stop reporting in early 2006. Let me stipulate: this nomenclature is nerdspeak. The average American would take M1 to mean the standard U.S. Army carbine of World War II, while the average Briton would think of M2 as a major English motorway. And for all I know, M3 may also be the name of a Toronto rock band. Nevertheless, anything that may be creating a parallel monetary universe, serving finance but having an uncertain, possibly disruptive effect elsewhere in the U.S. economy, is worth a brief comment.

The Federal Reserve Board, committed to the premise that the public regarded inflation as "anchored" and under control, doubtless found the earlier U.S. M3 measurement pesky. Given the time frame set out by Harvard's El-Erian—that the liquidity factories started production back in 2005—ducking that impact may have influenced the Fed's cutoff timing. According to the ongoing private computations published by ShadowStats.com, the M3 data started diverging from the other two measurements and soaring around the time the Fed decided to drop it. For 2007, the U.S. M3 numbers show runaway inflation in the annual range of 14 percent. In Canada and Australia, M1 measurements for June 2006 to June 2007 were very close to those for M3; in the United States, by contrast, from September 2006 to September 2007, M3 was a full 13 points higher than M1! I will come back to these implications, but for the moment, suffice it to say that (1) something quite unusual has taken place in the U.S. financial sector, and (2) these numbers provide even more support for believing that the U.S. consumer price index understates inflation.

For now, let us return to the crisis in housing and mortgage finance, which appears to have been abetted and deepened by the demand for more and still more mortgages unleashed by of the securitization process in the United States of 2001–6.*

HOUSING: THE 2007–12 POLITICAL AND ECONOMIC BATTLEFIELD

As the 2008 election season began, optimists insisted that the housing market would hit bottom late that year or in early 2009, and then start recovering. Contrarians pointed out that the prior U.S. housing decline dating from 1989 and 1990 didn't make a strong recovery until 1997, and that the much deeper housing slump unleashed in 1929 had hung on for nearly a decade.

Less debatable, though, has been the political and economic fact that the passion for homeownership—with all its consequences—runs highest in the English-speaking nations: Britain, Ireland, Canada, Australia, New Zealand, and the United States. The notion that an Englishman's

---

* In November 2007, Goldman Sachs estimated that "innovation in U.S. security markets, coupled with demand for yield, has driven up to 80% of subprime lending (c. US$1.2 trillion over two years)." Fitch, in turn, estimated that during 2005 and 2006, 50 to 60 percent of the collateral in structured finance CDOs was subprime-mortgage-backed securities.

home is his castle dates back to Sir Edward Coke in the mid-seventeenth-century, and the U.S. version to comments by James Otis in 1761. In Australia, homeownership is the fourth pillar of national retirement policy. To be sure, the rise of trailer parks has forced an addendum: if a man's home is his castle, his mobile home is (merely) his chattel. However, the underlying psychology remains in place.

This connection helps to amplify a vital corollary, widely discussed during the late-summer credit panic debate. Yale economist Robert Shiller, fearful that in some parts of the United States home prices could fall by as much as 50 percent, emphasized the usual prominence of housing slumps leading into U.S. recessions.[22] Merrill Lynch chief economist David Rosenberg, predicting a nationwide fall in housing prices of 15 or even 20 percent, explained a double underpinning. By 2007, a $23 trillion asset class was involved, and "there is nothing on the planet as big as that." Moreover, he said, "there has never been a real estate deflation in this country that failed to end in a destabilizing recession."[23]

Martin Feldstein, president of the National Bureau of Economic Research, which declares and measures recessions in the United States, told the important August 31 conference sponsored by the Kansas City Federal Reserve Bank that the sort of collapse already visible in new home construction had been " a precursor to eight of the past 10 recessions," so that there was "a significant risk of a very serious downturn."[24] Speaking at the same conference, Professor Edward Leamer, of UCLA's Anderson School of Management, set out his own theory, that the U.S. economy was guided not by a business cycle but by a consumer cycle particularly driven by housing. He added, "The historical record strongly suggests that in 2003 and 2004 we poured the foundation for a recession in 2007 and 2008 led by a collapse in housing we are currently experiencing. Only twice have we had this kind of housing collapse without a recession, in 1951 and in 1967, and both times the Department of Defense came to the rescue, because of the Korean War and the Vietnam War. We don't want that kind of rescue this time, do we?"[25]

The potential in California appeared particularly gruesome. As figure 4.4 (page 114) shows, home prices in the nation's largest state had tripled between 1995 and 2006. By mid-2007, in turn, five of the ten markets projected by Moody's Economy.com to undergo the largest peak-to-bottom home price declines were in California—Stockton, Modesto, Fresno, Oxnard-Ventura, and Sacramento.[26] If anything, the earlier explosive growth shown in the figure hinted at the possibility of a decline of a related magnitude.

But back in 2000–2001, as the NASDAQ stock market bubble was bursting, an appreciation of housing's enormous national weight—besides being a $20 trillion asset class, it was also the principal wealth repository for most American families—may well have spurred a new strategy on the part of the Federal Reserve Board and the President's Working Group on Financial Markets. Several specific motivations have been bandied about. First, the Working Group logically went into high gear to stimulate the U.S. economy after 9/11. Also, there was the belief, attributed to Greenspan in particular, that home-price inflation could be tapped to stimulate the larger national economy by home-owners who raised spendable dollars through refinancing. In a related vein, others have speculated that Greenspan's incremental 2001–3 rate

FIGURE 4.4

The Tripling of California Home Prices, 1995–2006

Single-Family Median Home Prices

Source: California Association of Realtors.

cuts partly sought to rescue Washington's two giant government-sponsored mortgage enterprises, the Federal National Mortgage Asssociation (Fannie Mae) and the Federal Home Loan Mortgage Corporation (Freddie Mac).[27] Both had been caught up in scandals related to improper accounting and management of financial derivatives. The crippling of either institution could have added home-price weakness to the deflation of financial assets in the wake of the high-tech and stock market crash.

Uncomplicated explanations also resonated. Stephen Roach, the chief economist of Morgan Stanley, described Fed chairman Greenspan as "a serial bubbler." Monetary lubrication was the chairman's principal shtick. Others have mustered arguments that as technology stocks came unglued in 2000, and telecommunications and energy-merchant (Enron) scandals hit the headlines in 2001, the financial services industry had good reason to turn to housing, an asset category that paused in 2000 but then resumed growing during 2001. Clever minds in the public and private sectors may simply have thought alike.

As figure 2.2 on page 32 shows, banks had steadily been raising the share of their earning assets that were mortgage-related since the 1960s, with particularly notable spurts in the 1970s and late 1980s. The surge that began in 2000 was comparable, and it ballooned the banks' reliance on mortgage-related assets from just over 50 percent to just over 60 percent. Major players included holding companies and banks like Citigroup, Wells Fargo, JPMorgan Chase, HSBC, and Bank of America. As a further backdrop, we can append the parallel expansion of activity by the pivotal government-sponsored mortgage enterprises. The total volume for mortgage lending by Fannie Mae, Freddie Mac, and the Government National Mortgage Association (Ginnie Mae) grew from $370 billion in 1985 to $1 trillion in 1990, then reached $2.5 trillion in 2000, and was estimated to top $4 trillion in 2007. By year's end, both Fannie and Freddie were posting multibillion-dollar third-quarter losses, worrying some observers that one or both would be unable to provide additional liquidity to the mortgage market or to fulfill their role as the U.S. housing sector's lenders of last resort.

To put a further exclamation mark after the home-mortgage focus of the big banks and investment banks, consider these statistics from the

Mortgage Bankers Association. For 2006, total mortgage origination was about $2.5 trillion, three times what it had been in 1997. Of this $2.5 trillion, three-quarters had been securitized into mortgage-backed securities. For asset-backed securities, a distinct and different category, the home-equity loan component back in 2002 had represented about 35 percent of all asset-backed securities, barely ahead of auto loans. But by 2006, home-equity loans had ballooned to 65–70 percent of the ABS total, shrinking auto loans and credit card debt to a *combined* share just over 20 percent.

What is more, opportunity was also global. In 2003, the United States had accounted for 90 percent of worldwide securitization issuance, and as recently as 2005, that share was 83 percent. Export markets were plums, and Wall Street had dreams that the whole alphabet soup—CDOs, MBSs, and ABSs—could become one of the biggest and most successful U.S. exports. As of mid-2007, Deutsche Bank estimated that although foreign investors owned only 28 percent of the total U.S. market for asset-backed securities, in the larger mortgage-backed category (including subprime) foreigners owned nearly 40 percent. Among these two-fifths, moreover, almost six out of ten were held by West Europeans, led by the British, Dutch, and Germans. Some of all flavors, analysts surmised, had been sold to less-sophisticated small and mid-sized institutions hungry for safe-rated high yield.[28]

Alas, several had been sold to money market funds operated by the large French bank BNP Paribas. On August 8, BNP Paribas announced that it was suspending redemptions in the three affected funds, which sparked a sell-off in Europe based on the realization that the subprime crisis had now crossed the Atlantic.[29] The marketing fallout was painful. Instead of riding to glory in the export markets, mortgage securitization (and its crippling blend of risk and opacity) now fed a globalizing credit crisis. It was no longer related only to American mortgages and housing; complex U.S. financial exports had suffered a particular black eye.

It is important to isolate those two words "risk" and "opacity." Within a few weeks, they convinced policymakers from Treasury Secretary Paulson to Mortgage Bankers Association leaders to foreign central bank heads and national financial regulators that this latest crisis could not end as quickly as the ones in 1987 and 1998. Even in September, a major complication had been foreshadowed in the closure of a London hedge fund. It had not failed, but it closed shop because market illiquidity led to a "bitter, secretive fight with Barclays Capital, its prime broker, about valuation issues—how to price the debt instruments the fund held," in the words of the *Financial Times,* and "a much bigger battle about valuation . . . still rages behind the scenes in numerous offices at banks, hedge funds, and accountancy firms on Wall Street and in the City of London."[30] In New York, pressure also took the form of finagling the books to avoid recognition of losses in the third quarter of 2007, delaying as much as possible until the year's end. To guard their own interests, the major accounting firms, through the U.S. Center for Audit Quality, notified financial firm managers and company directors that the auditors would all be obliged to follow strict accounting rules for valuing illiquid assets. Top government officials had good reason to expect a drawn-out crisis.

Treasury Secretary Paulson chose to emphasize the chronology of mortgage-payment resets when he told one financial meeting that "the subprime market will take longer than other markets because of a number of these resets taking place over the next 18 months to two years." North of the border, Bank of Canada governor David Dodge explained that "the re-pricing of credit risk is an ongoing process. Unfortunately, it may take somewhat longer than in previous periods, because of the opacity and legal complexity of so many of these structured products."[31]

Regulators in Britain, Germany, France, and the European Union queried securitization itself. The view from the United Kingdom's Financial Services Authority was that, in addition to opacity, the amount of securities produced for sale and the diversity of their purchasers had far outstripped the infrastructure and expertise needed to monitor them. French finance minister Christine Lagarde opined that "transparency with regard to the actual packaging process of securitisation should be heightened. However, once it reaches a certain degree of complexity, assessing the associated risks may prove to be impossible or too costly. A certain degree of standardisation may therefore be necessary."[32]

The divergence is instructive. Paulson chose to talk about a regulatory challenge confined to real estate lending, and from the U.S.

standpoint, historical precedent clearly supported a real estate preoccupation. The analyses of potential housing-led recessions and possibly
severe housing price drops offered by Greenspan, Feldstein, Shiller,
Rosenberg, Leamer, and others in August and September left little
doubt. The scope of these disruptions is more likely than anything else
to determine the political climate of regulation and recrimination in the
United States. In late 2006, Paul Kasriel, chief economist at Chicago-
based Northern Trust, neatly framed the negative scenario: "U.S. banks
currently hold record amounts of mortgage-related assets on their
books. If the housing market were to go into a deep recession resulting
in massive mortgage defaults, the U.S. banking system could sustain
huge losses similar to what Japanese banks experienced in the 1990s. If
this were to occur, the Fed could cut interest rates to zero but it would
have little positive effect on economic activity or inflation."[33]

Kasriel was early. Even so, by late 2007 others also found themselves
haunted by the ghosts of the earlier Japanese bubble and crash. Yale's
Robert Shiller raised the parallel, as did Japanese economist Tadashi
Nakamae and Asia-based Bloomberg columnist William Pesek.[34] And
on New Year's Day, Gillian Tett, the astute capital markets editor of the
Financial Times, pondered the analogy by seeing a similar origin in bad
loans, loss of confidence in the banking system, and inclination to delay
the day of reckoning. Few Americans were willing to credit these parallels, but Tett quoted Timothy Ryan, vice chairman at JPMorgan, as
saying "Former U.S. bank regulators like me feel a bit responsible because we used risk-adjusted capital rules to push riskier assets off balance sheet—but we never expected that it would lead to the creation of
things such as the SIVs and complex leveraged CDOs. . . . This was financial engineering that went too far."[35] Moreover, the U.S. housing
market was not the only one at risk; a report by the International Monetary Fund also saw overvaluation in Britain and Ireland, two other
countries with vulnerable bubbles.[36]

Be that as it may, the precedents seem most foreboding for the
United States. Much reference has been made to the home-price movements that began in 1989–90 and 1929. In his September testimony before Congress's Joint Economic Committee, a pessimistic Robert Shiller
thought the first comparison already inadequate: "The housing boom

since the late 1990s was clearly bigger than the one that preceded the 1990–1991 recession, and the contraction in residential investment since last year is sharper. I am worried that the collapse of home prices might turn out to be the most severe since the Great Depression."[37]

In the United States, real estate slumps drag out longer than the nine-to-eighteen-month stock market declines associated with mild-to-middling recessions, and the current home-price downturn looks like the biggest in memory. But we must still hope that Shiller's real estate evaluation and the Japanese analogy are too pessimistic.

FIVE

Peak Oil

A Potential Pivot of the 2010s

The meek shall inherit the earth, but not its mineral rights.

—Oil billionaire Jean Paul Getty

The oil boom is over and will not return. All of us must get used to a different lifestyle.

—King Abdullah of Saudi Arabia, 2007

Getty, the international oilman, knew what he was talking about. Might often makes right—at least in the sense of mineral rights. Resource wars, open or covert, are familiar policy tools. The English-speaking powers have a long history of might-enabled mineral acquisitions.

Being precise about how often Britain and the United States have invaded Iraq because of petroleum—or, for the naive among us, intervened to establish or secure democracy—isn't easy. In 1991, of course, and arguably in 2003. The first British military incursions, during World War I, took place while oil-rich Mesopotamia was still a province in the Ottoman Empire. In 1941, just before Hitler's troops invaded Russia and reached as far as the Caucasus, British troops went into Iraq to stave off an oil-motivated German attack abetted by the Vichy French regime next door in Syria. Clearly, we can't count the 1959 plot by the Central Intelligence Agency to kill Iraqi strongman Abdul Karim Qasim—incredibly, the young Saddam Hussein was among those enlisted by the CIA—because that did not involve an actual invasion.[1] Neither did Washington's success, way back in the 1920s, in persuading Britain to cut the United States in for a partial share of the oil in what had become

British-occupied Iraq. Petroleum-driven Anglo-American interest in the Persian Gulf goes back a long way.

Denying that the motive is oil is often wise, though, and sometimes even necessary. Lord Curzon, the British foreign secretary, drew mockery in the press and in Parliament for insisting such in 1924, although similar assertions by the U.S. president and the British prime minister in 2003 were treated respectfully. In 2007, former Federal Reserve chairman Alan Greenspan caused a stir when he stated matter-of-factly that the 2003 invasion had been about oil. Perhaps he knew, as did others, about the amount of time that Vice President Richard Cheney's high-powered task force on energy had spent studying the maps of the various Iraqi oil fields. In Cheney's mind, it was probably always about oil.

In any event, the apparent American attempt to make U.S. energy policy from bomb bays and guided-missile cruisers misfired in 2003. The botched occupation of Iraq boiled up into a serious local insurgency, destroying Washington's private dream of throwing open Iraqi oil spigots, driving down oil prices, and breaking the power of OPEC and its state-owned oil companies. Predictably, these producers more than shared the worldwide dismay over U.S. actions, and not just because they feared competition. By 2006 OPEC and non-OPEC petroleum exporters were also becoming more concerned about the peak-oil thesis, inasmuch as global crude oil production seemed to plateau after 2005 despite increasing world demand.

What Cheney may have feared about supply and upward price pressure in 2001 seems to have taken place, and then some. During the five years after the invasion, petroleum prices ballooned from $25 per barrel to the $100 range. This was the cause, but also the *effect,* of a steady slippage in the value of the U.S. dollar. The burden for the United States of having to import two-thirds of the oil it consumed became more and more costly. The price of oil rose, and Washington's credibility declined, and this double blow undermined the dollar's long-standing role in global petroleum sales—since 1974, greenbacks had been the semiofficial currency of international oil transactions. The dollar's weakening only increased interest within a number of producing nations in two possible responses: reducing or ending the role of the dollar as the world's reserve currency, or pricing petroleum sales in some other currency or combination of currencies. Watchful experts in the United States knew that if producers did either, it would only add to a perception of U.S. weakness.

That growing appearance—the sense elsewhere in the world of the United States as a paper tiger with papier-mâché leadership—helped to transform the relatively placid landscape of international oil rivalry circa 2001 into a seething jungle of regional and global energy plots, anti-American alliances, and realigning spheres of influence. Threats to U.S. oil interests arose in places Washington had long taken for granted: Latin America, the Arabian Peninsula, in small ways even Canada.

Also ominous was another commercial reality—the twenty-first-century upheaval reshaping the global oil business from one dominated by Western international oil companies (the so-called Seven Sisters of the 1960s) to one controlled by state-owned companies with increasingly nationalist agendas. The new seven were Saudi Aramco, Gazprom (Russia), PetroChina, the National Iranian Oil Company, Petrobras (Brazil), Petronas (Malaysia), and Petróleos de Venezuela. As of 2007, these and other state-run firms collectively controlled some 75 to 80 percent of estimated world petroleum reserves. For many, growing resource nationalism was only fed by further talk about a production peak, which made producers reluctant to sell from finite resources (national reserves are often much overstated) for anything but the highest possible prices. Furthermore, many oil-producing nations, enriched by recent high prices and happily anticipating more of the same, also encouraged so-called sovereign wealth funds—government vehicles for using burgeoning revenues to earn higher rates of return and to buy up companies and other assets in the older, developed nations.

The irony is as rich as 2007 oil prices. Five years after the United States and Britain invaded Iraq in 2003, the outcome—much of it a direct consequence of inept Washington strategizing—has been a massive transfer of wealth, through escalating oil prices, to many of the same nations Washington and London had sought to stymie on an individual basis and by curbing OPEC.

A concurrent—but by 2006–7 fast-growing—challenge to the United

States came in the displacement of market economics and the return of economic nationalism. Spreading attention to peak-oil calculations presumably encouraged resource nationalism and buoyed the importance of state-run oil companies. However, broader trends were also at work: a renewal of localism and statism, mercantilist mentalities, and the revenue hunger of national goverments. Obviously, besides undercutting the traditional market preferences of the United States and Britain, these developments reduced the growth of their four major international oil companies: ExxonMobil, Chevron, BP, and Shell. Through nationalizations and seizures, these companies' overseas operations were curtailed, from Venezuela, Bolivia, and Ecuador to Russia. French-owned Total was also squeezed.

Political imperatives being what they are, the temptation of conservative civilian leaders in the United States to pursue oil-related military action against targets like Iran is easy to understand. Such action would be more tempting still had U.S. incompetence in Iraq not encouraged so much skepticism about prospects in Iran, a more difficult target and a more difficult conflict to contain. Moreover, if one looks along the borders of Iraq and Iran to Syria, Turkey, Afghanistan, and Pakistan, rising regional tension with the United States is beginning to seem as contagious as a mortgage-stuffed collateralized debt obligation. The tinder is almost perfect for a war or military strike rooted in the frustration of a great power in decline.

Which brings us to a too-little-examined dimension of our current energy predicament: how the prior eminence of the United States in global petroleum matters has left not only an outdated infrastructure but a spectrum of disabilities, unwarranted smugness, vested interests, and booby traps. These range from currency vulnerabilities and lack of a serious national energy strategy to apparent policy inertia in Washington, where many officeholders seem unable to understand how much has changed for the United States over the last decade.

OIL: THE ALL-AMERICAN FUEL

Periodic denunciations of "Big Oil" have been a staple of U.S. politics, much as diatribes against Standard Oil were a century earlier. But it is a mistake to ignore the simultaneous romance that many Americans, especially those from producing regions, have had with fuel oils, lubricants, and illuminants over the centuries. Doubters can visit the many local and state museums, from Pennsylvania to California, from Alaska to Texas.

One of these displays, in West Virginia, claims George Washington as the nation's first energy speculator—he bought some local oil spring acreage in 1771. These seepages and springs were part of early North American folklore from Spanish conquistadores to Seneca Indians, from Appalachia to Wyoming and California. Indeed, New England's famous eighteenth- and early-nineteenth-century whaling industry built up the markets for illuminants and lubricants that, as the whales grew fewer, beckoned New England investors to underwrite drilling of the first serious oil well in Pennsylvania in 1859. The Civil War was the first U.S. conflict in which oil played a role—in 1863, Confederate cavalry torched the Northern-controlled Burning Springs field near what is now Parkersburg, West Virginia. And come the twentieth century, vast, unmatched American oil resources provided the vital fuel for newly mechanized combat that brought Allied victory in two world wars. Washington was the first president to take a business interest in oil and gas, Lincoln was the first to relate oil exports to the war effort, Franklin Roosevelt was the first to make oil the pivot of U.S. policy in the Middle East, and nobody matched Dwight Eisenhower in building roads for a motorized America. Visiting British journalists, especially back in the 1920s and 1930s, took home a succinct analogy: the Americans do oil like we in Britain do coal.

This is not tangential economic history; it is *central* economic history. Since the emergence of modern Europe in the wake of the Renaissance and the rise of capitalism, idiosyncratic energy regimes have been important to the making of the three successive leading world economic powers: wind and water to the seventeenth-century Dutch, coal to late-eighteenth-century Britain, and oil to the early-twentieth-century United States. By "idiosyncratic," I mean a leading-edge energy source or fuel in which a particular nation was not simply well endowed but made expert by a unique acquaintance and economic and cultural interaction. Dutch and British history makes both interrelationships quite clear.[2]

Surrounded by wind and water, the coastal Dutch made both forces work for them as no other people had managed. Wind was captured for power on sea and land alike, through sails and windmills—and unmatched skills in science, engineering, ship design, and navigation. Water management was also necessary in a country that depended on fishing and waterborne commerce and where some of the land was below sea level. Extraordinary pumps run by windmills enabled the Dutch to recover from the sea about one-quarter of the land mass of the present-day Netherlands. The windmill-studded Zaandam became the most advanced industrial district of early-eighteenth-century Europe, and Dutch maritime supremacy circled the world with colonies and stations from Japan and the East Indies to Brazil, New Amsterdam (later New York), and the Cape of Good Hope. It represented an extraordinary achievement.

The British did as well with coal, of which they had abundant deposits. Early English use of it for heating, ironworking, and other ventures impressed one historian enough to posit a first industrial revolution of sorts in the sixteenth and seventeenth centuries. Most economic historians, however, date the coal-fueled Industrial Revolution in Britain from the late eighteenth century, when coal production provided the laboratory for development of the steam engine, large-scale iron and steel output, and railroads.

Neither the Dutch nor the British could prolong their global lead when a new energy regime helped to usher in a new leading world economic power. For Britain, demotion came when the United States rode oil to the top, both militarily and industrially, during the first half of the twentieth century. The United States has its own idiosyncratic relationship with oil, as profiled several paragraphs back. The unfortunate probability confronting early-twenty-first-century U.S. policymakers is another iteration of the same vulnerability: being too closely intertwined with oil to maintain leadership amid an upheaval likely to lead to a new global energy regime.

The extent to which the United States has a dated, ghost-of-glories-past petroleum infrastructure is all too evident. The major U.S. oil companies, ExxonMobil, Chevron, and ConocoPhillips, are wealthy but aging behemoths, hard-pressed to maintain production levels, despite large exploration outlays, and no longer enjoying the access to overseas oil fields they once commanded. Oil production in the United States peaked in 1971. ExxonMobil, the largest publicly traded international oil company in the world, in 2006 was only the twelfth-largest upstream (exploration and production) company worldwide, ranked by booked reserves. Venezuela squeezed out both Exxon and ConocoPhillips in 2007, and Ecuador used troops to dispossess Occidental. The big ten are all state-owned national oil companies (NOCs), and these days nearly four-fifths of the world's petroleum reserves are under the control of thirteen NOCs disinclined to share them. Residually, however, the oil industry continues to enjoy most of the energy preferences from the federal government—in terms of taxes, subsidies, and political influence—awarded during the industry's heyday in the 1950s and 1960s. U.S. residential and transportation infrastructure, critically defined during those same oil-enabled decades of suburban homebuilding and unflinching commitment to automobiles and highways, air travel, and airports, has continued to expand in much the same high-fuel-consuming directions. Sensible as those decisions seemed four and five decades ago, the three main fuels involved—gasoline, aviation gasoline, and heating oil—account for some 80 percent of U.S. oil consumption. Much of the enormity of U.S. oil use, including the painful cost of imports, is a legacy of profligate residential sprawl.

If the overall U.S. government's inertial commitment is to oil rather than alternative fuels, that is also true of the Pentagon, oil-dependent out of necessity. Forty years ago, the overseas disposition of American military forces reflected some attention to energy supply factors—air force bases in Saudi Arabia, for example—but was mostly focused on Communist enemies. Washington's preoccupation back then was with the Soviet Union. These days, analysts like Michael Klare explain the proportion of military dispositions close to critical foreign oil fields, offshore deepwater drilling areas, pipelines, terminals, and vital sea lanes by suggesting that the services have increasingly become an oil-protection force. Last but not least, even the role of the U.S. dollar as the world's reserve currency is indirectly tied to oil, a relationship too few citizens understand.

When President Richard Nixon "closed the gold window" in 1971—this entailed ending sales of the precious metal to foreign central banks, the last authorized purchasers—his action ended the U.S. currency's one remaining tie to gold. But in 1974, when the OPEC producers demanded and got much higher prices for their petroleum, the U.S. government arranged a condition with Saudi Arabia—the Saudis agreed that OPEC would price its oil sales in dollars. Because oil buyers would need dollars for their purchases, this linked the U.S. currency to oil (although the connection was weaker than in the 1950s, when the United States was still the world's top oil producer). Should the uncertainty of the dollar and indeed of overall U.S. international influence eventually prompt OPEC and the other oil producers to drop the greenback's oil-purchase or reserve-currency role, the effects could be painful.

In short, oil's position as the all-American fuel, for so many years a badge and shield, is now in some ways a potential liability. The benefit to the United States of an oil-supported currency is an endangered prerogative, especially if that commodity's production is close to a peak that obliges a transition in the world's energy regime.

(PARTIAL) PEAK OIL AND POLITICIZED MARKETS

If the argument for an imminent oil-production zenith—the thesis that a peak of worldwide petroleum output has recently occurred or is only a few years away—commands little sympathy or even acknowledgment in Washington, the reasons go beyond embarrassment and stubbornness. Keeping mum has a logic of sorts. Past-peak oil, if and when confirmed, will inevitably call to mind other U.S. past-peak possibilities, from currency preeminence to trading patterns and military alliances. Old alignments cannot be expected to continue as before.

Thus the significance of the considerable rise in peak-oil discussion, given a new respectability by events between 2005 and 2008. The most important change in thinking came among upper-echelon executives of the U.S. international oil companies, all too mindful of stagnant global production, the minimal payback for their own expensive explorations, ballooning resource nationalism, and the deepening sway of state-owned petroleum companies. Although none of these developments constituted geological as opposed to circumstantial evidence, all were compatible with what might be expected of a creeping peak-oil-is-almost-here psychology.

Much of the new respect and credibility seemed to firm up between the spring and autumn of 2007. Data suggested a three-year stagnation of global production, and also supported findings of individual national output peaks in Norway, Mexico, and Kuwait. Between Easter and Thanksgiving that year, despite worldwide demand growing by only a percentage point or so, the price of a barrel of light, sweet crude jumped from $60–$70 to a record $90–$100. In early July, the Paris-based International Energy Agency (IEA) issued the *Medium-Term Oil Market Report*, which, despite already high oil prices, predicted "increasing market tightness beyond 2010." Besides high demand, the IEA recognized that new projects were lagging while output was falling faster than expected in mature fields from Mexico to the North Sea.[3] A week later, the U.S. National Petroleum Council, a respected business-government group headed by former ExxonMobil chief Lee Raymond, weighed in with a report entitled *Facing the Hard Truths About Energy: A Comprehensive View to 2030 of Global Oil and Natural Gas*. Zealous "imminent peak" proponents countered that the NPC document evaded more hard truths than it faced, but at least one establishment journal, the *Financial Times,* called the report "a defining moment in the history of the global energy industry."[4]

That perception of a watershed was mostly because Raymond's report strayed from the Bush administration's line in its candor on global warming, vehicle fuel economy standards, and the likelihood that future oil supplies would not be able to keep up with global consumption. But there were some bold paragraphs. By 2030, oil supply would match demand only if there was considerable intervening reduction in demand. And conceivably, supply could become inadequate as early as 2015. True, the NPC report did evade peak questions in favor of a demand-side emphasis, in contrast to an earlier analysis by Britain's Centre for Global Energy Studies, which identified current prices as being driven by a shortage of supply and not by consumer appetites.[5] Savvy peak theorists counted their gains. If the energy establishment and prestige press focused on market pressures, that was only to be expected.

Besides, in some places demand was growing rapidly, and that tendency prominently included internal consumption rates within the OPEC nations themselves. There were many reasons—government subsidies that made gasoline and oil cheap to residents, cars and more cars, and attempts to diversify national economics away from oil dependence. By some calculations, OPEC itself was responsible for a quarter of the new demand, a trend expected to continue.

Centrists in the press and energy industry were anxious to sidestep the identification and timing of national and worldwide production peaks, a political and strategic minefield. Peak proponents, for their part, were divided between hawks who thought a non-OPEC or global peak had *already* occurred or was about to, and others who believed it might be as much as fifteen years off. Even many senior oil industry executives were discussing potential supply-demand imbalances in similar time frames. Practical distinctions between them could be blurry. There was merit in the wry observations among peak advocates that industry executives preferred to speak in code, admitting that "the era of easy oil is over," or acknowledging that "the supply-demand balance would remain tight."

Senior ExxonMobil and Chevron executives, who had orchestrated the NPC study, would sometimes let candor slip out. If former ExxonMobil chief Raymond avoided peak talk, the company's current chairman, Rex Tillerson, told the *Financial Times* that he believed production from sources outside OPEC could have "a little more growth," but would soon level off.[6] Chevron chairman David O'Reilly ducked offering any chronology, but the company's chief technology officer, Don Paul, who had chaired the NPC's task group on oil supply, later told a Dow Jones energy conference that many people expected a peak by

2020. "The question is will there be peak oil? Yes. But will it be the disaster [some people] expect? I don't think it has to be. We have other ways of making fuel." He named biofuels, tar sands, and coal.[7]

The one-two punch of the IEA and NPC reports further legitimized candor. At September's annual international conference of the Association for the Study of Peak Oil and Gas (ASPO) in Ireland, Lord Oxburgh, the retired chairman of Shell UK, predicted that oil would climb to $150 a barrel, while former U.S. energy secretary and CIA director James Schlesinger, in one of a number of pithy comments, said, "The battle is over, the oil peakists have won. Current U.S. energy policy and the administration's oil strategy in Iraq and Iran are deluded."[8] October brought two more major conferences—one in Texas cosponsored by the University of Houston and the U.S. section of ASPO, the second thematically named "Oil and Money" and held in London. Once again, blunt comments flowed. Speaking at the ASPO meeting in Houston, oilman T. Boone Pickens and Texas investment banker Matthew Simmons agreed that 2005 had been the global production peak year, with Simmons also reiterating his widely reported doubts about Saudi Aramco output claims.[9]

Conference-goers in London heard experts from two OPEC nations—Sadad al-Husseini, former chief of exploration and production at Saudi Aramco, and Shokri Ghanem, chief executive of Libya's National Oil Company. Ghanem told the audience that world production could not go above 100 million barrels a day, and that when that ceiling was reached—optimistic U.S. officials projected that level of output by 2015 to 2020—global production would start to decline.[10] Al-Husseini was even more provocative. In one of the interviews he gave at the London conference, the candid Saudi more or less agreed with the Pickens-Simmons thesis. He indicated that world production was in the process of making a 2005–7 top and would plateau for ten to fifteen years at roughly the same level, assuming prices were raised some $12 a year to incentivize the continued output of oil and other related liquids. He further suggested that world oil reserves were inflated, and that 300 billion of the 1.2 trillion barrels—mostly in the OPEC countries—should be reclassified as speculative resources.[11]

Two more major reports rounded out what was an extraordinary October. The German-based Energy Watch Group, including both scientists and members of the German parliament, concluded that global oil production had peaked in 2006 and would likely decline at the rate of several percent a year. By 2020 and even more by 2030, the group argued, global oil supply will be dramatically lower.[12] This study, influenced by German Green Party parliamentarians, had no business backing and was regarded by mainstream U.S. peakists as a worst-case scenario. In the meantime, the School of Engineering at Case Western Reserve University in Cleveland published its second survey of oil economists, geologists, investors, and political decision makers from around the world, taken between May and August 2007. This updated its first "Peak-Oil When?" survey conducted in 2005. In that first compilation, geologists had warned about peak oil, but the others had dissented. In the follow-up, all of the respondent categories saw global peak oil by 2010. Among all the participating oil experts, 47 percent thought it virtually certain and another 31 percent chose highly likely.[13]

No one can definitively prove that this six-month barrage of conferences, surveys, agency and advisory group reports, and press stories— followed with increasing attention by hedge funds and brokerage firms—helped to loft the price of oil futures (Brent and West Texas Intermediate) between April and December 2007. Still, the connection does seem plausible. And helped by the seasonality of spring and summer motorists' demand for gasoline, oil-price pressures put themselves on an escalator to come alongside housing and mortgages in the August credit market panic. But before turning to the financial and foreign exchange markets and their various reflections of oil-price pressures, it is appropriate to turn to another global petroleum tension—the extent to which oil alliances around the world were beginning to realign, with the potential for new political and even military conflict.

A NEW ROUND OF OIL WARS?

In the grand sense, the term "oil war" is probably used too lightly. Still, both world wars had significant petroleum-related dimensions, and in recent years it has also been easy to point to nations—Nigeria, Sudan, Iraq, Indonesia, and Colombia—where localized fighting has had real oil-supply connections. Perhaps the best analogy is to the 1920s, when military confrontation rarely figured, but writers used "oil wars" to describe the various and sometimes fierce petroleum-related rivalries that engaged the major powers—the United States, Britain, France, and Russia—all of whom had understood oil's centrality in determining the outcome of the Great War of 1914–18.

A number of volumes have dwelled on the rivalry between Britain, the declining global hegemon, and the United States, the ascending one. French and Russian maneuvers were tangential by comparison. In the years right after World War I, Britain hoped to make a British-dominated Middle East her own equivalent of Texas. However, the United States thrust itself into the arrangement in Iraq, drew Saudi Arabia into what became a U.S. orbit, and dominated the Western Hemisphere. The British were handicapped by the new postwar clout of the United States as the world's top lender and creditor nation.

The partial parallel to the present decade leaps out. The United States, paired with Britain in twenty-first-century petroleum geopolitics, is the declining great power, weakened by ebbing oil production and declining financial leverage, while China is the would-be future hegemon, aided by its financial suasion as the principal global creditor of the embattled United States. One important caveat, though, is that China, unlike the United States of the 1920s, is not also the world's leading petroleum producer. For that matter, China is not even a front-rank producer. That nation became a net oil importer in 1993, and Beijing expects Chinese oil output to peak in 2015.[14] To realize its ambitions, China must become a preferred market for global oil exporters, especially the Middle East OPEC producers who by 2020 will have most of the remaining reserves and exportable surpluses.

Not that China has been the only player in the petroleum game reading up on Sun Tzu and Niccolò Machiavelli. Six others—major producers Russia, Iran, Venezuela, and Saudi Arabia, as well as top consumers Japan and India—are busy moving pieces on the petro-political chessboard. Since George W. Bush double-dared opponents with his

2002 proclamation of the "axis of evil," Washington's rumored plots to overthrow Venezuelan strongman Huge Chavez, and the 2003 invasion of Iraq, the opposition has been powerfully transformed into several actual and proposed new "axes of oil."

We can start with the Shanghai Cooperation Organization, conjoining Russia, China, and four central Asian republics formerly part of the Soviet Union. The SCO began in 2001 as an economic and energy group, and focused its 2007 summit on cooperation in oil and gas matters, despite mainstream press emphasis on the unusual joint military maneuvers held in border areas of Russia and China.[15] Oil-rich Iran has been courting both Russia and China, hoping to be invited into the SCO. The Washington-baiting Chavez, in turn, has promoted a South American energy entente of sorts including Venezuela, Ecuador, Argentina, Uruguay, and Bolivia. Saudi Arabia's recently installed King Abdullah, although a U.S. ally, made his first goodwill visits in 2006 to China, India, and Pakistan, thereafter hosting Iranian president Mahmoud Ahmadinejad in Saudi Arabia in early 2007. Two weeks later, the king decided to cancel a planned visit and state dinner at the Bush White House.[16] The Saudis, some experts said, were deciding to "look east" to Asia. These various alliances, groupings, visits, and dinner cancellations command interest because they contain hints or real evidence of plausible realignments, and because they smack of a New World Order quite contrary to the America-centered one imagined by two generations of Bush presidents.

The Saudi tiff is a good place to start. In the wake of the unpopular U.S. invasion of Iraq, the Saudis showed their displeasure by giving a major gas-development contract to French Total instead of Exxon-Mobil, while continuing to reduce oil sales to the United States. The *Washington Times* reported in September 2004 that after peaking at the equivalent of 1.7 million barrels per day in 2002, Saudi sales to the United States fell to 1.1 million barrels per day in May 2004. James Placke, a former deputy assistant secretary of state for Near Eastern affairs, explained that the Saudi turn away from the U.S. market began in late 2002 as the United States was preparing to attack Iraq. China soon jumped ahead of the United States in oil exports from the Saudi kingdom (and maintained that edge in 2007). To Placke, the shift represented "a slow recognition by the Saudi side that the 'special relationship' isn't so special anymore."[17]

Saudi Arabia, still claiming to have huge reserves, announced in 2007 plans to spend as much as $90 billion through 2012 to boost crude oil production by more than a third.[18] Others believed that some of those outlays were needed simply to maintain production. There were believers, but also questioners, including al-Husseini, the former exploration and production chief at Saudi Aramco. The Saudis must also be paying close attention to reports by the International Energy Agency and others that over the last eighteen months, two-thirds of the new demand for oil has come from China and India.

In 2004, as China became the world's second-largest oil consumer after the United States, Saudi Arabia and China decided to hold regular consultations. Sinopec, one of China's state oil companies, soon inked a deal to explore gas resources in the kingdom's vast Empty Quarter. A major Saudi investor, Aramco Overseas Company, agreed to put $750 million into a petrochemical complex in China's Fujian Province. In addition, Saudi Arabia and Kuwait agreed to participate in an $8 billion project for a new refinery in Guangdong Province. Something else the Saudis sought from China was advanced weaponry: in 1988, they obtained CSS-2 missiles and launchers; and more recently, they were said to be interested in al-Khalid battle tanks jointly developed by China and Pakistan, as well as K8 jet training aircraft with the same origins.[19] According to one report, the Saudis were interested in acquiring a package of Chinese-designed missiles and Pakistani nuclear warheads as a deterrent against possible attack from Iran.[20]

Some of the speculation about mutual motives is just that. Still, one thing is clear: the Saudis are to an extent looking at American oil purchases in the rearview mirror, while they see that the road ahead is Asian—bumper to bumper with cars. Only 17 out of 1,000 Chinese owned automobiles in 2007, compared to 860 of every 1,000 Americans. But by 2012, the International Energy Agency predicts, the Chinese collectively will buy as many cars as are bought in the United States—and from there on, Asian demand will dominate. Fatih Birol, the IEA's chief economist, predicts that demand for oil in China alone will, before long, equal the entire production of Saudi Arabia.[21] The Saudis, however, having no need to bet on China alone, were targeting a cluster of countries that also included Japan, India, and Korea, their other top Asian markets.[22] Japan, in fact, enjoyed the Saudis' biggest Asian shipments. For Persian Gulf marketers, East Asia is Tomorrowland.

China stands to be the world's largest oil market of the 2030s, possibly replacing the United States in that capacity by 2025. However, the leaders in Beijing want to maintain a diversity of suppliers. Based on monthly figures for September 2007, China got 18 percent of its oil from Saudi Arabia, 10 percent from Iran, 9 percent from Oman, 3 percent from the United Arab Emirates, and smaller amounts from Kuwait and Yemen. All told, some 46 percent of China's petroleum imports originated in the Middle East. Another 28 percent came from African countries, principally Angola and Sudan. A further 11 percent came from the former Soviet Union—Russia and Kazakhstan, whose president identifies the Shanghai Cooperation Organization as an "energy club." Not surprisingly, this geography of supply largely matches the tilt of China's supporting petro-diplomacy and overseas investment.[23]

Although the ratios of oil suppliers to the East Asian giant shift somewhat from month to month, three conclusions jump out. First, China's high-profile foreign-aid, oil, and investment emphasis on Africa seems to be paying off—60 percent of Sudan's oil now goes to China, as do rising shares from both Angola and Equatorial Guinea, with notable offshore production prospects in Nigeria. On the other hand, South African president Thabo Mbeki was moved to warn fellow leaders against falling into a "colonial relationship" with China.[24] Second, Beijing's imports from the Shanghai Cooperation Organization members seem to be steadying. Last, but certainly not least, China continues to rely heavily on shipments from the major Middle East members of OPEC—Saudi Arabia, Iran, and the smaller Persian Gulf states. Within that region, China's role as an arms supplier, most prominently to Iran, but also to Oman, the United Arab Emirates, Kuwait, and Yemen, constitutes an important backstop to help ensure future oil supplies.[25]

If Saudi Arabia is turning its attention eastward to the mass of Asia, something similar can be said of Vladimir Putin's Russia. The political drift of the former Soviet Union's Eastern European satellites into

Western alliances like the European Union and the North Atlantic Treaty Organization has almost of necessity turned Russian ambitions eastward. In central Asia, the Shanghai Cooperation Organization is already successfully consolidating a Russian and Chinese sphere of influence, with potential new members like Iran, Pakistan, and Turkmenistan queuing for entry.[26] Soaring oil prices, in turn, continue to pump money into Russia's economy and the Kremlin's rekindling military ambitions. Russian long-distance bombers have begun occasional flights over NATO territory in Europe and as far eastward as the U.S. island of Guam in the Pacific. Russia's naval chief, Admiral Vladimir Masorin, announced that Russia wanted to reclaim its old naval base in Syria to regain a naval presence in the eastern Mediterranean. To some independent media analysts, the nation's new posture represents "a confused mixture of realistic goals and unworkable Soviet-style symbolism," while others insist that "Russia is back" and aims to become "a formidable Pacific player," partly through oil and arms exports, but also by rebuilding its depleted Pacific fleet and Far East forces.[27]

For all that oil revenues are Russia's major enabler, the country's leaders also attach great importance to its sales of armaments and weaponry, especially to Asian buyers. Between 1998 and 2005, Russian officials signed agreements for arms sales in Asia totaling $29 billion. These represented 37 percent of the market, well ahead of the United States, with China and India the major customers. In 2007, Russian president Putin visited Indonesia to finalize a $1 billion arms deal that included two Kilo-class submarines, forerunners of a planned small fleet. This sale followed earlier arrangements to provide advanced Su-27 and Su-30 combat fighters to Indonesia, Malaysia, and other Asian nations.[28]

As the world's number one or number two oil exporter, Russia is making a lot of money—the country's oil revenues are opaque, but net gains since 2000 must be $700 billion to $800 billion or more.[29] Looking ahead, some experts are skeptical as to how long Russia will be able to export large amounts of oil from its present fields.[30] Thus the Kremlin's great interest in developing additional resources in the Caspian Sea, in deep-sea drilling in portions of the Arctic claimed by Russia, in solidifying relations with the former Soviet Central Asian republics, and in the possibility of admitting Iran to SCO membership and fuller status in the

Russo-Chinese orbit. Overall, a balanced view seems to be that Russia, although unable to pursue a Saudi-like role as a swing producer for the global oil market, has been effectively using its oil resources and clout, especially in central Asia and East Asia.[31]

Russia's leaders may be just as focused on gas. Vladimir Putin's choice to succeed him as president in 2008, Dmitry Medvedev, served as the chairman of state-owned Gazprom—Russia's and the world's biggest natural gas company—even while he held the office of first deputy prime minister. Another of Putin's top Kremlin associates, Aleksei Miller, also functioned as a senior executive of Gazprom. Late 2007 press reports suggested that when Medvedev became president and Putin switched to the prime minister's position, Putin himself would take over as chairman of Gazprom. That company is certainly a pillar of Russia's global energy strategy. Not only does Russia boast the world's largest natural gas reserves, with Iran ranked second, but Gazprom concluded 2007 with bold moves aimed at Nigeria, Africa's biggest oil and gas producer (ranked number seven globally in gas reserves), and Venezuela and Bolivia, possessors of the two largest natural gas reserves in South America. Already close to Venezuela—Gazprom hopes to invest in Hugo Chavez's proposed "gas pipeline of the south" from Venezuela through Brazil to Argentina—the company proposed a major natural-gas-and-energy infrastructure-development agreement to Nigeria and discussed a $2 billion arrangement with Bolivia, which recently nationalized its gas industry. In each case, Gazprom pitched its fraternal state-owned status versus the alleged exploitive capitalism of the Western international oil companies.

Iran and Venezuela, the other two ambitious major oil producers, have leaders famous for noisy anti-Americanism and an oil-powered foreign policy. Neither country bears real resemblance to a world power. Still, Iran under President Ahmadinejad, beyond trying to ally with Russia and China in Asia, has also pursued joint energy projects with members of the nascent anti-American axis in Latin America. His 2007 visits to Venezuela, Bolivia, Ecuador, and Nicaragua yielded a natural gas accord with Bolivia and a joint pledge by Iran and Venezuela to build a $350 million seaport for Nicaragua.[32] This tilt, along with Tehran's nuclear ambitions, has cost Iran support in Europe—Germany and Italy have cut back trade. But Iran has shifted its orientation toward Asia, and China is expected to replace Germany as the leading exporter of goods to Iran.[33]

In Venezuela, strongman Hugo Chavez has likewise turned his nation's large but ill-maintained oil resources into a political weapon. Most of his efforts have been centered in Latin America, where over several years he has arranged energy-related deals and joint ventures with Bolivia, Argentina, Uruguay, and Ecuador. For the most part, they have centered on energy supply, refineries, natural gas separation and distribution, resource exploration, or petrochemicals.[34] At OPEC's 2007 summit meeting in Saudi Arabia, Ecuador, just readmitted to the producers' cartel, supported the Venezuela-Iran faction. At more or less the same time, Venezuela announced that it had set up a multibillion-dollar joint investment fund with China.[35] Chavez and Ahmadinejad may be hard to take seriously in some circles, but oil boosts their stature.

These realignments, if they persist into the next decade, must affect the ability of the United States to secure needed oil imports and uphold its oil-power status during a high-risk decade, when the word "intense" will probably fail to describe global petroleum rivalries. Thirty years ago, Saudi Arabia and Iran were allies of the United States and suppliers who sent the bulk of their oil exports westward to North America and Europe. Venezuela was in the American camp. Since then, Iranian oil has been lost, while the Saudis have sometimes put China ahead of the United States as a customer. Venezuela was (and remains) a major supplier of oil to the United States, but its political hostility to Washington could change that. In early 2008, Chavez halted Venezuelan exports of asphalt to the United States, saying it was needed for road building at home. Meanwhile, Venezuelan shipments of oil to China began to climb.[36] Also, Chavez threatened to cut off oil to the United States should Washington strike at Iran. As figure 5.1 shows, of the eight principal 2007 suppliers of petroleum to the United States as of August, only one, Canada, could be called secure and reliable. Nigeria and Iraq are unstable; Saudi Arabian production might turn out to be weaker than expected. Russia, anxious to price its oil exports in rubles, hardly qualifies as politically dependable, nor does Algeria. As for Mexico, a longtime major exporter to the United States, its oil production has clearly peaked. According to CIBC World Markets, Mexico's exports have been falling since 2004 and could easily become insignificant by 2012.[37] Moreover, in 2007 antigovernment insurgents, the Popular Revolutionary Army, blew up oil and natural gas pipelines of the government petroleum monopoly, PEMEX, in four Mexican states.[38]

ANTIDOLLAR DIPLOMACY

Beginning in 1909, during the administration of President William Howard Taft, U.S. officials used the term "dollar diplomacy" to describe a commitment to increase U.S. trade by promoting American investment and enterprise in Latin America and China. A century later, we can fairly identify an emergence of "antidollar diplomacy"—the machinations of U.S. foes and rivals to undercut the dollar and curtail its longtime dual status as the currency in which foreign central banks hold their reserves, and international oil sales are priced.

If China, Iran, Venezuela, Saudi Arabia, the Persian Gulf states, and Russia had only oil and gas to plot and strategize over, that would be jeopardy enough. But during the last decade, they also accumulated huge quantities of dollars—some held as central bank reserves, others

FIGURE 5.1
The Principal Suppliers of Oil to the United States: A Hint of Vulnerability?

Crude oil imports (thousands of barrels per day) for 2007, year to date through August

Canada	1,853
Mexico	1,448
Saudi Arabia	1,427
Venezuela	1,120
Nigeria	1,025
Angola	524
Algeria	509
Iraq	481

Source: Energy Information Administration, release of October 30, 2007.

banked day to day as oil revenues, and still others flexing their muscles in so-called sovereign wealth funds. The latter, now much in global headlines, are the investment units—think of them as government-owned hedge fund equivalents, but bigger—deployed by countries that hold large reserves of currency (China, Saudi Arabia, Kuwait, Singapore, Abu Dhabi, and others). Their task is to pursue profit-maximizing financial strategies and undertake foreign direct investment and share-holding beyond the proper function of central banks.

Many of these dollar holdings can be modified or redeployed quickly. Central banks in Beijing, Dubai, and Damascus can decide to further diversify their reserves, selling off a percentage of dollars in order to reinvest in euros, yen, or a basket of currencies. Sovereign wealth funds, some given wide discretion by their governments, can buy exotic securities, bid to purchase foreign companies, or speculate for or against foreign currencies. State-run oil companies, hesitant to take weak dollars for ever-more-valuable oil, can insist instead that payment be made in yen, euros, or something else. Antidollar diplomacy comes in all of these forms, and it has been shaping and eventually enlarging since 2000, when Iraqi strongman Saddam Hussein, chafing under United Nations sanctions and periodic U.S. bombing attacks, decided that international purchases of oil from Iraq should be paid for in euros, not dollars, and that OPEC should consider a similar change.

In recent years, as oil prices have rocketed and the dollar has lost value, world wealth has been significantly realigning to Asia. By one calculation, each year something like 1 percent of the world's gross domestic product is being redistributed from the world's oil-consuming countries to the world's oil-exporting nations.[39] Goldman Sachs posits that since 2001, importing countries transferred $3 trillion more to OPEC nations than would have been the case had oil prices stayed in the $20-per-barrel range.[40] The principal beneficiaries have been obvious: Russia and the Middle East. This comes on top of the late-twentieth-century wealth shift occasioned by the surge of manufactured exports, information technology resources, and huge trade surpluses in China, India, and Southeast Asia. A further addendum to these wealth shifts has been a rumbling and even grinding in the tectonic plates of worldwide monetary interconnection.

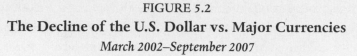

FIGURE 5.2
The Decline of the U.S. Dollar vs. Major Currencies
March 2002–September 2007

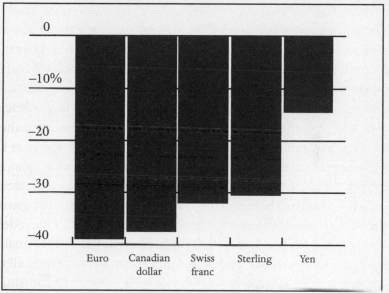

Source: "US Dollar," *Financial Times*, September 25, 2007.

The principal loser has been the American dollar, overtaken by the widespread perception, in the words of the *Toronto Globe and Mail,* that "for too long, Americans have been gorging on cheap credit and foreign oil, and all the things that go with the lifestyle—monster homes, big cars and big-screen TVs. For 15 years, the U.S. economy has been a magnet for global products and credit. Now the patient is over-indulged; his credit card maxed out."[41] Economists and financial pundits have offered more measured words and sophisticated analyses. According to Sebastian Mallaby of the *Washington Post,* foreigners "sent their money to the United States because they thought the U.S. financial system was transparent and sound; the subprime mortgage mess forced them to think differently. They sent their money to the United States because the greenback was expected to hold its value, but its purchasing power has fallen sharply against oil, metals and other commodities."[42] As for U.S. political culpability, former undersecretary of commerce Jeffrey Garten dismissed the White House's ostensible preference for a strong dollar as "an empty mantra, for the Bush administration continues to rely almost entirely on an ever weakening dollar as the central thrust of its international economic policy."[43] It is hard to disagree.

Figure 5.2 shows the dollar's 2002–7 decline against a group of major currencies. The year 2005 proved a brief hiatus because of rising interest rates and a tax-encouraged repatriation of profits accumulated by U.S. companies overseas, but otherwise the decline has been steady. The greenback's path over two to three more years may well be decisive.

To some commentators, the currency markets in the autumn of 2007 were behaving as if the dollar were forfeiting its status as the world's reserve currency.[44] Such thoughts were no echo of August, because the initial, temporary reaction that month as the panic spread around the world had been a flight to safety—the old and familiar safety of U.S. dollars and treasury bills. Not until two reconsiderations took hold—better understanding of the U.S. credit crisis as a dollar-*negative* rather than dollar-*supportive* event, and appreciation of the importance of dollar weakness in promoting oil price rises—did the dollar start to plummet, pushing to the forefront questions about its possible global dethronement.

This possibility, in turn, directed attention to historical precedents. Long-established reserve currencies do not hit the skids overnight; more often, inertia keeps them in place long after the deterioration begins. It would be convenient if neat, reliable timetables existed, but they do not. Even so, only one prior dethronement has any real relevance: the displacement of Britain's pound sterling by the U.S. dollar over some three decades during the first half of the twentieth century. Arguably, the clock started ticking for sterling, albeit remotely, when the neutral United States decided to continue on the gold standard—i.e., to maintain the convertibility of dollars into gold—as World War I broke out in 1914. The United Kingdom was the only major belligerent not to suspend gold convertibility, and a few wise Britons suspected that gold-minded U.S. officials were already calculating the credibility needed to mount a postwar challenge to British financial supremacy.[45] Ultimately, it took thirty to thirty-five more years for the dollar to complete its triumph, a drawn-out time frame worth keeping in mind.

Sterling did, in fact, tremble and dip several times between the momentous summer of 1914 and the war's end in 1918. Still, no major decline occurred until Britain temporarily took itself off gold in 1919 to wring out wartime inflation. That surprise departure sent sterling down by 30 percent against the dollar, a serious tremor. When Britain officially reattached its currency to gold in 1925, major damage had already been done, and in mid-Depression 1932, London suspended gold convertibility for good, causing another valuation dip. As we have seen, World War II completed the damage that the 1914–18 war had started. Nevertheless, in 1945, prestige minded British officials set a peacetime exchange rate for the pound at $4.03. That was soon unsustainable—the British economy of 1949, pallid and stressed, was still implementing wartime food rationing, and the government was forced to devalue to a humbler $2.80 exchange rate. So much for a onetime reserve currency. Thirty-five years had passed since the early warnings of 1914, not too different from Americans in 2008 harking back thirty-seven years to when a Vietnam-wearied United States closed the gold convertibility window for foreign central banks.

My point is that the dollar crisis has been taking shape for many years. Any abandonment of the greenback as the world's reserve currency could hardly occur "overnight." Unfortunately, a second yardstick is also relevant, one that the pound did not have to confront back in the first half of the twentieth century—the semiofficial link between U.S. currency and a strategic energy commodity. To review what happened back in 1974, three years after the greenback had lost its last small tie to gold: Saudi Arabia had just led OPEC to a major oil price increase. But in a collateral bargain with President Nixon and Secretary of State Kissinger, the Saudis agreed that international sales of oil would take place in dollars. Moreover, many of those dollars would be recycled through purchases of U.S. treasury bonds and notes. By and large, the arrangement worked.

In recent years, a handful of commentators, financial pundits, and disgruntled Asians have applied two related descriptions—in one, the U.S. dollar turned into the "petrodollar," and in the second, the United States put itself on the "oil standard." Washington acknowledges no such thing. However, by late 2007 the oil-dollar connection had

become a prime-time news story. Spokesmen for OPEC pointed out
that even though oil prices were going up, OPEC's real receipts were
declining. That was because the producers got paid in dollars—and the
declining value of those dollars shrank their net. "The adjusted 'OPEC
basket price' averaged only $43.60 in June compared with $44.30 a barrel in the same month last year [2006]," according to the *Financial
Times*.[46] In the words of OPEC president Mohammed bin Dhaen al-
Hamli, the cartel "was concerned about the continuing weakness of the
U.S. dollar" because "this is having a significant effect on the purchasing
power of oil-producing countries." Eric Chaney, an economist at Morgan Stanley, estimated that a 10 percent drop by the dollar against major currencies trimmed the purchasing power of OPEC's Persian Gulf
members by some 5 percent.[47]

To one group of observers, as mentioned, the United States had effectively put itself on an "oil standard," while others preferred the petrodollar phraseology. Although neither term developed any broad
usage, both shared a partial but meaningful validity. By late 2007, economists freely discussed a changing relationship between the value of the
dollar and the price of oil. "A long-term link between the dollar and the
oil price has broken down," said *Financial Times* investment editor John
Authers. "A high oil price used to mean a strong dollar as oil exporters
put their money in dollars. But now we have record crude prices and
the weakest dollar in decades." In this changed regime, the dollar tended
to fall when the price of oil went up.[48] Equally to the point, OPEC officials and economists explained a further nuance. Because the OPEC
producer nations were paid in dollars, the greenback's especially sharp
declines against the euro and pound throughout much of 2007 obliged
the producers to raise oil prices in order to maintain their purchasing
power in Europe and Britain, from which most (excluding the Saudis)
bought a large share of their imports.

The concept neatened if one thought in terms of the old currency
standard. After going off a limited gold standard in 1971, Washington
had hopped to a quasi oil standard in 1974. Now the United States,
down to producing only 37 percent of the oil it consumed, was losing
its control of global oil markets and in some danger of being forced off
its quasi oil standard. Or to put matters differently, if global oil produc-

tion had peaked or was not far from doing so, the dollar probably also had its own oil-related "peak" problems.

In fact, the dollar had four or five. In the first place, foreign central banks were beginning to sell varying quantities of dollars in order to diversify their reserves toward stronger currencies. Next came the potential reversals by some of the foreign nations—not least China, Hong Kong, Saudi Arabia, and most of the Persian Gulf oil sheikhdoms—that had earlier pegged (or in the case of China, semipegged with a band of allowable variation) their own currencies to the ups and downs of the now embattled greenback. Vulnerability number three, of course, was that OPEC or individual oil-producing nations might stop selling oil for dollars and start demanding euros or yen. A fourth problem lay with so-called monetary mercantilism—the tendency among top oil producers or stalwart manufacturing nations to amass huge foreign-currency holdings far beyond any central bank reserve logic. Redeployment of these excess reserves, in turn, spotlighted the dollar's fifth weakness—vulnerability to the institutional firepower (over $2 trillion in late 2007) of the sovereign wealth funds being put into commission from Qatar to Russia to China.

In order to understand potential dollar vulnerability, some further measurement of the way wealth was being realigned to Asia was in order. Of the more than $5 trillion worth of foreign-currency reserves in the world, up fivefold in ten years, roughly two-thirds had accumulated in Asia. Of the seven sovereign wealth funds with assets of over $100 billion, six (all save Norway's) flew Asian flags. Figure 5.3 displays both power rolls. As of 2007, the entirety of sovereign funds, some three dozen, had assets in the $2.2 trillion to $2.5 trillion range, up from $500 billion in 1990. Predictions for five to fifteen years ahead were stunning. Merrill Lynch projected $7.9 trillion of assets by 2011; Standard Chartered Bank, $13.4 trillion by 2017; and Morgan Stanley, $12 trillion by 2015 and $27.7 trillion by 2022.[49] Obviously, this included a lot of oil-price guesswork.

Although OPEC's recent take from high oil prices can be exaggerated by failure to recognize the erosion of the declining dollar, the annual receipts and estimates remain substantial: $506 billion in 2006, $508 billion in 2007, and $530 billion in 2008, according to the London-

FIGURE 5.3
Central Bank Reserves and Sovereign Wealth Funds:
The Heavy Hitters, 2007

Countries with sovereign wealth funds holding $100 billion or more		Top nine central banks by foreign currency reserves[†]	
Abu Dhabi	$625 bil.	China	$1.46 tril.
Norway	327 bil.	Japan	955 bil.
Singapore	323 bil.	Russia	455 bil.
Saudi Arabian Monetary	218 bil.	India	270 bil.
Agency*		Taiwan	266 bil.
Kuwait	213 bil.	South Korea	257 bil.
China	200 bil.	Brazil	173 bil.
Russia	128 bil.	Singapore	158 bil.
		Hong Kong	142 bil.

Source: International Monetary Fund official reserve assets. (The figure for each bank is for September, October, or November 2007.)

*Besides being Saudi Arabia's central bank, SAMA is also the Saudi investment authority, managing the country's foreign assets, including those held overseas.

[†]Euro-zone central bank foreign currency reserves totaled $483 billion.

based Centre for Global Energy Studies. A different series issued by the U.S. Energy Information Administration put the 2007 figure at $658 billion and the 2008 estimate at $762 billion.[50] "There's never been anything like this on a sustained basis the way we've seen the last couple of years," asserted Harvard economist Kenneth Rogoff. Oil prices "are not spiking; they're just rising."[51] Over the next twenty years, and despite probable production plateaus or declines, the OPEC members in the Middle East, with most of the longer-lived reserves, can presumably expect receipts of $5 trillion to $10 trillion.

The acceptability of such changes depends on whether one is Asian or American. We can most logically begin with the near-term scale of foreign central bank divestments of dollars and dollar-denominated assets. Between 1999 and the end of 2006, the greenback's share of global foreign-exchange reserves fell from 71 percent to 66 percent, The selling concentrated among the central banks of OPEC members, where the proportion of reserves held in dollars declined from 75 percent in the third quarter of 2001 to 61.5 percent three years later. This was substantially in response to U.S. foreign policy and banking practices re-lated to the Middle East.[52] The first nine months of 2007 brought another fall, with the dollar dropping from 66 percent of global reserves to an estimated 63 percent as divestment intensified during August's sharp sell-off. During that month, China, Japan, and Taiwan made large reductions in their holdings of marketable U.S. bonds.[53] Other an-nouncements of intended divestments also came from less important nations like Vietnam and Sudan.

Some caution is in order. Most nations that undertook diversification nevertheless retained substantial dollar reserves as part of a basket, often because the euro, the most plausible alternative currency, raised its own doubts. Among the weaknesses often cited were that the euro area was more identified with the European Central Bank than with any real po-litical entity; that Britain (and thus the global financial center of London) did not belong; and that the euro area lacked any military muscle.[54] Real-istically, for nations like Japan, Korea, Taiwan, Saudi Arabia, and the Per-sian Gulf emirates, the sheltering military might of the United States in the Persian Gulf or the Pacific would affect monetary allegiance; the United States fielded the world's strongest armed forces, while the European Union had a parliament, but nothing remotely resembling a Pentagon.

Nevertheless, former Federal Reserve chairman Alan Greenspan told the German magazine *Stern* that although the dollar is still ahead of the euro, "it doesn't have all that much of an advantage" anymore, so the euro could replace the dollar as the reserve currency of choice. More to the point was the nature of dollar wobbliness in a June 2007 survey conducted among central bank currency reserve managers by UBS, the Swiss bank. Only 47 percent expected the dollar still to be the most important reserve currency in twenty-five years, whereas 23 per-cent expected an Asian currency, 21 percent opted for the euro, and 8 percent chose gold.[55] Perhaps the euro and an Asia-wide currency to-gether could push the dollar down to 40 percent of central bank re-serves by 2025; the euro would be hard-pressed to do so alone.

As for the nations that had earlier tied their currencies to a more vigorous dollar, experts assumed that some would reconsider those "pegs" in new and trying circumstances. Kuwait dropped its peg in mid-2007, unhappy about how the dollar's decline was fueling Kuwaiti inflation. By year's end, inflation continued, but the Kuwaiti dinar had strengthened. Speculation arose that Saudi Arabia and the smaller Persian Gulf states would follow suit, but was denied on several occasions. Then autumn saw Sultan bin Nasser al-Suwaidi, governor of the central bank of the United Arab Emirates, OPEC's third-largest producer, glumly acknowledge that the UAE had "reached a crossroads now with a further deterioration in the U.S dollar and expected further weakening of the U.S. economy."[56] The UAE, he said, in consultation with the other members of the Gulf Cooperation Council (GCC)—Saudi Arabia, Kuwait, Qatar, Bahrain, and Oman—would consider switching its thirty-year-old peg to the dollar to a peg to a broader basket of currencies.

Because of the region's great economic influence, any wide-ranging currency realignment in the Persian Gulf would be a watershed event. Currency changes have often figured prominently in major economic upheavals. University of California economist Brad Setser, a respected commentator, set the scene: "The Gulf currencies have already depreciated substantially in nominal terms against many of their trading partners. The GCC currencies, for example, have depreciated by over 40% against most European currencies over the last five years. Shifting a dollar peg now doesn't correct for the dollar's past fall. . . . That is why Standard Chartered—among others—is calling for a large revaluation of the GCC currencies, and a much broader reassessment of their currency regimes. I agree. . . . The discrepancy between the monetary policy that is right for the US and the monetary policy that is right for the Gulf and China is particularly obvious right now."[57]

To currency experts, the Persian Gulf pegs to the dollar and China's "crawling peg" had increasing aspects of self-entrapment. Pegs bound these nations to stimulative U.S. policies when their actual local need was to deal with overheating economies and rising local inflation. Standard Chartered Bank economist Stephen Green, in a report entitled *The Dollar Isn't Funny Anymore,* agreed that risks to Asia and the Gulf would rise without policy changes to manage dollar weakness.[58]

Such analyses drew attention to the so-far-invisible political and economic elephant in the room—the possibility that OPEC or individual oil-producing nations would stop pricing their oil in dollars. The debate was a surprisingly old one, going back to April 2002, when a senior

OPEC representative had raised the possibility. Discussion began again after the U.S. invasion of Iraq, when Muslim nations like Malaysia advocated switching to euros, and the European Union's energy commissioner, Loyola de Palacio, said that she could see the euro replacing the dollar as the principal currency for pricing oil.[59] On the other hand, the initial ease with which the United States took over Iraq in 2003 cooled some speculation because the U.S. occupiers quickly reversed the earlier changeover to euros by Saddam Hussein, restoring the dollar's former status. Saudi Arabia continued to trim its oil sales to the United States, and some OPEC nations reduced their central banks' dollar holdings. However, changing OPEC's oil pricing from dollars to euros was left alone.

On an individual-member basis, though, within a few years Iran and Venezuela had picked up where Saddam Hussein had left off. Both nations' leaders, Iranian president Ahmadinejad and Venezuelan president Chavez, barnstormed from continent to continent baiting the United States and its unpopular president. By mid-2007, Iran had reduced the dollar's share of its central bank reserves to just 20 percent, while the National Iranian Oil Company had demanded that oil buyers in Japan pay for their barrels in yen, not dollars.[60] By autumn, Nippon Oil and several other large Japanese refiners had agreed to do so.[61] Among Chinese firms, most importers from Iran had already shifted to payments in euros, including Zhuhai Zhenrong Trading, a government-run firm ranked as the world's top buyer of Iranian crude.[62] Although U.S. economic sanctions hurt Iranians, a combination of rising oil revenues and the profitability of shifting from dollars to euros and yen minimized what might otherwise have been greater home-front jeopardy for Ahmadinejad.

If anything, Chavez was a more active and strident American foe. Venezuela's central bank had moved some of its reserves into euros in 2006, and in late 2007, Chavez instructed Petróleos de Venezuela, the state-owned oil company, to shift its investment accounts from dollars to euros and several Asian currencies to reduce risk. He called the dollar a "bubble" currency. Days earlier, Energy and Oil Minister Rafael Ramirez had announced that Venezuela and China would collaborate in a multibillion-dollar plan to construct six refineries and a shipping company to turn Venezuela into one of China's top suppliers.[63] Two months later, Ramirez was the one to tell reporters that the OPEC summit meeting about to be held in Riyadh, Saudi Arabia, would consider proposals by Venezuela and Iran to shift OPEC's oil pricing from dollars to a basket of currencies.[64] The fuse was now lit.

However little the Saudis hosting the OPEC summit liked it, there was no muzzling Chavez or Ahmadinejad, and when the meeting had adjourned, the unexpected had taken place: the eleven producers had agreed to study the case for pricing oil sales in a basket of currencies rather than in dollars alone. As the dollar steadied in late 2007, pressures to revalue eased, at least for the time being. However, surveys at year's end showed that businesspeople in the six GCC nations expected some kind of revaluation against the dollar in 2008.

Outside the framework of OPEC, Russia had its own far-reaching—and now crystallizing—currency ambitions. In 2006, President Vladimir Putin, in his state of the nation address to parliament, said Russia should launch an oil exchange of its own to trade petroleum products and futures in Russian rubles. It was then decided in autumn 2007 that futures for REBCO—Russian Export Blend Crude Oil—would trade in a new commodity market under the aegis of the St. Petersburg Stock Exchange.[65] In light of government signals that Russian companies should trade through the exchange, Western analysts assumed that Putin's unspoken goal was to see 10 to 20 percent of world oil and gas trade—some of it in Europe—become ruble-denominated.

In the meantime, observers disagreed on which tactics—diversification of central bank reserves, depegging from the dollar, or repricing oil to be paid for with a broader currency mix—held the biggest threat for the greenback or for the overall interests of the United States. Several experts partially exonerated central bank diversification sales, blaming "real money" managers (pension funds, insurance companies, and corporate treasurers) or funds. Mansoor Mohi-uddin, head of foreign-exchange strategy at UBS, suggested that the main threats "come not from central banks but real money or sovereign wealth funds fueled by very high oil prices selling the dollar aggressively."[66] Without some kind of currency magic, the fireworks were just beginning.

PETRO-PERILS AND POSSIBILITIES

For such a short word, oil seems awfully long on consequences—the future of the U.S. energy supply, the value of the dollar and American purchasing power, global warming and the fate of the world's climate. Unfortunately, all three predicaments seem to be converging in a relatively proximate time frame. This was part of what I wrote about in my last book, published as 2006 opened. Part of why the "peril and politics" of these issues seemed tricky was because of time closing in. In several sections, I suggested five time lines and countdowns. The first involved oil and the possibility that "not only had American oil production peaked but global oil production outside of OPEC might be within five to ten years of doing so."[67] The second involved the concern of the U.S. oil giants over slackening discoveries, stagnant production, and the need for huge new reserves like those in Iraq.[68] The third set of jitters involved precarious debt levels and the dollar—"a handful of Americans, aware of the interplay of oil and currency flows, worried about OPEC's potential threat to the dollar," and as for debt, "some who observe financial and credit markets see a speculative credit bubble, a housing bubble and $4 trillion of U.S. international indebtedness triggering a crisis within much the same time frame."[69] With respect to the global-warming countdown (the fourth), "particularly concerned climatologists talk about the 2010s."[70]

The fifth time line involved the evolution of radical religion, the excitement over the millennium, and the important Republican constituency that saw biblical prophecy and Armageddon unfolding in the Middle East and "had its own rapture chronometers and apocalypse monitors reporting how many months, days, and hours remained."[71] The 2006 elections collapsed the hopes of the extreme preachers, especially in pivotal Ohio, where a religious Right enthusiast running for governor on the GOP ticket was beaten 60 percent to 40 percent, and the failure in Iraq cooled evangelical fascination with the Middle East. For now, barring another huge-scale terrorist attack, this watch can stand down.

No one, however, can stand down with respect to the other four sequences: the rising near-term possibility of peak oil; the inability of the big U.S. and British oil companies to do more than run in place while state-owned oil companies take charge; the converging financial triangulation of the vulnerable dollar, the housing bubble, and the debt and credit crisis; and the onrush of global climate dangers. A clash between energy-supply worries and climate-change fears seems nearer than ever. Two years ago, I said I couldn't "remember anything like this multiplicity of reasonably serious calculations and warnings. It is as if the United States, like the [carriage of the] poet Oliver Wendell Holmes, is about to lose all its wheels at once."[72] The religious wheels, luckily, seem better attached now, but the other problems are two years nearer and starting to close in. Certainly this is true of chapter 5's twin subjects: increasingly scarce and expensive oil, and the increasingly embattled dollar.

If some degree of peak oil is widely accepted among geologists, its open acceptance still lags elsewhere. Much of the energy establishment prefers to explain the current pressures by emphasizing soaring demand rather than declining output. Thus, acknowledgment by groups like the National Petroleum Council and the International Energy Agency that pressures could become acute by 2015 or even 2012 still sidesteps the debate over the various production-peak hypotheses. This evasion leaves at least several years to plan—or to continue to equivocate.

Peak advocates already tugging at the alarm bells have a strong case,

FIGURE 5.4
Could Peak Oil Now Be Past Tense?

World Crude Oil Production
Thousands of barrels per day

- In 78 months of global crude oil production (1997–June 2007), only 4 months saw crude output exceed 74 million barrels per day.
- April 2005   74,140
- May 2005   74,298*
- Dec. 2005   74,268
- July 2006   74,076

Source: EIA International Petroleum, September 2007, Simmons and Company.
* All-time record crude production (thus far)!

based on official production data from a wide variety of sources. Figure 5.4 shows the calculations and interpretations of one of those pessimists, Texas investment banker Matthew Simmons, author of *Twilight in the Desert* (2005), his attempt to look behind the facade of Saudi reassurances over both reserves and production.[73] Simmons, as noted, is convinced that world production of crude oil peaked in 2005. So is Texas oilman T. Boone Pickens, while Germany's semiofficial Energy Watch Group dates the peak to 2006. The Case Western University survey of global energy experts capsuled earlier found some three-quarters expecting a peak no later than 2010. The editor of *Petroleum Review* says 2011. Profiles of OPEC crude oil production between 2005 and 2007 do show a plateau, but the Saudis, pouring money into exploration and development, insist that output is already increasing. Another question, though, seems to be: output of exactly what?

Here we must turn to a second semantic issue—the extent to which energy terminology has begun to change in a highly significant way. Professor Michael Klare summarizes it this way: In May, the Energy Department "stopped talking about 'oil' in its projections of future petroleum availability and began speaking of 'liquids.' The global output of 'liquids,' the department indicated, would rise from 84 million barrels of oil equivalent (mboe) per day in 2005 to a projected 117.7 mboe in 2030—barely enough to satisfy anticipated world demand of 117.6 mboe."[74] Peak-oil stalwarts like Simmons have made the same point: *crude-oil* production is what has peaked, and the liquids—from tar sands, oil shale, biofuels, coal-to-liquids, and gas-to-liquids—must now be included to keep things on track. Perhaps they can do so; certainly they can for several years. But that is not the only issue. If crude production has peaked, with its many ramifications, that in itself conveys an enormously significant message.

It is not a happy message. The economics are precarious, the geopolitics is dangerous, but the domestic U.S. politics stand to be awful. If a loosely defined peak, instead of being ten to fifteen years away—which leaves some time for innovation—is actually close at hand, the inadequacies of latter-day American governance could become as important as any geological challenge or technological solution. Energy has become the prime arena of an early-twenty-first-century incapacity to which we must now turn—the politics of evasion.

SIX

The Politics of Evasion

Debt, Finance, and Oil

It has emerged as one of the more intriguing subplots of the Democratic presidential primary to date: watching the minuet under way among the candidates when it comes to issues involving Wall Street, the industry providing a disproportionate share of the financial support for four of the party's contenders [Clinton, Obama, Edwards, and Dodd].

—"The Trail: A Daily Diary of Campaign 2008,"
Washington Post, August 8, 2007

The energy IQ of our Congress is 55. If you think there's a problem in getting oil company CEOs to address the problem (peak oil), try convincing a politician to address it.

—Energy consultant Tom Petrie, 2007

Rarely in U.S. history has a president, especially a two-term president, been so unpopular at a time when the Congress, captured in the midterm elections by the opposition, is held in no greater regard. In such a case, the norm is for the two to fight, with one side gaining the edge. But that has not been true of George W. Bush and the Democratic Congress elected by running against him in 2006.

The two sides have gone after each other in a fashion, but more often they have simply talked past each other to their separate party constituencies, repeating familiar commitments to keep the true believers on each side somewhat more contented than the unimpressed independents—those who bulk so large in the 60 to 70 percent of voters convinced that the country is on the wrong track. Most officeholders on both sides seem to rest easier if everyone stays away from uncomfortable themes, even ones in the headlines, like costly U.S. overreach in the Middle East; the reckless expansion of private debt, as well as the federal budget deficit variety; the new economic (and political) dominance of the financial sector; and the mounting probability that the nation will have to choose between desirable energy supplies and global warming measures. After all, what you can sidestep today might go away tomorrow. True, the public is not impressed—"no guts" and "living in a dream world" are frequently heard descriptions of politicians. However, most big party contributors tend to donate based on established relationships and sympathies or on nonideological desire for access, not on philosophical engagement.

No parallel to the simultaneous public distaste for a president *and* his opposition Congress comes to mind, but then modern polling goes back only to the 1930s. Let me stipulate: despite the obvious salience of predicaments like oil, climate, the volatile dollar, run-amok debt and credit, the housing bubble, and imperial overinvolvement in the Middle East, I would be the last to say that any more than 5 to 10 percent of the electorate would favor a 2008 debate over American decline. Average voters do not. In these matters, history does not merely urge caution; it demands skepticism—and about *both* public attention and likely governmental achievement. A few pages hence, we will turn to how politics in earlier leading world economic powers was unable to deal with national decline. First, however, it is necessary to consider two other symptoms of weak, even failed U.S. politics: the entrenchment in Washington of a staggering array of interest groups, which has engendered a soulless political dynamic of perpetually raising and dispersing campaign funds; and the further, bipartisan trend toward what can only be called a politics of inheritance and dynasty.

MONEY POLITICS AND ENTRENCHED INTERESTS

The English-speaking peoples, when filling in new lands, had a certain naïveté about the power of entrenched interests and how these could be subdued by locating a political capital in a remote federal preserve far from the existing centers of (corrupting) urbanity and wealth. The capitals were thus located in backwaters at a time when geography trumped media (Washington, D.C., Ottawa, and Canberra); but today, those names have become shorthand in their respective electorates for (1) metropolitan areas with strikingly high (and recession-resistant) per capita incomes; and (2) hothouses of seething interest-group concentration where elected representatives, shedding whatever grassroots fealty they may once have possessed, often train to retire after ten or twelve years to triple or even quintuple their salaries by becoming lobbyists.

As an aspiring theorist four decades ago, I developed a belief that the realignments seen in U.S. presidential politics every generation or so had an (idealized) cleaning-up component. The victors, with a mandate of sorts from an annoyed electorate rearranged in new party coalitions, came to the capital city and purged it of the used-up elites of the crowd that had just been voted out. Some of that occurred after Thomas Jefferson's election in 1800, Andrew Jackson's in 1828, Abraham Lincoln's in 1860, and Franklin D. Roosevelt's in 1932.

At any rate, it didn't happen after the 1968 election, although Republicans held the White House for twenty of the next twenty-four years. And it certainly hasn't happened since. Congress and the White House have been in the hands of different parties two-thirds of the time since 1968, so the United States has progressed to a new kind of interest-group influence: the simultaneous entrenchment in Washington of the used-up, don't-want-to-go-back-to-Peoria elites of *both* major parties. This electoral duopoly is in turn protected by various state and federal election and campaign-finance laws that make it hard for new parties to take hold or flourish. It's not that there aren't differences between the parties; it's just that they are limited differences and ones often reflecting cultural polarization.

In the early 1980s, an American sociologist by the name of Mancur Olson published a book called *The Rise and Decline of Nations*.[1] Its thesis was that decline comes because after many years of success, a nation's political and economic arteries get so clogged with special-interest groups that its life-giving circulation of ideas and elites is impaired. Countries that are beaten in wars and occupied receive a new lease on life because their old interest-group structures get uprooted. He dwelled on Britain, the United States, Australia, and New Zealand, none successfully invaded or occupied over the last few centuries, as examples of impaired political and economic circulation. Olson misjudged the links between inflation and political failure, but his interest-group focus may have a partial utility in explaining political and governmental entrenchment and decline. If one goes back and looks at the capital cities of the four previous leading world economic powers, in later eras attempts were made to divide, abandon, or relocate them. Capitals in both Rome and Spain were relocated—in the fifth century A.D. the Roman capital moved to Ravenna, and Spain's for a while moved from Madrid to Valladolid. Concern about elites that were calcified and verging on permanence worried people then, too.

Parties and factions can also run out of creativity. British party politics was chaotic in the decades between the two world wars, which limited innovation and complicated any prospect of renewal. There is little more to be said for U.S. party politics in the early 2000s. The Republicans were discredited by eight years of failure in war, diplomacy, and fiscal honesty, and the Democrats won no laurel wreaths for effective opposition. Institutionally, the 180-year-old Democratic Party and the 150-year-old Republican Party have, over the last 40 years, uprooted themselves from what were their constituencies and allegiances as late as the 1960s. Gone on the Democratic side is the southern and western geography of opposition to northeastern financial elites under the aegis of Thomas Jefferson and Andrew Jackson, Franklin D. Roosevelt and Harry S. Truman. Instead, there is a new Democratic politics of new national elites—financial, high-tech, and communications. The Republicans, in turn, have lost many of their old, post–Civil War northern and western constituencies and biases, turning to the South and the interior West and a combination of old-line northern business elites and the Sun Belt power structure so ascendant in the late twentieth century. For both parties, the bottom line is usually the same: *the bottom line.* Fundraising. Money. Comparative rootlessness makes it easy.

Contemporary Washington abounds with nonprofit institutes, centers, and other think tanks dedicated to publishing periodic reports on which industries and individuals have spent what amounts to fund or lobby members of Congress, parties, and presidential aspirants. Beyond underscoring that finance has taken a long lead, this book will leave most of the detail to these organizations' Web sites and press releases.

If money talks, opposition to its influence also has a voice. But it is probably fair to say that never before have so many spent so much on so relatively few. And now, on a bipartisan basis—making it all the more worrisome—a new vehicle of entrenched interest has emerged: the political dynasty.

DYNASTY: A REPUBLICAN AND DEMOCRATIC TRAGEDY?

Let me make clear what the heading just above cannot. Yes, the development of ruling political dynasties is a Republican tragedy and conceivably a Democratic one. But in the larger sweep of U.S. political history, it is also a tragedy for our republic and for democracy itself. In 1801, Thomas Jefferson was correct when he said that we were all democrats, all republicans, in the small-*d* and small-*r* way. Nominally, that is still true. Realistically, perhaps not. Something has happened to the democratic and republican fidelities that underpinned America's origins. And it has happened with Democratic and Republican complicity.

Four years ago, my book *American Dynasty*, although focused on the reasons why a Bush family dynasty was a particularly unworthy idea, devoted several early chapters to a sociological and cultural explanation-cum-indictment. Important elements of middle- and upper-middle-class opinion in the United States and indeed around the world were turning away from egalitarian ideas toward a taste for bits and pieces of luxury, paintings of supposed grandparents, and office seekers who represented some (or a lot) of the same. In Europe, the change included a surge of support for putting former royal families back on thrones—successful in Bulgaria and Romania, with a small prospect in Italy. In the United States, it was reflected in a kind of Ralph Lauren faux-aristocratic taste— an upgrading of first-generation money through everything from genealogical fascination and membership in societies emphasizing ancestry, to participation (vicarious or actual) in expensive travel and leisure, upscale architecture and design, wine-cellaring, gourmet cuisine, and elite sports like polo and skeet shooting. By most measurements, economic stratification grew. In vocation after vocation, from manufacturing to Hollywood to newspaper publishing, lineage counted more and nepotism grew.

That certainly included politics. Celebrity was a boon to fund-raising, if not necessarily to competence. Among the 535 members of the 107th Congress, elected in 2000, 77 were relatives of senators, representatives, governors, judges, state legislators, or local officials. In Rhode Island, after Republican Lincoln Chafee was named to his father's U.S. Senate seat, Democratic congressman Patrick Kennedy made this joke at a local roast: "Now when I hear someone talk about a Rhode Island politician whose father was a senator and who got to Washington on his family name, used cocaine and wasn't very smart, I know there is only a 50-50 chance it's me."[2]

The election of George W. Bush to the presidency in 2000 was a milestone. Although the United States had seen dynasties before, there was a huge difference. John Quincy Adams was elected president in 1824, but that was twenty-four years after his father, John Adams, failed to win reelection, and the two Adamses belonged to different parties. Benjamin Harrison was elected president in 1888, forty-eight years after his grandfather, William Henry Harrison, but the two Harrisons also belonged to different parties. Franklin Roosevelt was elected in 1932, twenty-four years after the last election of his distant cousin Theodore Roosevelt. They, too, were in different parties. In short, nothing in these situations resembled a dynasty of direct succession.

The Kennedy brothers could have been the first. After Democratic president John Kennedy was assassinated in 1963, his brother Robert waited until 1968, ran for the Democratic president nomination that year, but of course was himself assassinated. Edward Kennedy, the youngest, waited until 1980, then ran in that year's primaries against weak incumbent Democratic president Jimmy Carter. Kennedy, with a flawed reputation, lost in a defeat that apparently ended the line. Possibly the legend they left helped to make the next dynasty more plausible, even though it turned out to be conservative and Republican.

When I criticized the Bush dynasty at length in 2004, that was unpopular with most Republicans and conservatives, who were still licking George W. Bush's cowboy boots. Many Democrats were also cautious, understanding that they, too, had their family lines. There were the Kennedys, of course. But Bush's opponent in 2000, Albert Gore, was himself the son of a U.S. senator. And Massachusetts senator

John Kerry, the 2004 Democratic nominee, had strong Kennedy ties. (In addition, Kerry had served as lieutenant governor to Massachusetts governor Michael Dukakis, the Democrat who had lost opposing George Bush senior in 1988.) It was also clear enough in 2004 that New York senator Hillary Clinton was preparing to seek the 2008 Democratic presidential nomination.

Since 1996, the Democratic and Republican presidential contenders and hopefuls have included a brace of other heirs: Malcolm S. "Steve" Forbes (third publisher by that name of *Forbes* magazine), Senator John McCain III (son and grandson of four-star admirals named John McCain), former governor Mitt Romney (son of former governor George Romney), Senator Evan Bayh (son of former senator Birch Bayh), and Senator Elizabeth Dole (wife of former senator and 1996 GOP presidential nominee Bob Dole). And of course Mrs. Clinton.

This, obviously, would put the *d* in dynastic. George W. Bush's becoming the next Republican president after his father could have been a fluke. Hillary Clinton's becoming the next Democratic president after her husband, however, would begin to suggest a new historical norm. Pundits could be expected to follow any Hillary Clinton inauguration with at least pro forma attention to which Bush—George W.'s brother Jeb or nephew George P.—could potentially roll the dice for the White House in 2012.

The other possibility, some Republicans thought, was that the dynasty aspect could turn out to be Hillary Clinton's undoing in 2008. George H. W. Bush had not seemed like a giant in 1992 when he went down to defeat with just 38 percent in a three-way race. Huge numbers of Republicans had been among those who abandoned him. There was little reason to assume that Bush family genes were the stuff of rule by inheritance—and they turned out not to be. Because the Republican version of dynasty had lost credibility after three terms, that did raise some jitters about Hillary Clinton. Many opinion molders shared some nervousness about the wisdom of completing a quarter century in which Bushes and Clintons succeeded each other in the White House.

With little remaining hesitancy about bruising George W. Bush's feelings, in 2008 some Republicans prepared to make the incumbent nepotist, in essence, a subliminal anti-Hillary symbol. Grover Norquist, a prominent conservative lobbyist and strategist, huddled with conservative legal scholars and came up with a triumph of chutzpah: a proposed constitutional amendment to prohibit nepotism in the presidential succession. Norquist suggested that "both Republicans and Democrats see this amendment as sending a message about the other party's abuse of familial power." In fact, many independents—also, many independent-minded Democrats and Republicans—saw a *simultaneous* abuse.[3]

Although Norquist and other Republicans suffered from convenient blindness and inattention in 2000 and 2004, George W. Bush from the first represented an extension of his family's biases and favoritisms. He also had family access to a huge GOP big-contributor base, was committed to Texas and oil-industry interests, and was willing to pander to the religious Right. He respected his family's long-standing alliances with the Saudis and other Persian Gulf elites, inherited the family's personal grudges against Saddam Hussein, and had an intense desire to attack Iraq. In winning back the White House, he also brought along employment commitments to a plethora of family political retainers, GOP lobbyists and fixers, loyal fund-raisers, and others, frequently above and beyond the usual duties and engagements of a presidential nominee. Most of the connections and commitments were visible from the start—the big-contributor contacts smoothed the way to nomination—although the younger Bush's intoxication by Iraq and the religious Right turned out to be particularly self-defeating.

Drawing up a similar list of the familial baggage of Hillary Clinton is in some ways easier but in other ways more difficult. In contrast to George W. Bush—during his father's four-year term from January 1989 to January 1993, the younger Bush was mostly back in Texas and not taken very seriously—Mrs. Clinton during her husband's eight years in office was very openly and closely involved in White House policymaking. No one could call her inexperienced or unskilled. On the contrary. Indeed, the most prominent analyses published in 2007—*A Woman in Charge* by Carl Bernstein and *Her Way* by *New York Times* reporters Jeff Gerth and Don Van Natta Jr.—elevated her role to being almost a co-president or suggested that the Clinton blueprint had always involved a commitment to his presidency first, followed by hers.[4] For better or worse, and despite her independent career after 2000, that legacy in itself hinted at a continuity between the policies and people of January 1993 to January 2001, and the probable policies and people should a Clinton again occupy the White House between January 2009 and January 2013. Dynasty became more of an issue in 2008 than it had been in 2000.

THE POLITICS OF LEADING WORLD ECONOMIC POWERS IN DECLINE: A STUDY IN TOO LITTLE, TOO LATE

Few people prominent in U.S. politics want to embrace anything like an agenda to manage and minimize a trajectory of U.S. global decline, however much they might recognize elements of that predicament in private conversation. That is smart—few could do well enough to profit from such candor and advocacy. For those members of Congress with alert electorates, such a venture would be like strolling across a minefield. But having no inhibiting position, I would underscore the vulnerability of the national administration in office between January 2009 and January 2013 to a convergence of U.S. problems outlined in this book: debt and credit, currency weakness, asset losses, oil supply, climate change, potential resource wars, and the costs of overinvolvement in the Middle East. No matter what their alleged mandate, any governing-party coalition is likely to come under huge strain.

Before offering a much-condensed history of how and why prior nations were unable, despite darkening clouds, to adequately prepare for or cope with decline, let me offer a hopeful context. Spain, Holland, and Britain are far more prosperous today than they were at the heights of their global reach. The severe trial for each came in the thirty to fifty years between each nation's peak as a world power and that country's eventual reemergence as a mere nation-state, for the most part shorn of imperial glory, pushed back from its globe-girdling military ambition and denied yesteryear's determining influence on world trade, finance, and currency.

What's useful about the category of leading world economic power is that it denies a limited primacy based on continental military rather than global economic sweep. Thus, continental military powers like France under Louis XIV or Napoleon, as well as twentieth-century Russia or Germany, lack the breadth to make the list. The limited downside is that most histories discuss the decline of Hapsburg Spain, the maritime Dutch Republic, or the British Empire from a perspective centered on what went wrong economically. Figuring out how and why the *politics* of those same periods came up short in reform or restoration attempts has been a subordinate or even missing theme.

Over the last few years, analogies to Rome have been appearing, a logical enough response to the short-lived U.S. imperial pretense and breast-beating and its subsequent international embarrassment. Former *Atlantic* editor Cullen Murphy's *Are We Rome?* saw Americans understanding we were not, while MarketWatch columnist Paul Farrell hit a small bull's-eye with the article "If We Are Rome, Wall Street's Our Coliseum."[5] Rome was certainly a leading world economic power, and eighteenth-century British historian Edward Gibbon titled his famous chronicle *The History of the Decline and Fall of the Roman Empire*. Rome's late-stage politics—the waning of the Senate and the rise of tyranny, corruption, and abuses of legalism—seems analogous to our own, but I am no expert, so these pages will omit them.

The more recent disabilities of politics and reformist agendas in Spain, the Netherlands, and Britain constitute our subject matter. The Roman precedent, overlapping Spain's own territory, unnerved a gloomy seventeenth-century Iberia. The Spanish precedent was very well known to the Dutch, and the precedents of the Hollanders were often discussed in Britain. Not a few influential Americans are well aware of how fast Britain fell from the global economic glory of 1914 to the ignominy of 1949. And not a few influential Britons are beginning to wonder if the United States might not follow suit.

By the early 1600s, four generations into imperium, the high-and-mightiness of Hapsburg Spain—which through the 1580s had dominated half of western Europe and most of South America, amassed great wealth from gold and silver, built Europe's biggest fleet and best-trained army, and displayed the hauteur of being God's chosen nation—had begun to give way to *desengaño* (disenchantment) and worry about *declinación* (decline). The reformist lament was that Spain had precious metals by the galleon-load, but no real agricultural or producer economy to speak of. The country had hardly any middle class but was divided between poor people and the idle rich. And even the Castilian parliament protested that foreign financiers were siphoning off much of the money while debt had become a culture. Reformers also thought that the Catholic Church had too much wealth and patronage.[6] Conceivably, they gloomed, Spain's future had already been lost. Rome had also controlled half of Europe, much of the Mediterranean, and part of North Africa, yet it had declined.[7] To the more puritanical, Madrid, the capital, was beginning to be as luxury-minded and decadent as the Rome of Nero or Commodus.

In 1618, the fall of a weak Spanish first minister led to a burst of activism, and several years later, many of the arguments put into books and documents by reform-minded "projectors" or *arbitristas* were taken up by the king's new first minister, Don Gaspar de Guzmán, count-duke of Olivares. For some two decades, he promoted reforms—sometimes contradictory—in economic policy, domestic affairs, and foreign policy, broadly intended to restore Spain's sixteenth-century greatness.[8] Prominent among them were attempts to regain military *reputación* in Europe, to establish a so-called Union of Arms—an arrangement to better share the cost of military upkeep—and to reform both taxation and rentier habits of living off bond interest. Others sought to reform morals and to reduce the entrenchment in Madrid of the Church, high-living nobles, and bureaucrats.

Many of these reforms were blocked. The ones officially promulgated, like dress codes and the closing of brothels, had little effect. The interests of the Church, the nobility, and the bureaucracy prevailed. When the expensive and financially draining Thirty Years' War ended in 1648, Spain's years in the sun were over.

For much of the sixteenth century, the United Provinces of the Netherlands, as they styled themselves, had been Hapsburg territories under the rule of Spain. Even as they secured their independence and then consolidated world maritime supremacy during the seventeenth

century, awareness of Spain's decline was part of their history. As early
as 1670, despite the Dutch Republic's "golden age" riches and its huge
fleet and maritime outposts from Japan and South Africa to India and
Brazil, some observers began to worry about how so many great merchants now lived on interest income and rents, rather than actively
continuing earlier commercial and maritime activities.[9] Then from 1688
to 1713, the Netherlands fought a series of wars—in retrospect, more
beneficial to the future of their ally England, newly ruled by a king who
was also a Dutch prince—that wound up costing the Hollanders, who
were subordinate in war strategy, vital trade and trade routes while
quintupling the Dutch debt. By the 1730s, it was reasonably clear that
the Dutch Republic was starting to decline, and by the 1750s, as current-
day historians like Simon Schama and Jonathan Israel have detailed
with such thoroughness, there was malaise in the air, a sense of too
much dependence on finance, a renewed fascination with the late-
sixteenth-century Dutch revolt against Spain, and a yearning to somehow re-create the lost golden age.[10]

So was reform pursued? Was financialization curbed? Did Dutch
politics rise to the occasion? A quick answer is: no, no, and no. To use
the phrase currently employed by pollsters, most Dutchmen agreed that
the country had lost its way and was on the wrong track. The trouble
was the deepening psychological divide between the main Dutch political factions of the 1750s through the 1780s: the Orangists, loyal to the
Dutch princely house and to the old militant Reformed Church; and the
Patriots, religiously more ecumenical in reaching out to Dutch Catholics, Jews, and Lutherans, and more at one with the revolution brewing
in France. Both sides attacked corruption, invoked popular rule and past
greatness, and deplored one elite or another, but cultural and religious
cleavages kept them apart. By the late 1770s and 1780s, the Orangists
looked more to Britain, while the Patriots favored the colonists in the
American Revolution and then leaned in the French revolutionaries'
direction by the time Parisian mobs overran the Bastille.[11]

Here we can usefully consider another way that the Dutch attempted to stem their decline—in the arena of effective revenue politics
and management—because Spain had faced a similar problem (and

centuries later, so would Britain and the United States). In administrative terms and divisions, the Hapsburg union of Iberia, parts of Italy and Flanders, and the United Provinces of the Netherlands were both somewhat loose federations. They were conjoined by early nationalism and momentum, but poorly positioned to raise revenues as times became more difficult. The Spain of 1550, it must be remembered, was a stunning study in territorial amalgamation. In 1492, the same year that Columbus sailed to the New World, Spain completed a grueling, bloody, and bitter three-century reconquest of the Iberian Peninsula from the Moors—from Islam. Castile was thereby joined not only with León and Aragon, but with Valencia, Catalonia, and Granada (Portugal would be added later in the sixteenth century). In 1516, Spanish king Ferdinand died, and eventually a sprawling multinational Hapsburg inheritance put Italy, parts of Austria and Germany, Burgundy, and the Low Countries under the rule of the new king of Spain, Charles I, who also became Holy Roman Emperor.

All of a sudden, a Castile-centered Spain, soon to be vastly enriched by treasure ships, found itself in a dynastic package with the most sophisticated citadels of the Renaissance—Italy, Rhenish Germany, and Flanders. By the early seventeenth century, the imperial boundaries had changed, but the legal and jurisdictional problems long pushed aside had become acute. Castile, the core of Spain, had the power but also bore a disproportionate share of the imperial financial burden, and was beginning to stagger under it. Here, too, the chief ministers of the king who ruled both Castile and Spain couldn't get the other parts of Spain nominally within their jurisdiction to assume portions of the expense that Castile, by 1620 or 1640, could no longer handle.[12]

The Dutch—and keep in mind their polity's full name: the United Provinces of the Netherlands—had a similar problem in the 1720s and thereafter because the religious, commercial, and revolutionary nationalist electricity that united the seven provinces in 1580 and still in 1640 had given way in the eighteenth century to new currents of depopulation, shrinking enterprise, and dissatisfaction. The largest province, Holland (including Amsterdam), had more of the wealth than before, but refused to accept an increase in its share of taxes based on much earlier calculations.[13] The upshot, despite concentrated private wealth, was too little Dutch national revenue. We will return shortly to the problems in federalism and burden sharing that ultimately faced the United Kingdom of Great Britain and Ireland and the United States of America.

For the moment, though, it's back to the political disabilities that crippled British ability to head off the decline so apparent between 1914 and 1949. These include, but also go beyond, the effects of two disruptive and expensive world wars. As early as the 1860s, prominent Englishmen held up the Dutch maritime and financial example as a caution. Bestselling books of the 1890s included tomes warning of the economic challenges from the United States and Germany. Then the fierce debate in the early 1900s over trade policy in Parliament and the press made clear to serious observers that Britain had lost her huge mid-nineteenth-century economic and manufacturing lead and was facing at least "the experience of relative decline," to quote one well-regarded analysis.[14] From yet another perspective, three internal crises—deep worker unrest, women's suffrage, and a potential army mutiny over Irish home rule—were tearing Britain apart in the summer of 1914 before everything was subordinated by the outbreak of war.

My own view is that a fair part of what blocked British reform between 1914 and 1939 was a politics—and crumbling party system—that reflected or magnified many of these other problems and precluded any far-reaching policy transformation. For Americans, this idea is especially worth pursuing because of the partial analogies to the entrenchments and incapacities in contemporary Washington.

As late as 1882, the musical team of Gilbert and Sullivan had one of their characters in *Iolanthe* explain how every British child was born either "a little Liberal or a little Conservative." By 1910, however, some offspring were being born little Labourites, and the Liberal Party, with roots going back to 1832 and even 1688, was seen by some as being in peril. The inability of the incumbent Liberal government to deal with the military and strategic challenges of World War I as it unfolded soon obliged party members in Parliament to enter a wartime "National coalition" with the Conservatives, whose greater forcefulness soon made them ascendant, although a nominal Liberal, Lloyd George, served as prime minister. He and other coalition leaders called and won a quickie postwar "Khaki election" in 1918, and the coalition, now lopsidedly Conservative in makeup, continued in power through 1922.

To find a comparably confused and disordered period in U.S. party politics, one has to go back to the 1850s, another era famous for being unable to achieve long-term national solutions. But as Britain's Liberal-Conservative party system dissolved, national elections between 1922 and 1935 produced electoral chaos, two different coalition governments, uninspired thinking, and a series of second-rate prime ministers—Bonar Law, Ramsay MacDonald, Stanley Baldwin, and Neville Chamberlain, whose names could probably not be sequentially identified today by more than one British university graduate out of ten. Devoting any more space to these elections might only add to the confusion, so let me use 1924 for a conclusion. So woolly was the labeling that in addition to Conservatives, Liberals, and Labourites, several MPs migrating between parties ran as "Constitutionalists," Winston Churchill being the best known.[15] No sound blueprint for national renewal could ever have chopped its way through this between-the-wars muddle. Present-day Americans intrigued by talk of a bipartisan coalition or "national unity government" in Washington should consider this earlier record in London.

The other, less obvious price paid by twentieth-century Britain had to do with—shades of Spain and Holland—the problem of inadequate revenues and proposed (and rejected) burden sharing. Federalism was already a problem—the Welsh wanted to disestablish the English Church and the Irish wanted to disestablish English rule. As Britain entered the new century, some officials well aware of the wealth and potential of Canada, Australia, New Zealand, and South Africa doubted that Britain could prevail in the many contests unfolding without greater access to the revenue potential of these dominions and the rest of the empire. So a conference was held in London in 1902, keynoted by an emotional plea from Colonial Secretary Joseph Chamberlain. "The Weary Titan staggers under the too vast orb of its fate," he lamented. "We have borne the burden for many years. We think it is time that our children should assist us to support it." Charts were prepared to make the point.[16] Some help was given, but much less than the government had hoped. Once again, burden sharing was not a salable concept.

Twenty-first-century Americans, too, face deepening economic problems of federalism and imperial burden sharing. In 1973, Richard Nixon had implemented so-called revenue sharing through which $30 billion was returned to the states to use as they saw fit. But by the first decade of the new century, the states were insatiable in their demands for Washington to pick up huge medical care costs, which soon bulked large in the forecasts for ballooning federal budget deficits in the 2010s and 2020s.

International burden-sharing dimensions, vaguer, were also becoming troublesome. Since the 1970s, the United States had pursued a series of implicit burden-sharing arrangements. As we have seen, one with the Saudis and OPEC provided that oil would be priced in dollars and that the Persian Gulf producers would recycle their profits by investing in U.S. government bonds and other assets. A second, even more informal, had foreign nations aided or protected militarily by the United States—Japan, Korea, and Taiwan—indirectly share those costs by buying and holding huge quantities of U.S. treasury and agency debt in their reserves and otherwise supporting the dollar. In still another, even less formal arrangement nicknamed "Bretton Woods II" in 2003, China and other high-saving nations that exported vast quantities of goods to the United States, unofficially collaborated by holding large central bank balances in U.S. treasury debt to support the dollar. But as we will see in chapter 7, that unofficial burden sharing is now in doubt, politically and financially. A lot of old international relationships are up in the air.

THE RISE OF FINANCE IN U.S. POLITICS AND GOVERNANCE

A decade and a half has passed since Robert Rubin, a Wall Streeter about to become treasury secretary, theorized that if the Democrats became effective money managers, they could become the preferred national party of a politically centrist financial sector. Believed and implemented by Bill Clinton, this realignment possibility fell off the charts between

2001 and 2004, a period dominated by the politics of terrorism and Iraq. But it began to reappear in 2005 and 2006 as Democratic election prospects brightened. By some lights, Democrats believe their objective is back on track. The financial sector, once a Republican bastion, is the Democratic Party's biggest contributor. Moreover, Blue America—the Democratic-leaning Northeast, Great Lakes, and Pacific Coast regions—substantially overlaps with the urban citadels of U.S. finance and money management: New York, Boston, Philadelphia, Chicago, San Francisco, and Los Angeles. This is no accident of geography.

Indeed, during the boom years of the late-nineteenth-century Gilded Age and the Roaring Twenties, Democrats from New York and its environs were often Wall Street supporters and found on the conservative side of intraparty politics. Conservative New York Democrat Grover Cleveland, elected president in 1884 and again in 1892, was a good example. During the 1920s, two of the Democratic presidential nominees—John W. Davis and Alfred E. Smith—had New York bases (Davis was a Wall Street lawyer), and by 1936 conservative aspects of their politics put them so much at odds with the New Deal that they opposed Franklin D. Roosevelt's reelection. What the Democrats have *not* managed before, however, is a presidential majority coalition based in New York and the other money-center states—a coalition in which a working majority of financial leaders and donors are Democrats or independents moving away from prior Republican adherence.

The political geography is clear enough. Democratic presidential candidates carried all five money-center states in each of the four presidential elections between 1992 and 2004, and in 2008 nine of those states' ten incumbent U.S. senators were Democrats. Further confirmation comes from the increasingly Democratic tilt of financial-sector political contributions. In 2004, the cutting-edge hedge-fund industry gave 71 percent of its outlays to Democrats, with New York senator Charles Schumer the leading beneficiary.[17] Then in 2006, the Private Equity Council gave 69 percent of its campaign largesse to Democrats, while the hedge funds favored the Democrats by some three to one. As another national campaign got under way in 2007, with the Democrats widely expected to win, the early contributions from hedge funds and private-equity firms broke sharply their way. Hedge-fund employees' contributions to the Senate Democratic Campaign Committee out-numbered those to its Republican rival by roughly nine to one, while Democrats raked in four-fifths of the money in House races.[18] Democratic presidential hopefuls were not far behind.

In New York, besides the pro-Democratic top management at Citigroup (Sandy Weill and Robert Rubin), JPMorgan Chase (Jamie Dimon and Michael Cavanaugh), and UBS Americas (Robert Wolf), support for Hillary Clinton was forthcoming from old-line Republicans like John Mack of Morgan Stanley, Lehman Brothers chairman Richard Fuld, and former American Express chairman James Robinson. These men and their companies were disillusioned with George W. Bush. In fact, the entire sector's comfort level with the Democrats had grown during the late nineties. Some of this stemmed from Bill Clinton's embrace of the bull market and participation in Wall Street's summer circuits on Martha's Vineyard and in the Hamptons; further satisfaction came from Rubin's handling of global financial crises and from White House support of the sector's much-desired repeal of the Glass-Steagall Act, the 1930s legislation that blocked common ownership of banks, investment firms, and insurance companies. Besides Glass-Steagall repeal, other 1990s deregulation and court holdings permitted new holding companies, loosened structure in the telecommunications and energy industries, and unleashed credit card operators. This led to booms not just in stocks but in mergers and acquisitions, to massive financial and buyout-related debt issuance, and to aggressive marketing and interest-rate practices by credit card issuers. For expansionist financiers, it was Shangri-la.

The new profinance Democrats were not the same as the older profinance Republicans. They were more engaging, less out of the Union League of Philadelphia or 1950s *New Yorker* cartoons. Behind the scenes, some might contentedly bail out endangered bondholders, put impoverished nations through the behavioral wringer of the International Monetary Fund, or operate consumer finance units that bilked a low-income clientele. But in their public personas, most took a different tack. In deference to their multiple Democratic coalition-mates, they donated to the NAACP; joined the boards of environmental groups; embraced technology, education, free trade, and globalization; and worried about the growing international gap between the rich and the poor as well as the gap in the United States. There was also, as we have seen, another, broader enabler: the new popular acceptance of finance.

As Daniel Gross hypothesized in *Bull Run: Wall Street, the Democrats, and the New Politics of Personal Finance* (2000), a new "democratization of money"—the convergence of pension fund power, broad public ownership of mutual funds, and supposed Clinton administration talent had turned the mass of individual investors into the new "monied interests," displacing the *New Yorker* cartoon figures as the principal beneficiaries of the stock market. Thus, he argued, "the Democrats can be the party of Wall Street and Main Street, of the rich and the poor," while the Republicans paint themselves into a southern and culturally non-cosmopolitan corner.[19] Although the new-economy utopian pretenses generally disappeared after the 2000–2002 stock market crash, major legacies of this new Democratic economic contemplation remained relevant in 2008.

A Washington-to-Boston geography, with a New Jersey–New York–Connecticut center of gravity, grew even more vivid. Besides the Clintons' taking on New York coloration, Jon Corzine, the former co-chairman of Goldman Sachs, became the Democratic governor of New Jersey. Connecticut's favorite-son candidate for the Democratic presidential nomination, Christopher Dodd, was also the chairman of the Senate Banking Committee. Unsurprisingly, he has been well financed by the hedge funds thronging suburban Greenwich. Like New York's Schumer, Dodd stands out as a defender of the hedge fund and private equity interests. The old Republican loyalties of Wall Street, being further eroded on all sides by new meritocratic, quantitative, technological, and international employee origins, seem unlikely to reassert themselves, especially with the national GOP committing itself to southern and hinterland conservatism.

Indeed, GOP disenchantment with the sector could increase without a pro-finance Republican national administration. The appeal of two outsider GOP presidential candidates in the early 2008 primaries and caucuses—former Arkansas governor Mike Huckabee, who criticized Wall Street, and Texas congressman Ron Paul, who advocated the abolition of the Federal Reserve Board—hinted that southern and western Republicans could be expected to be less supportive of New York finance and multinational corporations (especially if their leaders were trending Democratic). Some analysts saw potential disarray in the role of Huckabee, a Southern Baptist minister, in mobilizing now-Republican evangelicals and fundamentalists on behalf of populist economic themes that hearkened back to what their forebears, then Democrats, had embraced in the years of William Jennings Bryan and Franklin D. Roosevelt. The somewhat shaky underlying coalition of cultural and economic conservatives could be at risk.

Which brings us to the question of how the party taking the White House in 2008 can manage the 2009 reform and reorientation of a culpable financial sector in the wake of a housing downturn unlikely to yet have hit bottom. If there is little reason to suppose that another Republican administration would know where to turn, there is not much more for expecting tough policymaking—to say nothing of two-fisted reregulation—from a Democratic Party bitterly condemned by many of its own reformers in 2007 for lacking even a whisper of steadfastness. Consider the words of former Democratic secretary of labor Robert Reich: "You might think that Democrats would do something about the anomaly in the tax code that treats the earnings of private equity and hedge fund managers as capital gains rather than ordinary income, and thereby taxes them at 15 percent—lower than the tax rate faced by many middle-class Americans. But Senate Democrats recently backed off a proposal to do just that. Why? It turns out that Dems are getting more campaign contributions these days from hedge fund and private equity partners than Republicans are getting. They don't want to bite the hands that feed."[20]

Any restoration of the Clinton dynasty to the White House would add a further layer of complication. The Clintons and former treasury secretary Rubin, whose authorship has been attached to 1995–99 economic policy ("Rubinomics"), held themselves out in 2007 and 2008 as having presided over a unique and renewable politics of prosperity, even though the technology and stock market bubble popped messily in the spring of 2000, more than half a year before Clinton retired. On leaving Washington, Mr. and Mrs. Clinton made a beeline for New

York, where the just-elected Democratic senator courted her new financial constituency. The former president himself made speech after speech to financial institutions, and signed up as a consultant to the family of funds run by the Yucaipa Companies, a private equity firm owned by one of his friends, billionaire Ronald Burkle.[21] Daughter Chelsea eventually went to work for Avenue Capital Group, a hedge fund whose owner, Marc Lasry, was a major Clinton contributor.

Not that the other Democratic presidential contenders were different. A tabulation of political contributions by employees of the top ten U.S. investment firms during the second quarter of 2007 showed over $1.4 million going to the Democrats versus $900,000 to Republicans Giuliani, Romney, McCain, and the rest.[22] Senator Barack Obama of Illinois led Hillary Clinton, who placed second. Former senator John Edwards, who placed third, had been a consultant to the hedge fund Fortress Investment Group. Obama was heavily funded by Chicago hedge fund billionaire Kenneth C. Griffin of Citadel Investment Group, and the more or less pro forma 2008 presidential candidacy of Connecticut senator Dodd had drawn half of its early funding from Greenwich-based SAC Capital Partners.[23]

In Republican and Democratic national politics, the notion of a breath of fresh air has become almost a contradiction in terms. One could argue that in place of the vital center praised by historian Arthur Schlesinger a century ago, the changes of the last several decades have pushed us toward a venal center.

REPUBLICANS, DEMOCRATS, AND HARD CHOICES BETWEEN ENERGY AND THE ENVIRONMENT

In 2007, Christopher Skrebowski, editor of the *Petroleum Review,* made an intriguing prediction. Global oil production would reach its global peak about two years after the inauguration of the next U.S. president. He didn't explain his early-2011 target date that way, but my doing so makes a worthwhile point. The successors to George W. Bush are unlikely to be able to repeat his nonchalance about the need for a national energy strategy. Indeed, his languor has disappointed erstwhile supporters.

Texas investment banker Matthew Simmons, a Republican who served on Vice President Richard Cheney's top-priority energy task force in 2001, voiced deep regret in 2005: "As far as I know, there is not a single contingency plan in place or currently being written by any of the think tanks of the world that sets out a model illustrating how the world can continue to function smoothly once it is clear that Saudi Arabian oil has peaked. In a nutshell, it is this total lack of any 'alternative scenario thinking' that makes this unavoidable event so alarming."[24]

Flynt Leverett, a former aide on Bush's National Security Council who left for the New America Foundation, wrote in 2006 that "U.S. foreign policy is ill-suited to cope with the challenges to American leadership flowing from the new petropolitics. Current policy does not take energy security seriously as a foreign policy issue or prioritize energy security in relation to other goals."[25]

In late 2007, two major oil company chief executives, James Mulva of ConocoPhillips and Clarence Cazalot of Marathon Oil, endorsed the need for a decisive federal energy strategy. Mulva told *BusinessWeek* editors that "we don't have a national energy policy," while rival nations are amassing power. "The Chinese have a very coordinated strategy that allows them to support economic growth."[26] In a demonstration of how the industry's planning sense far exceeds that of the Bush White House, Mulva emphasized four priorities: developing new energy sources, stepped-up federal investment in energy technology, conservation, and federal regulation of carbon emissions.

Possibly the invasion of Iraq was the Bush administration's principal, albeit unacknowledged, oil strategy. If so, it has fallen radically short. Its poor implementation and the botched, drawn-out U.S. occupation angered OPEC and most individual producing nations instead of eliminating their oil production and currency leverage. Far from increasing Iraqi output, the invasion decreased local production because of the insurgency. Overall, U.S. miscalculation and mismanagement helped prices to soar and the dollar to weaken, jeopardizing the unofficial "oil standard," while U.S. embarrassment and embroilment in the Middle East soured allies and encouraged the scheming of rivals from Tehran and Caracas to Moscow and Beijing. It remains possible that four decades of U.S. hubris, periodic military intervention, and overreach in the Middle East will be perceived as playing the same role for Washington as did the Thirty Years' War (1618–48) for Madrid, the 1688–1713 wars for Holland, and two successive world wars for Britain.

If a continuing U.S. presence in Iraq produces no upsurge in Iraqi oil output during the critical 2009–12 period, the negative effects just listed should continue to dominate any evaluation of the war's impact on energy costs and related financial and currency matters. However, considering the alternative chronologies predicted for peak oil—from "already happened" to a still imminent 2010 or 2011, or, under the industry's worst-case scenarios, trouble between 2012 and 2015—coping with a faster-than-expected peak could produce shockwaves. The Republicans, who have energy constituencies to please, nevertheless have prepared no emergency blueprints. And on the Democratic side, the pre-2008 emphasis on environmental issues and constituencies has locked in a politics focused on global warming and greening, not peak oil.

True, a few states that have been voting Democratic for president have substantial energy production within their boundaries—such as California (oil) and Illinois (coal). But even in those states, nonenergy industries vastly outweigh these activities. Absent an energy supply crisis, Democratic election strategies and blueprints for national governance will continue to emphasize energy consumers and environmental constituencies. On the Web site HillaryClinton.com, the one-and-a-half-page outline of her popular energy program, "Powering America's Future: New Energy, New Jobs," never uses the word "security" or the phrase "energy security." By contrast, the word "green" is used ten times. Proposals include a "green building industry," $20 billion in "green vehicle bonds," promised new "green collar jobs," and a new "Connie Mae" agency to help low- and middle-income families "to buy green homes and invest in green home improvements."[27] Moreover, going green isn't just an energy nuance; it's a potential opportunity for national uplift and economic mobilization (including five million jobs) on the heroic scale of World War II.

Barack Obama, from Illinois, where coal abounds, was broadsided by environmentalists in mid-2007 for supporting legislation to promote coal-to-liquid-fuel efforts. Little attention was paid to Obama supporters' explanation that "Illinois basin coal has more untapped energy potential than the oil reserves of Saudi Arabia and Kuwait combined."[28] In Congress, the Senate majority leader, Harry Reid of Nevada, speaking against the construction of three proposed major coal-fired power plants back home, explained with a political correctness more usual in Vermont: "I want to help Nevada become the national leader in renewable energy and energy independence. We have vast wind, solar and geothermal resources and we're wasting energy every day we're not tapping into those free, clean, and reliable power sources. . . . As proposed, these coal plants are old news, the way of the increasingly distant past."[29] In many circles, nuclear power is even less acceptable.

If the Democratic national coalition of the early twenty-first century is overbalanced toward financial-sector centers and contributors, in terms of striking an overall national energy policy balance, that coalition is overbalanced against energy-industry production centers, viewpoints, and expertise. In terms of voter sentiment, however, polls show that the Democrats have the cutting edge of the public-opinion blade. With respect to hits on the Internet, one June 2007 sampling found global warming pulling far, far ahead of peak oil, although this came just before the surge in conferences where peak oil was discussed.[30]

To be sure, there is some overlap between ardent believers in peak oil and persons worried about emissions, global warming, and a dangerous climatic tipping point. Many in both camps agree on the need to cut back on the 50 percent of U.S. oil consumption that is required to gas up fuel-guzzling automobiles. But there's much less concurrence on new fuel sources—oil sands, coal-to-liquids, nuclear power, and the like. If one of the two energy-related showdowns can be shown as holding off until 2030 while the other lay just ahead, priorities could develop. But if one worries about both, in proximate but unknowable time frames, the pressures and potential politics get tough. Assuming that both concerns have merit, but that there is some leeway, perhaps 2016–20 could see a double dimension: rising seas and small islands going under, oil-linked civil wars in Africa, $8.75-a-gallon gasoline in California, abandoned housing in U.S. towns where commuting is no longer affordable. However, if the true believers are right about problems being nearer at hand, then the tension could intensify between

2012 and 2016. Or if the most panicked experts are correct, then the regime taking over Washington in 2009 will face the crisis.

Electorally, of course, these scenarios would spotlight three different U.S. administrations. The time frame nearest at hand would probably see the greatest political tension and combat because national preparation would have been minimal. That minimalist description certainly applies to the eight Republican years ending in 2008, during which global warming was denied, market forces and utopias were exalted, sober energy realpolitik was ignored, weapons-of-mass-destruction and nuclear threats in Iraq and Iran were grossly exaggerated to support actual or possible energy-related invasions, and world opinion was offended. Over the last few decades, however, political ineptitude and misjudgment have been bipartisan phenomena. Energy, debt, and currency realpolitik has been missing among the Democrats, too, lost in their fund-raising prowess and heavy petting with hedge funds; naïveté about the pseudo-greening of Chinese, Indian, and Brazilian economic growth, and troubling faith in their own party's brand of job growth; and utopianomics: Put on your green collars, Americans, and if your parents or grandparents supported the New Deal way back when, have we got a Green Deal for you now!

SEVEN

The Global Crisis
of American Capitalism

As international investors wake up to the relative weakening of America's economic power, they will surely question why they hold the bulk of their wealth in dollars. . . . The dollar's decline already amounts to the biggest default in history, having already wiped far more off the value of foreigners' assets than any emerging market has ever done.

—*Economist*, December 2007

"If We Are Rome, Wall Street's Our Coliseum"

—Paul Farrell, MarketWatch, August 2007

Well, that was quick. In 2003, the idea of empire became fashionable in Washington, D.C. But the flirtation has lasted a little more than three years. The imperial eagles are being put back in the cupboard.

—Gideon Rachman, *Financial Times*, November 2007

Looking back a decade, we can now understand that a perverse incarnation of millennial utopianism crested in a form that critics have since labeled "market triumphalism"—the belief that history was "ending" because near perfection had been achieved through the enthronement of English-speaking democratic capitalism. Smugness paraded across a bipartisan spectrum.

Newt Gingrich, the Speaker of the U.S. House of Representatives, envisioned a politics in which major questions could be resolved by asking "our major multinational corporations for advice." Technology guru George Gilder theologized that "it is the entrepreneurs who know the rules of the world and the laws of God." Thomas Friedman, the *New York Times* columnist, enthused, "International finance has turned the world into a parliamentary system" that allows initiates "to vote every hour, every day through their mutual funds, their pension funds, their brokers." Even historian Francis Fukuyama, normally sober, burbled that "liberal democracy combined with open market economics has become the only model a state could follow."[1]

The Holy Grail had rarely been pursued with more passion than market-bewitched academicians brought to seeking financial capitalism's roots in furthest antiquity. Dissatisfied that Max Weber and others had pursued the economic origins of the market back only to the era of Calvin and Luther, zealots figuratively competed to find its antecedents in the hills around Lascaux or the Great Rift Valley. To believers, the all-knowing, all-comprehending market hailed by initiates had always been incipient, always evolving toward some ultimate moment when the Dow Jones Industrial Average would cross 10,000 and breathless quantitative strategists at Morgan Stanley (or wherever) would imagine the first synthetic collateralized debt obligation. Millennial utopianism was happy to oblige.

The muse of history, though, had contrarian inclinations. In unfashionable places like authoritarian Singapore, post-Communist Russia, and still-Communist China, state capitalists angry with American and International Monetary Fund hauteur during the 1997–98 financial crises embraced mercantilist principles as they quietly started to accumulate huge foreign-currency reserves. These would ultimately run into the trillions of dollars and spill over to fill the arsenals of sovereign wealth funds. From Venezuela to the East Indies, countries and colonies that had once bowed to Standard Oil or Royal Dutch Shell purred as state-owned oil companies controlling 80 percent of world petroleum reserves began to socialize global oil production. Wave good-bye to Venezuela, Exxon; stiff upper lip about Sakhalin, Shell. Some of the state oil companies even preferred to negotiate with one another and skip the marketplace. In China, with its $1.4 trillion holdings, comments on how Beijing might or might not view the anemic U.S. currency sometimes came from officials of leading Communist Party bodies.[2] Something went wrong in the 1990s after "the fall of Communism"; somebody forgot to explain the New World Order to the Russians and the Chinese.

Instead, Anglo-Saxon speculative capitalism—in a grand misreading that may yet turn out to match the cupidity of the French Bourbons in 1789—decided to celebrate "the end of history" and the perceived vacuum of serious economic rivalry by staging the largest-ever orgy of debt and credit. If history had ended, thereby assuring the triumphal invulnerability of asset-backed securities and structured investment vehicles, well, then, let 'em roll. Of course, we now know that history had not ended; the muse had merely started learning Mandarin, Hindi, and Arabic, rereading Karl Polanyi and Hyman Minsky, and pondering what might befall a leading world economic power that so worshipped its markets as to entrust them to hedge funds, bad quantitative mathematics, and banks like Citigroup. As the economists at Standard Chartered Bank quoted in chapter 5 wrote about the dollar in late 2007, it "isn't funny anymore."

THE CENTURY OF THE SIX-PACK

Back in the late 1980s, the widespread notion that a surging Japan would become the next global hegemon by displacing the United States turned out to be mistaken thinking. Present-day analysts offer a caveat that the prominence of Chinese companies in current-day global top-ten lists may not be any more predictive. In any event, they say, a Chinese displacement of the United States is not just around the bend.

No, certainly not just around the bend. But the pivotal contrast between Asia in 2008 and Asia in 1988 is this: two decades ago, the power of Asia beyond Japan still did not bulk very large. China had only a few tall buildings, and the India of that day had more water buffalo and camels on the roads than private vehicles. The Soviet Union, half of which was Asian, was falling apart. The precursors of the Taliban were pro-American, and Iran and Iraq had just spent eight years at war with each other. The economies of Southeast Asia, although shooting up in size, remained untested adolescents. Circumstances in the rest of Asia did not support the emergence of Japan as the leading world economic power.

Today's transformation, by contrast, backstops four predictions: First, Asia as a whole ought to dominate the global economy by 2030. Second, a commercially alert China—with the help of Southeast Asian nations in which overseas Chinese play a prominent economic role—is the best bet to be the dominant power in Asia. Third, some city with a large Chinese population, but not necessarily *in* China, will emerge as Asia's leading financial center, competitive with London and New York. And fourth, the premier currency in Asia will have a leading global reserve function by 2030, albeit probably not alone. This book is about the United States and an Anglosphere still financially hegemonic, rather than about Asia. However, the multidecade challenge that the English-speaking world's politics and finance must confront in analyzing their own vulnerabilities is essentially Asian—clearly in matters relating to energy access and rivalry, almost as certainly in currency and wealth management, and presumably in matters geopolitical and strategic.

Perhaps it is in order to define "Asia." The continent's western boundary (with Europe) is more loose than precise. Partly for this reason, I would include Russia because of its three-quarters Asian landmass and despite its Western window on the Baltic. For now, at least, Russia appears to be in another eastern-facing mode, and its authoritarian style of governance—to say nothing of its brusque but successful KGB or kommissar kapitalism—fits better in a partially Asian framework. Having no academic background to curb me, I have conceived Asia as a kind of "six-pack"—the half dozen key containers nestled among the humdrum binding being the Greater Persian Gulf (Saudi Arabia, Iraq, Iran, and the Gulf oil emirates); the FSU, or former Soviet Union (minus the six former western republics now inclining toward Europe, but including the Caucasian and central Asian republics); the Indian subcontinent; China; Southeast Asia (including overseas China); and Northeast Asia (Japan and Korea). The six-pack doesn't do too badly as a layout if you place the northern can (Russia, central Asia, Siberia) horizontally on top. What most commends the six-pack image, though, is the sheer mass, powerful differentiation, and growing economic clout of its half dozen units. Taken separately, each would rate as a major power. Which is why we may be looking at their century.

THE AMERICAN FINANCIALIZATION GAMBIT

In a new-economy milestone, the precise timing of which is unrecorded, financial services pulled ahead of manufacturing as a percentage of the U.S. gross domestic product in the mid-1990s. The sector had floated across the economic finish line on a half-decade freshet of federal rescues and bailouts such as the 1989–92 quarter-trillion-dollar insurance-like deliverance of failed savings and loan associations by the newly formed Resolution Trust Corporation, and the $1.5 billion Saudi cash infusion arranged by the New York Federal Reserve Bank for an almost insolvent Citibank. Other government support included extraordinary Federal Reserve Board rate cuts between 1990 and 1992 that rescued junk bonds and real estate, and the Clinton administration's 1994 use of special government funds to rescue the Mexican peso and provide life support for Wall Street investments in high-paying peso bonds. The national income accounts duly confirmed the hospital treatments, and confirmation of the patient's welcome weight gains came in GDP figures.

Proponents of this sectoral assistance, including Clinton adviser Robert Rubin, saw finance leading the nation into a new postindustrial era in which services, especially the lucrative financial ones, would replace manufacturing, just as the latter had ushered out a shrinking agricultural sector. Finance was the next great elevator ascending into the luminous temple of global progress. The hour had come, and the United States, caught up in its own market millenarianism, would take the lead.

Skeptics invoked a warning that went against the tide: this faith in finance was not new, but old—and it had played wayward pied piper to prior leading world economic powers. On the edge of decline the Spanish had gloried in their New World gold and silver; the Dutch, in their investment income and lending to princes and czarinas; and the British, in their banks, brokers, and global financial network. In none of these situations, however, could financial services succeed in upholding the national preeminence that had been earlier built by explorers, conquistadores, maritime skills, innovative science and engineering, the first railroads, electrical dynamos, and great iron and steel works.

Invariably, power and greatness passed to new explorers, innovators, and industrialists.

Several of my own books have dwelled on these arguments, and similar or related themes—finance as a late-stage economic and societal tendency to luxuriate, debt as a principal predictor of leading world economic powers' debilitation—have been put forward by others from Brooks Adams and Fernand Braudel to Paul Kennedy and David Landes. I will not pursue history's seeming lesson here, save to close with a favorite quotation. Joseph Chamberlain, the British colonial secretary, made the following statement to bankers in 1904: "Granted that you are the clearing house of the world, [but] are you entirely beyond anxiety as to the permanence of your great position? . . . Banking is not the creator of our prosperity, but is the creation of it. It is not the cause of our wealth, but it is the consequence of our wealth."[3]

In fairness to advocates, there is good reason to think that finance in the twenty-first century, somewhat like manufacturing in the late nineteenth, must rise as a share of GNP in major nations. What is unlikely in this 2010–50 framework, to take one example, is that the emerging BRIC group of nations—Brazil, Russia, India, and China—will see the percentage of their GNP represented by finance exceed or even approach the shares represented by their burgeoning manufacturing and extraction industries. Of course, there will be, as in China and the Persian Gulf, major buildups in central bank reserves and sovereign wealth funds earned by high-profile manufactures and oil revenues. But that does not go to the basic point.

The notion that, as in America, financial sectors will come to outweigh other sectors in the world's new growth economies seems implausible. Chinese finance, including the country's biggest banks and brokerages, has gained world-class status based on bubblelike stock market capitalization, but its share in China's GDP is much smaller. We must keep in mind that finance also lags far behind manufacturing in present-day First World export economies like those of Japan, Germany, and even bank-flavored Switzerland. The potential U.S. embarrassment, which this chapter must weigh, is whether the emergence of a reckless, hubris-driven financial sector in early-twenty-first-century America is a sunset phenomenon like the lesser versions of Edwardian and pre-1914 Britain, eighteenth-century Holland, and early-seventeenth-century Spain, economically centered on the gold and silver entrepôt of Seville and its port of Cadiz.

In the United States, the 2008–10 portrait of the financial services sector, including commercial banks, investment banks, consumer finance, insurance, and the mortgage and financial aspects of housing, is still no more than a glimmer in the eye of computers that are years from even receiving the official data. But we already know that over a hundred U.S. mortgage lending firms have failed or stopped making many types of loans, and that home values are in what some call the sharpest decline since the 1930s. The profits of banks and investment banks have slumped, and chief executives have been replaced at major firms like Citigroup and Merrill Lynch. Foreign demand for U.S. corporate debt securities and structured financial products plummeted in mid-2007, and their future marketability went under a cloud. So did the reputation of financialization and its apostles in both government and the private sector.

The so-called secondary sector, or shadow banking system, home to some of the most controversial institutions—structured investment vehicles, conduits and the like (used by banks to end-run lending limitations), and the "liquidity factories" that used latter-day magic wands to turn financial leverage into nonbank "candyfloss" money—faced diminished credibility and shrinkage. The prevailing expectation ran to a crop of bankruptcies and the trimming of sails by vessels still afloat. Banks, it was assumed, would be pressured to take many of the dubious enterprises and operations back onto their books, accepting some losses to themselves and their shareholders. In November 2007, HSBC Holdings, Europe's largest bank, decided to fold two SIVs and take their $45 billion in assets back on the bank's books.[4] Other banks followed. These actions were seen as reflecting a lack of confidence in the "SuperSIV" being promoted by Treasury Secretary Henry Paulson on behalf of Citigroup, Bank of America, and JPMorgan Chase, and the proposal was withdrawn.

Two other high-profile elements of the secondary sector—private equity groups and hedge funds—were also expected to face contraction. Financial executives surveyed near the end of 2007 by the accounting firm of Grant Thornton UK predicted that leveraged buyout pickings would drop for twelve to eighteen months, given how many recent LBO bonds had eroded to only 82 to 85 percent of their face value, while banks still held about $283 billion of LBO debt they had planned to sell.[5] A few insiders were more pessimistic.

David Rubenstein, cofounder of the U.S.-based Carlyle Group, suggested that U.S. operators would face tougher competition especially in Asia. The new scale of riches being accumulated there, he thought, would enable government-run sovereign wealth funds to displace U.S. private equity through new local private equity groups staffed by professionals but financed with government money.[6]

Hedge funds, many believed, had become less vulnerable after several major frights in August because the drawn-out aspect of the financial crisis gave clever managers a chance to shift to new strategies. Even so, Peter Clarke, the head of Man Group, the world's biggest listed hedge fund manager, predicted in late 2007 that new fund launches would drop by a third, and one out of ten existing funds would go out of business.[7]

The plight of some major U.S. banks constituted a special situation because of their long history and their current position on the ethical, political, and regulatory edge, heightened by uncertainty about how much more value they might lose between 2008 and 2010. For many, already unnerved by the August credit crisis, a new round of air-raid sirens went off in November: jumping prices for the credit default swaps that measured their perceived vulnerability, tightening focus on their quarterly reports of so-called Level Three category illiquid assets, and estimates by Goldman Sachs that unwinding mortgage leverage could substantially shrink 2008 lending by financial institutions.

But the larger dilemma involved what one security analyst called "one of the slowest-moving train wrecks we've seen." Mortgage-backed securities and the CDOs containing them would be unable to find footing so long as the expected volume of defaults on subprime was only incipient, not actual. Christopher Whalen of California-based Institutional Risk Analytics told a late-2007 conference that the default rate was still moving up. At the end of August, only $46 billion in subprime loans had gone bad, but according to one bank tabulation, that number would more than triple to $143 billion by the middle of 2009 and ease off only in 2010 at $270 billion, representing some 1.52 million homes.[8]

In the meantime, the mortgage and credit industries were developing another set of institutional problems. Although the analogy is far from perfect, Fannie Mae and Freddie Mac—the two federally sponsored giants organized to buy mortgages up to a certain value and facilitate the U.S. mortgage market—are sometimes called the Federal Reserve system of the housing industry. This reflects their broader institutional role as the mortgage-market lender of last resort. During the great real estate boom of 2001–6, Fannie and Freddie were the main distribution system for liquidity. As of mid-2007, the two owned or guaranteed $4.8 trillion of mortgages, the world's largest pool. But they operated by raising money cheaply through their federally sponsored status and AAA ratings, and then leveraging those funds. Fannie, for example, owned or guaranteed $2.8 trillion with a mere $40 billion capital base; Freddie did the same for another $2 trillion from a base of only $34.6 billion. On top of the multibillion-dollar losses they were now reporting, Fannie and Freddie also had to keep an eye on a probe by the New York State attorney general's office into the lending practices of the banks that sold mortgages to the two entities.[9]

That included most major banks. In the second quarter of 2007, Fannie and Freddie owned or guaranteed 40 percent of the national mortgage total. Then, as crisis struck, banks and finance companies started confining themselves to the smaller mortgage originations they could sell to the two federally connected agencies. In this new context, the share guaranteed by Fannie and Freddie rose from 40 percent in mid-2007 to 60 percent in the third quarter and 70 percent in October. "With secondary markets for private-label mortgages still paralysed," reported the *Financial Times*, "the prospect of a pullback from Fannie and Freddie could remove the life-raft that lenders such as Countrywide and Residential Capital have been relying on."[10] Any such eventuality would be devastating.

In the meantime, those money watchers convinced that the Federal Reserve Board under Alan Greenspan had over the years indulged in serial bubbling, dropping rates to pump up mortgage finance while the spattered liquid of the tech bubble was still drying, found some more

evidence. James Stack of Montana-based InvesTech Research, an early
prophet of the housing bubble, circulated an overlay of its 2000–2007
market-related contours set against the earlier profile of the 1995–2002
Internet-stock eruption and collapse. Figure 7.1 shows his technical por-
traiture of the extraordinary similarity between the two successive
bubbles. Put together, they suggest a startling and probably not coinci-
dental sequence. Stephen S. Roach, the chairman of Morgan Stanley
Asia, concluded that the Federal Reserve had "mismanaged the biggest risk of our times. . . . Over time, America's bubbles have gotten

FIGURE 7.1

The Internet Bubble and the Housing Bubble:
A Comparison, November 2007

The InvesTech Internet Index, 1995–2002,
and the InvesTech Housing Bubble Bellwether Index, 2000–2007

Source: InvesTech Research, *Market Analyst,* Whitefish, Montana, November 16, 2007.

bigger, as have the segments of the real economy they have infected."
Now higher interest rates are needed—"the only hope America has for
breaking the lethal chain of endless asset bubbles."[11]

In the meantime, the overseas sales of sophisticated financial products now all but marked "Made in Wall Street" were drying up like
West Texas in a drought. Just months earlier, New Economy publicists
had enthused over how corporate bonds, mortgage-backed securities,
CDOs, and suchlike could replace yesteryear's manufactured exports.
Their sales volume alone was enough to offset half of the $800 billion
current account deficit. Then came the crisis.

Scattered late-June and July credit-market tremors had begun the
disruption to debt security sales—and beyond them to trade and the
dollar. Year to year through April, foreign investment in U.S. corporate
bonds had brought in $509 billion in investment inflows, but that wilted.
In July, Alan Ruskin, chief international strategist at RBD Greenwich
Capital, commented, "One reason why the dollar has [recently] re-
sponded in such a negative fashion is that corporate bond inflows have
made up half of the current account financing in the past year." By the
end of July, David Bloom, director of currency strategy at HSBC, estimated that the month's new doubts over U.S. corporate debt had wiped
off 2.5 percent of the dollar's value against the euro, dropping the dollar
to an all-time low against the European currency.[12]

For a short time, the August panic induced a financial flight to
safety—the Gibraltar-like reliability of U.S. treasury issues—and that
movement boosted the dollar. Over the entire month, however, what
had been surface bleeding turned into a severe hemorrhage. During the
second quarter of 2007, foreigners had been net buyers of long-term
U.S. securities to the tune of almost $240 billion. But during the third
quarter, they became net *sellers* by $77 billion. University of California
economist Brad Setser, while accepting that the September numbers
were better than those for August, said, "At least to my mind, the right
headline for the September data is the continued absence of foreign
demand for U.S. assets, not the (relative) improvement from August."
September's foreign net purchasers, he said, were *official*—foreign central banks and the like. As for the remaining transactions, "Bottom line:
private demand for U.S. financial assets has disappeared."[13] Sales re-

sumed in October as the U.S. stock market briskly rebounded, but soft-
ness returned in November.

Other signs supported skepticism, not least in the fast-growing Asian
market. "Just a decade ago," said a late-2007 research report from
Greenwich Associates, "Asian fixed income was a dollar-denominated
business." But after the 1997 Asian currency crisis, nations in the region
began developing debt markets in local currencies to minimize cross-
pressures on local businessmen who disliked owing debt in dollars. This
shift away from dollar-denominated debt toward debt in local currencies has so far mostly brought fragmentation—yen issues in Japan, ring-
git issues in Malaysia, and so on.[14] But the message for U.S. marketers
was negative.

A further irony for Wall Street lay in the emergence of what might
be called an Islamic nationalist bond market, mostly in Asia. Moody's
Investors Service drew attention to the phenomenon in August, noting
that Islamic bonds, or *sukuk* (securities made religiously acceptable by
avoiding interest payments or investment in the alcohol, tobacco, pork-
packing, and gaming industries), were gaining stature. Intended or actual issuance was spreading beyond overwhelmingly Muslim nations
like Indonesia and Pakistan to mixed-faith countries like India, Malaysia, and Singapore.[15] By November, Hong Kong and Japan were also
moving toward Islamic financial products, as was the British treasury
(Britain has four licensed Islamic banks, the only ones in Europe or the
United States). The *Financial Times* noted that government "ministers
appear to have regained their appetite for a product that would help
give London another edge over New York in its fight for supremacy as
a financial centre."[16]

That is at least possible. Although issuance is only beginning, Standard & Poor's has estimated the potential of the Islamic finance market
at $500 billion. Others think that the flow of oil money into Muslim na-
tions will make the market even bigger, and the Malaysia-based Islamic
Financial Services Board—probably overenthusiastic—estimated the
potential by 2015 at nearly $3 trillion.[17] One must assume that this, too,
will reduce the U.S. share of the Asian fixed-income market.

Because the Chinese stock market boom in 2007 exaggerated the
top-tier global rank of four large Chinese banks and the country's two

principal brokerage firms, it may be wise to emphasize other yardsticks of Asian financial prowess. Standouts include the burgeoning investment in foreign financial institutions by major sovereign wealth funds, and small, tentative indicators of a rising Asian monetary policy coordination that might hint at a continental economic union or common currency.[18] Indeed, by the end of the year, investments by Asian sovereign wealth funds started playing such a prominent role in bailing out shaky or troubled U.S. banks and investment firms—Citigroup, Bear Stearns, and Morgan Stanley—that a new wisecrack made the rounds of Manhattan trading floors: "The joke is: Shanghai, Dubai, Mumbai or goodbye."[19] The last thing that wobbly, negligent U.S. capitalism needs is that wobbly negligence facilitating the rapid emergence of a rival continent.

OIL AND RISING WATER

Every book has a part that is difficult to write for a pivotal reason. This is that section, shaped by the difficulty in simultaneously interweaving the realpolitik of oil and the greenpolitik of global warming and rising seas. They are two different worlds even when they meet—as in the Arctic Ocean, where global warming is most at work.

Kivalina, a small U.S. Eskimo village north of the Arctic Circle on the Chukchi Sea, lies not too far from the Bering Strait, which separates Alaska and Russian Siberia. This threatened enclave is known to environmentalists because rising waters from the melting polar ice cap will soon require evacuation before the village is submerged. In all likelihood, few people preoccupied with the imminence of peak oil will even have heard of Kivalina.

On the other hand, perhaps one green activist in five will know about Russian president Putin's decision to pressure Shell and Exxon out of their previously agreed-upon roles in developing the rich oil fields of Siberia's Sakhalin Island. Fewer still will be familiar with the Russian government's insistent claims to an energy-rich underwater shelf in the Arctic on the basis—by most accounts far-fetched—that the 1,200-mile Lomonosov Ridge is an extension of a Russian mountain range and geologically linked to Siberia's continental shelf. The submerged area in question, somewhat bigger than Texas, is said to contain twice the oil of Saudi Arabia.[20] In mid-2007, a Russian scientific submarine placed a flag on the seabed at the North Pole, purporting to stake a territorial claim.

Several million Americans know that Putin once headed the KGB, the Soviet Union's onetime secret police. But only a relative handful know that in 1997 the future Russian leader defended the equivalent of a Ph.D. dissertation at Russia's St. Petersburg State Mining Institute. Two years later, he marshaled some of the same material in a lengthy article entitled "Mineral Natural Resources in the Strategy for Development of the Russian Economy."[21] George W. Bush was in the oil business for two decades, but as president, his strategic achievement in petroleum has seemed as minimal as Putin's rebuilding of Russia as a global oil power has seemed masterful. Ploy or not, Putin probably had the Lomonosov Ridge up his sleeve for years. As a measure of the gap between petroleum black and environmental green, Russia has one strategy for the Arctic ice cap—somehow controlling the oil and natural gas underneath it—while Washington Democratic leaders have a second: to keep it from melting, by cutting enough carbon emissions quickly enough. For Americans to pay attention to Russian goals would also be good for a second Arctic environment—the region's competitive geopolitics.

Leaving the Arctic behind, there is China, absolutely pivotal in any 2010–30 strategies to deal with global warming. Not only does China have the world's largest population, but it is now passing the United States in carbon emissions. Before China can lead the world economically, analysts expect it to build a much greater lead—to become, in essence, the Great Emitter. The People's Republic faces major internal dislocations from global warming, but even so, Beijing officials make clear their belief that most of the carbon dioxide in the atmosphere was released 50 to 150 years ago during the British, American, and Western European industrial maturations. Indeed, Westerners also know the history—of London circa 1858, when the city was nicknamed "the Smoke"; of soot-layered Pittsburgh or the Ruhr circa 1908; and of the petrochemical stench enveloping Houston circa 1958 being called "the smell of prosperity." The BRIC nations—not just China, but also

Brazil and India—have every intention of insisting that the nations of the long-since-industrialized West make the contemporary sacrifices, while the current aspirants have two or three decades of opportunity comparable to the West's from the 1890s through the 1950s.

Besides their sense of environmental history, the BRIC states come well armed financially. Of the five largest foreign-currency reserves in the world, three are maintained by China (number one), Russia (number three), and India (number five), and each nation is a big exporter. Not only do the Chinese command $1.46 trillion of foreign-currency reserves, but their commitment to oil geopolitics has made Beijing a rare official adherent to peak-oil theory and strategy. Officials of the Association for the Study of Peak Oil noted that a peak-oil workshop was held on October 26, 2007, at Beijing's China University of Petroleum, attended by representatives of the three Chinese national oil corporations, the president and secretary of ASPO International, the vice director of the Strategy Office (China Energy Office) and the chancellor and vice chancellor of the China University of Petroleum. The latter two public officials were elected president and vice president of ASPO-China, and "it was unanimously agreed that ASPO China should be formed and that Peak Oil research and modelling is essential to China. As seven of the nine new leaders of China have been engineering students it is expected that Peak Oil will feature in future government policy-making decisions."[22]

Despite the skepticism of U.S. Asian specialists, evidence is building of meaningful energy-related collaboration between China and India. In a 2006 article, "India, China, and the Asian Axis of Oil," Siddharth Varadarajan, the deputy editor of the *Hindu*, a leading Indian newspaper, discussed how agreements signed between India and China to place joint bids for overseas energy projects and acquisitions could create a framework for relationships that might support an Asian energy union.[23] The New America Foundation's Flynt Leverett, in his "The New Axis of Oil," grumbled about that. On top of China's "Going Out" strategy of encouraging its three national oil companies to buy equity stakes in overseas exploration and production companies and projects, Beijing's state-capitalist rather than market-capitalist approach was serving as a model for India's Oil and Natural Gas Corporation. Even the Japanese,

Leverett noted, were debating whether they should take "a more statist approach to external energy policy to meet the Chinese challenge."[24]

Still another example of Chinese-Indian collaboration lay in the two nations' teaming up to rebuild the Burma Road of World War II fame. China has already made a six-lane highway out of its portion of the road from Chinese Kunming to India's state of Assam; India's two-lane construction was running somewhat behind. Mari Shankar Aiyar, India's federal minister for the northeast region, voiced his own sense of alliance: "If the Japanese could be defeated because you are able to link Assam with south-west China, can't we defeat the Japanese once again in the economic race by linking the north-east region with south-west China?"[25] Asians overall are more exultant over the growing interrelationships along what is being called "the New Silk Road," an abstract avenue of trade and mutual investment that reaches from the Persian Gulf through Mumbai and Chennai (India) to Kuala Lumpur, Singapore, Hong Kong, Shanghai, and Tokyo. But the demographics of a Sino-Indian entente would make it especially momentous.

India's approach to carbon emissions resembles the Chinese position in numbers games and wordplay. Prior to the December 2007 United Nations global-emissions summit, a senior Indian environment ministry official reconfirmed India's pledge to keep its carbon emissions per person below figures for the rich West. At the present, though, the average American emits twenty times more carbon than the average Indian.[26] But officials in New Delhi know that American politicians must answer to a large and persuasive green lobby.

Indian and Chinese officials seem to have a deep multitrack awareness. Indeed, the nonspecialist amateur is struck by the many agreements developing between nations within the megaregion of India, China, Iran, Russia, and central Asia. These include deals involving energy supplies and acquisitions, nuclear-power cooperation, pipelines, economic aid, and military organizations like the Shanghai Cooperation Organizations. Figure 7.2 represents a back-of-the-envelope sketch on which the curious Internet surfer might fill in scores of bilateral and multilateral connections. Perhaps it is even appropriate to invoke a hint of "Asianism" along the lines of the European Community sentiment appearing in the 1950s.

FIGURE 7.2

A "Back of the Envelope" Look at Russia, India, China, Iran, and Central Asia

Go online and fill in the various relationships: military, nuclear, commercial, in oil and gas supply, in joint ventures, in weapons supply, in pipelines and refineries, in regional cooperation, and in sovereign wealth-fund investments. Chart your own guide to the new "Great Game."

In the United States, political correctness, religious fundamentalism, and other inhibitions sometimes dumb down national debate. The race for the 2008 Republican presidential nomination reiterated the party's relationship with large Christian fundamentalist constituencies that insist on biblical creation rather than evolution as a backdrop to environmental policy. The Republican chairman of the Senate Committee on the Environment up through 2006, James Inhofe of Oklahoma, disbelieved in global warming because he shared this biblical worldview, which may also have influenced the Bush White House. To varying degrees, the same could be said of two 2008 White House hopefuls, former Arkansas governor Mike Huckabee and former U.S. senator from Tennessee Fred Thompson. The latter joked to a publication that warming on other planets has sparked people "to wonder if Mars and Jupiter, non-signatories to the Kyoto Treaty, are actually inhabited by alien SUV-driving industrialists who run their air-conditioning at 60 degrees and refuse to recycle."[27]

One result of this muddled opposition was to give the Democratic Party a large edge in the 2008 national debate over environmental policy, which in turn facilitated the candidates' intensive courtship of green activist groups and voters during the presidential delegate-selection process. As the major Democratic contenders acquiesced in some ongoing U.S. presence in Iraq after 2008, environmental issues gained even more centrality as a vehicle for appealing to party liberals. By contrast, oil geopolitics received little attention, and the large U.S. international oil companies became whipping posts. Ironically, these companies cannot defend themselves with the truth, which is that they are losing much of their former golden-age influence to the much-better-positioned state-run national oil companies.

During 2007, support for this downbeat assessment came from such disparate sources as Bloomberg News and oilman T. Boone Pickens. The latter, a peak-oil believer, contended that the stock buybacks by ExxonMobil, Chevron, and other companies were "telling the market that we can't grow." Pretty soon, he said, "the reserves will be gone and they're going to be refiners and processors."[28] Should Chevron keep buying back its stock at current rates, the company would be close to liquidation by 2023. Along with Conoco, Shell, BP, and Total, by 2011 ExxonMobil and Chevron may no longer be able to increase their production, which should start declining in 2014, according to longtime oil analyst Charles Maxwell. After a while, he said, "they'll be in liquidation."[29] State oil companies have most remaining global reserves so locked up, according to the *Oil & Gas Journal*, that the Canadian oil sands region now represents 50 to 70 percent of the reserves not barred to international oil companies because of government restrictions.[30]

However, a substantial percentage of environmentalists seem as opposed to developing the Canadian oil sands as they are to developing coal in southern Illinois or oil shale in the Rocky Mountains. Some hold all three positions alongside determined support for the idea of U.S. energy independence. Facilitated as these assumptions are by strong public preference for Democratic environmental positions and general dismissal of the Republicans, the net result may be less a green breakthrough than a green illusion. Many of the presumptions about alternative energy supply involved do not add up.

The International Energy Agency's report titled *World Energy Outlook,* issued in November 2007, put the conundrum in sharp focus: between 2000 and 2006,China and India together accounted for about half of the world's primary energy demand, some 85 percent of the world's primary coal demand, and almost two-thirds of the world's energy-related carbon dioxide emissions. The momentum of these demands stands to be huge. Even with radical measures to reduce the energy intensity of world growth, the IEA expects energy demand would keep growing at 1.3 percent a year, while carbon dioxide emissions would not stabilize until 2025, and then at a level almost 30 percent above 2005 measurements. And if governments stick with the same policies, the pressures will really worsen: world energy demand will rise 50 percent by 2030 (three-quarters of this coming from developing nations), and carbon dioxide emissions will jump 57 percent (with two-thirds coming from China, India, Russia, and the United States). Moreover, despite the fanfare about alternative energy sources, fossil fuels will account for 84 percent of the increased consumption.[31] According to estimates from Goldman Sachs, nonconventional fuels from oil sands and shale, ethanol and biomass, coal, and natural gas liquids were projected to meet 3.5 percent of demand by 2015, up from 2.8 percent in 2006, but to reach 10 percent only by 2030.[32]

In short, extraordinary challenges lie ahead. Too many complacent conservatives get their nonchalance about the energy supply from White House saber rattling in the Middle East or from the book of Genesis, and their environmental policy from sages like Inhofe, Thompson, or the occasional televangelist. And on the other side, too many progressives and environmental activists, dismissing energy security, have imbibed the duty of a great moral challenge (ignoring Russia, India, and China) and of a U.S. opportunity to achieve energy independence by abandoning fossil fuels and relying instead on some combination of geothermal, solar, and wind power. In theory, some fairly sophisticated fusion of energy realism and climate consciousness ought to be achievable, but the history of previous leading world economic powers is the opposite of reassuring.

What makes it worse, of course, is the other set of economic perils and incompetencies that have built up under the aegis of speculative finance.

THE GLOBAL CRISIS OF AMERICAN CAPITALISM

The crisis is no longer in the future, but upon us. The debacle started in August, when collateralized debt obligations, built in part around bad debt and distributed globally by Wall Street, began making a slow train wreck relating to weak sections of the U.S. mortgage market into a crisis of top American banks and of the global credit markets. The crux, beyond unsafe mortgage lending, was the recklessness of the speculative mind-set that lay at the heart of Anglo-American finance in an era when the rest of the world was beginning to look for capitalism more rooted and conscious of its responsibilities.

It is often said that the nature of American capitalism reaches back into Europe as a whole less than into the particular ethos of eighteenth- and nineteenth-century Britain. Here I would not single out, as some do, the process described by historian Karl Polanyi in *The Great Transformation*. To Polanyi, an upheaval in late-eighteenth- and early-nineteenth-century Britain yanked the nation's financial markets from a previous position of being embedded in society and religion and stood them on their own—the rise of the unregulated and self-correcting market, which Polanyi discerned in economic developments and also in the theories of David Ricardo and Thomas Malthus, with some reference back to Adam Smith.[33]

Much more was involved than just that. Over more than two decades of studying the circumstances of the three leading world economic powers that preceded the United States, I have been drawn to see other origins—a kind of passing of the baton that initially included non–Anglo-Saxons. As we have seen, the Spain to which the gold and silver treasure ships of the Americas sailed was also the linchpin of the Hapsburg Empire, which included Europe's most sophisticated financial centers—Genoa, Florence, and Venice in Italy; Augsburg and other southern German towns; Portuguese Lisbon; and Hapsburg Burgundy and Flanders. The money shipped from the New World lured bankers and traders from these venues to Madrid, Seville, and Cadiz, and as religious warfare and persecution grew in the sixteenth century, so did the migration of commercially skilled refugees, along with the important revolt of the Protestant Netherlands against Catholic Hapsburg overlordship. As Spain's power declined, some of those commercially minded refugees—Flemish Protestants from Antwerp, German Protestants, French Protestants (Huguenots), and Spanish and Portuguese Jews—moved on to the Dutch Republic, where they played a major role in commerce and speculative finance. By dint of Protestant religion and North Sea geography, Holland had ties to England.

In 1689, the Dutch prince William of Orange became king of England, and during the eighteenth century more and more Dutch money moved into English investments. The England of this period followed the Dutch model in setting up a stock exchange and a central bank. Ultimately, many Flemings, Huguenots, and Jews also moved there, to play a major role in British commerce and banking. The future United States from the start drew immigrants from England, Holland, Scotland, and Protestant sections of Germany, as well as Huguenots, Flemings, and Jews, so when the baton of economic leadership passed to the United States in the twentieth century, there was a notable continuum of financial and commercial custom. Admittedly, this portrait is quickly drawn. But I think that appreciating the partial continuum is important because it is hard to see how any major twenty-first-century shift of power to Asia can occur without a major discontinuity unless a financial Anglosphere—the United States, the United Kingdom, Canada, Ireland, Australia, New Zealand, and perhaps the Netherlands—can remain a coequal power center for at least three or four decades.

In these few pages, I do not aim to refight the battle of distinguishing between English-speaking speculative capitalism, with its corollary of according financial and cultural importance to homeownership, and the somewhat different continental model. As already noted, historian Charles Kindleberger, in his classic *Manias, Panics, and Crashes,* included a chart of such events over three centuries—and an easy majority had their beginnings among the Dutch, the British, or the Americans. Present-day French, German, and Italian economists and writers tend to invoke a similar cleavage in which the English-speaking nations often indulge in speculative finance while unhappy continentals deplore the hedge funds, currency speculators, mortgage-backed securities, and CDOs involved. That was certainly true in late 2007 when French president

Nicolas Sarkozy spoke to a joint session of the U.S. Congress and used the occasion to indict "vagaries and excesses of a financial capitalism that currently leaves too much room for financial speculation."[34]

The underlying question before us in this last chapter is whether the housing and credit crisis expected to span the 2007–10 period constitutes *the* global crisis of American capitalism, in the sense of being the one that signals the Great Transferal to Asia. Based on the points I have made in this book, that outcome certainly seems possible. Global respect for the United States slumped drastically in 2002 and following the invasion of Iraq, and then again in 2005–7 as the survey data in the appendix so unfortunately illustrates. The value of the U.S. dollar has followed pretty much the same course. Between the deepening dislike of the United States in much of the Muslim world and the decline of the greenback, Persian Gulf states that once reinvested most of their oil revenues in U.S. bonds and kept their currencies pegged to the dollar no longer believe that Washington is a capital city that keeps faith. Given U.S. dollar policy in 2007, it is easy to see why.

Ill repute from selling "contaminated" mortgage-backed securities and structured investment packages has been a body blow to Wall Street, damaging bank profits and prestige. For some months, foreign skepticism also dried up the foreign purchases of long-term U.S. securities that financial leaders had trumpeted as vital to offset the U.S. current account deficit. The plummeting dollar, for its part, has given new impetus to proposals within OPEC that oil sales be conducted in some other currency better able to keep its value. And reaction against Washington and "market triumphalist" posturing by American financiers and politicians is now being accompanied by a global countertide of state-run national oil companies, resurging mercantilism, spreading "resource nationalism," the rise of massive state-funded foreign investment funds, and a general retreat of what used to be strong demand for U.S. financial products.

We can attempt a rough calculus of the damage to American finance, beginning with housing and mortgages. Should home prices decline 15 to 20 percent from their peak, at least $3 trillion in homeowner value will be lost, and mortgage finance will shrivel. The year 2007 was estimated to show the biggest decline in new home sales since 1963. As

2008 began, the Mortgage Bankers Association predicted that the year's mortgage originations would drop from $3.95 trillion in 2003 and $2.4 trillion in 2007 to just $1.86 trillion. Washington Mutual, a major lender, predicted a steeper decline to just $1.5 trillion in 2008 originations.

Turning to Wall Street and the major financial firms, the New York State comptroller's office, trying to plot 2008 tax receipts, tabulated in October 2007 that earnings at the seven largest financial firms based in New York City fell almost 65 percent in the third quarter of 2007 from a year earlier. Moreover, for many big firms and banks, the extent of damage from SIVs, CDOs, and the like had yet to be reported in actual earnings. Profits at private equity firms and consumer finance companies were sure to be shrinking.

For some of the big banks, potential loan losses would force them to either set aside more capital in reserves or substantially retrench. Having to take huge losses from SIVs and CDOs onto their books was bad enough, but by year's end, attention was also turning to potential corporate loan defaults. The *Financial Times,* comparing possible dimensions of the U.S. banking crisis to those of Japanese banks in the 1990s, calculated the earlier losses of the Japanese banks at $700 billion and speculated that if this decade's losses rose to $600 billion, that "might represent as much as one-third of the core (tier one) banking capital for U.S. and European banks."[35] What could even make things worse would be if defaults on sub-investment-grade corporate debt surged in 2008 because of a recession. Managers like "bond king" Bill Gross, who described credit default swaps as "perhaps the most egregious offenders" in today's banking system, predicted that they could cause losses of up to $250 billion in 2008.[36]

While this was all hypothetical, the effect could be to replace the old combination of bailouts and massive financial sector debt and leverage that had elevated the sector's share of the domestic product to 20 to 21 percent between 2003 and 2006. Instead, financial services could experience an unwinding strong enough to drop the sector's share to 16 to 17 percent. This, of course, could spark a long-needed debate over financialization—and what it has meant and might continue to mean for the United States.

Similar debates may develop in the other English-speaking countries.

Former Federal Reserve chairman Alan Greenspan and others on both sides of the Atlantic commented during 2007 on the vulnerability of British home prices, banks, and household debt levels, and housing prices in Ireland and New Zealand were also widely believed to be in bubbles. With a taste of their own for speculation, Australians are anxious to make their country one of the world's leading centers of financial management. Fourth ranked now with $1 trillion in assets, they hope to have $1.8 trillion in hand by 2015.[37]

A conundrum unique to the United States, however, involves the apparent weakening in recent years of the various monetary arrangements by which countries obliged to the United States for agreeing to higher oil prices, providing regional umbrellas of military protection, or keeping the world's largest consumer market open to huge quantities of manufactured imports undertook certain explicit or implicit obligations to support and protect the U.S. dollar. Back in 1974, Saudi Arabia and the Persian Gulf oil states agreed to sell oil in dollars and to recycle many of the dollars received into purchases of U.S. treasury debt. In the 1980s, Taiwan, Korea, and especially Japan, dependent on the U.S. Pacific defense umbrella, generally cooperated with the United States in currency matters and kept much of their growing foreign currency reserves in U.S. treasury debt. In the late 1990s, as Chinese manufactures poured into the United States, Beijing's mushrooming dollar accumulations became the focus. And in 2003, a trio of economists coined the term "Bretton Woods II" to describe a new benign state of affairs in which countries like Japan and China accumulated large reserves and recycled those reserves into treasury debt to provide low-cost financing for America's huge current account deficits.[38] These presumptions, in turn, led to a set of reassuring theories: that the United States was simply taking advantage of Asia's excess savings, and that the huge U.S. current account deficit, being manageable for that reason, was harmless and not an economic and political vulnerability.[39]

The catalyst for a critical reassessment by foreign dollar-holders came in 2007 when the deterioration of the U.S. dollar, visible since 2002, began to accelerate, with the greenback tumbling roughly 10 percent against the euro and pound sterling in 2007 alone. Nations holding large stocks of dollars in their reserves took a wicked beating, and those that pegged their currency to the declining U.S. greenback found their inflation rates heating up. A concerned Kuwait, for one, dropped its dollar peg in May, thereby soon bolstering its local currency. The weekly *Economist* observed that "international investors" must "question why they hold the bulk of their wealth in dollars."[40] European financial columnist Wolfgang Munchau, surprised by the third-quarter 2007 slump of global demand for U.S. long-term securities, followed up with the key question: Was this, he asked, the end of Bretton Woods II?[41]

History will have to be the judge of to what extent Washington policymakers were blindsided by these convergences. Some almost certainly were not. Alan Greenspan's critical memoirs were being typeset well before the August panic, and Treasury Secretary Henry Paulson, shortly after being named to that position in 2006, reestablished regular meetings for the President's Working Group on Financial Markets. This was the unit more colloquially known as the Plunge Protection Team. Even by its formal name, though, the Working Group represented a de facto admission that far from being rational and efficient, U.S. financial markets were periodically volatile and unstable—hardly desirable characteristics in the nation's dominant economic sector.

As suggested in chapter 2, a case can be made that Washington partially shifted to policies of financial mercantilism as early as the 1980s. This happened through that decade's series of federally orchestrated domestic and international bailouts, accompanied in 1988 by the presidential order to set up the Working Group, with its probable covert mandate to repeat where necessary the interventions employed during the tense days of the October 1987 crash. At very least, both the facts and the inferences suggest a mockery of strict free-market economics.

No one should be surprised to read someday that during the eighties, senior officials established at least vague guidelines for a policy of maintaining national assets. Such an intention would have stretched from bank, credit, and currency bailouts to a collusive monetary policy designed to drown any threatened asset deflation in liquidity and never, ever to pop an asset bubble. Here Greenspan and his successor, Ben Bernanke, put themselves at odds with views elsewhere in central banking circles that asset bubbles should indeed be popped—and that U.S. unwillingness to do so might even imperil global markets. We have certainly had the bailouts and off-and-on gushes of liquidity, and the most freewheeling treasury secretaries of the last two decades, Henry Paulson and Robert Rubin, have shown a rare protectiveness toward the sanctity of stock market advances. Even Paulson's de facto soft-dollar policy of 2006 and 2007 makes sense if one takes a Machiavellian view of a commitment to maintain assets.

The cynic's explanation is this: A weak dollar stimulates exports, thereby narrowing the trade deficit. A weak dollar also allows multinational corporations to (1) show larger overseas earnings (as local currencies translate into more dollars) and (2) increase the worth of their foreign holdings and subsidiaries as stated in dollars. For Americans, a cheap currency also keeps up the nominal value of the Dow Jones, the S&P 500, and other U.S. stock market averages. Measured in euros, British pounds, or Brazilian reals, these indexes did much less well over the last five years than when measured in (cheap) dollars. *Financial Times* columnist John Authers half joked that "whether they realise it or not, investors' positive sentiment in the U.S. may rest on the weak dollar."[42]

To be sure, any serious treasury secretary would have a point in declining to leave real-world U.S. asset management to the sort of market triumphalism that flourishes in few places beyond the editorial pages of the *Wall Street Journal*. The last several years have seen mounting evidence of a global mercantilist or state-capitalist resurgence in more than a dozen economic dimensions: spreading resource nationalism, government-run national oil companies; a shrinking private oil market; internal energy subsidies; energy alliances that double as military organizations (the SCO); export subsidies; currency pegging; mercantilist buildups of Asian central bank currency reserves; the overshadowing of private investors by Asian sovereign wealth funds; the enlargement of foreign state-owned portions of Western commercial banks and investment banks; the mimicry of early-twentieth-century dollar diplomacy by twenty-first-century renminbi, ruble, and even Venezuelan bolivar diplomacy; political reregulation of capital flows; and apparent Third World success in hobbling or stalling two market triumphalist enforcement mechanisms—the International Monetary Fund and the World Trade Organization. Some of this countertide flowed from the arrogance of wealthy Western capitalism during the various Asian, Russian, and Argentine financial crises of 1997–2003 and from the sense of many oil-producing nations that the invasion of Iraq was oil-motivated. The question of just how much more of a countertrend is still to come can be expected to spur hundreds of Ph.D. theses from Buenos Aires and Caracas to Moscow and Kuala Lumpur.

Even within the United States, market preferences are unlikely to block the emergence of some government-sanctioned energy strategy or hybrid of an energy and global-warming strategy, nor are they likely to block a considerable amount of financial reregulation, not least in the area of securities transparency and valuation. Other reregulation, as suggested by commentators like Martin Wolf and Henry Kaufman, could also include a rethinking of the legal status of megabanks. To Wolf, "What we have [in banking] is a risk-loving industry guaranteed as a public utility." If banks are to be rescued because they are too big to fail, they must also become, in the manner of a regulated public utility, too suitably behaved and too responsible to fail.[43]

This chapter cannot turn away from the role of unstable and speculative finance in jeopardizing America's position in the world of the early twenty-first century without considering two particular failures. The first is the malfeasance of speculation-driven innovation in matters relating to mortgage securitization and the larger arena of financial debt and debt products. Unprecedented expansion of financial sector debt, the experiments in designing and selling exotic mortgages, the ballooning of CDOs and other flawed structured products, and the role of so-called liquidity factories at least begin the list of innovations central to this latest credit crisis. Obviously, this represents a much larger scale of backfiring or negligent innovation than the impact of so-called portfolio insurance in 1987 or the shortcomings in hedge-fund quantitative mathematics in 1998. And if these multiple abuses overlap with the great unwinding of the 1982–2007 debt bubble, then they—and the financial sector that created, promoted, and so greatly profited from them—will have much to answer for.

The nature of English-speaking capitalism as practiced especially by Wall Street but also by the City of London is drawing fire. Martin Wolf, the chief economic commentator at the *Financial Times,* noted at year's

end that "what is happening in credit markets today is a huge blow to
the credibility of the Anglo-Saxon model of transactions-orientated financial capitalism. A mixture of crony capitalism and gross incompetence has been on display in the core financial markets of New York and
London."[44] On the other side of the Atlantic, the iconic American investor Warren Buffett summarized his criticism: "You can't turn a financial
toad into a prince by securitizing it. . . . Wall Street started believing its
own PR on this—they started holding this stuff themselves, maybe because they couldn't sell it. It worked wonderfully until it didn't work at
all. Wall Street is reaping what they've sown."[45]

Foreigners were even more blunt. Besides French president Sarkozy, former German vice chancellor Franz Münterfering had famously
joked about foreign hedge funds as locusts, and chief executives in
France and Italy told the press that the state-owned funds in Asia would
probably be better long-term investors, in effect pesticides to deal with
the private sector locusts.[46] In the oil-producing nations, especially in
the Persian Gulf, criticism of hedge funds and other speculators tended
to reach a crescendo before OPEC meetings because these speculations
were widely blamed for exaggerating oil price movement both up and
down. Energy and finance ministers who took this view presumably
found it somewhat harder to keep losing money by holding dollars.

If speculative excesses represent an albatross for the U.S. financial
sector, the prospective burden of quantitative mathematics represents
a black albatross. Or perhaps we should say a bevy of black swans, author Nassim Nicholas Taleb's shorthand for mathematical impossibili-
ties that cannot occur in hedge funds' quantitative strategies but always
manage to occur two, three, seven, or eleven times in the real world of
every significant financial crisis.[47] The idea that policymakers have allowed the U.S. economy to be guided by a financial sector increasingly
dominated by black box makers and algorithm vendors itself seems like
a black swan—an impossibility, save that it's happening. According to
one U.S. consultancy, by 2010 algorithmic trading, an aspect of "quant"-
based investing, is expected to account for half of all trading in U.S.
equity markets.[48]

There is no better distillation of the harm inflicted—and probably yet to be inflicted—than that of hedge fund manager Richard Book-staber in his 2007 volume, *A Demon of Our Own Design: Markets, Hedge Funds, and the Perils of Financial Innovation*. His underlying point is that even though financial strategists can keep dreaming up new instruments, it's not a good idea to do so, because each innovation adds layers of increasing complexity, tight coupling, and risk. By way of comparison, "consider the progress of other products and services over the past century. From the structural design of buildings and bridges, to the operation of oil refineries or power plants, to the safety of automobiles and airplanes, we learned our lessons. In contrast, financial markets have seen a tremendous amount of engineering in the past 30 years, but the result has been more frequent and severe breakdowns. . . . The integration of the financial markets into a global whole, ubiquitous and timely market information, the array of options and other derivative instruments—have exaggerated the pace of activity and the complexity of financial instruments that makes crises inevitable."[49]

Countertrends toward realism and greater regulation may well become excessive and overreach, much like the market excesses and Anglo-American hubris they now challenge. But it is well to understand the provocation offered by the blind-to-human-nature, history-ends-with-us millennial capitalism profiled at the beginning of this chapter. My summation is that American financial capitalism, at a pivotal period in the nation's history, cavalierly ventured a multiple gamble: first, financializing a hitherto more diversified U.S. economy; second, using massive quantities of debt and leverage to do so; third, following up a stock market bubble with an even larger housing and mortgage credit bubble; fourth, roughly quadrupling U.S. credit-market debt between 1987 and 2007, a scale of excess that historically unwinds; and fifth, consummating these events with a mixed performance of dishonesty, incompetence, and quantitative negligence.

How fully the complicit politicians will investigate the culpable regulators and financial architects remains to be seen. But there will be many further market events, energy and climate problems, books, essays, congressional hearings, and political campaigns to guide us.

THE ROAD AHEAD

This chapter does not seriously consider other yardsticks of the United States as an empire in decline, because they range too far afield.

The collapse of the housing bubble may leave some U.S. cities permanently blighted, with large new boarded-up areas—Cleveland and Detroit lead the list. Expensive homes in some areas may be given up. Urban portions of the Netherlands were blighted in the eighteenth century, and books have been printed showing some of the large houses abandoned in England and Ireland after both world wars.

Anger at immigrants or trouble over ethnic minorities has been a problem before. Spain expelled its Moriscos—nominally converted Muslims—during the early seventeenth century, and provincial parliaments complained about foreign merchants and profiteers. Dutchmen disdained immigrant German workers, willing to work for less. The British and Irish had each other to dislike.

Recent polls in the United States by Zogby/New Global Initiatives show an unprecedented 1.5 million Americans having already decided to leave the United States and another 1.8 million calling themselves likely to leave.[50] Emigration was also pronounced from declining Spain (to Spanish colonial America), from eighteenth-century Holland (to Dutch colonies, and by professionals and skilled workers to Britain and Sweden), and from declining rural and industrial areas of Britain in the first half of the twentieth century (to the colonies, the dominions, and the United States).

New York may lose ground as an international financial center, falling behind London, which shares Manhattan's language but not its less popular nationality, currency, and financial products. Over the next two decades, the biggest gainers are foreseen to be Asian, but great expectations are divided among Singapore, Hong Kong, Tokyo, and Shanghai, probably prolonging the English-speaking centers' lead.

No previous leading world economic power has enjoyed a full-fledged manufacturing renaissance after becoming unduly enamored of finance. However, should the United States decide to imitate the commitments of high-value-added manufacturers and exporters like

Germany, Japan, and Switzerland, some success would be likely, especially given dollar weakness.

As for education, shortcomings and calls for renewal have received attention in the past as national decline threatens, especially from progressives—the British Liberal Party of 1900 to 1910 comes especially to mind—who sought a rebuttal to trade proposals emphasizing reciprocity, imperial preference, or protection. This works politically because progressives are also usually associated with educators and education interests. Overall, though, improved education has been no more of a nostrum than airy schemes to rebuild lost industrial glories.

Instead of listing any more leaden linings, let me close with a silver lining. The thirty- to forty-year tumble from national preeminence that made life more glum for most folk in seventeenth-century Spain, eighteenth-century Holland, and the Britain from the 1910s to the 1950s may be somewhat moderated for the United States because of its position as a North American continental economic power with a large resource and population base rather than a weaker European maritime periphery. And further abandoning the hubris of military and financial imperialism would also help because both postures represent drags on the American future.

Afterword:

Speculative Capitalism Endangered:
The Domestic and Global Consequences

The trite phrase "playing for high stakes" doesn't begin to describe the economic and political obstacle course confronting the United States over the next decade and a half. Political leaders have trouble dealing with watersheds of the sort now approaching because such changes trample too many existing beliefs and nostrums.

The crisis of the U.S. financial sector detailed in the preceding pages is not an isolated event. Even the late 2008 U.S. National Intelligence Council report "Global Trends 2025: A Transformed World" sees Wall Street's failure speeding up the reordering of the international economy to the disadvantage of the United States. In economic terms, Asia is moving to the forefront, and the Shanghai Conference Organization, which conjoins Russia, China, and central Asia, may be emerging as a military counterbalance to the North Atlantic Treaty Organization. To our south, Latin America no longer seems to be the U.S. sphere of interest proclaimed in the Monroe Doctrine. And the increasingly relevant precedents of previous leading world economic powers do nothing to ease the chill.

WALL STREET AGONISTES

Official measurement of the shrinkage of the financial sector must await publication of its back-to-back shares of gross domestic product for the years 2008, 2009, and 2010. By then, the bulk of the deepest Wall Street upheaval and home-price collapse since the Great Depression will have echoed through the U.S. economy. The catch is that these numbers or others like them probably will not be available before 2012.

Much national policy, then, will have to be made with preliminary information. Should the U.S. financial sector be rebuilt, whatever the cost, to its swollen, abnormal dimensions of 2006–2007? Or is serious surgery in order to cut back its size to pre-bubble levels of, say, 1983 or 1984? Is it even possible to make and implement this kind of decision? Can we expect our national leadership to beat back financial sector pressures? Or can we assume that entrenched interests and wealth will prevail?

Even now, data is regularly available to show 1) the financial sector's share of overall stock market capitalization as represented by the Dow-Jones Industrial Average or the S&P 500; and 2) the financial sector's share of current profits. Near the peak of the Multi-bubble in 2004, Raymond Dalio of Bridgewater Associates, an unusually candid money manager, described the extreme circumstances prevailing: "The money that's made from manufacturing stuff is a pittance in comparison to the amount of money made from shuffling money around. Forty-four percent of all corporate profits in the U.S. come from the financial sector compared with only 10 percent from the manufacturing sector." Readers who do not carry the relevant statistics and trends in their memories should turn back to Figure 2.1 on page 31. These numbers and graphs portray a culture and an economy on the cusp of ruinous instability.

In terms of stock market capitalization, the financial sector's 2008 swan dive, propelled by bankruptcies and write-downs, was ignominious. From its strong 2004 grip on first place, it had dropped to a weak third. Profits, indeed, were in minus territory. However, this degree of embarrassment was only temporary; a rebound would come. By 2012, gross domestic product share, however debatable its methodology, would probably offer a better measure of the sector's new weight. From 20.6 percent in 2004, that share might—and this is pure guesswork—wind up falling to 18.9 percent in 2008, 18.1 percent in 2009, and 17.4 percent in 2010. Even with this degree of shrinkage, it is fair to assume that the data for 2009–2010, when released, would still show finance far ahead of manufacturing. Any major hard-goods rebound would take years.

Meanwhile, however much the nation's political leadership tries to keep mum or duck, the future place of the financial sector in the U.S.

economy poses a vital debate—to keep bailing out or not to keep bailing out, to rely on finance or seek to roll it back. At my writing in December 2008, that national conversation had not even begun. The
economic view looking out into 2009 was cheerless. Housing prices,
down some 20 percent from their 2006 peak, were not expected to
bottom until late 2009 or 2010. By then, U.S. banks would probably
have written off some $1.5 trillion worth of toxic or trashy mortgages,
mortgage-backed securities, or more exotic financial products.

If banking must pay for its broken romance with mortgage finance,
the American economy can also expect to lose ground. According to one
study, for every 10 percent decline in home prices nationally, real GDP
would fall by 1 percentage point, triple the effect of the same ebb in financial wealth. The value of owner-occupied housing in the United
States, some $23 trillion at its peak, might bottom at $15–16 trillion,
causing as big a dollar loss as U.S. stocks had chalked up by late 2008
from their previous high in October 2007. That kind of wealth effect—
a steep reduction in consumer spending based on fears generated by
shrinking household assets—could prolong the downturn.

Besides the bloodbath in home prices, mortgage finance, and related
exotic and toxic products—by 2010 conceivably yielding a loss of 2–3
percentage points of GDP—the financial sector faced other painful diets
and downsizings. I will not even try to estimate the shrinkage among
banks, broker-dealers, private equity firms, hedge funds, and so-called
liquidity factories. The financial press keeps a count. Likewise for the
sector's anticipated 15–30 percent shrinkage in wages and workforce,
plus even larger reductions in the annual bonuses that bulk so large in
the economies of New York, London, and lesser centers.

One limitation is that while we have some comparisons for effects
during the mid-range financial travails of 1989–92 and 2000–2002, the
relevant federal statistics for finance circa 1929–1933 are thin. Back
then, moreover, finance was a relative sideshow—some transient ballyhoo in an overall U.S. economy that remained firmly rooted in manufacturing. Now finance is the epicenter of distorted national
commerce—the biggest sector in the private economy, headed down
but to an unknown degree. Here we must look to government data,
but as the preface has indicated, the federal GDP calculus, with its

artificial imputations of income, "birth and death of businesses" guess-work, and erratic "deflator," is nothing anyone should rely on. Wall Streeters, in particular, scoffed at its second-quarter 2008 claim of a surge in financial profits when in fact, those profits had collapsed (see the preface, p. xlviii).

Many details of the multi-trillion dollar bailout orchestrated by the Treasury and Federal Reserve in 2009 were withheld, which compli-cates several problems of identification, to wit: how much was given to what portions of the financial sector on what terms and with what col-lateral; what were the rules; how many trillions worth of exotic loans and arcane products are still to be written off; and how much inflation is about to course through the system in despite 2009–2010 Fed insis-tence to the contrary.

While the Obama administration was a regime-in-waiting, progres-sive commentators like Paul Krugman, Robert Kuttner, and William Greider expressed a number of pointed doubts about its economic and bailout policies. Congressional Democrats, although less central, did indeed help bungle the 2008 bailout along with Secretary Paulson and Chairman Bernanke. Over the larger twenty-five years of bubble-and-bail economics, my own rough calculation gives the Republicans 70 per-cent of the blame. The 30 percent allocable to the Democrats, though, was heavily concentrated in the late 1990s White House of Bill Clinton and in the Treasury Department of Robert Rubin followed by Law-rence Summers. Their earlier roles in blocking regulation of deriva-tives, promoting mergermania of the Citigroup variety, encouraging Wall Street debt excesses, and so on, received a new round of attention after Obama's election. The extent to which Clinton Era veterans— White House chief of staff Rahm Emanuel, ex–New York Fed President Timothy Geithner, and ex–Treasury Secretary Lawrence Summers— led the list of Obama economic appointments bespoke more continuity than reform and rethinking. Geithner, for one, was as centrally involved in the Republican-shaped origins of the 2008 bailout as Paulson and Bernanke.

This would be inhibiting. Even as the Obama people were taking office and wading through their briefing materials, the window for seri-ous reconsideration of a financial bailout strategy was narrowing.

OVEREXPANDED FINANCE: A NATIONAL SUNSET PHENOMENON?

Historically, it has been just that. But the relevance of those precedents in the fast-changing twenty-first century does deserve a new round of attention and examination. I have set out the detail in several past books: *Wealth and Democracy* (pages 171–200) and in the *American Theocracy* sections on debt and its burdens (pages 298–316). The lesson, as a number of historians have argued, is that notable economies often go through phases of development that wind up in a late-stage tendency to "luxuriate" in finance—or, as the case might be, to overreach militarily and geopolitically, and then be pulled down by excessive debt and unsustainable borrowing.

The conundrum for 2009–2010 can be simply stated: Does the frenetic rise of the U.S. financial sector to 20.6 percent of GDP as portrayed in the preface represent a new and reliance-worthy twenty-first-century architecture of leading world economies or is it another bad ending, luxuriation, or debt-binge in the manner of Hapsburg Spain, Holland (when New York was New Amsterdam), and early twentieth-century Britain?

The case for a new architecture could be made with some bravado in 1999 and possibly even in pre-Crash 2006. Its premise would be that post-industrialism is now globally established, with finance as its prime component. Such belief may have some relation to the sort of futurism that portrays twenty-second-century humankind with larger foreheads and brains. The idea that moving money around could safely dominate a leading world economic power's GDP must have seemed plausible to 1990s thinkers caught up in tech bubbling, market worship, and millennialism (these ebulliences are discussed on pp. 179–81). But there was little in-depth consideration. Then the return of human nature and greed to everyday conversation sharpened doubts about an overweening financial sector, as must current day speculation on possible successors to the United States. The notion of China, India, or Brazil having a GDP led by finance in 2050 or 2100 seems silly.

Which brings us back to the contemporary reiteration of finance as a late-stage luxuriation and sunset phenomenon. Previous leading world economic powers have displayed a wide range of symptoms. Spain, at its height in the 1570s and 1580s, was already deemphasizing normal agriculture, industry, and commercial activity to revel in the massive flood of gold and silver arriving from the Americas. Moneymen flocked to Spain from Italy, Portugal, and the Low Countries to partake of the gold-showered economy, and more and more of the Spanish upper classes began to live on the income from various kinds of debt instruments. Despite periodic royal bankruptcies, Madrid kept pouring money into the Catholic side of Europe's religious conflicts, and the Thirty Years' War of 1618–1648 completed Spain's fall. The Dutch of the late seventeenth century, for their part, also gave up the sea and shop counter where possible to become rentiers and live off bonds and securities. By the mid-eighteenth century, industry and overseas trade had declined, brokers had the palatial homes, the major banks and financial houses seemed to concentrate on foreign loans, and a rising frequency of financial panics and failures heralded Europe's imminent revolutionary era.

Pre–World War I British finance offers a less egregious example. Industry in the UK was slipping relative to both Germany and the United States. A few politicians groused that banking could not safely replace manufacturing. Upper- and upper-middle-class Britain, too, was increasingly living on grand-scale overseas investments and rentier income. Nevertheless, the fatal British miscalculation lay in imperial overreach and not understanding how the cost of two world wars would force liquidation of overseas assets, mushroom national indebtedness, and topple the British pound. As between the three nations, important common threads stood out: weakened manufacturing, the rise of rentier income, debt and banking, and military or imperial overreach. Over three decades of watching the United States for similar trends, I have seen the parallels grow and grow.

Does the financialization of the United States, culminating in the recent excesses and implosions, therefore reiterate the sorry pattern of finance as a luxuriation and sunset phenomenon? Almost certainly— and with far more greed and institutionalized speculation-cum-gambling on display than the British example a century ago. One acid portrait came in the mockery by Continental Europeans of the tunnel vision and smugness of the Wall Street leaders who attended the Davos-based World Economic Forum between 2003 and 2007, ignoring the financial warnings in favor of parties, client meetings, and "total psychological denial."[1]

In more serious terms, international disdain for Wall Street and Anglo-American capitalism is mounting. Major burdens on the future economic performance of the United States in terms of huge federal budget deficits and future inflation seem assured. U.S. financial exports have plummeted. So if this is ebb is real, wouldn't the wisest U.S. course be to reshape the 2008 bailout into an approach that puts principal emphasis on reforms, financial sector rollbacks, and alternative economic development strategies?

RENEWAL, COLLAPSE, OR SOMETHING IN BETWEEN?

History's evidence, alas, is that countries fail to dig out of these late-hour declines. Past attempts at reform or renewal haven't succeeded, as pp. 162–68 amplify. Minor recoveries in manufacturing are possible—Britain's new industries in the 1930s, for example—but never on a scale to renew leading world economic power status. In theory, if the financial sector's share of GDP slipped to 16 percent, a massive Washington "manufacturing strategy" might rebuild the hard goods sector to 16 or 17 percent. In practice, though, finance is the politically best-connected U.S. sector, and there is little likelihood it will consent to economic disestablishment. That kind of renewal seems almost impossible.

Because of the escalating mathematical and probability-theory aspects of Wall Street practice, not a few observers have hypothesized partial or substantial "collapse" possibilities. In 2006, Emil W. Henry, the U.S. Treasury's assistant secretary for financial institutions, raised the idea of financial havoc emerging out of contagious complexity in U.S. mortgage finance. The size of the GSE mortgage portfolios ($1.5 trillion), coupled with ineffective pricing of GSE debt and the interconnectivity of world financial institutions, could produce a crisis. *New Scientist* magazine, in turn, noted that "Many people dismiss any talk of collapse as akin to the street corner prophet warning that the end is nigh," but scientists take the possibility seriously. Complexity—derivative financial instruments and the like—is making "our society . . . ever more vulnerable."

Biology and health provide another frame of reference. Some historians have described finance as a national or societal old age, while words like "toxic" and "contagious" were widely used to explain how the 2007–2008 crisis developed. More telling, the financial sector or the larger U.S. economy are described as having metastasized—a word generally used with respect to the growth of cancer, which science only began to really understand in the twentieth century. Interestingly, on the American Cancer Society's Web site, their short "History of Cancer" begins as follows: "Cancer develops when cells in a part of the body begin to grow out of control. Although there are many kinds of cancer, they all start because of out-of-control growth of abnormal cells." Such cells develop because of damage to DNA, usually among older adults. Then "cancer cells often travel to other parts of the body where they begin to grow and replace normal tissue. This process, called metastasis, occurs as cancer cells get into the bloodstream or lymph vessels of our body." Perhaps the Frankenstein finance of the last two decades— the crazed borrowing, pseudo-science, frenetic growth, greed, and gambling—did something similar to the once-normal cells of the American economic corpus.

Collapse-related concerns may lurk vaguely in the background of the gigantic bailouts. More plausibly, though, the five, six, or seven trillion dollars pumped through various federal bailout pipelines will smother any financial collapse scenario, thereafter leading to a reduced-growth economy hobbled by stagflation and debt. The parallel of Japan during the 1990s does not quite fit, though. The United States lacks both Japan's strong manufacturing export sector and high-saving population. Also, private debt as a share of U.S. GDP was far higher in 2008 than comparable measurements for Japan circa 1989. Tokyo had no twenty-five-year mega-bubble to deleverage. Beyond this, it is unwise to speculate, save that interest group entrenchment and party politics in the United States will to some degree re-enact the previous leading world economic powers' inabilities to cope with decline.

FALSE ALARMS VS. PROBABLE REALITIES

Americans inclined to dispute books and periodicals theorizing about U.S. global decline make a valid point about prior false alarms—most recently, the widespread late 1980s belief that "Japan Inc." was about to grab the economic lead. It did not. Moreover, there were two earlier misapprehensions—one at the end of the 1960s, the second in the mid- and late 1970s after the fall of South Vietnam.

On one hand, this should caution pessimists. On the other hand, by a second yardstick, this backdrop cautions optimists. If one examines the previous leading world economic powers for comparable nervousness and false alarms, the resemblances have a message—the norm has been a gestation period of some forty to sixty years during which early fears and unjustified concerns slowly morph into unpleasant reality.

For the United States, that trouble-filled horizon now looms. The report published in November by the U.S. National Intelligence Council foresaw a troubled countdown to 2025 during which the United States loses global stature and clear economic financial and currency preeminence. Energy problems will get worse, too. The NIC's various timetables are plausible enough. However, the spectacular 2008 failure of the oversized, overambitious U.S. financial sector problems may speed things up, as NIC chairman Thomas Fingar commented in separate remarks.[2]

Our first major wave of leading-power self-doubt came in the late 1960s, running the gamut from statistical indications of U.S. economic weakness to cultural exhaustion and the perceived retreat of American global power. Andrew Hacker, a political scientist at Cornell, penned articles and a book entitled *The End of the American Era*. His view was that the United States "has been embarked on its time of decline since the closing days of the Second World War," and that "only a few decades remain."[3]

The Washington correspondent of the *Times* of London, Henry Brandon, in 1972 pinpointed the detente motivation of Nixon–Kissinger foreign policy in "the fact that the retreat of American power is happening faster than any other in modern history—faster even than the British or the French."[4] Another compendium of interpretations of the first

Nixon administration foreign policy was provocatively titled *Retreat from Empire?* National Security Adviser Henry Kissinger was himself a historical pessimist of the first order, and besides intriguing journalists, his worldview and access to the president infuriated many conservative admirals and generals.

Apprehensions about diminished U.S. economic, trade, and currency strength in 1970–1971 did indeed reflect cautioning developments. As American military involvement in Vietnam boosted government spending, U. S. inflation accelerated, and European central banks began—as they were still allowed—to redeem their dollars for gold at the U.S. Treasury. Within the Nixon administration, Treasury Secretary John Connally and Peter Peterson, executive director of the Council for International Economic Policy, circulated memoranda detailing "America's diminishing share of world output, her slower rate of economic growth compared to all other developed nations, her dead last ranking in gross investment, and her shrinking proportion of the world's export trade."⁵ These trade and currency problems came to a head in 1971 when Nixon shut the U.S. gold window, froze consumer prices, and imposed a 10 percent import duty. For several years before and after, these episodes supported a glum interpretation on both sides of the Atlantic.

A second wave of American-decline speculation followed the final collapse of Vietnam in April 1975, renewing its momentum during the administration of Jimmy Carter. He was blistered in the 1978 elections for insisting on transferring control of the Panama Canal to Panama, and the U.S. ebb seemed even more worrisome in 1979 after three additional blows—Iran taking hostage the U.S. Embassy staff in Tehran, the Soviet Union invading and taking over Afghanistan, and OPEC implementing a second round of oil price increases following its first demands in 1973–74.

The Reagan administration, more aggressive in confronting the Soviets, talked about "Morning again in America" and blunted the decline argument. Then a third wave of worry built in the late 1980s around Japan's perceived economic rivalry. During the 1988 presidential campaign, several hopefuls took up the challenge. Republican Senator Robert Dole updated Reagan's "Morning again" slogan by saying it was now

"High Noon," drawing on the famous Western gunfight movie. Several books stirring economic fear of Japan became bestsellers. By 1989, polls showed national opinion opposing foreign investment in the United States, and several found majorities believing that Japan had already displaced the United States in world economic leadership.[6] In 1992, Senator Paul Tsongas, running in that year's Democratic presidential primaries, quipped that the United States was not the main economic beneficiary of the Soviet Union's recent implosion: "The Cold War is over—Japan and Germany won."

Worries continued for several years. But as the Japanese economy slipped into a decade of stagnation in the 1990s, optimism returned, especially after 1996. Soaring high technology stocks fanned belief in a new era of U.S. global economic supremacy—at least until the tech bubble itself popped in 2000. The terrorist attacks on New York and Washington in 2001 produced a great patriotism and rallying round effect, but that also dissipated within a few years.

So to what year can we backdate the latest wave of concern—the fourth—over U.S. decline? Probably to 2005–2006, following short-lived pride in invading Iraq and initial half belief in a new Imperium and Pax Americana. This psychology ebbed as the Iraq war bogged down, oil prices climbed, and the U.S. dollar tumbled against other major currencies. After the earlier premature warnings, it remains possible that the fourth wave is another such.

This time, however, our chronology of doubt stretches back four decades. Also, major apprehensions are repeating and threading together—weakness in the dollar, ballooning trade deficits, embarrassment or defeat in Asia, oil predicaments, the emergence of stronger Asian challenges and rivals. The persistence itself now argues against a false alarm. Arguably, it is now the "recovery" periods that seem transient.

Indeed, the same slow, ambivalent onset preceded earlier leading world economic power downfalls. I have dwelt more on these chronologies and decline patterns in previous books. Still, there does seem to be a pattern of nervousness that begins not too long after a national zenith. Then perception of dangers flows and ebbs over forty to sixty years. These precedents are not auspicious for the United States.

To work backward beginning with Britain, the latter gained clear global supremacy after Waterloo in 1815. However, some Britons began to worry in the 1850s that the nation's huge share of global manufacturing was beginning to slip, and in 1865 Matthew Arnold voiced his famous fear of Britain becoming another Holland (merely financial and commercial). By the 1890s, popular books gloomed over the industrial challenges of Germany and the United States. Between 1903 and 1905, Conservative Party leaders, concerned that manufacturing was being displaced by finance, proposed to substitute reciprocal trade for free trade, which failed. On going to war in 1914, Britain was the leading financial power. By 1919, Britain had emerged as one of the victorious allies in the First World War. No longer, though, was she the world's leading creditor nation, and British manufacturing was on the skids. Decline was well underway.

Or take the Dutch, who became the world's leading economic power by the 1610s or 1620s. By the end of that century, Amsterdam traders were complaining that whereas the town regents had previously been active merchants, now they "derived their income from houses, lands and money at interest." The wars between 1688 and 1713 broke Holland as a naval power and forced interest rates up to 9 percent, the highest since its independence. During those same years, the Dutch national debt quintupled. By the 1720s and 1730s, the Dutch ceased to dominate some of their prime trading routes, and local financiers preferred to loan money abroad rather than at home. Midcentury brought obvious economic decline. This chronology was not very different.

Spain, the previous leading world economic power, probably reached its heyday in the 1550s, started losing self-confidence after the defeat of the Spanish Armada in 1588, and by the early 1600s was in the clutch of a malaiselike *desengano*. So-called Arbitristas, concerned about Spain's future, laid out reforms, some of which the government in Madrid tried to promote in the 1610s and 1620s, but with little success. Hugely in debt, Spain was all but bankrupted by the Thirty Years' War (1618–1648).

Interested readers can flesh out these short summaries in well-known history books. What I would underscore here is that decline does not come out of the blue. There are always early warnings, dismissed as false alarms. Today's four-decade U.S. pattern is cause for concern.

ANGLO AMERICA DECLINING, ASIA RISING

Some scholars date the rise of European world supremacy and the subordination of Asia to sixteenth-century explorers and renaissance technology, especially the maritime prowess of Spanish, Portuguese, Dutch, and English ships bristling with cannon manned by skilled gunners. On the sea, at least, the European advantage was too great to be overcome. Within fifteen years of the first arrival of Portuguese ships in Indian waters, so triumphant were they that the King of Portugal could style himself "Lord of the Conquest, Navigation and Commerce of Ethiopia, Arabia, Persia, and India."[7]

Now we may be on the threshold of a comparable or greater turnabout. The early twenty-first century will likely be remembered as a watershed period during which that five-century European–North American advantage began to reverse amid a new weight of Asian population, urbanization, wealth, natural resource advantage, and rapid economic growth.

The speculative nature of Anglo-American finance, already a major global complaint, also furnishes a convenient 2008 measuring stick. Countries with the greatest predisposition toward and later actual write-down of toxic assets clustered in the Anglo American or New York–London orbit. Besides English-speaking nations like Australia, Canada, New Zealand, and Ireland, several others were closely tied to New York–London finance—Iceland, Holland, Belgium, Switzerland, and Germany. Taken together, this financial "Anglosphere" accounted for some 85 percent of the first trillion dollars worth of asset write-downs. Big British, Swiss, and German banks like UBS, HSBC, and Deutsche Bank figured prominently in this camp.

The places less affected were Mediterranean Europe, Eastern Europe, Latin America, Africa, and, most important, Asia. Within the latter, a Morgan Stanley analysis found an exception in Singapore, where banks already injured by investments linked to the U.S. housing market expected further trouble with nonperforming loans.[8] As of early November, Asian banks had taken only 4 percent of the global write-downs, and half of that total was in Japan.[9, 10]

Although this hardly represented full-fledged economic "decoupling," it probably reflected some lesser separation or deviation: Other circumstances, too, argued for Asia being less affected. The *Wall Street Journal's* case against "the death knell of decoupling" emphasized the International Monetary Fund's November projections of 2009 year-to-year changes in economic growth. In contrast to negative predictions for Japan, the United States, Germany, and Britain came these positive anticipations: China +8.5 percent, India +6.3 percent, the Middle East +5.3 percent, and Brazil +3.0 percent.[11]

Part of the presumed strength, for China and India in particular, lay in the enormity of their new middle classes and their great potential to increase domestic consumption. Senior economic officials in both countries made their stimulative intentions clear. Indian Finance Minister Palaniappan Chidambaram summed up: "We need to insure that our domestic economy, or at least the insulated parts of the domestic economy, continues to grow at a rapid rate. It's the external sector that's causing us problems, so we will have to compensate that. If exports decline, we will have to compensate that by stimulating domestic consumption."[12]

All three Asian high-growth areas had economies in which expansion was more energy- and commodity-intensive than that of the advanced nations. Consumption was often promoted by subsidizing or capping food and fuel prices. In consequence, according to IMF data, "emerging and developing economies as a group have accounted for about 95 percent of the growth in oil demand since 2003 and two-thirds of the growth in demand for the major food crops (the remainder being due to biofuels)."[13] Barclays and several other banks calculated that continuing high Chinese demand would play a major role in raising oil prices again in 2009.[14]

Yet another bolster of Asia's relative strength, in sharp contrast to its weakness during the crisis of the late 1990s, was a large decline in individual nations' short-term external debt relative to their currency reserves. In China, Malaysia, Thailand, India, and the Philippines, reserves exceeded short-term external debt by more than two to one, although the favorable ratio was less in Indonesia and South Korea.[15] Likewise worth passing note is the rapid rise within Asia of Islamic banking, which heeds religious (sharia) law and practice, and bans interest and trading in debt. One Islamic banker dwelt on the difference: "In Islamic finance, you cannot make money out of thin air. Our dealings have to be tied to actual economic activity, like an asset or a service."[16]

As for Japan, a detailed Bloomberg survey explained how "almost two decades of sub-par growth and an aversion to business and consumer debt have produced a leaner economy. The country's banks are cash-rich and still able to lend, exporting manufacturers such as Toyota Motor Corp. have increased their efficiency and households have mountains of savings that should buoy spending during the downturn."[17] One local money manager added that "The banks didn't globalize. It was kind of a lucky play for them." Still, Japan, like Singapore, was manifestly tied to Western circumstances.

Asian drum beaters liked to talk about the continent's various global leads—the world's tallest building (in Dubai), its biggest movie industry (India's Bollywood), and its biggest casino (in Macao, which recently overtook Las Vegas). But its momentum in wealth creation, according to a survey by Merrill Lynch and Capgemini, was more to the point: the highest rate in 2007 of adding millionaires (22 percent in India, 20 percent in China) and five of the world's ten fastest-growing markets. In terms of the combined wealth of millionaires, Asia was third at $9.6 trillion, trailing North America ($11.7 trillion) and Europe ($10.6 trillion).[18] The decisive aspect, said one principal at Capgemini, was that "The growth of their wealth is outpacing the growth of their population, and that's a trend that's going to continue in coming years."

Parenthetically, Latin America is a lesser and smaller version of much the same thing. Its central bank reserves have climbed as its external debt had diminished. In a mid-October visit to India, Brazilian President Luis Ignacio Lula da Silva said, "It's unacceptable that we will pay for the irresponsibility of speculators that transformed the world into a gigantic casino and at the same time they give us lessons on how we should govern our countries. We are the victims of a financial crisis generated by the rich countries."[19] Argentina, Brazil, and Mexico are G-20 nations equally anxious to displace the old G-7.

Disbelievers in any serious decoupling do have some solid arguments. India and China could find it more difficult to stimulate large-scale increases in domestic consumption than they expect. The principal Achilles' heel, wrote Richard Duncan in the *Far East Economic Review*, is that, "At best, Asia is facing a severe recession. September 2008 may mark the end of the era of export-led growth, rather than just the beginning of a more typical global recession. Asia's export-led economic model is just as threatened as the Anglo-Saxon model of highly leveraged capitalism."[20] But that analogy, if not the basic caution, is overdrawn. The Anglo-Saxon speculative model now described as American actually goes back four hundred years to Holland and the following late seventeenth and eighteenth century continuum between Dutch and English finance. By contrast, the Asian export-led model takes up just one forty-year stretch in the long economic history of several of the world's most commercial peoples. Chinese residents overseas are also the businessmen and shopkeepers of Southeast Asia.

The critical comparison may be between Asian state capitalism or Confucianomics and the Anglo American mode. Thanks to financial recklessness and negligent government regulation in both the United States and Britain, the speculative model now staggers while the Asian mode seems better fitted for an early twenty-first-century interregnum of neo-mercantilism and economic nationalism. Numerous current-day trends support this interpretation. First, the global surge in state economic activism and control. Next, the self-discipline exemplified, over the decade since Asia's late 1990s meltdown, by its nations' commitment to accumulating some $4.4 trillion of currency reserves, almost two-thirds of the global total. Seven of the ten largest reserves are Asian, according to recent tabulations. China leads with $1.9 trillion, Japan is second with $969 billion, and India, Taiwan, South Korea, Singapore, Hong Kong, and Malaysia follow.[21] In a related vein, China (with $653 billion of U.S. Treasury securities) and Japan (with $586 billion) are the two largest creditors of the United States.

Asian preeminence extends to the sovereign wealth funds some twenty governments have created to carry out international investment strategies not necessarily suitable for central banks. Figure 5.3 on p. 146 gives the details. On a broader political dimension, Asian nations have clearly begun thinking in strategic terms. Beijing's participation in the global interest rate reductions of October 2008, conspicuous while Japan initially abstained, was read as evidence that China, with its huge reserves, is unmistakably Asia's "big enchilada."

Moreover, Beijing's management of those reserves appears to be politicizing. Already the world's leading gold producer, the Land of the Middle Kingdom appears ready to put new emphasis on gold bullion. Responding to discussion of potential U.S. record budget deficits and inflation, the vice chairman of the China Gold Association commented that "China should have at least several thousand tons of gold in its reserves, five to six times the officially announced 600 tons."[22] In 2007, national demand for gold jumped 23 percent, making China the world's second largest consumer. Were Beijing to put $20–$50 billion a year into gold purchases, it could soon counter the current anti-gold policies of Western central banks and wield the yellow metal as a weapon.

Asian aggrandizement already includes upgrading the Association of Southeast Asian Nations (ASEAN) and promoting the G-20 group of nations to supplant the essentially Western G-7. The potential, at least, is getting attention. Two of the ASEAN nations with lesser central bank reserves, the Philippines and Thailand, have made various proposals that the ten ASEAN nations, together with Japan, China, and South Korea, pool up to $350 billion, or 10 percent of their foreign currency reserves, to help protect regional currencies and to promote intra-Asian trade, investment, and tourism. For now, the Chiang Mai Initiative only allows for currency swaps between two nations.[23]

As for possible world attention on the G-20 as opposed to the G-7, Western as well as Asian observers take the group seriously. While the G-7 includes only Japan from among Asian countries, the G-20 adds seven more Asian and largely Asian countries—China, India, Indonesia, Russia, Saudi Arabia, South Korea, and Turkey—as well as nearby Australia.[24] Ignoring that heavy Asian representation won't be plausible for very much longer.

The last symbol of a rising economic nationalism keynoted by Asia lies in the escalating role of state-owned oil companies that control an ever-growing percentage of the world's oil production. Their role—and its importance to the global emergence of state capitalism—is discussed in more detail on pp. 122–23.

By 2009, most of Asia—Japan and Singapore were two major exceptions—knew that much of the continent's economic future was substantially tied to energy (oil and natural gas alike), food production, and natural resources. To put matters another way, the growth they needed for their substantially third-world populations was commodity intensive, no longer true of development in Europe and North America. Not only was Asia the number one oil producing continent, but from China to the Persian Gulf virtually all the regional oil firms were state-owned companies that viewed oil patrimonially, politically and strategically. If there was not too much left, then stretch it out—cut production if the current price wasn't high enough. OPEC was Asian-dominated, and any OPEC equivalent organized around natural gas would be, too—Iran, Russia, and Qatar were three of the nations with the largest reserves.

Not surprisingly, many Asian nations' commodity-conscious view of the world also included gold as a tactical auxiliary to paper money. The populations of India and China were the top private buyers of the yellow metal, but when it came to government-owned gold, most of that was in North America and Europe—the United States, Germany, and France had the biggest official reserves. During 2008, a growing minority of Asian economists started to think that was a mistake. In an inflationary 2009–2010 global economy flooding with an overprinting of U.S. dollars, gold reserves in Beijing, Mumbai, or the Middle East could be more strategic than dollar reserves. In November, wire services reported that the Peoples Bank of China—the nation's central bank—was considering raising its official gold reserves from 600 tons to 4,500 tons in order to diversify its present dollar-based holdings. With that increase, Beijing's gold position wouldn't be far behind that of the United States. For now, it would be stretching to describe Asia as taking a commodity-based approach as an against Anglo American financial assets strategy, but it's not silliness.

Compared with a similar economic, financial, and energy profile back in 1989 or 1999, these paragraphs bespeak a huge realignment of power. Anybody who had predicted as much in ten years earlier would have been laughed at. Now, in the wake of the partial implosion of City of London and Wall Street credibility, even some financial regulation re-alignment is possible. In the global arena, much of Asia, Latin America, and Continental Europe (France and Germany, in particular) would like to put English-speaking speculative capitalism over a barrel, but lack an obvious framework. German Chancellor Angela Merkel has proposed regulating hedge funds and curbing bonus packages for bank-ers through a new European Union "constitution" governing financial markets, and British Prime Minister Gordon Brown has lobbied for cross-border financial oversight that places the world's thirty largest banks under the supervision of a panel of regulators.[25]

The mid-November meeting of the Group of Twenty, with its heavy Asian and Latin American representation, went beyond the relative centrism of the European Union. Finance ministers and central bankers from the G-20, meeting preliminarily in Brazil, focused on the pre-dominantly American banks and investment houses that had indulged in irresponsible risk-taking, especially through credit and currency de-rivatives. They agreed in blaming the crisis on "excessive risk-taking and faulty risk-management practices in financial markets," and urging action to correct "deficiencies in financial regulation and supervision in some advanced countries."[26] The tenor of that gathering and the follow-up full meeting of the G-20 convinced many observers that reliable Western dominance of global financial organizations like the Interna-tional Monetary Fund was about to end.

At the national level, substantial new regulation is assured. In China, Hong Kong, and Korea, senior officials discussed restricting the use of over-the-counter derivatives. Wu Xiaoling, former deputy governor of the Chinese central bank, had told an earlier conference that "The U.S. crisis reflects regulatory problems in the U.S. and innovative products that ignored basic economic rules. The U.S. crisis today would be China's tomorrow if financial products such as securitization are introduced without proper risk-control measures."[27] Commercially, some major foreign markets may close to the sort of U.S. financial products once seen as having huge export potential.

If U.S. budget deficits and Federal Reserve Board balance sheets do start displaying pervasive red ink and trillion-dollar entries here and there, still another new derivative product—credit default swaps— could provide an ironic litmus. Investors can now buy credit swap protection against defaults on debts of sovereign nations and states, and the cost of insuring Uncle Sam's credit has been rising—although not as sharply as the premiums for insurance against defaults by Michigan, New York City, California, or Great Britain. One can only wonder what the swap would cost if and when an annual federal budget deficit hits not just $1.2 trillion but $1.5 trillion.

OIL, FOOD, AND A SECOND PRICE REVOLUTION

Early modern Europe's famous price revolution, first felt in the late 1400s, caught hold in the mid-1500s and plateaued in the early 1600s. Not just a watershed in rising prices—up 300–400 percent in western Europe—it was an important chapter in world history. The events and circumstances drawn together in this upheaval—unprecedented far-flung European maritime exploration; enough gold and silver from America to massively expand Europe's money supplies; significant population growth; the rapid expansion of cities; the cultural dynamism of the Renaissance; European control of Asian trade routes, spices, and luxury goods; technological innovation in war, commerce, and navigation alike; huge new commercial fortunes; and much expanded consumer markets—signaled a new European centrality in the world. Asia, more populous and hitherto richer, fell behind. Prices did not always go up everywhere in Europe, but their general trajectory was upward. Centrally involved countries like France and Spain saw price indexes four or five times higher in 1620 than they had been in 1500.

Inflation, we might say, was a kind of transmission system. Although almost everybody got more nominal money, for the poor worker or farmer, it bought a lower standard of living than fathers or grandfathers in similar vocations had enjoyed. Observations in this vein fill the economic histories. But for those with capital, skills, or education, opportunities were vast. Economic inequality and polarization grew steadily.

Wars alone served to mushroom inflation in Europe and North America during the eighteenth, nineteenth, and first half of the twentieth century. And no major spikes occurred over a broad region in *peacetime*. Which brings us to 1965 and the huge price changes that have unfolded since then. If they represent another continental emergence like the one four to five hundred years ago, as opposed to a pair of shorter, individual commodity cycles, the implications would be enormous—certainly for Asia, but also for the United States.

Even a ten to twenty year commodity inflation cycle could be interrupted by a couple of years in which commodity prices fall. However, if Asia is really at the center of a new Price Revolution II, this could be something even more powerful. We could see an overall fifty-, sixty-, or seventy-year upheaval—able to run another twenty or thirty years—like the one that cut such a swath across early modern Europe.

If 2009–2010 global growth is weak, the prevailing expert assumption is that it will be less weak in Asia and more weak in North America and Western Europe. Prices in Asia may fall and be deflationary for a quarter or two, but few expect that Chinese and Indian data will be deflationary on a mulityear basis. Otherwise, it's hardly likely to cut short the "broadest and most buoyant commodity price boom since the early 1970s" identified by the IMF in the summer of 2008.

Here is where the enormity of Asian emergence comes in. Although the rise of North America in the nineteenth century was important, Europe was much more populous, enough so that even in 1900, North America was only an adjunct. By contrast, Asia's rise over the last fifty years, and especially the last twenty, represents a much larger mass and enterprise than Europe ever did. Asia had 56 percent of the world's population in 1950 and 59 percent in 1980, and is expected to have 61 percent in 2010 and about the same in 2025. Goliath is coming.

The summation of the National Intelligence Council's landmark survey is blunt: "In terms of size, speed and directional flow, the transfer of global wealth and economic power now underway—roughly from West to East—is without precedent in modern history."[28] Indeed, the flow of oil revenues to Asia in the last decade, which should soon resume, may be akin to the early stages of the flow of new world gold and silver to Europe four hundred-odd years ago. A parallel consumer-market dimension—the explosive emergence of the global middle class from 440 million now to 1.2 billion in 2025, most of it occurring in Asia—could have equal importance in recasting economics and price levels.[29]

However, before returning to the global food- and energy-driven momentum of Price Revolution II, it's appropriate to jump back more than six decades and recall the increasing Asianization of major influences on the United States. Take the wars fought by the United States during that period. They mostly involved Asia—Japan (World War II), Korea (1950–53), Vietnam (1965–73), the Gulf War with Iraq (1991), Afghanistan (2001–), and Iraq (2003–). Only the first was a clear success. Or consider the origin of the economic shocks directed against the United States: 1973–74 (OPEC-Oil), 1978–79 (OPEC-Oil), 2001 (Al-Qaeda—World Trade Center/Wall Street). On top of which, it's also fair to say that the four major U.S. inflations had significant roots in Asia: post-1965 (Vietnam War), post-1973 (OPEC-Oil), post-1978 (OPEC-Oil), post-2002 (oil and food). In recent years, moreover, as the preface shows (p. liii), Asia has been generating most of the world's highest inflation rates—and in many nations, these are expected to continue.

Like Price Revolution I, Asia's twenty-first-century economic transformation has a sprawling root system. The Asian version, however, involves a bigger share of the world population and an unprecedented expansion of middle-class consumer markets with their explosive, if stereotyped, new demand for energy, food, and clothing. Demand for tillable cropland grew in sixteenth-century Europe, but the market created by twenty-first-century Asia's upsurge will tower over the earlier example. Similarly, NIC projections of the extent to which pressure for oil in 2015 or 2025 will greatly exceed the supply, absolutely dwarf the analogy to sixteenth- and seventeenth-century Western European forests being depleted by wood-burning.

Of the fifty largest cities in the world, twenty-eight are Asian. The educated classes of Philadelphia, Liverpool, or Toronto have heard of Shanghai's astonishing new skyline and the giant sprawl of Tokyo and New Delhi. Few, though, could name the dozens of new Asian cities with 2–3 million populations. Here are five whose size really surprised me—Bandung, Indonesia; Inchon, Korea; Izmir, Turkey;

Pyongyang, North Korea; and Tashkent, Uzbekistan. That really brings home the urbanization factor.

Of the last three decades of growth within Asia, some has been fueled by oil profits and some by high-powered manufacturing aimed at export markets. Much has also come from activist governments practicing a form of state capitalism. In China, for example, a 2008 *Wall Street Journal* survey of building roads, airports, railroads, housing, and factories—some 30,000 miles of expressway were built just in this decade (versus a U.S. interstate system *totaling* 47,000 miles!)—found that government "domestic investment contributes far more to growth" than do exports. "In recent years, spending on everything from public works to housing to factory equipment has accounted for about four to six percentage points of China's 10 percent average annual growth rate."[30]

If public works-centered investment keynotes China's expansion, wealth and growth in the Middle East has disproportionately come from energy—oil and gas. The output of some Asian producers—Yemen, Oman, Indonesia, and Syria—is already in decline, and in others production levels have flattened: Brunei, Malaysia, China, India, and Qatar. Even so, the NIC study concludes that "only six countries—Saudi Arabia, Iran, Kuwait, the United Arab Emirates, Iraq (potentially), and Russia—are projected to account for 39 percent of total world oil production in 2025."[31] Like the International Energy Agency, the NIC report avoids use of "peak oil" terminology but assumes that world energy demand will outstrip supply. Furthermore, the national oil companies prevalent in Asia "have strong economic and political incentives to limit investment in order to prolong their production horizon. Keeping oil in the ground provides resources for future generations in oil states that have limited their horizons." This is peak oil by another name, and it explains the greater willingness of OPEC producers to cut output.

As noted in the preface, many leaders of the Persian Gulf oil producing nations angrily blamed speculators in the Western nations for pushing up per-barrel prices to excessive levels in the $140-range in the first half of 2008 and then helping to drive them down beyond any sustainable level in November and December. In July, just before oil prices peaked, Saudi King Abdullah put "speculators who play the market out of selfish interests" first in his explanation of who was to blame and what was happening.[32] By mid-December, with prices tumbling into the $40–50 a barrel range, oil ministers from Saudi Arabia and the various Gulf states, still unhappy about speculators, commented freely on how new investment would not earn a return unless oil sold at a minimum of $70–80 a barrel. Environmentalists, for their part, understood how too-low prices for oil served to undercut prospects for alternative energies. From wind to solar, low-carbon technologies became economic only when oil prices were reasonably high. Even in late October, Fatih Birah, chief economist of the International Energy Agency, had explained that in two years' time "we could see much higher prices than we saw three months ago, if [oil and gas] investments are not going through."[33] Another backstop for this sharp rebound thesis involved the widening gap between spot prices or prices for near-term futures in comparison to more expensive futures dated six months, fifteen months, or two years out. The latter reflected a widespread sense that energy costs might soon be rising again. On December 17, OPEC delegates meeting in Algeria decided to cut production by 2.2 million barrels to support prices.[34]

Across much of Asia, not least China and India, food is the principal component of government-measured inflation, which remains high. Obtaining more and better eatables is one of the greatest challenges facing Asia and Latin America, both in price and developmental priorities. Assumptions in the NIC report were that Asia, Africa, and Latin America would account for almost all of the world's population growth over the next twenty years, with only 3 percent coming in the West. This growth will pressure "energy, food, and water, and demand is projected to outstrip easily available supplies over the next decade or so." Because of "rising affluence and the shift to Western dietary preferences by a large middle class," demand for food will rise by 50 percent by 2030. To complicate matters, many countries will have to juggle conflicting energy and food security concerns. Among the major grain exporting nations, the United States, Canada, Argentina, and Australia, biofuels were predicted to command more cropland and water, and this "fuel" farming pressure will "force grain prices in the global markets to fluctuate at levels above today's highs."

Building agriculture's costly new infrastructure—land, water, top-soil, fertilizers, credit, facilities, and transportation—has raised food costs worldwide. Some multiple measure of the upheaval in China, for example, can be had from two facts: milk consumption in China has quadrupled since 1999, and Michelin has now just published its first red guide for restaurants in China (so far, just in Hong Kong and Macao).[35] In the western Brazilian state of Mato Grosso, where agribusiness is surging, the total cost of producing the three main crops—cotton, corn, and soybeans—was calculated to have increased 42 percent in 2008 over 2007.[36] Huge new appetites are emerging.

Even in the United States, where the press takes commodity defla-tion seriously, there is little pretense that food and restaurant costs are not continuing to rise. A major November profile of the food industry by the *New York Times* underscored that prices for packaged goods and meat were holding firm or increasing. Consumers, the analysis said, should not expect lower costs in grocery markets or restaurants.[37] Fore-casts by the Agriculture Department were for food prices to "increase 3.5 to 4.5 percent in 2009, compared with an estimated 5 to 6 percent increase" for 2007. At the National Restaurant Association, chief econo-mist Hudson Riehle told the *Times* that "our operators are being forced to raise menu prices at the highest rate since 1990."

In the agricultural sector, though, the plus side of record food prices is that they have a history of encouraging innovation, be it in farm equipment, technology, seeds, or fertilizer. The same has been true in energy, where 2006–2008 prices spurred development of previously un-economic resources—heavy oil, shale oil, and the Canadian oil sands region. This is why the idea of an Asia-centered Price Revolution II is so compelling. Price upheavals and progress may require each other.

One prospect that troubled the National Intelligence Council was the apparent resurgence of state capitalism, resource nationalism, and forms of mercantilism. I see similar trends, which are developed at greater length in pages 54–58 and 180. Even in the United States, the quasi-nationalization of finance in the 2008 bailouts and the heavy-handed role of Washington in picking economic winners and losers bespoke that same global trend. If history winds up supporting the notion of Price Revolution II in Asia, no one should be surprised to see a further institutionalization of state economic activity. The first Price Revolution in the sixteenth century, accompanying as it did the rise of European nation-states, was in fact the nursery of the original mercantilism in Spain, Portugal, France, and England, even though the "mercantile system" did not actually get its name until the activities of French controller-general Jean-Baptiste Colbert in the 1660s.

This prospect has enough ramifications to be a book, and not just a subchapter. But let us draw matters to a close. Inflation is the global threat. Asia, where the United States has geopolitical interests literally all over the map, and especially in the quadrant from Turkey to Israel and the Red Sea east to the Gulf of Arabia and the roof of Asia in Pakistan and Afghanistan, is the part of the world into which the United States is pouring the most money and from which Washington is most likely to be pressured and squeezed. During and after the first Price Revolution, Asia and Islam were pushed from Europe—Spain expelling the last Moors, central Europeans holding Vienna then forcing the Turks to retreat, and Russia advancing south and east to Tartary and the Urals. If Asia is the twenty-first-century continent, the United States could be at risk of a costly military overcommitment of the magnitude that dethroned the three preceding leading world economic powers. Perhaps it can still be avoided.

Appendix

Global Public Opinion and the Loss of Respect
for the United States, 2003–7

Part of the arena in which the United States must fight its energy, climate, financial, and currency battles includes global opinion, which has become skeptical and in many places hostile to American interests—much more so than in 2001 and 2002.

My last book detailed how much of this dissatisfaction and sourness related to the invasion of Iraq and the reelection of George W. Bush to a second term, both events that were regretted around the world. In 2005, the Pew Global Attitudes Project found startling foreign majorities saying that their views of the United States had become less favorable after Bush's reelection. For example, 77 percent of Germans said so, as did 75 percent of Canadians, 74 percent of the French, and 62 percent of Britons. Other surveys elaborated similar sentiments.

If anything, this lack of international respect intensified during the 2005–7 period, as we will see in a number of samplings. Another new mind-set also deserves note: the growing evidence from surveys taken within the United States that Americans, too, have come to worry about their nation's loss of standing in the world and to favor major changes in the U.S. position in the world. A late 2007 roundup by Voice of America News reported that surveys taken earlier in the year by Gallup had found 61 percent of respondents describing themselves as dissatisfied with the U.S. position in the world, while an autumn sampling for the German Marshall Fund of the United States found that American support for the idea that the United States should support promoting democracy around the world had fallen from 52 percent in 2005 to just 37 percent in 2007. Another U.S. opinion survey, taken in 2006 for the Chicago Council on Global Affairs, found 76 percent of respondents opposing the idea of the United States' taking the leading global role in trying to solve international problems.[1]

In sum, the hubris-driven American unilateralism of the 2002–3 variety no longer commands popular support on the home front, and the realities of foreign disrespect are beginning to sink in.

Two dimensions of that disrespect—an overview and then some national and regional specifics—tell much of the tale.

AN OVERVIEW OF 2007 SURVEYS

The 2007 Strategic Survey of the International Institute for Strategic Studies
"The US has suffered a significant loss of power and prestige around the world in the years since George W. Bush came to power, limiting its ability to influence international crises. . . . The 2007 Strategic Survey of the non-partisan International Institute for Strategic Studies picked the decline of U.S. authority as one of the most important security developments of the past year—but suggested that the fading of American prestige began earlier, largely due to its failings in Iraq."[2]

Trans-Atlantic Trends 2007
"A new poll . . . by the German Marshall Fund of the United States shows that Europeans are down on America right now and not seeing light over the horizon. The poll is part of the report 'Trans-Atlantic Trends 2007' that surveys 12 European countries in an attempt to gauge feelings about relations between the U.S. and Europe. When it comes to Europeans' views of US President George W. Bush, his war in Iraq, and his foreign policies, 77 percent disapprove of him and his policies, while 17 percent voiced approval. This compares with American views, which show an approval rate of 32 percent and disapproval rate of 63 percent, according to an August survey released by the Gallup Poll. Teasing out whether the issue was the US war or Bush himself, the Europeans seemed divided in the trans-Atlantic survey, with 38 percent choosing the war and 34 percent Bush himself."[3]

The Pew Global Attitudes Project, 2007
"Global distrust of American leadership is reflected in increasing disapproval of the cornerstones of U.S. foreign policy. Not only is there worldwide support for a withdrawal of U.S. troops from Iraq, but there also is considerable opposition to U.S. and NATO operations in Afghanistan. Western European publics are at best divided about keeping troops there. In nearly every predominantly Muslim country, overwhelming majorities want U.S. and NATO troops withdrawn from Afghanistan as soon as possible. In addition, global support for the U.S.-led war on terrorism ebbs ever lower. And the United States is the nation blamed most often for hurting the world's environment, at a time of rising global concern about environmental issues."[4]

Chicago Council on Global Affairs Multinational Survey, 2007
"A multinational poll finds that publics around the world reject the idea that the United States should continue to play the role of preeminent world leader. Most publics say the United States plays the role of world policeman more than it should and cannot be trusted to act responsibly. . . . This desire for a reduced American role may flow in part from a lack of confidence that the United States can be trusted to 'act responsibly in the world.' This lack of confidence was the most common view in 10 out of 15 countries. Two Latin American countries show the

highest numbers expressing this mistrust—Argentina (84%) and Peru (82%), followed by Russians (73%), the French (72%) and Indonesians (64%)."[5]

BBC World Service/Globespan Poll, 2007
"The global view of the United States' role in world affairs has significantly deteriorated over the last year according to a BBC World Service poll of more than 26,000 people across 25 different countries. . . . The poll shows that in the 18 countries that were previously polled, the average percentage saying that the United States is having a mainly positive influence has dropped seven points from a year ago—from 36 percent to 29 percent—after having already dropped four points the year before. Across all 25 countries polled, one citizen in two (49%) now says the U.S. is playing a mainly negative role in the world. Over two-thirds (68%) believe the U.S. military presence in the Middle East provokes more conflict than it prevents and only 17 percent believes US troops there are a stabilizing force."[6]

SOME FOREIGN NATIONAL AND REGIONAL IMPLICATIONS

Provoking world opinion in this manner would have been foolish even in 1950, when the United States was all-powerful, industrial pollution was barely an issue, the dollar reigned supreme, and so did U.S. oil production. Today, with the United States vulnerable in global currency markets, oil markets, credit markets, and climate conferences alike, this sort of unilateralism and bravado is little short of disastrous. The United States is the world's leading debtor, not its leading creditor as in 1950. Here are some economic and financial cautions:

The Organization of the Petroleum Exporting Countries
No poll was taken during 2007 in all of the nations that make up OPEC, but five were polled by the Pew Center: Indonesia, Malaysia, Kuwait, Venezuela, and Nigeria. The United States was widely disdained in Indonesia and Malaysia but somewhat liked in Nigeria (principally because of that nation's large Christian minority). The United States is correct to be putting more reliance on Nigeria as an oil supplier. Still, the overall balance of power in OPEC is held by Muslim countries, with the two heavily Christian nations—Venezuela and Ecuador—having joined with Iran in taking an anti-American stance at the most recent OPEC meeting.

Russia
Vladimir Putin, with a job approval in the 80s, is as popular in his nation as Bush is unpopular in the United States. Part of the reason is that Putin has strengthened Russia's global position, especially in energy, even as the circumstances of the United States have declined. Putin is now anxious to use Russian energy clout to boost the role of the Russian ruble against the U.S. dollar. Polls released in January 2007 by Russia's Public Opinion Foundation show Russians embracing the ruble and the euro and losing faith in the dollar. In 2002, 35 percent trusted the dollar more than the euro or ruble, and 37 percent preferred the ruble. As of January 2007, 63 percent trusted the ruble more, versus 15 percent choosing the euro and 5 percent opting for the dollar.[7]

The Alienating U.S. Presence in the Middle East
The numbers here are particularly depressing. Of the nine nations having the most unfavorable views of the United States in the 2007 Pew Center poll, eight are Muslim. Indeed, the three with the highest unfavorable to favorable ratios are three especially closely caught up in U.S. policy in the Middle East: the territory of Palestine, Pakistan, and Turkey. The latter two are former close U.S. allies whose people have come to dislike and distrust the United States. According to the German Marshall Fund survey, angry Turks are in the process of turning away from Europe and toward the anti-U.S. viewpoints of nations like Iran.[8] As for the alienation of Pakistan, a September 2007 poll conducted by WorldPublicOpinion.org found 75–80 percent public opposition to allowing foreign (U.S.) troops to enter Pakistan to attack Taliban or al Qaeda forces. Some 64 percent of Pakistanis opposed the government's 2007 crackdown on Islamic fundamentalists and 60 percent believed that Sharia (Islamic law) should play a larger role in Pakistan.[9] Data like these tend to support the notion of serious blowback against U.S. policy in the Middle East.

Argentina and Financial Bitterness at the United States
During the 1990s, the Argentine peso was interchangeable with the American dollar, but that relationship became unworkable when Argentina was caught up in inflation and international debts. In 2002, when banks were closed to stop withdrawals, some anti-American demonstrations took place. Ultimately, a new government turned to the left, repudiated its international debts (later paying them off at a bargained-for low rate), rejected the austerity proposed by the International Monetary Fund (backed by Washington), established relationships with Hugo Chavez and Fidel Castro, and restored a degree of prosperity through more populist economic policies. Hostility toward the United States and its economic policies has lingered.

Notes

PREFACE TO THE REVISED EDITION

1. pp. 33–34.
2. *American Theocracy*, pp. 272, 326.
3. Ibid, p. 294.
4. Ibid, p. 325.
5. Ibid, pp. 293–94.
6. Ibid, p. 325.
7. Ibid, p. 281.
8. Ibid, p. 327.
9. Ibid, p. 291.
10. "Citi's Taxpayer Parachute," *The Wall Street Journal*, November 5, 2008.
11. *The Politics of Rich and Poor*, p. 172.
12. Warren Buffett, Letter to Shareholders of the Berkshire-Hathaway Corporation, 2003.
13. "Brooksley Born Vindicated as Swaps Rules Take Shape," Bloomberg News, November 13, 2008.
14. Toni Straka, "Coming Soon: The $600 Trillion Dollar Emergency Meeting," Seeking Alpha, Oct. 13, 2008, Seekingalpha.com.
15. "Credit Markets' Frozen Corners Thaw—in Time," *Wall Street Journal*, February 14, 2008, p. C1.
16. Alan Katz and Ian Katz, "Greenspan Slept as Off-Balance Sheet Toxic Debt Evaded Scrutiny," Bloomberg News, Oct. 30, 2008.
17. Mark Pitman, "Evil Wall Street Exports Boomed with Fools Born to Buy Debt," Bloomberg News, October 27, 2008.
18. "Fed Chief Warns of Housing Froth," *Washington Post*, June 10, 2005.
19. Michael Lewis, "The End," *Portfolio*, November 11, 2008.
20. Gretchen Morgenson, "How the Thundering Herd Faltered and Fell," *New York Times*, November 9, 2008, page BU 1.
21. *American Theocracy*, p. 296.
22. Ibid, p. 292.
23. Katz and Katz, "Greenspan Slept."
24. Pitman, "Evil Wall Street Exports Boomed."

25. "A Quiet Windfall for U.S. Banks," *Washington Post,* November 10, 2008.

26. "In Praise of a Rocky Transition," *The Nation,* December 1, 2008.

27. "Truth or Consequences," *Barron's,* December 29, 2008, and "Credit Crunch: What Credit Crunch?" Reuters, December 11, 2008.

28. "Fed Official: Bank Mergers Must Not Lead to 'Financial Oligarchy,'" Bloomberg News, October 13, 2008.

29. "Up and Down Wall Street," *Barron's,* December 8, 2008.

30. William E. Leuchtenburg, "George, You Were No Herbert Hoover," *The New Republic,* October 22, 2008.

31. "Mr. Risk Goes to Washington," *BusinessWeek,* June 2, 2006.

32. "Bernanke Is Fighting the Last War," *Wall Street Journal,* October 18, 2008.

33. Ibid.

34. "Wall Street Bailout Questioned at Fed Event," Associated Press, August 23, 2008.

35. Gretchen Morgenson, "What a Deal: Trash for Treasuries," *New York Times,* May 18, 2008.

36. Ibid., and Gretchen Morgenson, "Regulators in Need of Rehab," *New York Times,* October 12, 2008.

37. "A Chaotic Sunday Opens Wall Street's Week" and "AIG Scrambles to Raise Cash, Talks to Fed," *Wall Street Journal,* September 15, 2008, p. C1.

38. "Ghosts of the Great Depression," *The Daily Reckoning,* Agora Financial, October 3, 2008.

39. Kevin Hassett, "Panic of 2008 Is Better Than the Alternative," Bloomberg News, November 3, 2008.

40. "Wall Street Bailout Questioned."

41. "Overheard," *Wall Street Journal,* November 13, 2008, p. C16.

42. Mark Gilbert, "Risk Drifts from Banks to Governments to You, Me," Bloomberg News, October 16, 2008.

43. "Treasury Draws Fire for Shift in Rescue," *Wall Street Journal,* November 14, p. A4.

44. "U.S. Treasury Shuns Banks That Need Cash Most," Bloomberg News, October 29, 2008.

45. "Senators Question Changes That Make Bank Mergers Easier," *Washington Post,* October 31, 2008.

46. "Fed Defies Transparency Aim in Refusal to Identify Bank Loans," Bloomberg News, November 10, 2008.

47. Gretchen Morgenson, "They're Shocked, Shocked About the Mess," *New York Times,* October 26, 2008.

48. "Paulson Credibility Takes Hit with Rescue-Plan Shift," Bloomberg News, November 14, 2008.

49. "The Key Numbers Behind the Bailouts," *Wall Street Journal,* December 13–14, 2008.

50. Austan Goolsbee, "The Unemployment Myth," *New York Times,* November 30, 2003.

51. "Former Federal Reserve Chief Volcker Warns on Inflation," Dow-Jones Newswires, May 15, 2008.

52. Fred Shannon, *The Farmer's Last Frontier* (Armonk, N.Y.: M. E. Sharpe, 1989), pp. 291, 349–352.

53. Aaron Friedberg, *The Weary Titan* (Princeton, N.J.: Princeton University Press, 1988), pp. 79–80.

54. Irving Bernstein, *The Lean Years* (Boston: Houghton Mifflin Company, 1960), pp. 267–268.

55. N. Gregoiry Mankiw, "Have We Learned Enough?" *New York Times,* October 26, 2008), business section pp. 1 and 6.

56. Alan Abelson, "Sizing Up Sarah," *Barron's,* September 1, 2008, p. 7.

57. Peter Schiff, "Damned Lies and Statistics?" *Asia Sentinel,* November 2, 2007.

58. John Williams, www.shadowstats.com, GDP data series, November 25, 2008.

59. Caroline Baum, "Output Without Income Is Like a 'Virgin Birth,'" Bloomberg News, September 8, 2008.

60. Abelson, "Sizing Up Sarah."

61. "Moody's Weighs Warning Labels for Its Ratings," *Wall Street Journal,* February 5, 2008, p. C1.

62. James Grant, quoted in "The Rude Awakening," Agora Financial, November 18, 2008.

63. John A. Garraty, *The Great Depression* (New York: Harcourt Brace, 1986), pp. 52–57.

64. "Brazil October Inflation Rate Rises to 3-year High," Bloomberg News, November 7, 2008.

65. "Mexico Inflation Soars to 7-year High in October," Reuters, November 7, 2008.

66. "China's October Inflation Matches Decade High of 6.5 Percent," Bloomberg News, November 13, 2008.

67. "Singapore Inflation Hits 16-year High on Food, Energy," Reuters India, November 23, 2008.

68. "Inflation in Pakistan at Near-30-year High," United Press International, November 11, 2008.

69. "Asian Interest-Rate Swaps Signal More Rate Cuts Are Coming," Bloomberg News, November 5, 2008.

70. "Indonesia's October Inflation," Reuters, November 3, 2008.

71. "Philippine Inflation Eases to 11.2 Percent in October," *Agence France-Press,* November 5, 2008.

72. "Russia's Inflation at 0.9 Percent in October," *RIA Novosti,* November 5, 2008.

73. "Turkey: October Inflation Reflects Bad News for Consumers," Turkish Statistics Institute, see europe.net, November 4, 2008.

74. "Inflation Sees a Slight Drop to 20 Pct.," *Egypt Daily News*, November 10, 2008.

75. "Saudi Inflation Falls to 10.9 Percent," Saudi Arabian Monetary Agency, October 12, 2008.

76. "Nigeria Oct. Consumer Inflation Rises to 14.7 Percent," Reuters, November 19, 2008.

77. "Inflation Pressures Easing in Australia," *International Business Times*, November 18, 2008.

78. "U.S. Inflation Understated, Pimco's Gross Says," *MarketWatch*, May 22, 2008.

79. CNBC. "Bailout Tally: $3.8 Trillion and Counting," thinkprogress.org/2008/11/17/17bailout.tally/.

80. "Tearing into the Fed and Treasury Plans," *Barron's*, October 27, 2008.

81. Ibid.

82. R. B. Wernham, ed., *The Counter-Reformation and Price Revolution, 1559–1610* (Cambridge: The Cambridge University Press, 1968), p. 3.

83. "Record Options Trading Slows as Hedge Funds Fold, Price Surge," Bloomberg News, November 20, 2008.

84. "S&P 500 Index Drop Leaves 64 Industries with Losses," Bloomberg News, November 21, 2008.

85. "U.S. Stock Volatility Will Soon Top 1929, Goldman Says," Bloomberg News, November 21, 2008.

86. Harold W. Stanly and Richard G. Niemi, *Vital Statistics on American Politics* (Washington, D.C.: *Congressional Quarterly*, 1994), p. 124.

87. "Obama Embrace of Wall Street Insiders Points to Politic Reforms," Bloomberg News, November 19, 2008.

88. "Obama Tilt Toward Rubinomics Stirs Warning from Organized Labor," Bloomberg News, August 18, 2008.

89. "Volcker Would Be Solid Treasury Candidate: Stiglitz," Reuters, November 5, 2008.

90. "Obama Embrace of Wall Street Insiders."

91. "Emanuel Pick Underscores Balancing Act Ahead in Reshaping Financial Industry," *Wall Street Journal*, November 8–9, 2008.

92. William Greider, "Establishment Disorder," *The Nation*, November 17, 2008, p. 16.

93. "Obama Embrace of Wall Street Insiders."

94. James Grant, "Why No Outrage," *Wall Street Journal*, Saturday/Sunday, July 19–20, p. W1.

95. "Incumbents Are Attacked for Rescue Plan," *Washington Post*, October 12, 2008.

96. "U.S. Consumers Lose Faith in Fed, Financial System," Reuters, October 10, 2008.

97. "Americans Want Regulation More Than Rescue," Gallup.com, November 11, 2008.
98. "Americans Oppose Bailouts, Favor Obama," Bloomberg News, September 24, 2008.
99. "Americans Turn Negative on Economy, Expect Recession, Poll Says," Bloomberg News, October 25, 2008.

1. INTRODUCTION: THE PANIC OF AUGUST

1. See Charles P. Kindleberger, *Manias, Panics, and Crashes* (New York: Harper Torchbooks, 1978), pp. 106, 254–56.
2. David Fromkin, *Europe's Last Summer* (New York: Knopf, 2004), p. 168.
3. "The Loan Comes Due," *New York Times*, August 5, 2007, Week in Review.
4. "Inside the Sub-prime Storm," *Schwab Investing Insights*, August 16, 2007, p. 2.
5. "Risk Returns with a Vengeance," *Fortune*, August 20, 2007; www.cnnmoney.com, August 21, 2007.
6. "Mortgage Fraud Is the Thing to Do Now," *Chicago Tribune*, September 22, 2007; www.foreclosurepulse.com, July 12, 2007.
7. www.ml-implode.com.
8. Niall Ferguson, *The Pity of War* (New York: Basic Books, 1999), p. 192.
9. "Loan by Loan, the Making of a Credit Squeeze," *New York Times*, Sunday Business, August 19, 2007.
10. S&P/Case-Shiller from "U.S. Home Prices Fell by Record in Second Quarter," Bloomberg News, August 28, 2007.
11. "Fed Gets 'F' for Failures on Housing," Bloomberg News, August 31, 2007.
12. "Debtor Nation," *Harvard Magazine*, July–August 2007, p. 42.
13. "Investors Opening Their Eyes to Widespread Credit Excesses of the Past," *USA Today*, August 7, 2007.
14. For details, see Greenspan's statements to the *New York Times* in 1978 and 1980, quoted in Fred Sheehan, "Currency Devaluation and House-Swapping," *Whiskey and Gunpowder*, September 5, 2007.
15. "The Houses That Saved the World," *Economist*, March 28, 2002.
16. Thomas Heibling, *The Real and Financial Effects of Bursting Asset Price Bubbles* (video essay), International Monetary Fund, Washington, D.C., April 3, 2003.
17. Kurt Richebächer, "Property Bubbles," quoted in *The Daily Reckoning*, Agora Financial, www.dr.com, August 17, 2007.
18. "Credit Market Has Pros Confused," *USA Today*, August 27, 2007; "Investor Mood Worsens on Housing Turmoil," Reuters, August 27, 2007.
19. Kevin Phillips, *American Theocracy: The Peril and Politics of Radical Religion, Oil, and Borrowed Money in the 21st Century* (New York: Viking, 2006), p. 337, for 2002–5; for 2006, see Kimberley Amadeos, "The U.S. Trade Deficit 2006—A Description," www.useconomy.about.com.

20. "Oil Prices: A Pause, Then Up," *Barron's*, October 16, 2006.
21. "James Schlesinger: Au sujet du pétrole, nous sommes tous piquistes désormais," http://contreinfo.info, September 19, 2007.
22. "The New Seven Sisters," *Financial Times*, March 12, 2007.
23. "Acceptability Is Total's Growth Model," *Financial Times*, September 6, 2007.
24. See, for example, "SCO Summit Focuses on Energy Cooperation," *Eurasia Daily Monitor*, August 17, 2007; "Central Asia's Military Extravaganza Puts NATO Allies on Notice," *Vancouver Sun*, August 17, 2007; and "Chavez Tour Ends in Energy Deals," *BBC News*, August 21, 2007.
25. John A. Garraty, *The Great Depression* (New York: Harcourt Brace, 1986), pp. 7–9.
26. Kindleberger, *Manias, Panics, and Crashes*, p. 5.
27. See, for example, Peter Tertzakian, *A Thousand Barrels a Second: The Coming Oil Break Point and the Challenges Facing an Energy Dependent World* (New York: McGraw-Hill, 2006).
28. Kevin Phillips, *American Dynasty: Aristocracy, Fortune, and the Politics of Deceit in the House of Bush* (New York: Viking, 2004).
29. "Bernanke's Pledge Fails to Dispel Pessimism at Jackson Retreat," www.bloomberg.com, September 3, 2007.
30. Robert Bruner and Sean Carr, *The Panic of 1907* (New York: Wiley, 2007).

2. FINANCE: THE NEW REAL ECONOMY?

1. "Paulson Says Sub-prime Woes Will Linger," Reuters, Sepember 12, 2007.
2. "Sustaining New York's and the U.S.'s Global Financial Services Leadership," Michael Bloomberg and Charles Schumer, U.S. Senate, Washington, D.C., January, 22, 2007.
3. Fred Sheehan, "Tin Men," *Whiskey and Gunpowder*, July 5, 2007.
4. "Merchants of Debt," *Time*, February 28, 1977.
5. Ibid.
6. Hyman Minsky, *Stabilizing an Unstable Economy* (New Haven, Conn.: Yale University Press, 1986).
7. Fred Shannon, *The Farmer's Last Frontier: Agriculture, 1860–1897* (Armonk, N.Y.: M. E. Sharpe, 1989), pp. 350–55.
8. William F. Hixson, *A Matter of Interest: Reexamining Money, Debt, and Real Economic Growth* (New York: Praeger, 1991), p. 81.
9. Kevin Phillips, *Post-Conservative America: People, Politics, and Ideology in a Time of Crisis* (New York: Random House, 1982), p. 9.
10. James Medoff and Andrew Harless, *The Indebted Society* (New York: Little, Brown, 1996), pp. 28–34.
11. Benjamin Friedman, "Sorting Out the Debt," *New Perspectives Quarterly*, vol. 4, no. 3 (Fall 1987).

12. Thomas W. Synnott III, "The Debt Explosion of the 1980s," *Business Economics,* January 1991.
13. "Deregulation Helped Turn S&L Problem into Crisis," *Miami Herald,* February 19, 1989.
14. Kevin Phillips, *Arrogant Capital: Washington, Wall Street, and the Frustration of American Politics* (New York: Little, Brown), p. 94.
15. Ibid.
16. Of the $11.6 trillion worth of public and private debt added in the United States between 1993 and 2001, $5.8 trillion—an extraordinary proportion—was private financial debt, according to federal Flow of Funds data.
17. Jane D'Arista, "Financial Sector Borrowing Drives the Credit Expansion," *Flow of Funds Review and Analysis,* Fourth Quarter 1999, p. 2.
18. Daniel Gross, *Bull Run: Wall Street, the Democrats, and the New Politics of Personal Finance* (New York: Public Affairs Press, 2000), p. 194.
19. Alan Greenspan, *The Age of Turbulence: Adventures in a New World* (New York: Penguin Press, 2007), chapter 2.
20. Michael Duffy and Dan Goodgame, *Marching in Place: The Status Quo Presidency of George Bush* (New York: Simon & Schuster, 1992), p. 66.
21. Bill Gross, "100 Bottles of Beer on the Wall," Investment Outlook, www.pimco.com, February 2007.
22. Nick Beams, "U.S. Indebtedness a Growing Threat to Global Stability," www.can.mailarchive.ca, May 23, 2005.
23. *New York Times,* September 22, 2006.
24. *Wall Street Journal,* June 27, 2006.
25. Ambrose Evans-Pritchard, "BIS Warns of Great Depression Dangers from Credit Spree," *Telegraph* (London), June 25, 2007.
26. Kurt Richebächer, "Inflate or Die," *Richebächer Letter,* January 2007, p. 3.
27. David W. Tice, Speech to Shareholders of Prudent Bear Funds Inc., New York, May 1, 2007.
28. Stewart Miller, "Is 'Private' Oil Threatening the NYMEX?" *Investment U. Letter,* www.investment.u.com, January 25, 2007.
29. See Phillips, *Arrogant Capital,* pp. 92–102; Kevin Phillips, *Wealth and Democracy: A Political History of the American Rich* (New York: Broadway Books, 2002), pp. 105–6.
30. William Greider, *Secrets of the Temple* (New York: Simon & Schuster, 1987), p. 93.
31. By January 2008, spreading weakness in the stock and credit markets was increasing sentiment that central banks should have kept the debt and credit bubble from attaining such size. See, for example, Paul de Grauwe, "Central Banks Should Prick Asset Bubbles," *Financial Times,* November 1, 2007.
32. Phillips, *Arrogant Capital,* p. 95.
33. Bret Fromson, "Plunge Protection Team," *Washington Post,* February 23, 1997.

34. Edward Chancellor, *Devil Take the Hindmost* (New York: Penguin, 2000), p. 276.

35. Robert Heller, "Have Fed Support Stock Market, Too," *Wall Street Journal,* October 27, 1989.

36. Alan Greenspan, speech in Louvain, Belgium, www.federalreserve.gov/boarddocs/speeches/1997.

37. "Monday View: Paulson Reactivates Secretive Support Team to Prevent Markets Meltdown," *Telegraph* (London), October 30, 2006.

38. "Fed to Prop Up Wall Street," *Observer* (London), September 16, 2001.

39. *Financial Times,* as quoted in John Crudele, "Greenspan, Fed Bailed Out Marts in September," *New York Post,* April 2, 2002.

40. Robert Brumby, *Australian Financial Review,* July 4, 2002.

41. "Did the White House Rig the Stock Market?" *U.S. News & World Report,* August 20, 2007.

42. See especially Jocelyn Pixley, *Emotions in Finance* (Cambridge, UK: Cambridge University Press, 2004).

43. John C. Edmunds, "Securities: The New Wealth Machine," *Foreign Policy,* Autumn 1996.

44. Minsky, *Stabilizing an Unstable Economy.*

45. "Monetary and Prudential Policies at a Crossroad?" Bank for International Settlements, Basel, Switzerland, 2006.

46. For the Forbes 400, see *Forbes,* September 20, 2007; for the survey of the twenty highest-paid hedge fund managers, see "Top Fund Managers Made 22,300 Times Average Wage, Study Says," www.bloomberg.com, August 29, 2007.

47. "Private Banks: Big Versus Small," *Barron's,* October 22, 2007, pp. 38–39.

3. BULLNOMICS: ITS FAVORITISM AND FICTIONS

1. Edward Chancellor, *Devil Take the Hindmost* (New York: Penguin, 2000), p. 234.

2. Ibid., pp. 17, 35, 38.

3. Thomas Frank, *One Market Under God: Extreme Capitalism, Market Populism, and the End of Economic Democracy* (New York: Doubleday, 2000), pp. 3–4.

4. Thomas Frank, "Markets 'R' Us," *New Statesman,* January 8, 2001.

5. See, for example, B. Mark Smith, *The Equity Culture* (New York: Farrar, Straus & Giroux, 2003), chapter 10; Chancellor, *Devil Take the Hindmost,* chapter 8.

6. Smith, *The Equity Culture,* p. 212.

7. Chancellor, *Devil Take the Hindmost,* p. 248.

8. Jim Chanos transcript, *Financial Times,* www.ft.com, June 7, 2007.

9. Smith, *The Equity Culture,* p. 235.

10. Philip Coggan, "Global Investment Fund Management: Underskilled in Underweighting," *Financial Times,* September 19, 2005.

11. "Efficient Market Hypothesis," www.wikipedia. org.

12. Susan Pulliam, Randall Smith, and Michael Siconolfi, "U.S. Investors Face an Age of Murky Pricing," *Wall Street Journal*, October 12, 2007.

13. Bill Gross, "Haute Con Job," Investment Outlook, www.pimco.com, October 2004.

14. Stephen Cauchi, "Food Shock As 'Agflation' Sees Prices Rise," *Melbourne Age*, September 30, 2007.

15. "UN Warns of Food Inflation Effects," *Financial Times*, October 29, 2007.

16. Richard Bernstein and Jose Rasco, "Global Agriculture & Agflation," Merrill Lynch research report, April 27, 2007.

17. Bill Gross, "How We Learned to Stop Worrying," Investment Outlook, www.pimco.com, May–June 2007.

18. W. Joseph Stroupe, "Caution: Inflation Is Higher Than You Think," *Asia Times*, June 27, 2006.

19. Kevin Phillips, *Boiling Point: Democrats, Republicans, and the Decline of Middle-Class Prosperity* (New York: HarperPerennial, 1994), pp. 10–11.

20. Stroupe, "Caution."

21. Timothy Aeppel, "An Inflation Debate Brews over Intangibles at the Mall," *Wall Street Journal*, May 9, 2005.

22. "GDP Deflator—Definition of GDP Deflator," *Labor Law Talk Dictionary*, http://dictionary.laborlawtalk.com/GDP_deflator.

23. Peter L. Bernstein, "In a Maze of Indexes, Finding Prices to Live By," *New York Times*, August 5, 2007.

24. "America: Banana Republic Watch," www.nakedcapitalism.com, May 6, 2007.

25. Charles Hugh Smith, "The Housing-Inflation Connection," www.seekingalpha.com, August 27, 2007.

26. John Wasik, "CPI's Lie on Household Inflation Doesn't Wash," Bloomberg News, September 24, 2007.

27. Wolfgang Munchau, "The Trouble with Inflation Indices," *Financial Times*, May 5, 2007.

28. Frederic Mishkin, "Globalization, Macroeconomic Performance and Monetary Policy," Domestic Prices in an Integrated World Economy Conference, Washington, D.C., September 2007.

29. Michael Shedlock, "Grossly Distorted Procedures," Global Economic Trend Analysis, http://globaleconomicanalysis.blogspot.com, May 11, 2005.

30. Kevin Phillips, *American Theocracy: The Peril and Politics of Radical Religion, Oil, and Borrowed Money in the 21st Century* (New York: Viking, 2006), pp. 251, 259, 102, and 365.

31. Ibid., p. 250.

32. "Does God Want You to Be Rich?" *Time*, September 10, 2006.

33. Ibid.

34. Eric Gorski, "Hispanics Transforming U.S. Religion," Associated Press, April 25, 2007.

35. See Lauren Sandler, *Righteous* (New York: Viking, 2006), pp. 126–46, for a discussion of black Republicans and rappers in suburban Atlanta churches.
36. "Does God Want You to Be Rich?"
37. Phillips, *American Theocracy*, p. 249.
38. "The Secret's Success," *Nation*, June 4, 2007, p. 5.
39. "Preaching a Gospel of Wealth in a Glittery Market, New York," *New York Times*, January 14, 2006.
40. *Ogden (Utah) Standard-Examiner*, August 26, 1989.
41. "Federal Regulators Call Money Scams a Cottage Industry in Utah," Associated Press, November 22, 2000.
42. James P. Pinkerton, "As Rove Moves On, It's Back to the Future," *Newsday*, August 14, 2007.

4. SECURITIZATION: THE INSECURITY OF IT ALL

1. John C. Edmunds, "Securities: The New World Wealth Machine," *Foreign Policy*, Autumn 1996.
2. International Financial Services, "Securitisation," *City Business Series*, March 2006.
3. Jacob S. Hacker, *The Great Risk Shift: The Assault on American Jobs, Families, Health Care, and Retirement and How You Can Fight Back* (New York: Oxford University Press, 2006), pp. 2, 31.
4. Elizabeth Warren, "The Middle Class on the Precipice," *Harvard Magazine*, January–February 2006, p. 28.
5. "The Federal Reserve Must Prolong the Party," *Financial Times*, August 21, 2007.
6. "Back to the Future for Asset-Backed Securities," *Financial Times*, September 4, 2007.
7. "Introduction: New Players Join the Credit Game," *Financial Times*, March 13, 2007.
8. "Banks See Growing Share of Profits from Use of Asset-Backed Securities," *Financial Times*, June 4, 2007.
9. John Crudele, "No Freedom of Information on the Plunge Protection Team," *New York Post*, May 15, 2007.
10. "Next in Line for Subprime Hit: Bonds?" Associated Press, September 9, 2007.
11. Michael J. Panzner, "Eau de Liquidity," www.financialsense.com, May 21, 2007. For obvious reasons, quick short-term profits usually worked to diminish the concern vendors would have over long-term stability.
12. Ibid.
13. "Nasty Side Effects of Debt Innovation," *Financial Times*, September 10, 2007.
14. John Authers, "Big Banks Are Moving Back to Center Stage," *Financial Times*, August 25, 2007.
15. "New Players Join the Credit Game," *Financial Times*, March 13, 2007.
16. The old individual quotations are no longer necessary now that the spreading

economic crisis has put a new spotlight on Greenspan's collusions and mistakes. For examples of this emerging genre, see "Roots of Credit Crisis Laid at Fed's Door," MarketWatch, October 24, 2007, and Edmund L. Andrews, "Fed and Regulators Shrugged as the Subprime Crisis Spread," *New York Times,* December 18, 2007.

17. "Credit Turmoil 'Has Hallmarks of Bank Run,'" *Financial Times,* September 2, 2007.

18. Mohamed El-Erian, "In the New Liquidity Factories, Buyers Must Still Beware," *Financial Times,* March 22, 2007.

19. David W. Tice, "Report to Shareholders," Prudent Bear Funds, Inc., April 30, 2007.

20. Satyajit Das, "Credit Crunch: The New Diet Snack of Financial Markets," www.prudentbear.com, September 5, 2007.

21. Bill Gross, "What Do They Know?"Investment Outlook, www.pimco.com, October 2007.

22. "Testimony of Robert J. Shiller Before the Joint Economic Committee of Congress," Washington, D.C., September 19, 2007, pp. 1–2.

23. "The R-Word Surfaces on Wall Street," *Financial Times,* September 10, 2007.

24. Ibid.

25. "A New Light on Housing's Role in U.S. Recessions," InmanBlog: The Inside Track on Real Estate, http://blog.inman.com, August 31, 2007.

26. "Double-Digit Home Price Drops Coming," www.cnnmoney.com, September 19, 2007.

27. The notion that Fannie and Freddie were part of what drove Greenspan's 2001–3 rate cuts did not get much attention, but some, like *Forbes* columnist Richard Lehmann, raised it in 2007 as the housing crash refocused attention on the controversial GSEs.

28. "Impact of U.S. Crisis to Linger in Europe," *International Herald Tribune,* September 6, 2007.

29. "Credit Fears Hit Global Markets," *Guardian* (UK), August 9, 2007.

30. "Wrangle Over Credit Pricing," *Financial Times,* September 12, 2007.

31. "Paulson Says Subprime Woes Will Linger," Reuters, September 12, 2007; "Dodge Says Opaque Securities Worsened Credit Crisis," www.bloomberg.com, September 12, 2007.

32. "Watchdogs Look for More Transparency on Securitisations," *Financial Times,* October 10, 2007.

33. Michael Shedlock, "Interview with Paul Kasriel of Northern Trust," http://globaleconomicanalysis.blogspot.com/2006/12/interview-with-paul-kasriel.html.

34. William Pesek, "Japan Ghosts of Bubbles Past Haunt U.S. in 2008," Bloomberg News, January 7, 2008.

35. Gillian Tett, "Japan Offers a Salutary Tale in Banking Crises," *Financial Times,* January 1, 2008.

36. "U.K. House Market Is Heading for Crash," *Times* (London), October 17, 2007.
37. "Testimony of Robert J. Shiller," U.S. Congress, Joint Economic Committee, September 19, 2007, p. 2.

5. PEAK OIL: A POTENTIAL PIVOT OF THE 2010s

1. Kevin Phillips, *American Theocracy: The Peril and Politics of Radical Religion, Oil, and Borrowed Money in the 21st Century* (New York: Viking, 2006), p. 73.
2. For details, see ibid., chapter 1.
3. "World Will Face Oil Crunch 'in Five Years,'" *Financial Times*, July 10, 2007.
4. "High Prices Threaten to Linger," *Financial Times*, July 18, 2007.
5. Toni Johnson, "Reading Oil's Tea Leaves," *Daily Analysis*, Council on Foreign Relations, www.cfr.org, July 26, 2007.
6. "Total Chief Warns on Oil Output," *Financial Times*, October 31, 2007.
7. "Chevron CTO Says Peak Oil Will Not Be a Disaster," *Energy Bulletin*, www.energybulletin.net, October 24, 2007.
8. Energy Watch Group, "Peak Oil Could Trigger Meltdown of Society, www.yubanet.com, October 23, 2007.
9. "Why 'Peak Oil' May Soon Pique Your Interest," *Christian Science Monitor*, August 16, 2007.
10. "Libya Oil Head: Global Oil Output Can Only Reach 100 Million B/D," Dow Jones Newswire, October 30, 2007.
11. Dave Cohen, "The Perfect Storm," *Energy Bulletin*, www.energybulletin.net, October 31, 2007.
12. Energy Watch Group, "Peak Oil Could Trigger."
13. Case Western Peak Oil Initiative, "Peak-Oil *When?*" *October 2007 Report*, www.peakoilwhen.org.
14. "China to Reach Peak Oil Production As Early As 2015," Interfax-China, October 29, 2007.
15. "SCO Summit Focuses on Energy Cooperation," *Eurasia Daily Monitor*, Jamestown Foundation, August 17, 2007.
16. See "Bush's Royal Trouble," *Washington Post*, March 28, 2007.
17. "Saudi Arabia Cuts Oil Sales to U.S., Ups China," *Washington Times*, September 15, 2007.
18. "Peak Oil Review," *Energy Bulletin*, October 29, 2007.
19. "Analysis: Mideast Oil and Chinese Arms," *Energy Daily* (UPI Hong Kong), October 26, 2007.
20. Washington Institute for Near East Policy, "Chinese-Saudi Cooperation: Oil but Also Missiles," *Policy Watch* no. 1095, April 21, 2006.
21. "IEA Says Oil Prices Will Stay 'Very High,'" *International Herald-Tribune*, October 31, 2007.
22. "Saudi Arabia and China Extend Ties Beyond Oil," *China Brief*, Jamestown Foundation, September 27, 2005.

23. "Saudi Arabia Tops China's September Crude Imports List," *Platt's*, November 8, 2007.

24. "China Leads Race for World's Riches," *Telegraph* (London), November 10, 2007.

25. See especially "Analysis: Mideast Oil and Chinese Arms."

26. "SCO Summit Focuses on Energy Cooperation."

27. "Fueled by Billions in Oil Wealth, It Looks to Reclaim the USSR's Status as a Global Military Power," *Christian Science Monitor*, August 17, 2007, and "Russia Arms Old and New Friends in Asia," *International Herald-Tribune*, September 5, 2007.

28. "Russia Arms Old and New Friends in Asia."

29. No appropriate data is available. A minimum measurement, however, would combine the $420 billion added to central bank reserves since 1999 with $150 billion set aside in Russia's oil-based main sovereign wealth fund.

30. See, for example, "Declining Exports from Big Oil Exporters Expected," *Canadian News*, September 28, 2007.

31. See especially Flynt Leverett and Pierre Noel, "The New Axis of Oil," *National Interest*, July 2006.

32. "Latin America Welcomes Ahmadinejad," *Christian Science Monitor*, September 28, 2007.

33. "China to Become Iran's Leading Supplier," *Financial Times*, September 13, 2007.

34. "Chavez Pushes Petrodollar Diplomacy in Uruguay," Associated Press, August 21, 2007, and "Venezuela Boosts Energy Ties with Other Nations," Xinhua, www.xinhuanet.com/english, August 10, 2007.

35. "China, Venezuela Contribute $6 Billion to Development Fund," Bloomberg News, September 26, 2007.

36. "Analysis: Venezuela Ups Exports to China," United Press International, October 2, 2007.

37. "America's Top Oil Suppliers Tightening Taps on Exports: CIBC World Markets," PR Newswire–First Call, October 2, 2007.

38. "Six Pipelines Blown Up in Mexico," *Los Angeles Times*, September 11, 2007.

39. "Oil Price Rise Causes Global Shift in Wealth," *Washington Post*, November 10, 2007.

40. "OPEC Can't Control Oil Prices, Risks Consumer Switch," Bloomberg News, November 16, 2007.

41. "The Dark Cloud? The U.S. Economy," *Toronto Globe and Mail*, September 21, 2007

42. Sebastian Mallaby, "The Dollar in Danger," *Washington Post*, November 12, 2007.

43. Jeffrey Garten, "How to Prevent a Rout of the Declining Dollar," *Financial Times*, October 10, 2007.

44. "The World's Currency Could Be a U.S. problem," *Financial Times*, November 9, 2007.
45. William L. Silber, *When Washington Shut Down Wall Street* (Princeton, N.J.: Princeton University Press, 2007), pp. 154–61.
46. "Falling Dollar Puts Pressure on OPEC," *Financial Times*, July 23, 2007.
47. Ibid.
48. John Authers, "The Short View: Falling Dollar," *Financial Times*, September 17, 2007.
49. "Sovereign Funds Bring Political Leverage, Jobs," Bloomberg News, October 23, 2007; "Thatcherism Is Out As China Vindicates Galbraith," Bloomberg News, August 8, 2007; and "Wealth Is the Name of the Game," *Gulf Weekly*, November 14–20, 2007.
50. "OPEC May Reject Calls for More Supply with Oil at $76," Bloomberg News, September 7, 2007; "Record Oil Prices Net OPEC $658 Bn," *Financial Times*, November 11, 2007.
51. "Oil Price Rise Causes Global Shift in Wealth."
52. "OPEC Sharply Reduces Dollar Exposure," *Financial Times*, December 6, 2004.
53. "Treasury Gain May Falter, Foreign Holders Flee Dollar," Bloomberg News, September 10, 2007.
54. "Dollar Is Battered and Bruised, Not Yet Out," Bloomberg News, November 9, 2007.
55. "Greenspan: Euro Gains As Reserve Choice," Associated Press, September 17, 2007; Justin Fox, "The U.S. Dollar Still Has a Few Fans Among Central Bankers," www.time-blog.com/curious_capitalist, June 13, 2007.
56. "U.A.E. to Drop Peg Only with GCC Agreement," Bloomberg News, November 16, 2007.
57. Brad Setser, "How Long Can the Gulf Countries Continue Their Dollar Pegs?" www.rgemonitor.com, November 15, 2007.
58. "How Jay-Z, Bundchen Got the Jump on Hedge Funds," Bloomberg News, November 16, 2007.
59. "EU Says Oil Could One Day Be Priced in Euros," Reuters, June 16, 2003.
60. "Iran Asks Japan to Pay Yen for Oil," Bloomberg News, July 13, 2007.
61. "More Japanese Oil Firms Pay in Yen," *Iran Daily*, October 10, 2007.
62. "Iran Presses Oil Customers to Pay in Currencies Other Than Dollars," Reuters, March 27, 2007.
63. "Petroleos de Venezuela to Convert Accounts Away from Dollars," Bloomberg News, September 17, 2007.
64. "Venezuela's Oil Minister: OPEC Leaders May Discuss Creation of a Currency Basket to Price Crude," Associated Press, November 16, 2007.
65. "St. Petersburg Bourse Selected as Trading Floor for Oil Prices," RIA Novosti, November 14, 2007.

66. "Mansoor Mohi-uddin, "View of the Day: US Dollar," *Financial Times*, September 11, 2007.
67. Phillips, *American Theocracy*, p. 87.
68. Ibid.
69. Ibid., p. 95.
70. Ibid.
71. Ibid., p. 96.
72. Ibid., p. 95.
73. Matthew Simmons, *Twilight in the Desert: The Coming Saudi Oil Shock and the World Economy* (New York: Wiley, 2005).
74. Michael T. Klare, "Beyond the Age of Petroleum," *Nation*, November 12, 2007.

6. THE POLITICS OF EVASION: DEBT, FINANCE, AND OIL

1. Mancur Olson, *The Rise and Decline of Nations* (New Haven, Conn.: Yale University Press, 1984).
2. *Mother Jones*, September–October 2002, p. 64.
3. Grover Norquist, "A Dynastic Disease in American Politics," *Financial Times*, November 20, 2007.
4. Carl Bernstein, *A Woman in Charge: The Life of Hillary Rodham Clinton* (New York: Knopf, 2006); Jeff Gerth and Don Van Natta Jr., *Her Way: The Hopes and Ambitions of Hillary Rodham Clinton* (New York: Little Brown, 2006).
5. Cullen Murphy, *Are We Rome?* (New York: Houghton Mifflin, 2007); Paul Farrell, "If We Are Rome, Wall Street Is Our Coliseum," MarketWatch, August 27, 2007.
6. J. H. Elliott, *Imperial Spain, 1469–1716* (New York: Mentor Books, 1966), pp. 296–316.
7. J. H. Elliott, *Spain and Its World, 1500–1700* (New Haven, Conn.: Yale University Press, 1989), p. 264.
8. For details, see Elliott, *Imperial Spain*, pp. 317–23; Elliott, *Spain and Its World*.
9. C. R. Boxer, *The Dutch Seaborne Empire, 1600–1800* (London: Penguin Books, 1965), pp. 34–35.
10. Simon Schama, *Patriots and Liberators* (New York: Vintage Books, 1992), pp. 25–58; Jonathan Israel, *The Dutch Republic* (New York: Oxford University Press, 1992), pp. 1067–97.
11. Schama, *Patriots and Liberators*, pp. 58–135.
12. Elliott, *Imperial Spain*, pp. 324–33.
13. Each of the seven Dutch provinces essentially devised its own tax system, and then from those receipts paid in a more or less fixed proportion of Dutch "federal" revenues. The province of Holland, which included Amsterdam, mostly taxed consumption rather than wealth or income, and between, say, 1670 and 1770, the Holland/Amsterdam share of Dutch wealth and income

grew while that elsewhere in the United Provinces shrank. Even so, Holland's share of the "federal" burden remained essentially what it had been in 1595 or 1658. See Jonathan Israel, *The Dutch Republic*, pp. 285–87, for details and Israel's assessment that the province of Holland was by comparison undertaxed.

14. Aaron L. Friedberg, *"The Weary Titan": Britain and the Experience of Relative Decline, 1895–1905* (Princeton, N.J.: Princeton University Press, 1988).

15. Michael Kinnear, *The British Voter: An Atlas and Survey Since 1885* (Ithaca, N.Y.: Cornell University Press, 1968), p. 46.

16. Friedberg, *"The Weary Titan,"* pp. 116–18.

17. Mark Shields, "Democrats Bought and Paid For by Hedge Funds, Private Equity Firms," www.onlineathens.com, September 21, 2007.

18. "Buyout Firms, Hedge Funds Look to the Senate," Bloomberg News, November 9, 2007.

19. Daniel Gross, *Bull Run: Wall Street, the Democrats, and the New Politics of Personal Finance* (New York: Public Affairs Press, 2000), pp. 21–25.

20. Robert Reich, "Pushback," www.economist.com, October 25, 2007.

21. "How a Billionaire Friend of Bill Helps Him Do Good, and Well," *New York Times*, April 23, 2006.

22. "Obama, Hillary Draw Wall Street Donors," Bloomberg News, July 22, 2007.

23. "Big Fish Shadow Obama's Small Fry," *Chicago Tribune*, July 26, 2007; "Dodd Defends Donations from Hedge Fund Industry," *Stamford (CT) Advocate*, August 13, 2007.

24. Matthew Simmons, *Twilight in the Desert: The Coming Saudi Oil Shock and the World Economy* (New York: John Wiley & Sons, 2005), p. 350.

25. Flynt Leverett and Pierre Noel, "The New Axis of Oil," *National Interest*, July 2006.

26. "The Trouble with Crude Oil," *BusinessWeek*, October 26, 2007.

27. "Powering America's Future: New Energy, New Jobs," Hillary Clinton for President, www.hillaryclinton.com/issues/energy.

28. "The Green Gripe with Obama," *Washington Post*, January 10, 2007.

29. Julia Whitty, "Coal Sponsors Tonight's Democratic Debate," *Mother Jones*, November 2007.

30. "Why Is Peak Oil Politically Incorrect?" *Energy Bulletin*, June 10, 2007.

7. THE GLOBAL CRISIS OF AMERICAN CAPITALISM

1. Thomas Frank, *One Market Under God* (New York: Doubleday, 2000), p. 58; Nelson Lichtenstein, "Market Triumphalism and the Wishful Liberals," in Ellen Schrecker, ed., *Cold War Triumphalism After the Fall of Communism* (New York: New Press, 2004), pp. 103–5.

2. "China Threatens 'Nuclear Option' of Dollar Sales," *Telegraph* (London), October 8, 2007.

3. Aaron L. Friedberg, *"The Weary Titan"*: *Britain and the Experience of Relative Decline, 1895–1905* (Princeton, N.J.: Princeton University Press, 1988), pp. 75–76.
4. "HSBC Will Take On $5 Billion of Assets from Two SIVs," Bloomberg News, November 26, 2007.
5. "Buyout Firms, Hedge Funds See Year-Long Credit Slump," Bloomberg News, November 29, 2007.
6. "U.S. Buy-Out Reign Under Threat," *Financial Times*, November 13, 2007.
7. "One Hedge Fund in 10 to Go Bust, Says Man," *Financial Times*, November 20, 2007.
8. "At Subprime Event, Too Early to Tell Who'll Survive," Bloomberg News, November 20.
9. Stansberry and Associates, *S&A Digest*, November 21, 2007.
10. "On Wall St: Subprime Flames Lick at Freddie," *Financial Times*, November 23, 2007.
11. Stephen S. Roach, "You Can Almost Hear It Pop," *New York Times*, December 16, 2007.
12. "Greenback Humbled by Concerns over US Economy," *Financial Times*, July 11, 2007; "Tough Times Not Over Yet for Unloved Dollar," *Financial Times*, July 26, 2007.
13. Brad Setser, "Another Bad TIC Release," *RGE Monitor*, November 19, 2007.
14. "Dollar Loses Grip on Asian Debt Sector," *Financial Times*, November 19, 2007.
15. "Islamic Bonds to Get Boost from Singapore, India, Moody's Says," Bloomberg News, August 30, 2007.
16. "Treasury Goes Ahead with Islamic Bond Scheme," *Financial Times*, November 17, 2007.
17. Ibid.; "Islamic Bonds to Get Boost"; "Hong Kong Enters the Race for Islamic Capital," *Financial Times*, November 21, 2007.
18. "Currency Blocs Fall into Place," *Financial Times*, November 22, 2007.
19. "Morgan Stanley Posts Loss," *New York Times*, December 20, 2007.
20. "Putin's Arctic Invasion," *Daily Mail* (London), June 28, 2007.
21. Harley Baker, "Vladimir Putin on Russian Energy Policy," *National Interest*, November 2005.
22. "ASPO China Is Formed," *Energy Bulletin*, ASPO International, October 30, 2007.
23. Siddarth Varadarajan, "India, China, and the Asian Axis of Oil," *Hindu*, January 24, 2006.
24. Flynt Leverett and Pierre Noel, "The New Axis of Oil," *National Interest*, July 2006, p. 7.
25. "Ghost Road to Boost India-China Trade," *Financial Times*, October 9, 2007.
26. "India to Tell West to Shoulder Climate Change Burden," Reuters, December 2, 2007.

27. "Climate Is a Risky Issue for Democrats," *Washington Post,* November 6, 2007.
28. "Global Oil Output Has Already Peaked, Pickens Says," Bloomberg News, October 19, 2007.
29. David Pauly, "Slow, Steady Liquidation of the World Oil Industry: David Pauly," Bloomberg News, October 1, 2007.
30. "No Real Alternative to Oil: Rise in Demand Seems Unavoidable," *International Herald-Tribune,* October 29, 2007.
31. "Welcome to a World of Runaway Energy Demand," *Financial Times,* November 13, 2007.
32. "No Real Alternative to Oil." A lot of the alternatives deemed plausible may be unrealistic.
33. Karl Polanyi, *The Great Transformation: The Political and Economic Origins of Our Time* (Boston: Beacon Press, 2001).
34. "Three Ways to Avoid Wall Street," *Money Morning,* November 9, 2007.
35. Gillian Tett, "Japan Offers a Salutary Tale in Banking Crisis," *Financial Times,* January 1, 2008.
36. Bill Gross, "Pyramids Crumbling," *Pimco Investment Outlook,* January 2008.
37. "The Race Is On to Be Asia's Number One for Finance," *Financial Times,* July 5, 2007.
38. Noriel Roubini and Brad Setser, "Will Bretton Woods 2 Regime Unravel Soon?" www.rge.monitor.com, February 2005.
39. Chris P. Dialynas and Marshall Auerbeck, "Renegade Economics: The Bretton Woods II Fiction," *Pimco Viewpoints,* September 2007.
40. "America's Vulnerable Economy," *Economist,* November 15, 2007.
41. "Dollar's Last Lap as the Only Anchor Currency," *Financial Times,* November 25, 2007.
42. John Authers, "The Short View: Weak Dollar," *Financial Times,* September 10, 2007.
43. "Why Banking Is an Accident Waiting to Happen," *Financial Times,* November 27, 2007.
44. Martin Wolf, "Why the Credit Squeeze Is a Turning Point for the World," *Financial Times,* December 11, 2007.
45. "Mortgage Crisis Perplexes Even Shrewd Investor Warren Buffett," *San Francisco Chronicle,* December 12, 2007.
46. "European Bosses Warming to Foreign Funds," *Financial Times,* December 11, 2007.
47. Nassim Nicholas Taleb, *The Black Swan* (New York: Random House, 2007).
48. "Does Not Compute: How Misfiring Quant Funds Are Distorting the Markets," *Financial Times,* December 9, 2007.
49. Richard Bookstaber, *A Demon of Our Own Design* (New York: John Wiley & Sons, 2007), pp. 5, 259–60.
50. Mike Muehleck, "Exit U.S.," www.agorafinancial.com//afrude/.

AFTERWORD: SPECULATIVE CAPITALISM ENDANGERED

1. "Out of Control Wall Street Chikefs Spurned Warnings at Davos," Bloomberg News, October 24, 2008.
2. "U.S. Clout Down, Risks Up by 2025—Intel Outlook," Reuters, November 20, 2008.
3. Andrew Hacker, *The End of the American Era* (New York: Atheneum, 1970), p. 3. Few other skeptics were so blunt.
4. Henry Brandon, *The Retreat of American Power* (New York: Doubleday, 1973), p. 3.
5. Allen J. Matusow, *Nixon's Economy* (Lawrence, Kan.: The University Press of Kansas), pp. 131–135.
6. *The Politics of Rich and Poor,* p. 220.
7. Carlo Cipolla, *Guns, Sails and Empires* (New York: Barnes & Noble, 1996), p. 137.
8. "Safe Haven Image Sparks Singapore, Switzerland," Bloomberg News, October 17, 2008.
9. "Templeton, Sydbank See Won, Rupiah, Rupee Bottoming," Bloomberg News, November 3, 2008.
10. "Japan's 'Least Ugly' Economy May Beat U.S. Europe in Crisis," Bloomberg News, November 18, 2008.
11. "Death Knell of Decoupling Rings Hollow," *Wall Street Journal,* November 18, 2008.
12. "India May Reduce Key Interest Rate as Inflation Slows," Bloomberg News, November 19, 2008.
13. Charles Collyns and Krikshna Srinivason, Inflation—Changing Dynamics, The International Monetary Fund, July 20, 2008, www.imf.org/external/np/vc2008/072008.htm.
14. "Euro May Gain 16 Percent as China Demand Drives Up Oil," Bloomberg News, November 21, 2008.
15. "For Asia, Crisis Takes a Different Turn," *Wall Street Journal,* November 1–2, 2008.
16. "Islamic Banking: Steady in Shaky Times," *Washington Post,* October 31, 2008, p. A16.
17. "Japan's Least Ugly Economy May Beat U.S., Europe in Crisis," Bloomberg News, November 1, 2008.
18. "India, China See Highest Jump in Millionaires: Survey," Reuters, June 25, 2008.
19. "India Joins Brazil, Russia in Injecting Cash in Banks," Bloomberg News, October 16, 2008.
20. Richard Duncan, "Time to Dump the Dollar Standard," *Far Eastern Economic Review,* October 2008.
21. "Templeton, Sydbank See Won."

22. "China Should Buy Gold for Reserves, Association Says," Bloomberg News, November 14.

23. "Thailand Proposes Asia Pool $250 Billion for Crisis," Bloomberg News, October 22, 2008.

24. William Pesek, "Asia's Economy Could Use Its Own Gordon Brown," Bloomberg News, November 1, 2008.

25. "G-20 Pits Bush versus Sarkozy-Merkel Regulation Push," Bloomberg News, November 8, 2008.

26. Ibid.

27. "U.S. Meltdown Reflects Regulators' Failures, Wu Says," Bloomberg News, September 18, 2008.

28. "Global Trends 2025: A Transformed World," National Intelligence Council, November 2008, www.dni.gov/nic/NIC_home.html.

29. Ibid.

30. "China Bets Highways Will Drive Its Growth," Wall Street Journal, November 11, 2008.

31. NIC, "Global Trends."

32. "Saudi King Blames Oil Prices on Speculation, Taxes," International Business Times, June 22, 2008.

33. "Oil Price Rebound Could Be Severe," Wall Street Journal, October 29, 2008.

34. "OPEC Cuts 2.2 Million Barrels," money.cnn.com, December 17, 2008.

35. "KKR Invests in Chinese Dairy Farm," Wall Street Journal, December 2, 2008.

36. "In Brazil, Credit to Farmers Dries Up," Wall Street Journal, November 29–30, 2008.

37. "No Relief on Food Prices," New York Times, November 27, 2008.

APPENDIX: GLOBAL PUBLIC OPINION AND THE LOSS OF RESPECT FOR THE UNITED STATES, 2003–7

1. Jela De Franceschi, "Defining America's Role in the World," Voice of America News, September 10, 2007.

2. "US Suffers Decline in Prestige," Financial Times, September 12, 2007.

3. "Europeans Tell Bush—Trans-Atlantic Bruises Linger," Spiegel Online International, September 7, 2007.

4. "Global Unease with Major World Powers," Pew Global Attitudes Project, Pew Research Center, Washington, D.C., June 27, 2007, p. 1.

5. "World Publics Reject U.S. Role as the World Leader," Chicago Council on Global Affairs, April 17, 2007.

6. "World View of US Role Goes From Bad to Worse," www.worldpublicopinion.org, January 2007.

7. http://bd.english.fom.ru.

8. "Iran Winning Turkish Hearts, Minds," Wall Street Journal, September 6, 2006.

9. "Less Than Half of Pakistani Public Supports Attacking Al Qaeda," www.worldpublicopinion.org, October 2007.

Index

Page numbers in *italics* refer to figures.

FOR MORE FROM BESTSELLING AUTHOR KEVIN PHILLIPS, LOOK FOR THE

American Theocracy
The Peril and Politics of Radical Religion, Oil,
and Borrowed Money in the 21st Century

From ancient Rome to the British Empire to twenty-first century America, global overreach, militant religion, energy dependency, and ballooning debt have been Achilles' heels of leading world economic powers. For America today, the new, added danger comes in how these same interests and biases—oil, religion, and money management—have combined to dominate the Republican electoral coalition which in turn now controls American politics and policymaking. With an eye on the past as well as the future, Phillips lays out in the bluntest terms how petro-imperialism has sunk empires before; how religious warfare has devastated powers as great as ours in history; and how being a debtor nation has left us in a precarious and vulnerable position in the global marketplace. In Phillips's uncompromising view, this is a powerful but highly combustible political combination which, if left unchecked, is likely to have catastrophic results not simply for the Republicans, but for America itself.

"A harrowing picture of national danger that no American reader will welcome, but that none should ignore. . . . The most alarming analysis of where we are and where we may be going to have appeared in years. . . . Extensively researched and . . . frighteningly persuasive."
        —*The New York Times Book Review*

"Everyone should have access to what *American Theocracy* so powerfully tells us about our country at this critical time. . . . Its brilliance is so abundant even its asides are insightful."
        —*Chicago Sun-Times*

ISBN 978-0-14-303828-3

American Dynastry
Aristocracy, Fortune, and the Politics of Deceit in the House of Bush

Intelligence, energy, and national security: the categories of Bush family operations have also been—no coincidence—the key enterprises of the American twentieth century. Kevin Phillips casts his keen eye upon the making of the Bush family dynasty across four generations, documenting how it has perfectly exemplified many of the growing trends in American political life—political and economic dynastization, favoritism to the top 1 percent even after a tight election, paper entrepreneurialism and crony capitalism à la Enron (Bush-Enron dealings go back to 1986), and the further rise of the military-industrial complex. In this devastating book, onetime Republican strategist Phillips reveals how four generations of Bushes have ascended the ladder of national power since World War I, becoming entrenched within the American establishment—Yale, Wall Street, the Senate, the CIA, the vice presidency, and the presidency—through a recurrent flair for old-boy networking, national security involvement, and political deception.

"Fresh and damning . . . Phillips's marshaling of evidence has cumulative power. None of the other recent critical, liberal books about George W. Bush have this sort of sweep or impact. *American Dynasty* is so sober and steeped in learning that readers will wonder how President Bush, or any man's family, could stand this depth of exposure. . . . Brilliant and important."
—*Chicago Sun-Times*

ISBN 978-0-14-303431-5